Claim Handling Principles
and Practices

Claim Handling Principles and Practices

Donna J. Popow, JD, CPCU, AIC
Assistant Vice President and Ethics Counsel
American Institute for CPCU/Insurance Institute of America

First Edition

American Institute for Chartered Property Casualty Underwriters/
Insurance Institute of America
720 Providence Road, Malvern, Pennsylvania 19355

© 2006

American Institute for Chartered Property Casualty Underwriters/Insurance Institute of America

All rights reserved. This book or any part thereof may not be reproduced without the written permission of the copyright holder.

Unless otherwise indicated, all examples used in this text are based on hypothetical situations and are for purposes of illustration only. Any names included in these examples are fictional and are not intended to represent any true-to-life person, place, product, or organization.

Information which is copyrighted by and proprietary to Insurance Services Office, Inc. ("ISO Material") is included in this publication. Use of the ISO Material is limited to ISO Participating Insurers and their Authorized Representatives. Use by ISO Participating Insurers is limited to use in those jurisdictions for which the insurer has an appropriate participation with ISO. Use of the ISO Material by Authorized Representatives is limited to use solely on behalf of one or more ISO Participating Insurers.

First Edition • First Printing • August 2006

Library of Congress Control Number: 2006928689

ISBN 978-0-89463-282-2

Foreword

The American Institute for Chartered Property Casualty Underwriters and the Insurance Institute of America (the Institutes) are independent, not-for-profit organizations committed to expanding the knowledge of professionals in risk management, insurance, financial services, and related fields through education and research.

In accordance with our belief that professionalism is grounded in education, experience, and ethical behavior, the Institutes provide a wide range of educational programs designed to meet the needs of individuals working in property-casualty insurance and risk management. The American Institute offers the Chartered Property Casualty Underwriter (CPCU®) professional designation. You select a specialization in the CPCU program with either a commercial or a personal risk management and insurance focus, depending on your professional needs. In addition to this specialization, the CPCU program gives you a broad understanding of the property-casualty insurance industry.

The Insurance Institute of America (IIA) offers designations and certificate programs in a wide range of disciplines, including the following:

- Claims
- Commercial underwriting
- Fidelity and surety bonding
- General insurance
- Insurance accounting and finance
- Insurance information technology
- Insurance production and agency management
- Insurance regulation and compliance
- Management
- Marine insurance
- Personal insurance
- Premium auditing
- Quality insurance services
- Reinsurance
- Risk management
- Surplus lines

No matter which Institute program you choose, you will gain practical knowledge and skills that will help you to grow personally and professionally.

The American Institute for CPCU was founded in 1942 through a collaborative effort between industry professionals and academics, led by the faculty members at The Wharton School of the University of Pennsylvania. In 1953, the American Institute for CPCU merged with the IIA, which was founded in 1909 and which remains the oldest continuously functioning national organization offering educational programs for the property-casualty insurance business. The Institutes continuously strive to maximize the value of your education and qualifications in the expanding insurance market. In 2005, the Institutes extended their global reach by forming the CPCU Institute of Greater China (CPCUIGC). In addition, many CPCU and IIA courses now qualify for credits towards certain associate's, bachelor's, and master's degrees at several prestigious colleges and universities, and all CPCU and IIA courses carry college credit recommendations from the American Council on Education (ACE).

The Insurance Research Council (IRC), founded in 1977, helps the Institutes fulfill the research aspect of their mission. The IRC is a division of the Institutes and is supported by industry members. The IRC is a not-for-profit research organization that examines public policy issues of interest to property-casualty insurers, insurance customers, and the general public. IRC research reports are distributed widely to insurance-related organizations, public policy authorities, and the media.

Our textbooks are an essential component of the education we provide. Each book is specifically designed both to provide you with the practical knowledge and skills you need to enhance your job performance and career and also to deliver that knowledge in a clear manner. The content is developed by the Institutes in collaboration with insurance and risk management professionals and members of the academic community. We welcome comments from our students and course leaders because your feedback helps us to continuously improve the quality of our study materials. Through our combined efforts, we will truly be *succeeding together*.

Peter L. Miller
Interim and Acting President and CEO
American Institute for CPCU
Insurance Institute of America

Preface

Insurance, at its core, is a promise to pay—a promise to pay the insured for incurred losses or claims that are covered by the policy. Claim representatives are the promise keepers within the insurance company. It is the job of a claim representative to investigate a loss, determine the amount of the loss, determine if the policy covers the loss, and, if so, to pay for the loss.

The AIC 33 text, *Claim Handling Principles and Practices*, reflects the belief that there are principles and practices of good claim handling that can be applied to any type of claim. This text describes the nature of risk and how insurance is used to manage it. It explains the vital role that claim representatives play in keeping the insurer's promise to pay and how the actions of a claim representative can affect the insurer's bottom line. This text examines policy analysis and the activities in the claim handling process. It explores various types of investigations, fraud detection, negotiations, and litigation management techniques. This text stresses good-faith claim handling, ethics, and professionalism. This combination of topics is designed to give students the claim foundation they need to become successful claim representatives and to pursue additional educational opportunities.

The Institutes appreciate the work and contributions of the following individuals who reviewed the curriculum, provided subject matter expertise, and offered valuable suggestions for improvement:

James A. Franz, CPCU, AIC, ARM

James Jones, CPCU, AIC, ARM

Richard Litchford III, CPCU, AIC

William McCullough, CPCU, CLU, AIC

James Sherlock, CPCU, CLU, ARM

Robert D. Stevens, Sr., CPCU, CLU, AIC

Christine A. Sullivan, CPCU, AIM

Their expertise, dedication, and perseverance made the finished work possible and are greatly appreciated.

For more information about the Institutes' programs, please call our Customer Service Department at (800) 644-2101, e-mail us at cserv@cpcuiia.org, or visit our Web site at www.aicpcu.org.

Donna J. Popow

Contributing Authors

The American Institute for CPCU, the Insurance Institute of America, and the author acknowledges with deep appreciation the work of the following contributing authors:

Elise M. Farnham, CPCU, ARM, AIM

Doris L. Hoopes, CPCU, AIC, AAI

Douglas J. Kent, Esq.

Kevin M. Quinley, CPCU, ARM, AIC

William C. Stewart, Jr., CPCU, AIC, RPA

Contents

1 Risk and Insurance — 1.1
- Insurance — 1.7
- Claim Function — 1.12
- Other Insurance Company Functions — 1.19
- Insurance Regulation — 1.23
- Summary — 1.36

2 Claim Handling Process — 2.1
- Insurance Policy Structure — 2.3
- Framework for Coverage Analysis — 2.12
- Claim Handling Process — 2.20
- Applying the Framework for Coverage Analysis and the Claim Handling Process — 2.47
- Summary — 2.49

3 Investigation of Cause of Loss, Liability, and Damages — 3.1
- Bases for Legal Liability — 3.3
- General Investigative Tools — 3.10
- Property Damage Claim Investigation — 3.44
- Bodily Injury Claim Investigation — 3.53
- Workers' Compensation Claim Investigation — 3.59
- Summary — 3.62
- Appendix — 3.65

4 Insurance Fraud — 4.1
- Importance of Insurance Fraud Detection — 4.3
- Types of Insurance Fraud — 4.4
- Motives for Insurance Fraud — 4.7
- Factors That Influence Fraud — 4.9
- Fraud Indicators — 4.10
- Anti-Fraud Efforts — 4.19
- Summary — 4.29

5 Good-Faith Claim Handling — 5.1
- Law of Bad Faith — 5.4
- Parties to a Bad-Faith Claim — 5.8
- Bases of Bad-Faith Claims — 5.11
- Damages Resulting From Bad Faith or Extracontractual Liability — 5.16
- Defenses to Bad-Faith Claims — 5.19
- Elements of Good-Faith Claim Handling — 5.25
- Summary — 5.34
- Appendix — 5.37

6 Ethics and Professionalism — 6.1
- Importance of Ethics and Professionalism — 6.3
- Ethical and Professional Dilemmas — 6.5
- Ethical and Professional Standards — 6.17
- Summary — 6.24
- Appendix A — 6.25
- Appendix B — 6.27

7	**Negotiation**	7.1
	Negotiation Styles	7.4
	Claim Negotiation Process	7.10
	Claim Negotiation Variables	7.13
	Claim Negotiation Techniques	7.24
	Negotiation Techniques to Avoid	7.35
	Common Pitfalls in Claim Negotiations	7.36
	Summary	7.38
8	**Managing Litigation**	8.1
	Managing a Third-Party Lawsuit	8.4
	Managing a Bad-Faith Lawsuit	8.32
	Managing Litigation Expenses	8.39
	Summary	8.43
	Appendix	8.47
	Index	1

Segment A

Insurance Claim Handling

Chapter 1: Risk and Insurance

Chapter 2: Claim Handling Process

Chapter 3: Investigation of Cause of Loss, Liability, and Damages

Chapter 4: Insurance Fraud

Chapter 1

Direct Your Learning

Risk and Insurance

After learning the content of this chapter and completing the corresponding course guide assignment, you should be able to:

- Explain how hazard risk differs from business risk and what risk management techniques can be used to manage risk.
- Describe the parties to, benefits of, and costs of insurance.
- Describe the claim department structure, types and functions of claim personnel, and claim personnel performance measures.
- Describe each of the different insurance company functions and their purposes.
- Summarize the following aspects of insurance regulation:
  - The three major federal statutes that regulate insurance and their significance
  - The role of the NAIC in insurance regulation
  - The purposes of insurance regulation
  - The activities of insurance regulators
  - The types of insurance regulation
- Define or describe each of the Key Words and Phrases for this chapter.

OUTLINE

Risk

Insurance

Claim Function

Other Insurance Company Functions

Insurance Regulation

Summary

Develop Your Perspective

What are the main topics covered in the chapter?

Any discussion of claim handling must begin with a discussion of risk. People and organizations face risk every day. They must choose a method of dealing with risk, and insurance is frequently the method of choice. This chapter explains how insurance works; what role the claim department plays in addressing risk; and how insurance regulation serves to protect consumers, maintain insurer solvency, and prevent destructive competition.

Identify different methods of managing risk.

- What informal methods do you use to manage the risks of daily life?
- If you have insurance, what risks does it cover?

Why is it important to learn about these topics?

To properly handle claims, claim representatives should understand what motivates people to purchase insurance and what their expectations are once a loss occurs. Additionally, claim representatives should understand how insurance companies and claim departments are evaluated and regulated, so that claim handling practices conform to company standards and goals and comply with insurance regulations.

Consider how a claim department's performance is measured and regulated.

- How do the activities of the claim department affect the company's loss ratio?
- With what state regulations does your claim department have to comply?

How can you use what you will learn?

Claim representatives must be aware of all the regulations with which the claim department and the insurer must comply.

Analyze your state's insurance regulations.

- How does your company ensure that it complies with regulations concerning unfair trade practices?
- How does your company ensure that it complies with regulations concerning unfair claim practices?

Chapter 1
Risk and Insurance

Few individuals or organizations can afford to bear the potential financial losses associated with their activities and property. For example, homeowners must repair or replace their homes if the homes are damaged or destroyed. Automobile drivers at fault in accidents must pay for injuries to others or for damage to others' property. Organizations can lose income if their property is damaged or destroyed. These losses could range from thousands to millions of dollars a year.

Individuals and organizations can use two methods to manage the risk of potential financial loss. They can control the risk (risk control) by taking steps to avoid loss, prevent loss, or mitigate loss; or they can finance the risk (risk financing) by having funds available to pay for a loss or by transferring the possibility of financial loss to others. Insurance is a risk financing technique. While explaining all of the risk management techniques, this textbook and the entire Associate in Claims curriculum focuses on insurance as a risk management technique.

Insurance, at its most basic level, is a promise; the insurer promises to pay the insured for a covered loss, or to pay a third party on the insured's behalf, when a specific event occurs. The claim representative (a generic title that refers to all who adjust claims, except for public adjusters) fulfills the promise to pay the insured or to pay on behalf of the insured by handling a claim when a loss occurs. The focus of this textbook is on the role of the claim representative, how it fits into the context of the overall insurance function, and the qualities and skills required of claim representatives.

Insurance is only one technique used to manage risk. This chapter begins by examining the concept of risk and risk management techniques to demonstrate how insurance fits into the broader picture of risk management. It describes what insurance is and the insurer's role in managing risk. Focus then narrows to the claim department and how it fits into the broader picture of insurance and into the even broader scope of insurance regulation.

RISK

The term "risk" has different meanings depending on the context. Many in the insurance business use the term to identify the insured or the property being insured. However, for the purpose of this text, **risk** is defined as uncertainty about outcomes, some of which can be either negative or positive. If an outcome is certain, there is no risk.

Risk
The uncertainty about outcomes, some of which can be either negative or positive.

Much of life is uncertain. The degree of uncertainty about something depends on subjective as well as objective information. This combination of perception and fact often determines whether people act on the uncertainty before them. If rain is a possibility, a person may take an umbrella. If an auto accident is probable, a party may buy auto insurance to protect against a possible loss. The terms "possibility" and "probability" are closely associated with the term "uncertainty."

Understanding the distinction between possibility and probability makes it easier to assess risk and determine how to manage it.

Possibility means something could happen. For risk to exist, two or more outcomes must be possible. If only one outcome exists, the result is certain and risk does not exist. The following are some examples of possibilities:

- While walking, a person could be struck by lightning.
- While driving to work, a person could be injured in an auto accident.
- While loading a truck, a person could be injured at work.
- While playing a slot machine, a person could win $1,000.

Each of the examples carries some risk because more than one outcome is possible, and one of the possible outcomes—incurring bodily injury or losing money—is negative.

Possibility does not quantify risk; it only verifies that risk is present. To quantify risk, one needs to know how often the possibilities can occur. Knowing that someone can win the lottery and become an instant millionaire does not provide enough information to quantify the risk. The potential risk-taker needs to know the likelihood of that possibility, that is, the probability of winning.

Possibility and Probability Compared

Probability is the mathematical likelihood that an event will occur in the long run. If something is possible, the likelihood of its occurring can be expressed mathematically as a number between zero and one.

Unlike possibility, probability is measurable. The possibility that a baseball team will win the Super Bowl does not exist. Therefore, the probability that a baseball team will win the Super Bowl is zero. The probability that a particular individual will win the top prize in the Powerball lottery is extremely low (1 in 120,000,000), and the probability of being killed in a fireworks accident is somewhat greater (1 in 620,000). In comparison to the lottery probability, the probability of being dealt a royal flush in a five-card hand of poker is still greater (1 in 40,000), and the probability of spinning a red number in roulette is significantly greater (1 in 2.05) than that of winning the lottery.

Understanding the probability of various outcomes helps focus risk management attention on the risks that can be appropriately managed. Probability is discussed in more detail in later chapters.

Hazard Risk and Business Risk

How someone manages risk is often determined by whether the risk is a hazard risk or a business risk. **Hazard risk** is the risk from accidental loss, including the possibility of loss or no loss. **Business risk** is risk that is inherent in the operation of a particular organization, including the possibility of loss, no loss, or gain. The risk of a fire to a home is a hazard risk. If a house burns, its owner suffers a loss. If no fire occurs, the owner's financial condition remains unchanged. A company that produces a new product is facing a business risk, as that new product may cause the company to lose money, break even, or make a profit. Sometimes owning an asset poses both hazard and business risks. For example, a homeowner may face the risk of a house fire, which is a hazard risk. The homeowner may also face market value risk upon sale of the home, which is a type of business risk. This chapter focuses on techniques for managing hazard risk because insurance is often used by individuals and entities to manage hazard risk.

Hazard risk
Risk from accidental loss, including the possibility of loss or no loss.

Business risk
Risk that is inherent in the operation of a particular organization, including the possibility of loss, no loss, or gain.

Risk Management Techniques

Risk imposes certain costs. It can cause worry and fear in individuals and organizations. It can deprive society of goods and services that are considered too risky to produce. Risk also restricts the use of money by creating the need for an emergency fund to pay for unexpected losses. If individuals and organizations set aside large sums of money for emergency funds, they are unable to use those funds for other purposes. Because of the various costs imposed by risk, individuals and organizations need to manage it. Risk managers do this by implementing a variety of risk management techniques that either control or finance risk.

Risk Management Techniques

Risk Control
- Avoidance
- Loss prevention
- Loss reduction
- Separation
- Duplication
- Diversification

Risk Financing
- Retention
- Noninsurance transfers
- Insurance transfers

Risk Control

Controlling risk is one method of managing risk. Risk control can involve several techniques.

Avoidance is choosing not to perform actions that would create a risk. Obviously, this technique will not be available for every risk. It is impossible to avoid the risk of death. However, it is possible to avoid the risk of dying in a plane crash by avoiding airline travel. Some businesses successfully use avoidance to manage risk. To avoid a risk that arises out of the manufacture of a hazardous material, a business can choose not to make the product. However, avoidance may not be the most practical means of managing risk. If the business finds that the hazardous material is a commercially viable product, it may be financially irresponsible not to manufacture the product.

Two other techniques of risk control are loss prevention, which is reducing the frequency or chance of loss, and loss reduction, which is minimizing the severity or adverse financial impact of any potential losses. A business can reduce the frequency of auto accidents by having fewer cars on the road. An individual can reduce the frequency of auto accidents by driving less. Despite these efforts, some losses will occur. However, drivers can reduce the severity of an auto accident by wearing their seatbelts at all times. A business or homeowner can also take steps to reduce the severity of potential loss. For example, a business may have a sprinkler system that will be triggered when a fire is detected, thereby minimizing the amount of inventory lost. A homeowner may have a device by the water heater that will sound an alarm should the heater start to leak, thereby minimizing water damage to the surrounding area.

Other techniques for controlling risk are separation, duplication, and diversification. These are more frequently associated with organizations rather than individuals. A manufacturer may store inventory in several locations (separation) rather than in one where it would all be subject to a single loss occurrence. An electric generating plant may have several generators working while maintaining a spare generator off-line (duplication), to be used if another generator fails. Finally, a business can diversify its products and services or geographically diversify its exposures to control risk. For example, an insurer that primarily issues policies for personal autos and homes can diversify by writing commercial business policies, or a large retail chain can diversify location by establishing distribution centers throughout the country rather than having only one location.

Risk Financing

The second method of managing risk is risk financing. This method ensures that funds are available to pay for or offset losses. One risk financing technique is retention, or the practice of assuming financial responsibility for one's own losses. **Retention** is a risk management technique by which losses are retained, rather than transferred, by generating funds within the organization to pay for losses. Retention, when used appropriately, can be a practical method of

Retention
A risk management technique by which losses are retained by generating funds within the organization to pay for losses.

handling risk. All or part of a risk can be retained. For example, in some states a business can decide to create its own fund to pay for injuries to employees. An individual can choose a large deductible on a home or auto insurance policy, thereby retaining part of the loss. Retention can be a conscious decision or it can occur without any thought, because of ignorance or indifference. For example, homeowners or farmers can retain the risk of polluting the ground water because they are unaware that the pesticide they are using is unsafe.

Noninsurance transfer is a risk financing technique by which the risk of loss is transferred to a person or an organization that is not an insurer. Two possible ways of accomplishing this type of transfer of risk are by the terms of a contract and by incorporation of a business. Risk transfer by the terms of a contract can be found in a variety of contracts. In a contract of sale, a purchaser can transfer the risk of repair or service back to the retailer by purchasing a service agreement. In a lease agreement, the risk of certain types of loss can be transferred from the owner of the building to the renter of the building. Risk transfer by incorporation occurs when a sole proprietor incorporates to protect his or her personal assets from creditors.

Finally, insurance is a risk financing technique that involves the transfer of risk.

Noninsurance transfer
A risk management technique by which the risk of loss is transferred to a person or an organization that is not an insurer.

INSURANCE

Insurance is a system for transferring risk from people and organizations to insurers that reimburse those people and organizations for covered losses. An **insured** is a person or an organization whose property, life, or legal liability is covered by an insurance policy. The insured pays a premium in exchange for the insurer's promise of coverage for specific losses; thus, insureds transfer the potential financial consequences of their loss exposures to insurers. Loss exposures are conditions, situations, or property that present the possibility of loss. A building, for example, is a loss exposure if the possibility exists that it can be damaged by fire.

To effectively complete the transfer of the risk, an insurer pools the premiums it receives from all of its insureds and uses that pool of money to indemnify (restore to pre-loss financial condition) the few insureds who sustain covered losses. In any given period, such as a year, a relatively small percentage of insureds suffer covered losses.

The accuracy of their projections is based on the **law of large numbers**. Insurers project the number of losses they will pay in any given period so that they can determine what premium is required to pay for those losses. The law of large numbers is a mathematical principle stating that, as the number of similar but independent exposure units increases, the relative accuracy of predications about future outcomes (losses) based on these exposure units also increases. Insurers underwrite a large number of similar loss exposures and project the dollar amount of all the losses that those insureds are expected to experience. Premiums are based on each insured's share of the projected losses plus the insurer's expenses and an allowance for profit.

Insurance
A system for transferring risk from people and organizations to insurers that reimburse those people and organizations for covered losses.

Insured
A person or an organization whose property, life, or legal liability is covered by an insurance policy.

Law of large numbers
A mathematical principle stating that, as the number of similar but independent exposure units increases, the relative accuracy of predications about future outcomes (losses) based on these exposure units also increases.

1.8 Claim Handling Principles and Practices

Principle of indemnity
The principle that insurance policies should provide a benefit no greater than the loss suffered by an insured.

The **principle of indemnity**, a fundamental principle of insurance, holds that insurance policies should provide a benefit no greater than the loss suffered by an insured. For example, if Jill purchases insurance for her five-year-old car and the car is later destroyed in an accident, under the principle of indemnity Jill should be paid (indemnified) for the value of the five-year-old car. Jill is not entitled to the value of a new car because that would put her in a better financial position than she was in before the loss occurred.

Insurable interest
An exposure that a party has to financial loss.

The principle of indemnity is reinforced by the requirement that a party must have an insurable interest to purchase property insurance. An **insurable interest** is a person's or an organization's exposure to financial loss, such as damage to or loss of an insured house. The insurable interest requirement prevents people from profiting from a loss. For example, if Joe purchases insurance for a house that he does not own or rent, he has nothing to lose financially from a loss. If a loss occurs, and if the insurer pays the claim, Joe profits by the amount of the loss payment because he has no incentive to pay to repair or replace the home. Such an arrangement is undesirable because having nothing to lose would encourage insureds to cause losses, which would result in higher premiums for all insureds.

Insurance policies cover losses only to the extent of the insured's insurable interest in the property. Suppose that Jerry owns 30 percent of an office building. The building is destroyed by a tornado. Jerry can collect insurance only on 30 percent of the building's value, even though the entire building was destroyed. This result prevents Jerry from profiting from the loss, supporting the principle of indemnity.

Parties to the Insurance Contract

The insurance contract (policy) involves two parties: the insured and the insurer. The insured is the first party to the insurance contract; the insurer is the second party to the insurance contract. A demand by an insured person or organization seeking to recover for a loss from its insurer is called a **first-party claim**. When an insured injures a third party or damages the property belonging to a third party, the third party's demand against the insurer, called a **third-party claim**, is based on the legal duties the insured owes to the third party.

First-party claim
A demand by an insured person or organization seeking to recover from its insurer for a loss that its insurance policy may cover.

Third-party claim
A demand by a third party against an insured based on the legal duties the insured owes to the third party; it seeks to recover from the insured's insurer for a loss that the issuing policy may cover.

Benefits of Insurance

The business of insurance provides many benefits to individuals, families, businesses, and society as a whole. These benefits include the following:

- *Payment for covered losses.* Payment for losses is the most obvious benefit of insurance. Without insurance, the effects of a loss may be financially devastating for an individual, family, or organization. Insurance enables individuals and families to maintain their homes and standards of living. Insurance enables businesses to continue operating after a loss, allowing employees to keep their jobs, customers to continue receiving goods and services, and suppliers to be paid.

- *Reduction of uncertainty.* The risk of loss produces fear and uncertainty. For example, a restaurant owned by two brothers employs the brothers' wives and their children, who have their own families. If the restaurant is destroyed by fire, many lives will be affected by the loss of income. By purchasing adequate insurance on the restaurant, the owners can eliminate such fear and uncertainty. If the restaurant is destroyed by a covered cause of loss, the insurer would pay to have it rebuilt, preserving the families' source of income. Therefore, insurance reduces anxiety and provides peace of mind.

- *Support for credit.* Before lending money for a large purchase such as a house, financial institutions want assurance that the money will be repaid. If the borrower does not repay the loan, the lender can repossess the house. But if the house is destroyed by fire, the lender cannot repossess it. Insurance would pay for the destroyed home and thus makes loans possible by reducing the lender's uncertainty about whether the borrower would be able to repay the loan.

- *Source of investment funds.* Insurers can use the premiums they receive from their insureds to make loans and investments until they need that money to pay for losses or operating expenses. The interest from those loans and the earnings from those investments help insurers meet operating expenses and reduce premiums. Additionally, loans and investments help generate other business activity, creating new jobs and resulting in new consumer products.

- *Loss reduction and prevention.* Insurers recommend loss reduction and prevention to reduce the severity and frequency of losses. Businesses take loss control measures to promote workplace safety. Individuals and families can benefit from loss control measures such as installing smoke and burglar alarms and deadbolt locks. Such measures save lives and protect property. These and other loss control measures benefit insureds by reducing the amount of money that insurers must pay in claims resulting in lower premiums. Insureds, insurers, and society as a whole are better served when losses are prevented than when losses are covered by insurance.

- *Efficient use of resources.* Without insurance, individuals and organizations would have to set aside contingency funds to pay for property damage, bodily injuries, and lawsuits. Money and other resources that could otherwise be used to produce and deliver goods and services would be tied up. Consumers would be less likely to make major purchases, and businesses would be reluctant to enter new ventures or expand their facilities. Insurance frees those contingency funds for consumer spending and business growth. Insurance premiums are much lower than the costs of contingency funds, so purchasing insurance allows insureds to use the remaining money more productively. Some organizations choose not to purchase insurance, but instead to pay for some or all of their losses with their own funds. That arrangement is called self-insurance, or retention. Self-insurance is actually not insurance because it does not involve risk transfer. Self-insured businesses save some of the administrative costs associated with insurance, but they must maintain sufficient resources to pay for losses that do occur.

- *Reduction of social burdens.* Accident victims who are not compensated for their injuries and individuals who lose all their belongings in a fire can be a serious financial burden to society. The families of these accident victims can become a burden if they depend on that victim for financial support. Insurance helps reduce that burden by compensating injured individuals for lost wages and medical expenses and by paying for damaged or destroyed property.
- *Satisfaction of legal and business requirements.* Some laws require individuals and organizations to purchase insurance. For example, in many states, automobile owners must prove that they have auto liability insurance before they can register their vehicles. State laws require employers to pay for the job-related injuries or illnesses of their employees, and employers typically purchase workers' compensation insurance to meet that financial obligation. Some business relationships require proof of insurance. For example, building contractors are usually required to provide evidence of liability insurance before they are granted a construction contract. In fact, almost anyone who provides a service to the public, such as landscapers, architects, doctors, and lawyers, may need liability insurance to contract for services. In this way, insurance protects both the public and business entities.
- *Source of employment and tax revenue.* The insurance business in the United States employs many people. In addition to the benefits of employment to the individual, governments benefit because those employees pay local, state, and federal income taxes. Insurers pay taxes on their profits and, in most states, on the premiums they collect from insureds. These taxes benefit society by paying for government services.

Costs of Insurance

The direct and indirect costs associated with insurance affect not only the individual or organization that must pay the premium; they also affect society as a whole. Dollars spent on premiums cannot be spent on other things that could be more beneficial to society. Direct and indirect costs of insurance include the following:

- *Premiums.* A direct cost of insurance is the premiums. Insurance benefits are not provided free of charge. Insurers charge premiums to have funds to pay claims and to cover their operations. Premiums can be substantial. However, the portion of the premium that is used to pay losses is not an additional cost to society. Most of those losses would have occurred and imposed a cost to society regardless of whether they were insured. The additional cost created by insurance is the portion of premium that is used to pay insurers' operational expenses.
- *Opportunity costs.* Opportunity costs are an indirect cost of insurance. Opportunities are lost when money is used to pay premiums. Insureds dislike spending money for mandatory insurance because they would rather use the money for some other purpose. Money spent on premiums may be used for other purposes that would be more productive for the

economy, such as investment in a small business or to help finance the down payment on a house. All purchases create opportunity costs for consumers. Because some insurance buyers believe that they do not benefit from insurance unless they suffer losses, they are sensitive to the opportunity costs associated with insurance.

- *Increased litigation.* Another indirect cost of insurance is increased litigation. Liability insurance sometimes pays large sums of money to protect insureds who may be responsible for injury to someone else or for damage to someone else's property. Many people, however, view liability insurance as a pool of money available to pay the claims of anyone who has suffered injury or whose property has been damaged, regardless of fault. The existence of insurance can encourage such persons to sue to recover for their injuries or damages.

- *Moral hazards.* Still another indirect cost of insurance is the economic incentive it provides for insureds to cause losses. **Moral hazards** are conditions that may lead a person to intentionally cause or exaggerate a loss. If moral hazards result in more or larger losses than would have occurred in the absence of insurance, they are an indirect cost of insurance. For example, an insured may intentionally burn an empty warehouse in what has become a dangerous section of a city and use the insurance proceeds to rebuild in a more favorable location. Exaggerated claims are a more common type of moral hazard than intentional losses such as arson or staged auto accidents. For example, an insured may claim that a stolen ten-year-old TV was new in order to obtain a larger claim payment.

- *Morale (attitudinal) hazards.* **Morale hazards**, also called **attitudinal hazards**, involve carelessness about or indifference to potential loss on the part of an insured. Insurance is available to pay for losses should they occur, so an insured may leave an expensive piece of jewelry or a laptop computer in an unlocked and unattended car, knowing insurance will cover any loss if the item is stolen.

Moral hazard
A condition that may lead a person to intentionally cause or exaggerate a loss.

Morale hazard, or attitudinal hazard
A hazard that involves carelessness about or indifference to potential loss on the part of an insured.

Exhibit 1-1 summarizes the benefits and costs of insurance.

EXHIBIT 1-1

Benefits and Costs of Insurance

Benefits
- Payment for losses
- Peace of mind
- Support for credit
- Funds for loans and investments
- Loss control
- Efficient use of resources
- Reduction of social burdens
- Satisfaction of legal and business requirements
- Source of employment and tax revenue

Costs
- Premiums
- Opportunity costs
- Increased litigation
- Moral hazard
- Morale hazard

The claim function has a significant role in helping policyholders achieve their risk management goals. It is responsible for keeping the insurer's promise to the policyholder to pay covered losses by providing prompt and professional claim adjusting services. How the claim function fulfills the insurer's promise to pay is discussed next.

CLAIM FUNCTION

Insurers have claim departments; however, claim departments can also be found in large business entities that self-insure, in companies called third-party administrators (TPAs) that handle the claims of others, and in agents' or brokers' offices. The claim representatives in a large business or at an agent's or a broker's office may or may not investigate and pay claims, just as a claim representative working at an insurer would. If they do not investigate and pay claims directly, their role is often that of an examiner, monitoring the actions of the insurer or third-party administrator. A **third party administator** contracts to provide administrative services to other businesses and is often hired to handle claims by organizations that have self-insurance plans. Claim representatives at a third-party administrator perform many, if not all, of the same claim-related activities as the claim representatives of insurers.

Third-party administrator
A firm that contracts to provide administrative services to other businesses and that is often hired to handle claims by organizations that have self-insurance plans.

This section focuses on the structure of an insurer's claim department and the various parties, policies, and performance measures that help the insurer fulfill its promise to pay covered losses.

Claim Department Structure

An insurer's claim department can be organized in several different ways. However, only one structure is used here to illustrate the various claim positions within the department. Usually a senior claim officer heads the claim organization and reports to the chief executive officer, the chief financial officer, or the chief underwriting officer. Exhibit 1-2 shows a typical organizational chart for a claim department.

The senior claim officer may have a staff located in the same office. This staff is often called the home-office claim department. Within the home-office claim department, any number of technical and management specialists can provide advice and assistance to any remote claim offices and claim representatives.

The senior claim officer may have several claim offices or branches countrywide or worldwide. Staff from remote claim offices can all report directly into the home-office claim department, or regional/divisional claim officers may oversee the territory. Regional claim officers may have one or more branch offices reporting to them. Each branch office may have a claim manager. Each branch office that reports to the claim manager may have one or more claim supervisors and a staff of claim representatives. Similar department structures are adopted by TPAs, large organizations that self-insure, and large agents and brokers.

EXHIBIT 1-2

Claim Department Organizational Chart

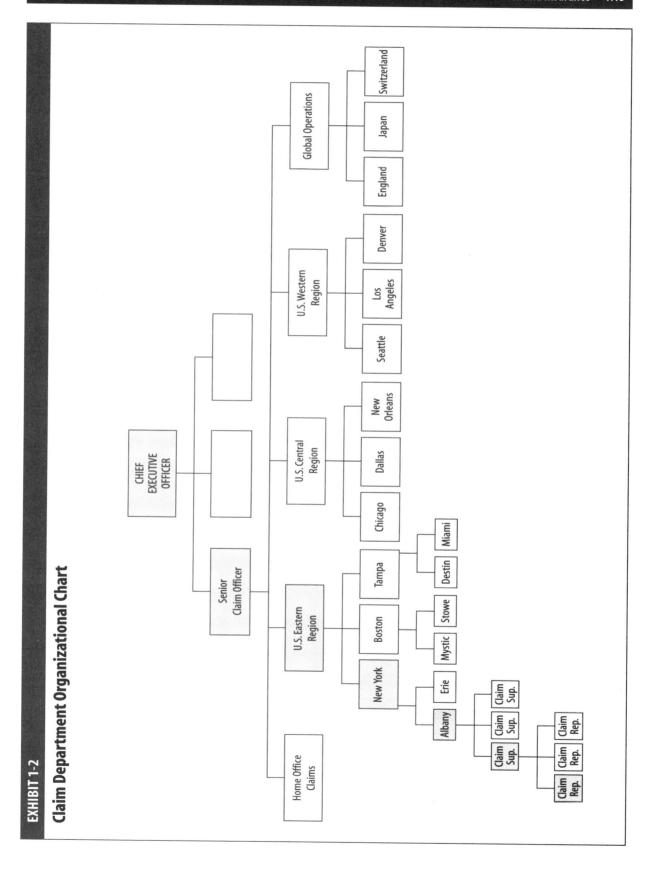

Claim Personnel

People who handle claims may be staff claim representatives, independent adjusters, employees of third-party administrators, or producers who sell policies to insureds. In addition, public adjusters also handle claims by representing the interests of the insureds to the insurer. This section discusses the different personnel who handle claims.

Staff Claim Representatives

Staff claim representatives are insurer employees, and they handle most claims. They may include inside claim representatives, who handle claims exclusively from inside an insurer's office, and field claim representatives, who handle claims both inside and outside the office. Field claim representatives, also called outside claim representatives, handle claims that require such tasks as investigating the scene of the loss; meeting with insureds, claimants, lawyers, and others involved in the loss; and inspecting damage. Staff claim representatives usually work from branch or regional offices rather than at the insurer's home office. If the branch or region covers a large territory, the insurer may set up claim offices in areas away from the branch office to enable the claim representative to serve insureds efficiently.

Independent Adjusters

Independent adjuster
An independent claim representative who handles claims for insurers for a fee.

A particular insurer may not find it economically feasible to set up claim offices. In this case, insurers may use **independent adjusters**, who handle claims for insurers in exchange for a fee.

Some insurers use independent adjusters for all field claim work. These insurers employ claim personnel in their home office or branch offices to monitor claim progress and settle claims, but independent adjusters handle all the field work.

Some insurers use independent adjusters when their staff claim representatives are too busy to handle all claims themselves. For example, when a tornado or hurricane strikes, staff claim representatives may need assistance to handle the large number of claims quickly enough to satisfy the insurer and its insureds. Insurers may also use independent adjusters to meet desired service levels or when special skills are needed. For example, some independent adjusters are experts in highly specialized fields, such as investigating aircraft accidents.

Some independent adjusters are self-employed, but most work for adjusting firms that range in size from one small office with a few adjusters to national firms with hundreds of offices employing thousands of adjusters.

Third-Party Administrators

Businesses that choose not to purchase insurance but to self-insure do not use agents, underwriters, or other typical insurer personnel. However, they do need personnel to handle the losses that arise. Self-insured businesses can employ their own claim representatives or contract with third-party administrators (TPAs) who handle claims, keep claim records, and perform statistical analyses. TPAs are often associated with large independent adjusting firms or with subsidiaries of insurance companies. Many property-casualty insurers have established subsidiary companies that serve as TPAs.

Producers

The term "producer" is used to describe anyone who sells insurance. This can include agents, brokers, employees of insurers, or intermediaries. **Insurance agents** are legal representatives of insurers for which they have contractual agreements to sell insurance. An **insurance broker** is an independent business owner or firm that sells insurance by representing customers rather than insurers. An insured who purchases insurance through a producer is likely to call the producer first when a loss occurs. Most insurers give some producers the authority to pay claims up to a certain amount, such as $2,500. Those producers can issue claim payments, called drafts, directly to insureds for covered claims, thus reducing the time necessary to pay insureds. In this capacity, producers function much like inside claim representatives.

If the producer does not have draft authority, he or she can report the loss to the insurer immediately, give the insured the telephone number of the insurer's claim office, and explain how the insured can expect the claim to be handled.

> **Insurance agent**
> A legal representative of one or more insurers for which the representative has a contractual agreement to sell insurance.
>
> **Insurance broker**
> An independent business owner or firm that sells insurance by representing customers rather than insurers.

Public Adjusters

If a claim is complex or if the settlement negotiations are not progressing satisfactorily with the insurer, the insured may hire a public adjuster to protect his or her interests. A **public adjuster** is an organization or person hired by an insured to represent the insured in a claim. Some states have statutes that govern the services public adjusters can provide. In general, the public adjuster prepares the insured's claim and negotiates the settlement with the staff claim representative or independent adjuster. The insured, in turn, pays the public adjuster's fee, which is usually a percentage of the settlement.

> **Public adjuster**
> An organization or person hired by an insured to represent the insured in a claim.

Because a claim department staff can be diverse and may be spread over a wide geographic area, insurers face special issues in evaluating and measuring their performance.

Performance Measures

Insurers are businesses, and, as such, they must make a profit in order to survive. Claim departments pay claims, which may be considered to reduce an insurer's profit. But claim departments play a crucial role in insurer profitability by paying fair amounts for legitimate claims and by providing accurate, reliable, and consistent ratemaking data. Fair claim payment does not conflict with insurer profit goals. Consequently, an insurer measures its underwriting and claim department's performance using a loss ratio, which is a profitability measure. A claim department's performance can also be measured by quality, using best practices, claim audits, and customer satisfaction.

Profitability Measures

To calculate the loss ratio to measure profitability, insurers must ascertain their incurred losses. **Incurred losses** are paid losses plus losses for which the insurer is liable but which the insurer has not yet paid. Earned premium is the proportion of written premium (total policy premium) that applies to the part of the policy period that has already occurred. For example, if the written premium is $120 for a twelve-month policy, then the earned premium for each month is $10 ($120 divided by 12). Assuming that the policy is written on a calendar year basis, the earned premium at the end of March would be $30, that is, $10 each for January, February, and March.

The **loss ratio** is an insurer's incurred losses (including loss adjustment expenses) for a given period divided by its earned premiums for the same period, as shown in the following calculation:

$$\text{Loss ratio} = \frac{\text{Incurred losses} + \text{Loss adjustment expenses}}{\text{Earned premium}} \times 100\%.$$

Loss adjustment expenses include the following:

- Salaries and expenses for an insurer's claim staff
- Costs of hiring lawyers to defend insureds in lawsuits
- Fees charged by service providers (for example, doctors' fees for independent medical examinations or engineers' fees to inspect damaged property)
- Costs of obtaining medical, police, and other types of reports

The amount of loss for which the insurer is liable but has not yet paid is the amount of loss reserve on a claim. **Loss reserves** are estimates of the amount of money the insurer expects to pay in the future for losses that have already occurred and that have been reported to the insurer. They are usually set on a per claim basis by the claim representative. When all the loss reserves are aggregated, they represent the insurer's liabilities. If the reserves are higher than necessary, the loss ratio appears higher (worse) than it actually is. When the loss ratio is high, underwriters tend to decline new risks or to increase premiums for new and existing risks. This practice can cause the insurer to become less competitive in its pricing.

Conversely, if the reserves are lower than necessary, the loss ratio may suggest that the profitability being measured is higher than it actually is. The insurer might aggressively pursue a line of business that is really unprofitable. For insurers to accurately assess their underwriting, claim representatives must consistently set accurate reserves and adjust them as appropriate.

The loss ratio is one component of the **combined ratio**, which represents an insurer's underwriting profitability. The combined ratio is calculated as follows:

$$\text{Combined ratio} = \text{Loss ratio} + \text{Expense ratio}.$$

Incurred losses
The amount equal to paid losses and losses for which the insurer is liable but has not yet paid.

Loss ratio
An insurer's incurred losses (including loss adjustment expenses) for a given period divided by its earned premiums for the same period.

Loss reserves
Estimates of the amount of money the insurer expects to pay in the future for losses that have already occurred and been reported.

Combined ratio
A profitability measurement calculated by adding loss ratio and expense ratio.

The expense ratio in this formula uses underwriting expenses and expenses other than claim-related expenses and is calculated as follows:

$$\text{Expense ratio} = \frac{\text{Expenses}}{\text{Earned premium}} \times 100\%.$$

Because claims usually do not occur immediately after a policy is issued and because they take some time to be paid, insurers can invest premiums to generate additional income until the premiums are needed to pay claims. Insurers select stocks, bonds, Treasury bills, and other securities to buy and sell. They seek to earn the highest possible return from investments while making sure that funds are available to meet their financial obligations. Insurers typically spend slightly more on operations (claims and other expenses) than they collect in premiums. Managing investments wisely enables insurers to earn a profit despite a loss on operations.

The following example illustrates the performance ratios and their implications. In fiscal 2005, the Atwell Insurance Company earned $25 million in premiums, incurred $16 million in losses and loss adjustment expenses, and incurred underwriting expenses of $7.5 million. Its combined ratio is calculated as follows:

$$\text{Loss ratio} = \frac{\$16 \text{ million}}{\$25 \text{ million}} = 0.64 \times 100\% = 64\%.$$

$$\text{Expense ratio} = \frac{\$7.5 \text{ million}}{\$25 \text{ million}} = 0.30 \times 100\% = 30\%.$$

$$\text{Combined ratio} = 64\% + 30\% = 94\%.$$

If the combined ratio is less than 100 percent, as for Atwell Insurance Company, the insurer has made an underwriting profit. For every $1.00 in premium, Atwell pays $0.94 in losses and operating expenses, leaving $0.06 for profit. If the combined ratio is 100 percent, every dollar that the insurer earned in premiums was used to pay losses and operating expenses. A combined ratio of greater than 100 percent means that the insurer has incurred an underwriting loss because it paid out more money in losses and operating expenses than it received in premiums. An insurer can have an underwriting loss and still be profitable if its investment income is sufficient to offset the losses. Therefore, by managing losses and controlling expenses associated with handling losses, the claim department plays an important role in an insurer's profitability.[1]

Quality Measures

Even though claim handling is more art than science, there are measures that can be used to evaluate the performance of a claim department. Three of the more frequently used quality measures are best practices, claim audits, and customer satisfaction.

Best practices can mean different things to different people. In the context of a claim department, best practices usually refers to a system of identified internal practices that produce superior performance. Best practices are usually maintained electronically or in written form and shared with every claim representative. An insurer can create best practices by studying its own performance or by studying the performance of similar successful insurers.

Claim department best practices are often based on legal requirements specified by regulators, legislators, and the courts. For example, a claim department may have a best practice that states "every claim will be acknowledged within twenty-four hours." This time frame may have been selected because of a regulation, law, or court decision that requires insurers to acknowledge a claim within twenty-four hours of receipt. Other best practices may relate to the following:

- Time allowed to make initial contact with the insured and claimant
- Timely responses to outside communications
- Timely and accurate loss reserving
- File documentation
- Timely payment of claims or timely denial of claims
- Complete explanation of payment or denial

Insurers use claim audits to ensure compliance with best practices, in addition to gathering statistical information on claims. A claim audit is performed by reviewing a number of open and closed claim files and evaluating the information contained in the files. Claim audits can be performed by the claim staff that works on the files (called a self-audit), or they can be performed by claim representatives from other offices or by a team from the home office.

Claim audits usually evaluate both quantitative and qualitative factors, examples of which are shown in the box.

Quantitative and Qualitative Audit Factors

Quantitative	Qualitative
Timeliness of reports	Realistic reserving
Timeliness of reserving	Accurate evaluation of insured's liability
Timeliness of payments	Follow-up on subrogation opportunity
Number of files opened each month	Litigation cost management
Number of files closed each month	Proper releases taken
Number of files reopened each month	Correct coverage evaluation
Percentage of recovery from subrogation	Good negotiation skills
Average claim settlement value by claim type	Thorough investigations
Percentage of claims entering litigation	
Percentage of cases going to trial	
Accuracy of data entry	

The quantitative and qualitative factors can be rated or graded individually as can the overall file. The quantitative information gathered can help identify trends that require corrective action. For example, information showing that a claim representative has a high number of files closed each month and has the highest number of files reopened each month may suggest that this claim representative is closing files prematurely. A claim manager would want to review these files to see if this is the case or if there is a legitimate reason for the reopenings.

The qualitative factors are used to determine if claim representatives are following the guidelines and best practices set by the insurer. They must be evaluated in the context of the overall claim file. The type of the claim will dictate how it should best be handled. Consistently poor results in a given area can indicate a need for training and supervision. For example, a consistent failure to correctly evaluate coverage indicates a need for training in coverage analysis.

The quality of a claim department's performance is also measured by its customer satisfaction. Claim supervisors and managers will usually keep track of any correspondence they receive about the performance of individual claim representatives. While compliments are usually acknowledged, supervisors or managers must respond to complaints, and most claim departments have procedures for doing so. Complaints may come directly from the insured, claimant, or vendor; or they can be submitted by a State Insurance Department on behalf of an insured, claimant, or vendor. However received, the complaint must be investigated by management and responded to in a timely manner. Complaints such as "I called a claim representative on January 24 and February 3 and never received a return phone call" may indicate legitimate service issues. Other complaints can simply indicate dissatisfaction with an otherwise valid claim settlement. Review of complaints received in a claim office can show whether problems exist with a particular claim representative, supervisor, or manager.

The claim function is only one part of a larger organization that provides insurance. An insurance company has parties who market and sell the insurance contract, underwrite the insurance contract, price the insurance contract, manage and gather data about a large number of insurance contracts, and ultimately pay the claims made against these contracts. These parties perform the major functions of the insurance company.

OTHER INSURANCE COMPANY FUNCTIONS

This section provides an overview of the principal functions of a typical insurance company, which allow the insurer to fulfill its promises to the insured. Some insurers may not have all of these functions; they may be combined, or they may be called something else. While each of these functions operates individually, each contributes to the insurer's overall effectiveness. The effective interaction of these functions is vital to the insurer's survival and continued success. Because the purpose of this text is to describe the claim function, it is discussed in more detail than the other functions.

Marketing and Sales

Marketing and sales are the functions that bring business in to the insurer. The terms "marketing" and "sales" are sometimes used interchangeably. However, marketing may encompass the broader perspective of actually delivering products or services to the customer, while the sales function is usually to contact the customer and bring the insurance application to the insurer. This distinction may vary depending on many factors, including the insurer's size and available financial resources, the lines of business written, and the marketing system used.

Many insurers market through producers who are independent agents and brokers and who represent several otherwise unrelated insurers. Some insurers market through exclusive agents, who represent only one insurer or group of insurers under common ownership and management. Others rely on the efforts of their own employees.

Insurers must develop marketing programs. Successful marketing programs are likely to include the following features:

- Market research to determine the needs of potential buyers and markets
- Advertising and public relations programs to inform customers about the insurer's products
- Training programs to prepare the sales force (either employees or independent or exclusive agents) to meet the customers' needs
- Production goals and strategies to achieve them
- Effective motivation and management of the producer network

Underwriting

Once an insurance application is received, the underwriting department determines if the application meets insurer guidelines. The goal of underwriting is to write a profitable book of business for the insurer, that is, to accept those applications (also called submissions) most likely to produce a profit for the insurer. Underwriters are involved in risk selection, pricing, and determination of coverage terms and conditions. Underwriters work with the marketing department. They can also work with the sales department to modify policy conditions or pricing to make an otherwise unacceptable application acceptable for coverage.

Applications from most mid-sized and large commercial organizations are handled by an underwriter. Applications from small commercial organizations and for personal insurance are often handled by computerized expert systems. Such systems are designed to replicate the thought process used by underwriters for risk selection, pricing, and determination of coverage terms and conditions. These systems are used to accept those accounts that clearly fall within the insurer's eligibility guidelines. Any applications that are not clearly within eligibility guidelines are referred to an underwriter for evaluation. This underwriter then reviews the application to determine if pricing or coverage modifications are needed. The underwriter may also consult with the sales department before rejecting the application because the rejection may adversely affect a business relationship.

Loss Control

The loss control function works closely with the underwriting function. Loss control specialists inspect businesses that apply for insurance and suggest ways to prevent losses and reduce the severity of those losses that cannot be prevented. Loss control is an important insurer function that continues to grow in importance as policyholder loss exposures become more complex.

Reinsurance

To underwrite policies, insurers must be financially able to pay claims. One way insurers can ensure that they have sufficient funds to pay claims is by sharing the premiums and potential losses with a reinsurer. A **reinsurer** is an insurer that assumes all or part of the insurance risk from the primary insurer. The reinsurance function within most insurer operations is responsible for establishing reinsurance programs and negotiating those programs with reinsurers or reinsurance brokers. The reinsurance department also establishes guidelines for reinsurance procedures, usually in conjunction with staff underwriters. Reinsurance also protects the financial solvency of primary insurers by enabling them to meet their obligations to policyholders and claimants.

Reinsurer
The insurer that assumes all or part of the insured risk exposures of the primary insurer in a contractual agreement.

Another reason reinsurance is important is that it permits the primary insurer to provide high limits of insurance. For example, a primary insurer that provides insurance for a multimillion dollar high-rise office complex can transfer all or part of that risk to other insurers around the world through reinsurance transactions. Reinsurance also helps cushion the effects of natural disasters on individual insurers and the insurance industries of individual countries. For example, in 1992, Hurricane Andrew caused more than $15 billion of losses in the United States. The insured losses from the 1994 Northridge earthquake totaled almost $13 billion. Without reinsurance, this level of losses would have had a significant effect on the U.S. insurance industry. The reinsurance process spreads the cost of the catastrophes throughout the worldwide insurance industry and therefore substantially softens their overall effects.

Actuarial

Actuaries are highly trained specialists who perform all the mathematical functions underlying insurance operations. Underwriters rely on the actuarial function to supply the information required to calculate insurance rates (the price of insurance for each unit of exposure that, when multiplied by the number of exposure units, determines a premium amount), to develop rating plans, and to estimate loss reserves. Actuaries may assist in corporate planning and in establishing corporate goals by compiling and analyzing statistical reports. They may also be involved in assessing the insurer's success in meeting these goals.

The actuarial function is also responsible for providing information for regulators and for the ratemaking process. At one time, final rates were developed by rating bureaus that are now called advisory organizations. Organizations such as Insurance Services Office (ISO) now provide loss costs rather than final rates to insurers. Loss costs are the actual or expected costs of claims. Insurance company actuaries are responsible for developing factors to reflect individual insurer expenses and anticipated profits. These factors are applied to loss costs to convert them to final rates.

Finance and Accounting

The finance and accounting function is important in any insurance operation. Policyholders pay premiums at policy inception and receive benefits later if a loss occurs. The insurer's finance and accounting function invests the premiums received until they are needed to pay for losses. Any funds not used to pay for losses or expenses of selling policies and running the company are considered profit. Many insurers lose money on their operations because losses and expenses exceed the premiums collected.

The finance and accounting function may also prepare the financial statements that insurance regulators use to evaluate the insurer's profitability and solvency. This function can also be responsible for the insurer's day-to-day cash operations.

Information Technology (IT)

The information technology function is responsible for providing the technological infrastructure that supports all the insurer's internal and external communications and provides for many rating, statistical, claim payment, and other processes. The IT function collects and stores data that are used by employees, customers, and regulators. To provide efficient and optimal claim services, insurers depend on IT to improve interactions between office and field staff as well as with customers and claimants.

Miscellaneous Functions

Insurance also involves a number of other equally important functions that are not discussed in detail here, including premium audit, human resources, training and development, and legal services. Each of these functions contributes to the overall effective operation of an insurer.

Though insurers serve society in many ways, their primary purpose is to facilitate the transfer of risk. Their other contributions to the economy, such as the preservation of human and material assets and the accumulation of investment capital, are incidental to that primary purpose. All of the foregoing functions must work together to fulfill the insurer's primary purpose and to achieve insurer goals, and they must do so within the framework of insurance regulation.

INSURANCE REGULATION

Insurance operations are closely regulated. Insurance regulators monitor the solvency of insurers to protect policyholders and members of the public who benefit from the existence of insurance. Regulation also extends to the rates and forms used by insurers. If filed rate increases are not approved by the applicable regulator, an insurer may not meet its profit goal. Also, policy form approval and the time constraints relating to the filing process may keep an insurer from fully meeting a customer's needs. Insurance regulation is complicated by the variance of requirements from state to state and by the added burden of meeting certain federal regulatory requirements. For example, each state may have its own set of unfair claim handling practices. To enhance understanding of the regulatory environment within which the claim representative must operate, a brief discussion of the evolution of insurance regulation is included.

Evolution of Insurance Regulation

The ratification of the U.S. Constitution, which gives Congress the right to regulate commerce among the states, marks the beginning of the history of insurance regulation in the U.S. The Constitution's Commerce Clause in Section 8 provides that "The Congress shall have power to…regulate commerce with foreign nations, and among the several states, and with the Indian tribes." The Constitution also provides that the powers it does not delegate to the federal government belong to the states. Consequently, by the mid-1800s, state insurance departments began forming and states began collecting financial information from insurers operating within their boundaries to collect taxes and fees. In 1869 the U.S. Supreme Court decision in *Paul v. Virginia* effectively ratified the power of the states, rather than the federal government, to regulate insurance.[2] Despite the Supreme Court's decision in the *Paul* case, the debate continued: Who should have the power to regulate insurance—Congress or the states?

In 1944 the Supreme Court reversed the decision of *Paul v. Virginia*. In *United States v. South-Eastern Underwriters Association* (SEUA),[3] the Court ruled that insurance was interstate commerce subject to federal antitrust laws. The Supreme Court answered the question of who had the power to regulate insurance by effectively saying "both Congress and the states." This ruling surprised those in the insurance industry because the states had been regulating insurance for decades.

McCarran-Ferguson Act

In response to the *SEUA* case, Congress passed the McCarran-Ferguson Act in 1945. The act stated the following:

- State regulation of insurance "is in the public interest."
- Insurers are exempt from federal antitrust laws if the states maintain their own comprehensive regulatory systems.
- Federal antitrust laws will apply if the business of insurance is not regulated by state law or in cases involving boycott, coercion, or intimidation.

The McCarran-Ferguson Act preserved the structure of existing state insurance regulation. At the same time, it clarified the federal government's power to step in and assume regulatory functions in the absence of state regulation. Today, insurance regulation remains primarily with the states, but the debate continues. In addition, some federal laws that have applications beyond insurance can affect insures in specific ways.

Insurance Fraud Protection Act

The Insurance Fraud Protection Act is part of a federal anti-crime bill titled "Violent Crime Control and Law Enforcement Act of 1994."[4] This broad legislation protects consumers and insureds against insurer insolvencies resulting from fraud.

The act identifies the following crimes as fraud involving the business of insurance:[5]

- Making false statements or reports to insurance regulators—including overvaluing assets—to influence regulatory decisions
- Making false entries in books, reports, or statements to deceive anyone about an insurer's financial condition or solvency
- Embezzling from anyone who is engaged in the business of insurance
- Using threats of force or "any threatening letter or communication to corruptly influence, obstruct, or impede" insurance regulatory proceedings

The act prohibits insurers, reinsurers, producers, and others from employing a person who has been convicted of a felony involving breach of trust or dishonesty.

Gramm-Leach-Bliley Act of 1999

The issue of state versus federal insurance regulation has never been completely resolved. Many times during the last fifty years, it seemed likely to resurface as a major legislative concern. The issue came to the forefront during the 1990s, when affiliations between banks and insurers began to form and questions arose about who would regulate these "bankassurance" organizations. Banking activities were traditionally regulated by the federal government and, in some cases, by the states, while insurance was regulated only by the states.

The Gramm-Leach-Bliley (GLB) Act of 1999, also called the Financial Services Modernization Act, addressed this issue. However, although the GLB Act answered some questions, it raised many others that have not been answered, at least as of the writing of this text.

Under the GLB Act, each segment of the financial services business is regulated separately. The act makes it clear that states continue to have primary regulatory authority for all insurance activities. However, the act prohibits state actions that would prevent bank-related firms from selling insurance on the same basis as insurance producers. Meanwhile, securities activities are regulated by securities regulators, and banking activities are regulated by banking regulators.

Information sharing among banks and insurance affiliates raises privacy concerns. The GLB Act addresses these concerns through a provision requiring banks to disclose to customers their information-sharing policies and practices. Because state laws can be more restrictive than federal laws, this provision could lead to some inconsistency in practice.

Role of National Association of Insurance Commissioners (NAIC)

One disadvantage of state regulation of insurance is the inefficiency that can result when more than fifty different insurance departments perform similar tasks and address the same issues and problems, each in its own way. The National Association of Insurance Commissioners (NAIC) was established to encourage coordination and cooperation among state insurance departments.

Regulators from the fifty state insurance departments and those of the District of Columbia, Puerto Rico, and Guam belong to the NAIC. Members meet periodically to discuss insurance industry problems and issues in insurance regulation. The NAIC itself has no direct regulatory authority, but it has a profound influence on the content and uniformity of state regulation. For example, the NAIC drafts model laws and regulations that state legislatures may adopt as written or modify as they see fit. Consequently, the states that have adopted the model laws and regulations share some degree of uniformity in their practices. In 1990, for example, the NAIC drafted the Unfair Claims Settlement Practices Act, which specifies wrongful claim settlement practices. Many states have either adopted this act or have used it as the basis for writing their own.

The NAIC model act lists fourteen actions that it defines as unfair claim practices. Some state laws list more than twenty unfair or illegal claim practices.

Purposes of Insurance Regulation

Insurance regulation serves the following three purposes:

1. To protect consumers
2. To maintain insurer solvency
3. To prevent destructive competition

Although these purposes clearly overlap, each is examined separately.

Protect Consumers

The primary purpose of insurance regulation is to protect consumers. When consumers buy food, clothing, or furniture, they can usually inspect the products before purchasing them to ensure that the products meet their needs. Even if consumers inspect the insurance policies they purchase, they may not be able to analyze and understand the insurance policy, a complex legal document. Regulators help protect consumers by reviewing insurance policy forms to determine whether they are fair contracts. Regulators can set coverage standards, specify policy language for certain insurance coverages, and disapprove unacceptable policies.

Insurance regulators also protect consumers against fraud and unethical behavior by responding to complaints about such alleged behavior. Departments of insurance receive complaints about behaviors, including the following:

- Producers have intentionally sold unnecessary insurance.
- Producers have misrepresented the nature of coverage to make a sale.
- Claim representatives have engaged in unfair claim practices, refusing to pay legitimate claims or unfairly reducing claim payments.
- Insurance managers have contributed to the insolvency of insurers through their dishonesty.

In addition to protecting consumers against such abuses, regulators also try to ensure that insurance is readily available, especially insurance that is viewed as a necessity. For example, all states now try to make continuous personal auto insurance coverage available by restricting the rights of insurers to cancel or nonrenew personal auto insurance policies. At the same time, regulators recognize that insurers sometimes must break long-term relationships with policyholders whose loss exposures no longer match those the insurer wants to cover. Cancellation restrictions aimed at promoting availability can therefore lead insurers to reject more new-business applications, which reduces insurance availability.

Insurance regulators also provide information about insurance matters so that consumers can make more-informed decisions.

Maintain Insurer Solvency

Another purpose of insurance regulation is to maintain insurer solvency. Solvency regulation protects policyholders against the risk that insurers will be unable to meet their financial obligations. Consumers and even some sophisticated businesspeople may find it difficult to evaluate insurers' financial ability to keep their promises. Insurance regulators try to maintain and enhance the financial condition of private insurers for several reasons, including the following:

- *Insurance provides future protection.* Premiums are paid in advance, but the period of protection extends into the future. If insurers become insolvent, future claims may not be paid, and the insurance protection already paid for may become worthless.
- *Insurer solvency is in the public interest.* Large numbers of individuals and the community at large are adversely affected when insurers become insolvent.
- *Insurers have a responsibility to policyholders.* Insurers hold substantial funds for the ultimate benefit of policyholders. Government regulation is necessary to safeguard such funds.

Insurers can become insolvent despite regulatory oversight. However, sound regulation can minimize the number of insolvencies.

Prevent Destructive Competition

Insurance regulation also seeks to prevent destructive competition. Regulators are responsible for determining whether insurance rates are high enough to prevent destructive competition. At times, some insurers underprice their products to increase market share by attracting customers away from higher-priced competitors. This practice drives down price levels in the whole market. When insurance rate levels are inadequate, some insurers can become insolvent, and others might withdraw from the market or stop writing new business. An insurance shortage can then develop, and some individuals and organizations may be unable to obtain the coverage they need. Certain types of insurance, such as products liability or directors and officers insurance, can become unavailable at any price.

Activities of Insurance Regulators

Day-to-day regulation of the insurance business is conducted by state insurance departments, which fall within the executive branch of each state government. State insurance departments enforce insurance laws enacted by the legislature. These laws regulate the formation of insurers, capital and surplus requirements, licensing of producers, investment of funds, financial requirements for maintaining solvency, insurance rates, marketing and claim practices, taxation of insurers, and the rehabilitation of financially impaired insurers or the liquidation of insolvent ones.

Every state insurance department is headed by an insurance commissioner, superintendent, or director appointed by the governor or elected by the voting public. Under the insurance commissioner's direction, a state insurance department engages in a wide variety of regulatory activities that typically include the following:

- Approving policy forms
- Holding rate hearings and reviewing rate filings
- Licensing new insurers
- Licensing producers, adjusters, and claim representatives
- Investigating policyholder complaints
- Rehabilitating or liquidating insolvent insurers
- Issuing cease-and-desist orders
- Conducting periodic audits of insurers, including claim and underwriting audits
- Evaluating solvency information
- Performing market conduct examinations
- Publishing shoppers' guides and other consumer information (in some states)

Many commissioners were employed in the insurance business before they entered public office, and many gain employment with insurers or insurance-related organizations after leaving office. The expertise in and understanding of insurance operations necessary to regulate effectively are most likely found in a person who has worked in the insurance business. However, those connections between insurance commissioners and insurers raise questions about whether some commissioners can act objectively when regulating insurers. In response to such questions, state insurance commissioners may point out that they frequently issue cease-and-desist orders, fine or penalize insurers for infractions of the law, forbid insurers to engage in mass cancellations, limit insurance rate increases, and take numerous other actions that benefit policyholders at the insurers' expense.

State insurance departments are partly funded by state premium taxes, audit fees, filing fees, and licensing fees; premium taxes are the major source of funding. Although state premium taxes are substantial, only a relatively small proportion is spent on insurance regulation. Premium taxes are designed primarily to raise revenues for the state as a whole.

Types of Insurance Regulation

State insurance departments regulate insurance through rate regulation, solvency surveillance, policy form regulation, and consumer protection.

Rate Regulation

Insurance rates are regulated to ensure that they are adequate to pay losses but are not excessive or unfairly discriminatory. Establishing appropriate rates can be difficult even with actuarial analysis. In an open, competitive market, inefficient insurers are allowed to fail. However, the failure of insurers is not in the public's interest. Insurers must be financially sound so that they can compensate insureds for losses for which premiums have been paid. Therefore, one role of regulators is to ensure that rates are sufficient for insurers to collect enough premiums to pay for losses and other expenses and to generate a reasonable profit. Even so, no method of rate regulation can guarantee that rates will be adequate.

Regulation also seeks to protect consumers from excessively high rates, which generate excessive profits for insurers. Regulators have considerable discretion in determining whether rates are adequate or excessive for a given type of insurance, and they use several approaches for doing so.

One such approach is to consider the fair rate of return. An insurer should expect at least some minimum rate of return on the equity invested in its insurance operations. An insurer's fair rate of return presumably should resemble the rate of return applicable to other types of businesses, especially if insurers are to attract investment capital. Another view is that the insurance business, by its nature, involves a higher degree of risk than many other businesses and that higher risks should generally be accompanied by higher returns. Given such varying viewpoints, the question about what constitutes a fair rate of return for insurers is far from settled.

Another goal of insurance rate regulation is to ensure that rates are not unfairly discriminatory. The word "discrimination," as commonly used, carries negative connotations, but the word itself is neutral, meaning only the ability to differentiate among things. Discrimination, in the neutral sense, is essential to insurance rating. However, insurers' discrimination must be fair and consistent; that is, loss exposures that are roughly similar regarding expected losses and expenses should be charged substantially similar rates. For example, two drivers age twenty-five operating similar vehicles in the same rating territory and buying the same type and amount of auto insurance from the same insurer should be charged similar rates.

Regulation prohibits only discrimination that is unfair. If loss exposures are substantially different in terms of expected losses and expenses, then different rates can be charged. For example, if a car is kept in an area that has a high incidence of car theft, the rate will be higher than if the car is kept in an area that has a much lower rate of car theft.

The trend, especially with respect to commercial insurance, is to deregulate rates, that is, to allow rates to be determined by competitive market forces. However, even in states in which rates are being deregulated, regulators continue to monitor insurer solvency.

Solvency Regulation

To monitor insurer solvency, state insurance regulators examine the insurer's financial condition and operations. The financial information collected is evaluated using Insurance Regulatory Information System (IRIS) ratios, designed by the NAIC to help regulators identify insurers in financial trouble. Such insurers are placed on a watch list and receive close scrutiny from regulators.

Why do insurers fail? Some insolvencies occur when an insurer is overexposed to losses resulting from a major insured catastrophe. However, usually no single event or mistake causes an insurer to become insolvent. Rather, poor management and adverse events combine to cause insolvencies. The following factors may contribute to insolvencies:

- Rapid premium growth
- Inadequate insurance rates and reserves
- Excessive expenses
- Lax controls over managing general agents
- Uncollectible reinsurance
- Fraud

Poor management is at the root of most of these factors. A combination of inadequate insurance rates and lax underwriting starts a deterioration in a book of business. If these problems are not detected and corrected promptly, the decline in the quality of the business accelerates.

Rapid premium growth precedes nearly all major insolvencies. Rapid growth by itself is not harmful, but it usually indicates bargain-basement insurance rates and lax underwriting standards. If insurance rates are inadequate and losses understated, net losses and capital deterioration rise faster than management can handle.

The rules governing an insolvent insurer's claim payments vary by state, but the following provides a general overview. An insurer that declares insolvency may be placed in liquidation and its assets and liabilities taken over by the state insurance commissioner. The insurance commissioner appoints a deputy receiver to gather the insolvent insurer's remaining assets. All funds payable to the insurer must be collected, including reinsurance and other debts and recoverables, agents' premium balances, and retrospective premium adjustments. The receiver notifies insureds, claimants, and other creditors of the liquidation order and provides proof of claim forms that must be returned by a specified date. The receiver determines whether to allow or disallow each claim and notifies the claimant. All debts and claims against the insurer (including claims for employee wages and administrative costs) are prioritized into classes. All claims for one class must be paid before payment of another class is allowed. Five to ten years can pass before losses are paid in insolvency. In most cases, those with claims are not paid the full amount of the loss. For example, the liquidator might offer forty-two cents on the dollar for property-casualty claims.

State **insurance guaranty funds** are another source for paying insolvent insurers' claims. The funds cover the unpaid claims of certain types of insolvent insurers licensed in the state. Insurers doing business in the state pay assessments to the fund. Insurance guaranty funds contract with claim representatives, such as independent adjusters, to handle the claims. The claim representative determines coverage, investigates the loss, and negotiates settlement as with any other claim.

Insurance guaranty funds
State funds that pay the claims of insolvent licensed insurers in the particular state.

Insurance Policy Regulation

Many states require that insurers file their policy forms with regulators for approval of policy language. Regulators scrutinize policy language with the goal of making insurance policies fair, clear, and readable so that consumers receive the coverage they expect from the policy. Some states require that insurers use prescribed policy language. Insurance policy regulation is considered necessary for the following reasons:

- *Insurance policies are complex documents.* Because most insurance policies are difficult to interpret and understand, regulating their structure and content is necessary.
- *Insurance policies are almost always drafted by insurers who sell them to the public on a take-it-or-leave-it basis.* Regulation can protect policyholders from policies that are narrow, restrictive, or deceptive.

Insurance policies are regulated through legislation and insurance departments' regulations, rules, and guidelines. Court decisions can also cause changes in policy language and forms. State insurance departments implement specific directives from the legislature or exercise the general authority they have to regulate insurance policies. Administrative rules and guidelines can be stated in (1) regulations communicated by the state insurance department to insurers, (2) informal circulars or bulletins from the same source, and (3) precedents set during the approval process. For example, the state insurance department might require specific wording in certain policy provisions or might notify insurers that certain types of policy provisions will be disapproved.

Although the courts do not directly regulate insurers, they clearly influence them by determining whether insurance laws are constitutional and whether administrative rulings and guidelines are consistent with state law. The courts also interpret ambiguous and confusing policy provisions, determine whether certain losses are covered by a policy, and resolve other disputes between insurers and policyholders over policy coverages and provisions.

Court decisions often lead insurers to redraft their policy language and to modify provisions. For example, based on the legal doctrine of concurrent causation, certain courts ruled that if a loss under a risk of direct physical loss (formerly "all-risks") policy results from two causes of loss, one of which is excluded, the entire loss is covered. As a result of this doctrine, insurers were required to pay certain flood and earthquake claims they had believed were excluded by their property insurance policies. Subsequent revision of the language in many such property policies explicitly excluded coverage for flood and earthquake losses in cases in which an unexcluded cause of loss contributed to the loss.

Consumer Protection

Generally, all insurance regulatory activities seek to protect insurance consumers. But some activities are designed to *directly* protect consumers. For example, state insurance departments respond to consumer complaints, and they also provide information to consumers in publications, such as insurance buying guides, and information about claim handling practices.

In most cases, state insurance departments lack direct authority to order insurers to pay claims when facts are disputed. Such disputes are best resolved through the courts. However, most state insurance departments investigate and follow up on every consumer complaint, at least to the extent of getting a response from the insurer involved.

Through consumer complaint bureaus, regulators monitor the conduct of insurer employees and representatives who interact with customers. If necessary, these bureaus hear formal complaints. Most states have laws addressing unfair trade and claim practices, which are usually modeled after the NAIC's Unfair Claims Settlement Practices Act.

Many states calculate complaint ratios, and some make them readily available to consumers through the Internet. To help make consumers understand the cost of insurance, some states publish shoppers' guides and other forms of consumer information and may also post such information on the Internet. Consumers can obtain information provided by state insurance departments by linking to each state insurance department's Web site from the NAIC Web site.

Each state has licensing requirements for insurers domiciled (legally headquartered) in the state and for other insurers conducting business in the state. These requirements concern the insurer's financial strength, including whether the insurer has sufficient surplus to meet its obligation to pay losses.

Some states also require licensing for many of the people who sell insurance, give insurance advice, or represent insurers, including producers, insurance consultants, and claim representatives. Such licensing requires passing an examination on insurance law and procedures. Renewing a license often involves completing a specific number of continuing education hours in insurance or related subjects.

Insurance producers must be licensed in each state in which they do business. Insurance producers operating without a license are subject to civil, and sometimes criminal, penalties.

Traditionally, lack of uniformity among the states' licensing requirements has been a source of frustration and expense for producers licensed in more than one state. Provisions in the GLB Act have led to greater licensing reciprocity among states. Regulators' ultimate goal is to move beyond reciprocity and to resolve issues related to uniformity in producer licensing. Meeting this goal will streamline the licensing process while retaining state regulatory authority over it.

States that issue a separate broker's license may use a different set of examinations than the ones used for other producers to test candidates' competence, or they may establish higher standards for the broker's license than for the agent's license. Some states require anyone taking the broker's examination to have been licensed agents for a specified period, such as two years.

Insurance consultants give advice and opinions about insurance policies sold in the state. Some states require insurance consultants to be licensed, and licensing requirements vary by state. Separate examinations are usually required for one to become an insurance consultant in both life-health insurance and property-casualty insurance.

Some states license claim representatives and adjusters because of the complex and technical nature of insurance policies and to protect claimants from unfair, unethical, and dishonest claim practices. Licensing also provides some assurance that claim representatives and adjusters are aware of prohibited claim practices and have minimum technical skills. Public adjusters, who represent insureds for a fee, are generally required to be licensed to ensure technical competence and to protect the public.

Another regulatory activity that protects consumers is monitoring market conduct. Sales practices, underwriting practices, claim practices, and bad-faith actions are market conduct areas that states regulate.

States have **unfair trade practices acts**, which specify certain prohibited business practices, to regulate the trade practices of the business of insurance as required under the McCarran Act. Unfair trade practices acts prohibit an insurer from using unfair methods of competition and engaging in unfair practices as defined in the acts. Most acts also authorize the insurance commissioner to decide whether activities not specifically defined in the law might result in unfair competition or might qualify as unfair trade practices. Currently, all U.S. jurisdictions and the District of Columbia and Guam have unfair trade practices acts.

Unfair trade practices acts
State laws that specify certain prohibited business practices.

Unfair trade practices cases can be decided by the commissioner of the state in which the activity occurred. An insurer that violates the unfair trade practices act is subject to one or both of the following penalties:

1. *Fine per violation.* The fine is often increased significantly if the activity is considered to be flagrant, with conscious disregard for the law.
2. *Suspension or revocation of license.* This usually occurs if the insurer's management knew or should have known that the activity was an unfair trade practice.

If an insurer disagrees with the commissioner's findings, it can generally file for judicial review. If the court agrees with the commissioner, the insurer must obey the commissioner's orders.

Producers are subject to fines, penalties, or license revocation if they engage in certain illegal and unethical activities. A producer may be penalized for engaging in practices, such as the following, that violate the state's unfair trade practices act:

- *Dishonesty or fraud.* A producer may embezzle premiums paid by policyholders or may misappropriate claim funds.
- *Misrepresentation.* A producer may misrepresent the losses that are covered by an insurance policy, which may induce a client to purchase that policy under false pretenses.
- *Twisting.* A producer may induce a policyholder to replace one policy (usually life insurance) with another, to the insured's detriment. This is a special form of misrepresentation.
- *Unfair discrimination.* A producer may engage in any number of acts that favor one insured unfairly over another.
- *Rebating.* A producer may engage in rebating, which is the practice of giving a portion of the producer's commission or some other financial advantage to an individual as an inducement to purchase a policy. Rebating is currently illegal in all but two states. The practice is especially problematic with life insurance policies for which the producer's first year's commission is sizable. If a producer rebates part of the commission to one policyholder but not to another, that act is considered unfair discrimination. If the producer rebates the same percentage of the commission to all policyholders, the act is not unfairly discriminatory, but it is still illegal.

Insurance regulators are concerned that improper underwriting could result in insurer insolvency or unfair discrimination against an insurance consumer. To protect consumers, insurance regulators do the following:

- *Constrain insurers' ability to accept, modify, or decline applications for insurance.* To increase insurance availability, states often require insurers to provide coverage for some loss exposures they might prefer not to cover.
- *Establish allowable classifications.* Regulators limit the ways in which insurers can divide consumers into rating classifications. For example, unisex rating is required in some states for personal auto insurance. This promotes social equity rather than actuarial equity.
- *Restrict the timing of cancellations and nonrenewals.* All states require insurers to provide insureds with adequate advance notice of policy cancellation or nonrenewal so that insureds can obtain replacement coverage. Insurers are typically allowed to cancel or nonrenew only for specific reasons.

Typical violations that are discovered during market conduct examinations of an insurer's underwriting function include the following:

- Discriminating unfairly when selecting loss exposures
- Misclassifying loss exposures
- Canceling or nonrenewing policies contrary to statutes, rules, and policy provisions

- Using underwriting rules or rates that are not on file with or approved by the insurance departments in the states in which the insurer does business
- Failing to apply newly implemented underwriting and rating factors to renewals
- Failing to use correct policy forms and insurance rates
- Failing to use rules that are state specific

All states prohibit certain claim practices by law. Apart from regulatory penalties, failure to handle claims in good faith can lead to claims for damages, alleging bad faith on the insurer's part.

Unfair claim practices acts prohibit unethical and illegal claim practices. The acts generally are patterned after the NAIC Model Unfair Claims Settlement Practices Act. Prohibited insurer claim practices typically include the following:

Unfair claim practices acts
State laws that prohibit unethical and illegal claim practices.

- Knowingly misrepresenting important facts or policy provisions
- Failing to properly investigate and settle claims
- Failing to make a good-faith effort to pay claims when liability is reasonably clear
- Attempting to settle a claim for less than the amount that a reasonable person believes he or she is entitled to receive based on advertising material that accompanies or is made part of the application
- Failing to approve or deny coverage of a claim within a reasonable period after a proof-of-loss statement has been completed

The NAIC Model Act and state unfair claim practices laws are more fully discussed in a later chapter. Strict regulatory controls on claim practices protect policyholders. Unfair claim practices tarnish the offending insurer's image and reputation, erode public confidence in the insurance industry, and deny claims to policyholders' detriment.

Valid and legitimate claims should be paid promptly and fairly with a minimum of legal formality. Conversely, paying fraudulent claims submitted by dishonest insureds should be vigorously resisted, and paying excessive claim settlements should be avoided.

In some cases, courts have ruled that an insurer's improper claim handling constitutes not only a breach of contract but also an independent tort (civil wrong), the tort of bad faith. **Bad faith** is a breach of the duty of good faith and fair dealing. An insurer that violates good-faith standards can be required to honor the policy's intent (by paying the claim) and pay extracontractual damages for emotional distress and attorney fees. These extracontractual damages—damages above the amount payable under the terms of the insurance policy—are payable by the insurer. Legal remedies for bad-faith actions can lead to both first-party actions (involving the insured) and third-party actions (involving the claimant).

Bad faith
A breach of the duty of good faith and fair dealing.

SUMMARY

Individuals and organizations can use several techniques to manage the risk of potential financial loss. How someone manages risk is often determined by whether the risk is a hazard risk or a business risk. Hazard risk is the risk from accidental loss, including the possibility of loss or no loss. Business risk is inherent in the operation of a particular organization, including the possibility of loss, no loss, or gain.

Risk can be controlled or financed. Insurance is a risk-financing technique; it transfers risk from people and organizations to insurers. This transfer is feasible because a large group of individual risks are pooled, and individual premiums contribute to a pool of money that is used to pay losses for the few who actually suffer them. The many other contributors who do not suffer a loss benefit from peace of mind, knowing that they are protected from potentially devastating financial loss.

In addition to payment for losses and peace of mind, insurance provides the benefits of support for loans, funds for loans and investments, loss control, efficient use of resources, reduction of social burdens, satisfaction of legal and business requirements, employment, and tax revenue. Insurance has costs, as reflected in premium payments. Indirect costs of insurance include opportunity costs, increased litigation, and the moral and morale hazards associated with losses.

In addition to claim departments, insurers have other functional areas, such as marketing and sales, underwriting, loss control, reinsurance, actuarial, finance and accounting, and information technology, which enable the insurer to obtain business and fulfill its policy obligations.

Claim departments can be found in insurance companies, in large businesses, in third-party administrators (TPAs), and in the offices of large agents and brokers. A senior claim executive is usually in charge of a claim department, which may also have several mid-level executives and several office locations staffed with claim representatives who directly handle claims.

Claims are handled by insurance company claim representatives, independent adjusters, TPAs, producers with claim settlement authority, and public adjusters, who act on behalf of the insured.

Claim department performance can be measured by mathematical means such as loss ratio. It can also be measured qualitatively through the use of best practices, claim audits, and customer service compliments and complaints. These performance measures are often tied to insurance regulations.

Insurance operations are closely regulated by states. Only a few federal laws and federal court cases regulate insurance operations. The McCarran-Ferguson Act preserved the structure of existing state insurance regulation but also clarified the federal government's power to assume regulatory duties in the absence of state regulation. The Insurance Fraud Protection Act protects consumers and insurers against insurer insolvencies resulting from fraud. The Gramm-Leach-Bliley Act preserves the states' primary regulatory authority for all insurance activities but prohibits state actions that would prevent bank-related firms from selling insurance on the same basis as insurance producers.

The National Association of Insurance Commissioners (NAIC) was established to encourage coordination and cooperation among state insurance departments. The NAIC drafts model laws and regulations that state legislatures may adopt as written or modify as they see fit. The organization has no direct regulatory authority in any of the states or countries it serves.

State insurance departments regulate insurance through rate regulation, solvency surveillance, and consumer protection. Rates must be adequate, not excessive, and not unfairly discriminatory. Most states have laws addressing unfair claim practices that are modeled after the NAIC's Unfair Claims Settlement Practices Act.

Understanding why people and businesses buy insurance and how insurance companies are structured and regulated provides the context for the next chapter's discussion of the claim handling process.

CHAPTER NOTES

1. The combined ratio discussed here is called the *statutory basis combined ratio*. Another version of the combined ratio, called the *trade basis combined ratio*, uses written premium rather than earned premium as the denominator for the expense ratio. The trade basis combined ratio is used more for underwriting purposes than for claim purposes.
2. *Paul v. Virginia*, 8 Wall. 68, 438 U.S. 531 (1869). A Virginia law required licenses for out-of-state insurance companies, and another required licenses for anyone acting as an agent for an out-of-state insurance company. Samuel D. Paul, a Virginia attorney, wanted to test the constitutionality of the laws. Several New York companies appointed Paul as their agent in Virginia. Paul's application for a license in Virginia was rejected because the insurers he represented had not deposited the bonds required by the law. Paul continued to write business, and he was indicted, convicted, and fined. He appealed on the basis that the U.S. Constitution forbids state governments from obstructing interstate commerce, and he argued that insurance is interstate commerce. The Supreme Court disagreed, holding that because an insurance policy is not an article of interstate commerce, the business of insurance is not interstate commerce, and, therefore, the states had the authority to regulate insurance.
3. *U.S. v. SEUA*, 322 U.S. 533 (1944). The SEUA was a rating bureau in Atlanta owned by 200 private fire stock insurance companies. In 1942, the Justice Department charged the SEUA and nine of its member insurance companies with restraint of trade in violation of the Sherman Antitrust Act. According to the Justice Department indictment, the companies that made up the SEUA controlled over 90 percent of the fire insurance business in six southern states. The case was dismissed at the federal district court level. On appeal, the U.S. Supreme Court ruled that insurance is commerce and is subject to federal antitrust laws.

4. 18 U.S.C. §1033 (1994).
5. Ann Monaco Warren and John William Simon, "Dishonesty or Breach of Trust in 18 U.S.C. §1033: Are *You* Criminally Liable on the Basis of an Associate's Record?" FORC *Quarterly Journal of Insurance Law and Regulation*, vol. 10, ed. III, September 12, 1998.

Chapter 2

Direct Your Learning

Claim Handling Process

After learning the content of this chapter and completing the corresponding course guide assignment, you should be able to:

- Describe the physical construction of insurance policies and the function of each of the insurance policy components.
- Describe the framework for coverage analysis and the information obtained by following it.
- Describe the activities in the claim handling process, including the following:
  - Acknowledging and assigning the claim
  - Identifying the policy
  - Contacting the insured or the insured's representative
  - Investigating and documenting the claim
  - Concluding the claim
- Given a claim, determine coverage for a loss using the framework for coverage analysis and the activities in the claim handling process.
- Define or describe each of the Key Words and Phrases for this chapter.

OUTLINE

Insurance Policy Structure

Framework for Coverage Analysis

Claim Handling Process

Applying the Framework for Coverage Analysis and the Claim Handling Process

Summary

Develop Your Perspective

What are the main topics covered in the chapter?

To properly handle claims, claim representatives must know how to analyze an insurance policy, and they must be able to apply that information to the facts they obtain during the claim handling process. This chapter provides the framework for coverage analysis and describes the claim handling process.

Review an insurance policy.

- What is the structure of that policy?
- Which policy components can you identify?

Why is it important to learn about these topics?

Claim representatives have an ethical obligation and a legal duty to use good claim handling practices on every claim they are assigned. Using a systematic approach to policy analysis and the claim handling process helps reinforce these good claim handling practices.

Examine how claims are handled in your office.

- What claim handling activities are performed?
- Who performs these activities?

How can you use what you will learn?

Analyze a closed claim and apply the framework for coverage analysis and the claim handling process to that claim.

- Do you agree with the coverage determination? Why or why not?
- What good-faith claim practices were used throughout the claim?
- Does the file contain sufficient documentation for you to answer the first two questions? If not, what information is missing?

Chapter 2
Claim Handling Process

To fulfill the insurer's promise to pay covered claims, claim representatives should follow a systematic process. A process is important because it creates consistency in claim handling and helps ensure that claims are handled in a manner that conforms with legal and ethical standards. This chapter describes the claim handling process, including the important step of analyzing an insurance policy. Although different types of claims may require unique treatment, the same basic activities are performed in every claim. These activities, listed in Exhibit 2-1, provide a framework for handling all types of property, liability, and workers' compensation claims.

EXHIBIT 2-1

Activities in the Claim Handling Process
- Acknowledging and assigning the claim
- Identifying the policy
- Contacting the insured or the insured's representative
- Investigating and documenting the claim
- Determining the cause of loss and the loss amount
- Concluding the claim

While these activities appear sequential, they are not always undertaken sequentially. A claim representative may sometimes undertake several activities concurrently and may repeat some activities as new information is uncovered.

INSURANCE POLICY STRUCTURE

There are many different types of insurance policies. Claim representatives must carefully examine the structure of each policy and read and analyze all policy provisions to determine if coverage applies based on the facts of a given claim. The following sections describe the physical construction of property and liability insurance contracts, their content, and the framework to be used when analyzing an insurance policy.

Physical Construction

Insurance policies can be classified according to their components, which make up the physical document. Three general ways to classify policies are (1) self-contained or modular, (2) package or monoline, and (3) preprinted or manuscript. Some documents, such as the application for insurance, may be physically attached to the policy; others may be added to a policy by a reference within the policy (incorporated by reference).

A self-contained policy, as opposed to a modular policy, is a single document containing all agreements between the applicant and the insurer. The policy identifies the insurer and the insured; the subject matter of the insurance; and the amounts, terms, and conditions of coverage. Endorsements, which are documents that amend a policy, may be used to add, eliminate, or modify coverages. Self-contained policies are appropriate for loss exposures that are similar among insureds. For example, a private passenger auto policy may apply to all of an insurer's individual auto policyholders in one or more states.

In contrast to a self-contained policy, a modular policy, commonly used in commercial insurance, is a mix-and-match set of components that can be assembled to meet the insured's unique combination of needs. It is designed around one basic policy component, often called a "policy jacket" (or "common conditions form"), that includes conditions, definitions, or other provisions that apply to, or match, all documents used with it. Every modular policy contains the common policy conditions and common declarations. An advantage of the modular policy is that a single policy can include several types of insurance, whereas using self-contained policies requires a separate policy for each of the coverages an insured requires.

Insurance policies may also be classified as either package or monoline. Package policies contain carefully designed and coordinated provisions in the various component forms that minimize the possibility of coverage gaps or overlaps. The terminology, definitions, and language of the components are consistent, and fewer forms are required than if a series of self-contained policies were used to provide the same coverage. Therefore, underwriting is simplified. An insurer can provide several types of insurance for one insured, offsetting the less profitable types of insurance. Insurers often offer a premium discount on package policies, an added benefit to the insured. An example of a package policy is the homeowners policy, which offers the homeowner coverage for both property damage and liability in a single package.

If the insured needs only one particular type of insurance, a monoline policy would provide that coverage. For example, the commercial property coverage policy includes a commercial property declarations (or information) page, the necessary commercial property coverage forms, and a commercial property conditions form. This combination of documents forming a complete policy for a particular type of coverage or line of business is called a monoline policy.

An insurance policy may also be classified as either preprinted or manuscript. Most insurance policies are assembled from one or more preprinted forms and endorsements. These ready-made policies are developed for use with many different insureds and are usually approved by state insurance regulators. An insurer sends the insured the entire preprinted policy with a declarations page that indicates the form numbers and edition dates of the forms that apply. The insurer and the insurance producer generally retain only the declarations page, often as an electronic document. They can review the appropriate coverages by referencing the preprinted forms listed. In contrast to the preprinted policy, a manuscript policy is a one-of-a-kind policy written to meet a unique coverage need. Because it is unique to one insured, the policy form is usually exempt from regulatory approval.

Insurance service and advisory organizations, such as Insurance Services Office (ISO) and the American Association of Insurance Services (AAIS), have developed standard insurance forms that are available for use by individual insurers. These standard forms are usually accompanied by endorsements that reflect necessary state variations or that customize coverage. Claim representatives should pay particular attention to the policy form numbers associated with a particular standard policy so that they are analyzing coverage for a particular claim using the correct policy form. It is common for an insurer to have several different editions of a policy form in use at the same time, often because that insurer does business in several states and the same forms are not approved for use in every state. For example, an insured with locations in four states can have different versions of the commercial general liability policy in each location, with different coverage supplied by each.

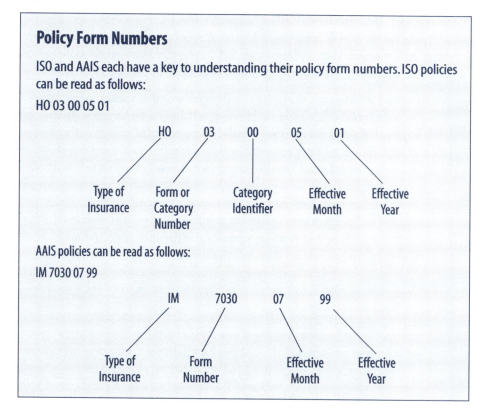

Policy Form Numbers

ISO and AAIS each have a key to understanding their policy form numbers. ISO policies can be read as follows:

HO 03 00 05 01

- HO — Type of Insurance
- 03 — Form or Category Number
- 00 — Category Identifier
- 05 — Effective Month
- 01 — Effective Year

AAIS policies can be read as follows:

IM 7030 07 99

- IM — Type of Insurance
- 7030 — Form Number
- 07 — Effective Month
- 99 — Effective Year

While ISO and AAIS develop standard policies, many insurers develop their own nonstandard, company-specific preprinted policies, often for high-volume types of insurance (such as auto or homeowners) or for coverages in which they specialize. The language and content in these nonstandard insurance policies can vary from provisions used by other insurers and from standard policy provisions. Many nonstandard policies contain coverage enhancements not found in standard policies.

Manuscript policies, as distinguished from preprinted policies, are nonstandard, custom policies developed for one specific insured or for a small group of insureds, such as a business association, with unique coverage needs. A manuscript policy can be specifically selected or drafted for a particular need, such as products liability coverage for a pacemaker manufacturer. Manuscript endorsements can also be used for covering insureds with specific needs. Most manuscript policy provisions are adapted from the language in standard contracts or other insurance contracts. Some manuscript policies' wording is developed through negotiation between the insurer and the insured.

> **Manuscript policies**
> Nonstandard, custom policies developed for one specific insured or for a small group of insureds, such as a business association, with unique coverage needs.

Other documents can become part of any policy by physical attachment or by reference within the policy. Some examples of attached documents are the completed application for insurance, endorsements, the insurer's bylaws, and the terms of relevant statutes. Examples of documents incorporated by reference are the rules and rates that have been approved by an insurance regulator, promissory notes (accepted by an insurer instead of cash premium payment), inspection reports, specification sheets, and operating manuals that describe safety equipment or procedures.

Policy Components and Their Functions

The various property, liability, and workers' compensation insurance policy components indicate the coverage that is provided, losses that are not covered, and the responsibilities of the parties to the contract. This section describes the functions of the following insurance policy components:

- Declarations
- Definitions
- Insuring agreements
- Exclusions
- Conditions
- Miscellaneous provisions
- Endorsements

The claim representative must review each of these policy components to determine if they apply to a given claim. The circumstances of the specific claim determine how often this review must occur. For example, if a loss to a building is reported as water damage, the claim representative would review the policy to see what type of water damage is covered. On investigation, the claim representative may learn that the water has entered the building as a result of rain that accumulated and backed up from a storm drain. With this information, the claim representative would again review the policy to see if coverage applies to water damage from that specific cause.

Declarations

A property, liability, or workers' compensation policy's declarations (information pages) are typically the first page(s) of an insurance policy. Declarations contain basic information about the insured taken from the insurance application, a description of the coverage provided under the policy, and information about what is unique to the policy.

> **Information Found in the Policy Declarations**
>
> A policy's declarations usually include the following information:
> - Policy number
> - Policy inception and expiration dates
> - Name of the insurer
> - Name of the producer
> - Name of the insured(s)
> - Mailing address of the insured
> - Physical address and description of the covered property or operations
> - Numbers and edition dates of all attached forms and endorsements
> - Dollar amounts of applicable policy limit(s)
> - Dollar amounts of applicable deductibles
> - Names of persons or organizations whose additional interests are covered (such as mortgagees, loss payees, or additional insureds)
> - Premium

Policy forms or endorsements may also contain information that qualifies as declarations. For example, a glass coverage endorsement may contain a narrative description or diagram of the covered glass so that it can be identified in the event of a loss.

> **APPLY YOUR LEARNING**
>
> **Adjusting Tip**
>
> Claim representatives should carefully check policy declaration information against information submitted in a claim. Any differences in the insured's name, address, building locations, and policy forms must be resolved with the underwriter and producer before the claim representative settles the claim.

Definitions

Another component of many property-liablity policies is the definitions section, which contains definitions of terms used throughout the policy or form. The purpose of the definitions is to establish a common understanding of what the terms in the policy mean. The definitions can be included anywhere in the policy or be presented in a glossary.

Examples of "definitions" vary. Many current policies explain that the term "we" is used to indicate the insurer and "you" to indicate the named insured. Similarly, policies may also describe the use of the pronouns "us," "our," and "your."

Many court cases rest on the definitions of words not defined in a policy. Courts and insurers follow the rules of contract interpretation to resolve such issues, as follows:

- Everyday words are given their ordinary meaning.
- Technical words are given their technical meaning.
- Words with an established legal meaning are given their legal meaning.
- Words that have local, cultural, and trade-usage meanings are considered, if applicable.

> **APPLY YOUR LEARNING**
>
> ### Adjusting Tip
>
> When analyzing coverage, a claim representative should consult the definitions, such as "bodily injury," "property damage," and "insured." When the claim's circumstances do not fit within the definitions, the coverage promised in the insuring agreement does not apply.

Insuring Agreements

Insuring agreement
A statement in an insurance policy that the insurer will, under described circumstances, make a loss payment or provide a service.

The **insuring agreement**, a fundamental component of any insurance policy, is any insurance policy statement indicating that the insurer will make a loss payment or provide a service under described circumstances. The insuring agreement broadly states the promises made by the insurer about coverage. For example, the insuring agreement of the standard Insurance Services Office (ISO) homeowners policy (HO-3)[1] reads as follows:

> We will provide the insurance described in this policy in return for the premium and compliance with all applicable provisions of this policy.

The insuring agreement of the liability coverage part of ISO's Personal Auto Policy (PAP)[2] begins as follows:

> A. We will pay damages for "bodily injury" or "property damage" for which any "insured" becomes legally responsible because of an auto accident.

The words and phrases enclosed in quotation marks in the policy are defined in the policy's definitions.

Policies can have more than one insuring agreement if they provides more than one type of coverage. For example, the Personal Auto Policy typically provides liability, medical payments, uninsured motorists, and physical damage coverages. Each coverage has its own insuring agreement, which states what the insurer agrees to do, subject to policy clarification.

> **APPLY YOUR LEARNING**
>
> **Adjusting Tip**
> Insuring agreements usually contain one or more defined terms, and the definitions are crucial to understanding the coverage provided.

Insuring agreements fall into the following two categories:

1. Comprehensive, all-purpose insuring agreements describe extremely broad, unrestricted coverage that applies to virtually all causes of loss. The broad coverage is clarified and narrowed by exclusions, definitions, and other policy provisions. An example of this type of insuring agreement can be found in an HO-3 policy, which provides protection against causes of loss that the form does not specifically exclude.

2. Limited or single-purpose insuring agreements restrict coverage to certain causes of loss or to certain situations, which are clarified, narrowed, or sometimes broadened by other policy provisions. An example of this type of insuring agreement can be found in an HO-1 or HO-2 policy, which provides named peril, specified peril, or specified cause of loss coverage.

Insuring agreements can also apply to extended, additional, or supplemental coverages. A coverage extension generally extends a portion of a basic policy coverage to apply to a type of property or loss that would not otherwise be covered. An additional coverage adds a type of coverage not otherwise provided. A supplementary payments coverage clarifies the extent of coverage for certain insurance expenses. Other policy provisions grant or restore coverage otherwise excluded. Therefore, these provisions serve as insuring agreements. They may appear within a definition, as an exception to an exclusion, or elsewhere in the policy.

Exclusions

Exclusions are policy provisions that state what the insurer does *not intend* to cover. The primary function of the exclusions component is to clarify the coverages granted by the insurer in the insuring agreement, and not to remove coverage from the insured. Adding exclusions to a policy is a legally enforceable way of clarifying property or situations that the insurer does intend to cover. For example, the ISO HO-3 policy contains the following exclusion:

A. We do not insure for loss caused directly or indirectly by any of the following....

5. Neglect

> Neglect means neglect of an "insured" to use all reasonable means to save and preserve property at and after the time of a loss.[3]

For example, during a storm, a tree falls on the insured's home, creating a substantial hole in the upstairs bedroom wall. After the storm ends, the insured has the tree removed but does nothing to seal off the hole in the wall. Another storm occurs and rain enters the bedroom, ruining the carpet. The damage to the carpet is caused by the insured's neglect and would not be covered under the HO-3 policy.

Six Purposes of Exclusions

Exclusions can serve one or more of the following purposes:

1. *Eliminate coverage for uninsurable loss exposures.* Some exposures (such as intentional acts) are not insurable loss exposures. Exclusions allow insurers to preclude coverage for those exposures.
2. *Assist in managing moral hazards and morale (attitudinal) hazards.* Exclusions help insurers minimize loss exposures that are affected by moral hazards. Some exclusions also force insureds to bear any losses that result from their own carelessness (from morale hazards).
3. *Reduce the likelihood of coverage duplications.* In some cases, two applicable insurance policies cover the same loss. Exclusions ensure that such policies provide complementary, not duplicate, coverage.
4. *Eliminate coverages not needed by the typical insured.* Exclusions sometimes allow insurers to decline coverage for loss exposures that typical insureds do not face. These exclusions eliminate the chance that all insureds would have to share the costs of covering substantial loss exposures of relatively few insureds.
5. *Eliminate coverages requiring special treatment.* These coverages might require rating, underwriting, loss control, or other treatment that is different from that normally applied to the insurance policy.
6. *Assist in keeping premiums reasonable.* Exclusions allow insurers to decline those loss exposures that would increase overall insurance costs. By declining such loss exposures, insurers can offer premiums that most insureds consider reasonable for their exposures.

Exclusions can appear straightforward; however, the meaning of an exclusion is often contested in court. If an exclusion (or any other policy component) is unambiguous, then it is usually enforced according to its common meaning. If an exclusion (or any other part of the policy) is ambiguous, courts typically hold that the exclusion does not apply, because ambiguities are construed against the writer, in this case, the insurer.

Conditions

Policy condition
Any provision that qualifies an otherwise enforceable promise made in the policy.

Another property-liability and workers' compensation policy component is the conditions. A **policy condition** is any provision that qualifies an otherwise enforceable promise made in the policy. In a policy's insuring agreement, the insurer promises to pay covered losses, furnish a defense, and provide other services to the insured only if the insured has fulfilled his or her contractual duties as specified in the policy conditions. If the insured fails to meet these requirements, the insurer is released from any obligation to keep its promises under the contract.

Some policy conditions are included in a "Conditions" section, while others are found in the forms, endorsements, or other documents in the insurance contract.

APPLY YOUR LEARNING

Adjusting Tip

Claim representatives must carefully read the applicable conditions throughout the policy to determine the duties, rights, and options of both the insurer and the insured.

Conditions cover a broad range of topics, including the following:

- The insured's duty to pay the premium
- The insured's duties after a loss occurs
- The geographic area in which coverage applies
- The way disagreements between the insurer and the insured can be resolved
- The procedures that should be followed to cancel the policy

For example, the "Loss Payment" condition of Section I of the HO-3 reads as follows:

> I. **Loss Payment**. We will adjust all losses with you. We will pay you unless some other person is named in the policy or is legally entitled to receive payment. Loss will be payable 60 days after we receive your proof of loss and:
> 1. Reach an agreement with you;
> 2. There is an entry of a final judgment; or
> 3. There is a filing of an appraisal award with us.[4]

These policy provisions are called "conditions" because each party's obligations under the policy are conditional. If either party fails to fulfill the required obligations, the other party is released from its obligations under the policy. For example, an important condition prohibits fraud committed by insureds, as indicated in the following excerpt from the HO-3:

> Q. **Concealment or Fraud**. We provide coverage to no "insureds" under this policy if, whether before or after a loss, an "insured" has:
> 1. Intentionally concealed or misrepresented any material fact or circumstance;
> 2. Engaged in fraudulent conduct; or
> 3. Made false statements;
>
> relating to this insurance.[5]

If the insured commits fraud, the insurance policy is void and the insurer is under no obligation to pay claims.

Miscellaneous Provisions

Miscellaneous provisions are a component of a property-liability policy that can be found throughout the policy. These provisions do not strictly qualify coverage as do declarations, definitions, insuring agreements, exclusions, or conditions, but they do affect coverage. They may describe the relationship between the insurer and the insured or establish procedures for implementing policy conditions. However, they do not have the force of conditions, meaning if the insured does not follow procedures specified in miscellaneous provisions, the insurer typically must still fulfill its contractual promises.

An example of a miscellaneous provision is a valuation provision that sets procedures for determining the value of losses covered by the policy. Other miscellaneous provisions may be unique to a particular type of insurer; for example, for a mutual insurer in which policyholders have voting rights, the miscellaneous provisions may describe the policyholders' rights to elect the board of directors.

Endorsements

Endorsements, a key component of many policies, become part of a policy when they are listed in the declarations and attached to the policy. An endorsement adds to, deletes, replaces, or modifies another policy provision. Other terms that refer to endorsements are "policy change," "addition," "amendment," and "codicil." Some endorsements have a descriptive title, such as "Loss Payable Clause." An endorsement can be preprinted, computer-printed, typewritten, or handwritten on a separate sheet of paper attached to the policy. An endorsement takes precedence over any conflicting terms in the policy to which it is attached. A handwritten endorsement supersedes a computer-printed or typewritten endorsement. These rules are based on the premise that an endorsement added to a policy, particularly if it is handwritten, tends to reflect the true intent of the parties more accurately than do other, preprinted policy terms.

Knowing the components of the policy and what each is meant to accomplish helps the claim representative analyze coverage applicable to a claim. In order to analyze coverage, claim representatives also need a framework.

FRAMEWORK FOR COVERAGE ANALYSIS

Coverage analysis is the process of examining a policy by reviewing all its component parts and applying them to the facts of a claim. A claim representative begins the process of coverage analysis by carefully reading the policy form and all endorsements. With experience, claim representatives learn to recognize the types of losses covered under the policy forms. They are aware of the types of losses that insureds and claimants often believe are covered, but are not. This policy knowledge aids coverage analysis. But experience does not remove the necessity for the claim representative to read the applicable policy forms carefully and to analyze coverage systematically.

A systematic framework for coverage analysis can guide the claim representative to the parts of the policy that may provide or exclude coverage. It also ensures that all of the component parts are reviewed and reduces the incidence of erroneous coverage determinations. The following questions outline a systematic framework for coverage analysis and the information it will yield:

- Is the person involved covered?
- Did the loss occur during the policy period?
- Is the cause of loss covered?
- Is the damaged property covered?
- Is the type of loss covered?
- Are the amounts of loss or damages covered?
- Is the location of the loss covered?
- Do any exclusions apply?
- Does other insurance apply?

The claim representative can follow this framework by answering the questions in the order they appear here. However, in some cases, the policy may prompt the claim representative to answer the questions in a different order. In any case, the answers help the claim representative make a coverage determination.

Is the Person Involved Covered?

Some policies cover only insureds named or listed in the policy. Most policies define "insured" broadly, so the claim representative must determine whether the persons who suffered the loss are covered. For example, the homeowners policy covers the financial loss that the insured suffers as the result of a fire. For coverage to apply, the policy must cover the person who has suffered the financial loss. For example, the PAP Part A—Liability Coverage defines "insured" as follows:

> B. "Insured" as used in this Part means:
> 1. You or any "family member" for the ownership, maintenance or use of any auto or "trailer".
> 2. Any person using "your covered auto".
> 3. For "your covered auto", any person or organization but only with respect to legal responsibility for acts or omissions of a person for whom coverage is afforded under this Part.
> 4. For any auto or "trailer", other than "your covered auto", any other person or organization but only with respect to legal responsibility for acts or omissions of you or any "family member" for whom coverage is afforded under this Part. This provision (B.4.) applies only if the person or organization does not own or hire the auto or "trailer".[6]

According to the PAP definition, a friend who borrows your car and drives it is an insured. A friend who uses your car and pays you for that use is not an insured because of the last sentence in Item 4.

In contrast, the HO-3 defines "insured" in part as follows:

> 3. "Insured" means:
>   a. You and residents of your household who are:
>   (1) Your relatives; or
>   (2) Other persons under the age of 21 and in the care of any person named above;...[7]

According to the HO-3 definition, a sixteen-year-old international exchange student who lives in the household is an insured. An independent twenty-four-year-old friend who visits over the weekend is not an insured. "Insured" may be defined differently in other sections of the policy. For example, the definition of "insured" is expanded for Part B—Medical Payments Coverage of the PAP to include:

> 1. You or any "family member":
>   a. While "occupying"; or
>   b. As a pedestrian when struck by;
>   a motor vehicle designed for use mainly on public roads or a trailer of any type.
> 2. Any other person while "occupying" "your covered auto".[8]

Most property insurance policies limit recovery to the amount of a person's insurable interest in the damaged or destroyed property. However, insurable interest alone does not guarantee coverage. For example, an individual may have an insurable interest in a building but not be considered an insured under the policy because the person's name is not listed in the declarations or on an endorsement. Claim representatives determine whether the person making the claim is entitled to coverage under the policy and whether that person qualifies as an "insured."

For example, Kathy owns a house jointly with her parents, who live in another state. All three have an insurable interest in the house, but Kathy is the only named insured on the policy. If a tornado damages the house, Kathy would be paid for the loss because she has an insurable interest in the house and is a named insured. Kathy's parents are not residents of the house or named insureds, so even though they have an insurable interest, they are not insureds under the policy.

APPLY YOUR LEARNING

Adjusting Tip

Claim representatives must determine whether others have an insurable interest in the property on which a claim is based. In Kathy's case, the claim representative, on discovering that Kathy's parents have an insurable interest in the house, should check with a supervisor or manager to determine how to handle the claim payment. Lienholders or mortgagees often have an insurable interest in property, and the claim representative must determine when they should be included as payees on any claim payments.

Did the Loss Occur During the Policy Period?

Many policies are written to cover only losses that occur during the policy period. The HO-3 states the following:

> P. **Policy Period.** The policy applies only to loss which occurs during the policy period.[9]

The policy period typically begins and ends at one minute after midnight (for example, from 12:01 AM on January 25, 2006, to 12:01 AM of January 25, 2007). The Loss of Use section contains an exception to the policy period provision. For example, if a fire leaves a home unfit to live in, the insured can claim expenses for living elsewhere, even if the policy expires the next day. However, the fire must have begun during the policy period.

The date and time of loss occurrence is used to determine whether a loss occurred during the policy period. However, court decisions have offered different interpretations of date of occurrence. For example, a court may determine that the date of occurrence for an occupational disease is the first date of exposure to the harmful condition that caused the disease, the last date of exposure to the harmful condition that caused the disease, or the date the disease was diagnosed.

Is the Cause of Loss Covered?

Covered causes of loss, or perils, vary by type of policy and may include fire, theft, hail, windstorm, collision, or a legal obligation to pay damages.

Specified causes of loss coverage, also called named-perils coverage, covers a loss only if it is a direct result of a specifically listed or named cause of loss in the policy. For example, in the HO-3 policy, personal property is covered for specified perils.

> **Specified causes of loss coverage**
> A named perils coverage that covers loss caused only by the specifically listed perils.

Causes of loss are not often defined in the policy because the definitions are subject to court interpretation and therefore vary by state. For example, fire may seem easy to define, but does fire include smoke or excessive heat with no actual flame? Does it include damage the firefighters cause while extinguishing the fire?

> **APPLY YOUR LEARNING**
> ### Adjusting Tip
> When the policy does not define a cause of loss or another term, claim representatives can use other resources to determine the meaning. For example, statutory provisions and court decisions have defined many terms that are not defined in policies. Standard dictionaries are also resources for defining terms.

Special form coverage, also called all-risks or open-perils coverage, covers every cause of direct physical loss that is not excluded. The HO-3 provides special form coverage on the dwelling and other structures. Section I—Perils

> **Special form coverage**
> Property insurance coverage covering all causes of loss not specifically excluded.

Insured Against in the HO-3 states, in part, "We insure against *risk of direct loss to property* described in Coverages A and B" [emphasis added].[10] Following that statement is a list of causes of loss that the policy does not cover, such as smog, rust, birds, and rodents. Any cause of loss that is not listed among the excluded causes of loss is covered.

> **An HO-3 Claim Example**
>
> An insured accidentally spills a caustic chemical in the kitchen. The chemical splashes on the linoleum floor, table, chairs, and area rug. Because spills are not excluded under special form coverage on the dwelling, the damage to the linoleum floor is covered. Because spills are not a named peril under specified perils coverage on the contents, the damage to the table, chairs, and area rug is not covered.

In answering the question "Is the cause of loss covered?", claim representatives should thoroughly investigate all the facts concerning the loss and apply them to the language in all the provisions of the policy.

Is the Damaged Property Covered?

In following the framework for coverage analysis, the claim representative must determine whether the damaged property is covered. Insurance policies may not cover all of the insured's property. Certain property must be specified in order for coverage to apply. For example, the PAP defines "your covered auto" as:

1. Any vehicle shown in the Declarations.
2. A "newly acquired auto".
3. Any "trailer" you own.
4. Any auto or "trailer" you do not own while used as a temporary substitute for any other vehicle described in this definition which is out of normal use because of its:
    a. Breakdown;
    b. Repair;
    c. Servicing;
    d. Loss; or
    e. Destruction[11]

If a claim investigation reveals that an auto involved in an accident does not appear in the declarations or fall within the definition of "your covered auto," a coverage question may exist. However, the question may be easily resolved if the insured can prove that the car was recently purchased but has not yet been added to the policy or is a temporary substitute vehicle.

In another example of property that must be specified for coverage to apply, the HO-3 describes the property covered under Coverage A—Dwelling as follows:

a. The dwelling on the "residence premises" shown in the Declarations, including structures attached to the dwelling; and

b. Materials and supplies located on or next to the "residence premises" used to construct, alter or repair the dwelling or other structures on the "residence premises".[12]

For example, if Jeff reported the theft of four bundles of shingles and two rolls of tar paper that were stored in his garage, and the claim representative's investigation revealed that Jeff planned to use those materials to repair his roof, then the stolen property would be covered based on the policy provision just mentioned. If the claim representative's investigation revealed that Jeff is a roofing contractor and planned to use those materials on a job, the loss would not be covered. Therefore, it is important to determine whether the damaged property is covered under the policy.

Is the Type of Loss Covered?

Losses can be classified as direct or indirect. **Direct loss** refers to reduction in property value resulting immediately and proximately from damage caused by a covered cause of loss. A crumpled car fender is a direct loss. **Indirect loss**, sometimes called consequential loss or time element loss, is difficult to define, but generally refers to a loss that arises as a result of damage to property, other than the direct loss to the property. Indirect losses reduce future income, increase future expenses, or both. For example, if fire destroys an insured's home, the cost of rebuilding the home is a direct loss. The rental cost for temporary living quarters for the insured while the home is being rebuilt is an indirect loss. The loss of earnings and the extra expenses incurred over a period of time after a fire damages a business are also indirect losses.

Many property policies cover direct losses only. Other policies cover some types of indirect losses. For example, homeowners policies cover increases in living expenses after a covered loss renders the home untenable.

Direct loss
A reduction in property value resulting immediately and proximately from damage caused by a covered cause of loss.

Indirect loss
A loss that arises as a result of damage to property, other than the direct loss to the property.

Are the Amounts of Loss or Damages Covered?

Claim representatives should always check the policy to determine whether the amounts of loss are covered. For property damage claims, the amount of loss payable is usually limited to physical damage to, destruction of, or loss of use of tangible property. The amount is usually based on the cost to repair or replace the damaged property with that of like kind and quality. Claims for indirect loss, such as loss of business income, can be payable if indirect loss coverage is included or has been added to the policy.

Compensatory damages
Compensation to claimants for their bodily injury or property damage.

Special damages
A monetary award to compensate a victim for specific, out of pocket expenses incurred because of a loss, such as medical expenses, wage loss, funeral expenses, or repair bills.

General damages
A monetary award to compensate a victim for losses, such as pain and suffering, that do not involve specific measurable expenses.

Punitive damages
A payment awarded by a court to punish a wrongdoer for a reckless, malicious, or deceitful act and to deter similar conduct.

For liability claims, damages for which the insured may be liable are of the following two types:

1. **Compensatory damages**, which include **special damages** (which pay for specific, out-of-pocket expenses, such as medical expenses, wage loss, funeral expenses, or repair bills) and **general damages** (which pay for losses, such as pain and suffering, and do not involve specific measurable expenses), reimburse or compensate claimants for their bodily injury or property damage.
2. **Punitive damages** punish a wrongdoer for a reckless, malicious, or deceitful act and deter similar conduct.

Exhibit 2-2 shows the types of damages.

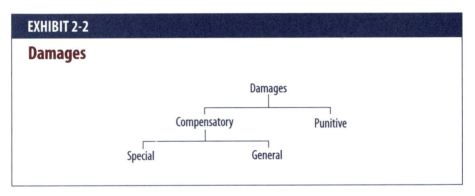

EXHIBIT 2-2

Damages

Some policies do not define or list the types of damages payable under the policy. For example, the insuring agreement for the PAP liability coverage section begins, "We will pay damages for 'bodily injury' or 'property damage' for which any 'insured' becomes legally responsible because of an auto accident."[13]

Generally, the term "damages" refers only to compensatory damages, such as expenses for medical bills, lost wages, and pain and suffering. In some states, the insurer is not permitted to pay for punitive damages because such payment by an insurer would not punish the insured. For example, if a manufacturer of a defective product has insurance for punitive damages, imposition of punitive damages would not have the same deterrent effect as forcing the manufacturer to pay the damages directly from its assets. Therefore, some policies expressly exclude coverage for punitive damages.

In a liability insurance policy, the insurer agrees to pay judgments and settlements up to the policy limit. In addition, some liability policies contain deductibles. They may also include coverage for certain expenses, such as defense costs and bail bonds, outside the limit of liability. Others may have a self-insured retention (SIR) in which the insured organization adjusts and pays its own losses up to the SIR level. Once that SIR is exceeded, the insurer makes payment. The claim representative must verify all the policy limits applicable to a loss before making a settlement to ensure that any payment made falls within the available limits of coverage.

In addition to ensuring that the type of loss and types of damage are covered, claim representatives must verify that the amount of damages is within the policy limits. A first party property policy will have limits of liability and may also have sublimits for certain types of property or types of losses. For example, the HO-3 contains a limit on the dwelling and contents as well as special limits for loss of money and theft of jewelry and silverware. First-party losses are also subject to deductibles, provisions that specify how the loss is to be valued (either actual cash value or replacement cost), and coinsurance clauses designed to ensure that the appropriate amount of insurance is maintained on the property.

Is the Location of the Loss Covered?

The location where the loss occurred must be within the policy's territorial limits and, for property policies, be shown on the policy as a covered location. To illustrate, the PAP defines policy territory as follows:

1. The United States of America, its territories or possessions;
2. Puerto Rico; or
3. Canada.

This policy also applies to loss to, or accidents involving, "your covered auto" while being transported between their ports.[14]

Accidents occurring in Mexico would not be covered because they are outside the territory covered by the policy. Property policies cover buildings only at the locations listed in the declarations, but personal property can be covered at other locations.

Do Any Exclusions Apply?

As stated earlier, some losses may be excluded in the policy. For example, the HO-3 excludes losses caused by deterioration, such as a wooden garage door that rots. The PAP excludes damage caused by wear and tear, such as the wear on a tire.

Exclusions to coverage can involve the following:

- Persons
- Causes of loss
- Types of property
- Types of damage
- Other circumstances

When claim circumstances fall within a specific exclusion, coverage does not apply. An exclusion applies even if other coverage requirements are met. For example, suppose that an insured uses his car as a taxi and is involved in an accident, severely damaging the driver's side door. The insured subsequently submits a claim. That claim appears to be covered according to the following criteria:

- *Is the person involved covered?* The driver is the named insured.
- *Did the loss occur during the policy period?* In this case, it did.

- *Is the cause of loss covered?* The policy covers physical damage to the insured's car.
- *Is the damaged property covered?* The vehicle is listed in the policy's declarations.
- *Is the type of loss covered?* The policy covers collisions.
- *Are the amounts of loss or damages covered?* The amount of the loss is within the policy limits but more than the deductible.
- *Is the location of the loss covered?* The loss occurred within the policy's territorial limits.

Then the claim representative would ask another question: "Do any exclusions apply?" On reviewing the exclusions, the claim representative would find that the PAP excludes loss that occurs while the car is used as a public or livery conveyance, and the claim representative would rightfully deny the claim.

Sometimes exclusions contain exceptions, meaning they clarify what is excluded. For example, the PAP excludes liability coverage for damage to property used by the insured. However, an exception in the exclusion states that the exclusion does not apply to property damage to a residence used by the insured. Claim representatives who carefully read the policy can avoid incorrectly denying coverage based on an exclusion when an exception applies.

> **APPLY YOUR LEARNING**
>
> **Adjusting Tip**
>
> A claim representative must make sure that the exclusion upon which the denial is based has not been declared invalid by a court having jurisdiction over the claim or by a state statute.

Does Other Insurance Apply?

Some policies are intended to apply only if no other insurance applies or only above the limits provided by other insurance. For example, the PAP states that coverage provided under that policy is excess over other collectible insurance for vehicles the insured does not own. In other cases, a policy may pay a portion of the loss based on the limit of insurance available from other policies.

Having answered all the questions in the framework for coverage analysis, the claim representative can apply the policy to the facts of the claim and make a coverage determination.

CLAIM HANDLING PROCESS

The claim representative has a responsibility to thoroughly investigate a claim to determine how coverage applies. However, investigation is only one activity in the claim handling process. To ensure that every claim is handled in good faith, from beginning to end, the claim representative should follow a systematic claim handling process that is discussed in the remainder of this chapter. The process is a group of activities that are standard for anyone who handles claims. The activities are not always sequential. Some can be performed concurrently, and some may need to be repeated as new facts are uncovered. Depending on the severity and complexity of the claim, the process may be completed quickly or it can take months or even years to complete.

> **Activities in the Claim Handling Process**
> - Acknowledging and assigning the claim
> - Identifying the policy
> - Contacting the insured or the insured's representative
> - Investigating and documenting the claim
> - Determining cause of loss and loss amount
> - Concluding the claim

The claim handling process is initiated when the insured reports the loss to the producer or directly to the insurer's claim center. If the loss is reported to the producer, the producer typically enters the loss information into the agency's claim information system, which then transmits the appropriate loss notice to the insurer. If the producer prepares a hard copy of the loss notice, he or she may fax it to the insurer. If the loss is reported directly to the insurer, claim personnel enter the loss information into the insurer's claim information system.

Losses can be reported using a loss notice form, which varies by type of loss. One of the most commonly used loss notice forms is the ACORD form. ACORD forms include basic information about the loss, such as the loss date and time, policy number, insured name and address, covered property, and loss description. For injury claims, the loss notice also includes the accident location, witness names and addresses, and the names and addresses of any injured persons.

However, not all losses are reported using a loss notice. Some losses may be reported in a letter or as part of a lawsuit. Regardless of how a loss is reported, the same information must be entered into the insurer's claim information system. If the first notice of the loss is a lawsuit, the claim representative must be aware of the deadline by which to respond to the lawsuit. The time allowed for response varies by state. The claim representative must turn the lawsuit over to counsel to answer, even while the initial investigation is underway.

Once a loss notice is received and the information is entered into the insurer's claim information system, the insurer begins the claim handling process.

Acknowledging and Assigning the Claim

Generally, the first activity of the insurer in the claim handling process is acknowledging receipt of the claim and assigning the claim to a claim representative. Some insurers acknowledge claims immediately upon receiving the loss notice by contacting the insured by phone, e-mail, letter, or postcard. Others acknowledge the claim after it is assigned to a claim representative. Many insurers transfer claim files to a claim manager for assignment to a claim representative. The claim manager may add comments to the file and then transfer the file directly to the assigned claim representative. The purpose of the acknowledgment is to advise the insured that the claim has been received. The acknowledgment also provides the name and contact information of the assigned claim representative and the claim number. Insurers acknowledge claims in this timely manner to comply with insurance regulations.

Insurers use different methods of assigning claims to claim representatives. Some insurers assign claims based on territory, type of claim, extent of damage, workload, or other criteria contained in the insurer's claim information system. The goal is to assign the claim to the claim representative who possesses the appropriate skills to handle it. Some states require claim representatives who handle claims in the state to have an adjuster license. These licensing requirements must also be considered when assigning a claim to a claim representative. For example, Texas law requires a claim representative adjusting a loss for a Texas insured or a loss that occurred in Texas to be licensed as an adjuster in Texas. Such statutes usually allow exceptions in the event of a catastrophe, such as a flood or tornado, that requires every available claim representative be sent into an area to handle the high volume of resulting claims.

After receiving the claim assignment, the claim representative contacts the insured, and possibly the claimant (if it is a third-party claim), to acknowledge the claim assignment and explain the claim process. For insurers that do not make contact immediately after receiving the loss notice, this contact serves as the claim acknowledgment. For some types of losses, the claim representative may give the insured instructions to prevent any further loss, such as to cover roof damage with a tarp. If the claim involves property damage, the claim representative may arrange a time with the insured to inspect the damage or the damage scene. As an alternative, the claim representative may advise the insured or claimant that an appraiser or an independent adjuster will be in contact to inspect the property damage. If the claim involves bodily injury, the claim representative should get information about the nature and extent of the injury.

Identifying the Policy

Another activity in the claim handling process is identifying the policy. The claim representative first identifies the policy in force upon receiving the assignment. Some insurers do this before they acknowledge the claim. Other insurers identify the policy in force before the claim representative begins the claim investigation. In either case, the claim representative must thoroughly read the policy, using the framework for coverage analysis described previously, to determine what types of coverage apply to the loss.

If it is apparent from the loss notice that coverage may not be available for the loss, the claim representative must notify the insured of this concern through a nonwaiver agreement or a reservation of rights letter. Both of these documents, discussed later in this chapter, reserve the insurer's and policyholder's rights under the policy.

Reserves

Often, in conjunction with identifying the policy, claim representatives establish claim or case (loss) reserves, although this can occur at almost any point in the claim handling process, depending on the insurer's internal guidelines. While the exact timing may differ among insurers, the setting of an initial reserve(s) usually occurs early in the claim handling process. A **reserve** is the amount the insurer estimates and sets aside to pay on an existing claim that has not been settled. The insurer's claim information system often determines the types of reserves that are established, such as one reserve for property damage and another for bodily injury. Some systems require separate reserves for each claimant in a claim, and some systems require separate expense reserves for the costs of handling the claim. For example, in a claim for an auto accident, an individual reserve may be set up for damage to the insured's vehicle, damage to the other party's vehicle, medical expenses for the insured, and bodily injury for the claimant. Setting accurate reserves is an important part of the claim representative's job. Reserves that are too high or too low can affect the profitability of the insurer. Establishing and maintaining adequate reserves is important for the insurer's financial health because reserves affect the insurer's ability to maintain and increase its business.

Reserve
The amount the insurer estimates and sets aside to pay on an existing claim that has not been settled.

Insurers can use different methods of setting reserves. Six common methods are discussed here.

Common Methods of Setting Case Reserves

1. Individual case method
2. Roundtable method
3. Average value method
4. Formula method
5. Expert system method
6. Loss ratio method

The individual case method and the roundtable method rely on the claim representative's judgment. The other methods rely on statistical analysis to set the reserve.

One method of setting claim reserves is the individual case method. Claim representatives set an individual or case reserve for each claim or cause of loss, based on the claim representative's expectation of what the insurer will pay. When the **individual case method** is used on each claim, the claim

Individual case method
A method of setting reserves based on the claim's circumstances and the claim representative's experience in handling similar claims.

representative estimates the loss reserve based on the claim's circumstances and experience in similar claims.

Because of the subjective nature of the evaluation, reserves can vary widely by claim representative. Factors that claim representatives may consider when using the individual case method for a bodily injury claim are shown in Exhibit 2-3.

EXHIBIT 2-3

Individual Case Method Considerations

Considerations a claim representative may use when setting reserves on a bodily injury claim using the individual case method include the following:

1. Claimant profile (factors in calculating economic loss)
    a. Age
    b. Gender
    c. Occupation
    d. Level of education
    e. Dependants, if any, their ages, and to what extent they rely on the claimant financially and for companionship

2. Nature and extent of the injury (factors in calculating general damages)
    a. Whether the injury is permanent
    b. Extent of pain and suffering
    c. Extent of disruption the injury creates in the individual's lifestyle

3. Special damages (factors in calculating special damages)
    a. Anticipated medical bills incurred to date and for future care
    b. Type of medical care that has been or is being provided; whether it includes diagnostic care or treatment
    c. Whether the claimant will lose any wages

4. Claimant representation (factors in determining the likelihood of a lawsuit and predicting general damages that could result)
    a. Whether the claimant is represented by a lawyer
    b. If so, the lawyer's reputation
    c. Typical value of local court verdicts

5. Liability factors (factors in calculating compensatory and/or punitive damages)
    a. Whether the case involves ordinary negligence or gross negligence
    b. Whether the case involves any comparative or contributory negligence
    c. Any legal limits to recovery, such as a cap on certain types of damages
    d. Any other parties' contribution to the loss or responsibility for contributing to the settlement

6. Miscellaneous factors
    a. General economic conditions in the geographic area (factor in calculating economic loss)
    b. Whether the insured's conduct in causing the loss was outrageous (factor in calculating compensatory damages)
    c. Whether drinking or drug use contributed to the loss (factor in calculating liability)
    d. The insured's credibility as a witness (factor in determining likelihood of successful lawsuit)
    e. The claimant's credibility as a witness (factor in determining likelihood of successful lawsuit)

Another method of setting claim reserves is the roundtable method. The **roundtable method** involves two or more claim personnel indepenedently evaluating the claim file, each suggesting a reserve based on his or her evaluation. Ideally, the claim personnel should not initially know the reserves the others have set. After the evaluation and a discussion, a consensus reserve figure may be reached, or an average of all the figures may be calculated. Because this method is time-consuming, it is not appropriate for setting initial reserves. However, for serious or prolonged claims, it is a suitable method to review initial reserves.

Roundtable method
A method of setting reserves by using the consensus of two or more claim personnel who have independently evaluated the claim file.

Claim representatives may also set claim reserves using the **average value method**, which uses a predetermined dollar amount that is set aside for a particular type of claim when it is reported. This method is useful when there are small variations in loss size for a particular type of claim and when claims can be concluded quickly. The average values are usually based on data from past claims and adjusted to reflect current conditions. For example, auto physical damage claims may be initially reserved at $1,500 based on an insurer's previous loss experience with those claims. That figure may remain the same until the claim has been concluded. For some claims, the initial reserve is set based on the average value method, but claim representatives are required to modify the initial reserve within a specified number of days to reflect each claim's circumstances.

Average value method
A method of setting claim reserves by using a predetermined dollar amount that is set aside for a particular type of claim when it is reported.

Another method of setting claim reserves is the **formula method**, in which the claim representative uses a mathematical formula to set reserves. For example, a formula may be based on the assumption that a certain ratio exists between the medical cost and the indemnity (or wage loss) in a workers' compensation claim. Based on an insurer's loss history with many similar claims, the indemnity reserve may be set at a certain percentage of the medical reserve. The formula method may also be used to set the additional living expense reserve under a homeowners policy if the home is destroyed by fire. The reserve may be set as a certain percentage of the coverage limit. The formula is determined by the insurer and is automatically created for the claim representative, based on the facts of the claim.

Formula method
A method of setting claim reserves by using a mathematical formula.

Expert system method
A method of setting reserves with a software application that estimates losses and loss adjustment expenses.

Claim representatives may also set claim reserves by the **expert system method**, using a software application containing business rules to assist in estimating losses and loss adjustment expenses (LAE). The details of a particular claim are entered into the computer, and the program applies the appropriate rules to estimate the amount of the loss and the LAE. An expert system can provide greater consistency in reserving than the individual case method. While similar in operation to the formula method, the expert system includes more subjective information, such as loss location or the name of the treating physician, in creating the reserve.

Loss ratio method
A method of setting reserves by establishing aggregate reserves for all claims within a type of insurance or a class of loss exposures.

The **loss ratio method** of setting claim reserves is used to establish aggregate reserves for all claims within a type of insurance or a class of loss exposures. The actuarial department uses this method when other methods of establishing claim reserves are inadequate. For example, in medical malpractice insurance for physicians and surgeons, claims are often reported long after the expiration date of the policy that provided the coverage. To ensure that the insurer has adequate reserves for those claims, the actuarial department may project reserves using the loss ratio method.

The NAIC Annual Statement is another example of the use of the loss ratio method of setting reserves. The Annual Statement requires minimum reserves for certain types of insurance such as workers' compensation. The minimum reserve is a specific percentage of the earned premiums for the year. For example, for workers' compensation insurance, the minimum reserve required by the Annual Statement may be 50 percent of earned premiums. If case reserves are lower than that amount, the Annual Statement uses the set percentage. If case reserves are higher than the set percentage, the Annual Statement uses the case reserves. Exhibit 2-4 illustrates how Annual Statement reserves are established in this situation.

EXHIBIT 2-4

Minimum Annual Statement Reserves

Minimum Statutory Reserve		50%
Earned Premiums		$40,000,000

	Case Reserve	Annual Statement Reserve
Example 1	$16,000,000	$20,000,000
Example 2	$22,000,000	$22,000,000

Additionally, insurers are required by law and good accounting practice to establish reserves for losses that have been incurred but not reported (IBNR). Although the name refers only to incurred but not reported losses, unreported losses account for only a part of the reserve in many cases. Often, the IBNR reserve also includes an amount for reported losses for which the case reserves are judged to be inadequate. A reserve for claims that have been closed and then reopened may also be included in the IBNR reserve.

Actuaries analyze the insurer's experience by comparing paid losses to case reserves to determine whether the insurer typically under reserves or over reserves claims. If the insurer typically under reserves claims, the IBNR reserve will be set at an amount to cover the ultimate cost of the claim.

Causes of Reserve Errors

Reserve adequacy and accuracy are important to an insurer's continued solvency and ability to write new business (capacity). Claim representatives can negatively influence solvency and capacity by undervaluing claim reserves. Although an occasional reserve may be inadequate or inaccurate with little or no effect on the insurer, consistently inaccurate or inadequate reserves on thousands of claims can distort the ratemaking process, eventually affecting an insurer's ability to write business competitively and ultimately affecting solvency.

Reserving errors can be caused in several ways. Initial reserves may be inaccurate because they are determined based on limited information. Thus, many insurers require that initial reserves be reviewed and adjusted for accuracy within a short time frame. In addition, most insurers require reserves to be evaluated whenever a claim file is reviewed. That evaluation ensures that reserves reflect the most current information contained in the claim file.

Reserve inaccuracy can also be the result of the claim representative's poor planning, lack of expertise in estimating claim severity, or unwillingness to reevaluate the facts. In these cases, the claim representative may set a modest initial reserve, but then raise the reserve by a few thousand dollars to issue payments. Later, the reserve is increased again when more bills arrive. This process is called stairstepping the reserve.

On a claim that concludes in thirty, sixty, or ninety days, stairstepping has little effect except to reveal the claim representative's poor claim handling practices. But if the claim remains open for several years, as many liability and workers' compensation claims do, the incremental increase in reserves during those years is not properly reflected in the insurer's ratemaking process.

This does not mean that claim representatives cannot adjust a reserve up or down during the course of a claim. However, they should make those adjustments because of new information or changes in the circumstances of the claim, not because of poor planning or other poor claim handling practices.

Stairstepping can be avoided if proper claim handling practices and reserving methods are used. For example, the roundtable method or expert system method may result in a realistic reserve that would prevent frequent stairstepping.

Because reserves should reflect the ultimate cost of a claim and not the claim's present value, the reserve should account for the claim's future settlement value. For example, a catastrophic injury claim may take years to settle. During that time, inflation may increase the cost of medical care, or new and expensive medical technology may be developed. The reserves for such claims should anticipate those increased costs.

Claim representatives may underestimate the future settlement value of a claim if they are overconfident of their ability to conclude the claim for a lesser amount. Reserves should always be based on the value of a claim, never on the perceived likelihood of successful negotiation and settlement. Analysis of verdicts rendered in similar cases helps show the potential value of a claim and discourages the tendency to base reserves on negotiation expertise.

Some inadvertent errors in setting reserves can be detected using computer software that stores claim information. Some claim information systems provide a data entry check. For example, the software might require that the reserve amount be entered twice to allow the person inputting the data a chance to verify the amount. Additionally, claim managers can review reports of reserves from the preceding day for unusual entries or reserves established in excess of authority. For example, a report listing all reserves of $100,000 or more might uncover a $10,000 reserve that was incorrectly entered as $100,000.

As claim representatives proceed with claim investigations and evaluations, they should increase or decrease the reserve amounts to reflect new information received. For example, if the estimate for car repairs is $5,000, the claim representative would set up a reserve of $5,000. If hidden damage is then found and the estimate is revised to be $10,000, the claim representative should change the reserve to reflect this increase in the repair estimate. Likewise, if an estimate to repair is lowered, the reserve should be changed to reflect the decrease. Because these changes are based on changes in the facts of the claim, they are not considered stairstepping.

Contacting the Insured or the Insured's Representative

Another activity in the claim handling process, which occurs soon after the loss is assigned to a claim representative and initial reserves are established, is contacting the insured or the insured's representative. This initial contact with the insured serves several purposes. It can reassure the insured that the claim will be investigated. It also provides the claim representative with an opportunity to explain the claim process and begin the claim investigation.

For some insurers or in certain claims as specified in the insurer's guidelines, this contact occurs at the same time as the claim acknowledgment. Generally, the claim representative reviews the initial loss report and policy and then contacts the insured and schedules a time to speak with the insured or a party representing the insured about the facts of the loss. This can be a face to face meeting at the insured's location or the loss location, or it can be a telephone discussion. If the loss involves a third-party claimant, then the claim representative also contacts the claimant and schedules a meeting with the claimant or a party representing the claimant to discuss the facts of the loss.

For some claims, the insured is represented by a public adjuster or an attorney. Public adjusters are active in some states and metropolitan areas, most often in property damage claims. Such adjusters charge a fee to help insureds present claims to insurers. The claim representative should discuss claim-related issues with the public adjuster or attorney until advised not to do so by the insured.

Not every claim requires a face-to-face meeting with the insured or claimant. Some claims can be handled by phone, supplemented by an exchange of documents. Most insurers have guidelines for claim representatives to determine which claims can be handled by phone.

Before making the initial contact with any of the parties, the claim representative should prepare a list of questions for the insured or claimant along with a set of instructions on how the claim will be handled and what actions the insured or claimant will have to complete as part of the claim process.

The first meeting or discussion with the insured sets the tone for the claim. For the insured or the claimant, the loss has mostly likely created a disruption resulting in strong emotions, such as anger or grief. Those who have never filed an insurance claim may be apprehensive or confused about how the claims will be handled. The claim representative should be aware of these factors and take them into consideration when initially meeting or speaking with the insured or the claimant.

APPLY YOUR LEARNING

Adjusting Tip

Claim representatives should be aware that their words and actions set the insured's or claimant's expectations about the claim. If the claim representative promises that something will be done by a certain date, the insured or claimant will expect it to be done by that date. Therefore, claim representatives demonstrate good-faith claim handling practices by meeting these deadlines.

At the initial contact, claim representatives frequently find that many insureds do not fully understand the details of their insurance coverages. The claim representative must be prepared to explain the policy terms and their meanings in relation to the loss. The claim representative must explain any possible policy violation, exclusion, or limitation that can affect coverage. Withholding such information can be considered a breach of the claim representative's or insurer's duties. The claim representative must be careful not to give the insured or claimant the impression that a claim will be paid if possible grounds to deny a claim exist.

Once contact is made, the claim representative should do the following:

- Tell the insured what is required to protect any damaged property and to document the claim. Be specific about what the insured must do and by when it must be done.
- Describe the inspection, appraisal, and investigation the claim representative will be conducting.

- Tell the insured what additional investigation is needed to resolve any potential coverage issues. Give complete and clear instructions if the insured is to provide any additional information.
- Explain potential coverage questions or policy limitations or exclusions and obtain a nonwaiver agreement, when necessary (to be described in a subsequent section).
- Obtain the authorizations necessary to get medical and wage loss information, if such information is part of the claim.
- Describe the time involved to process and conclude the claim.
- Supply the insured with a blank proof of loss form for property damage and any necessary written instructions, so the insured can document the claim.

> **APPLY YOUR LEARNING**
> **Adjusting Tip**
> When speaking with the insured, discuss all potential coverage issues, not just the ones most likely to apply. If the insured or claimant can overcome the first potential coverage issue and then is told of another that may apply, it can appear that the claim representative is trying to avoid paying the claim.

In some cases, the claim representative may conduct a recorded interview with the insured during the initial meeting or discussion.

Claim representatives must be aware of the legal implications of their words and actions when communicating with insureds. They must be careful not to mislead the insured or the claimant about the potential coverage for the claim or the amount of the claim payment. To avoid such pitfalls, claim representatives must understand three legal concepts: good faith, waiver, and estoppel.

Good Faith

Insurance policies are contracts of utmost good faith. When conducting a good-faith investigation, a claim representative must attempt to correctly and promptly resolve coverage issues. Many situations that present coverage issues require further investigation to determine whether the claim should be paid or denied. Until the coverage issues are resolved, the claim representative and insurer must avoid any conduct that would lead insureds or claimants to believe that the claim will be paid. Otherwise, the insurer may waive its right to legitimately deny coverage. While attempting to resolve the coverage issues, claim representatives must focus on the facts and decide if the facts support coverage. Claim representatives must also quantify the loss so that payment is not delayed if coverage is confirmed.

Waiver and Estoppel

Waiver
The intentional or voluntary relinquishment of a known right.

Waiver is the voluntary or intentional relinquishment of a known contractual right, such as one contained in a policy condition or exclusion. For example, a claim representative can waive a right contained in a policy condition or exclusion by telling an insured that a loss is covered before confirming that by checking the policy. The claim representative has waived the insurer's right to deny the claim if the facts later prove that there is no coverage.

Estoppel is a legal bar to asserting certain contractual conditions because of a party's previous actions or words to the contrary. Estoppel results when one party's action causes another party to rely on that behavior or those words with detrimental results. For example, a claim representative who tells an insured that damaged goods can be discarded before they are inspected cannot later deny the claim on the grounds that the damaged goods were not available for inspection. The claim representative is estopped from denying the claim on that basis.

> **Estoppel**
> A legal bar to asserting a certain contractual condition because of that party's previous actions or words to the contrary.

Example of Case Involving Both Waiver and Estoppel

An insured calls the claim service center of Atwell Insurance and reports that a large tree fell into her yard during a windstorm. The customer service representative who answers the call tells the insured to have a contractor remove the debris and send the bill to the insurer.

Two weeks later, the insurer receives a bill from the contractor for $1,200. The customer service representative is authorized to settle claims only up to $500, so she takes the bill to her supervisor. Her supervisor indicates that the policy does not cover this type of loss unless the tree damages the insured's house, fence, or other covered structure. The supervisor further explains that when a falling tree damages property, a $500 limit on debris removal applies.

The insured's policy does not cover this loss. However, the customer service representative waived this coverage defense by telling the insured to arrange for the debris removal and to send the bill to the insurer without first explaining the coverage under the policy. Because the insured relied on what the customer service representative told her and incurred expenses, Atwell Insurance may be estopped from denying coverage. Even though coverage does not apply to the original loss, Atwell may have to pay the $1,200 bill. The insurer's failure to notify the insured at the beginning of the claim process that coverage did not apply estopped it from later denying coverage.

Claim representatives use two common methods to avoid waiver and estoppel: nonwaiver agreements and reservation of rights letters.

Nonwaiver agreements and reservation of rights letters serve the following general purposes:

- To advise the insured that any action taken by the insurer in investigating the cause of loss or in ascertaining the amount of loss is not intended to waive or invalidate any policy conditions.
- To clarify that the agreement's or the letter's intent is to permit a claim investigation and that neither the insured nor the insurer will thereby waive any respective rights or obligations.

> **APPLY YOUR LEARNING**
>
> **Adjusting Tip**
>
> Claim representatives have a reasonable amount of time, usually specified in state unfair claim practices acts, in which to conduct an investigation and advise the insured of a coverage decision without waiving any of the insurer's rights. Thus, claim representatives should not obtain nonwaiver agreements and reservation of rights letters on every claim because most claims will not require them. If in doubt, claim representatives should proceed cautiously and obtain guidance from supervisors or managers.

Nonwaiver agreement
A signed agreement indicating that during the course of investigation, neither the insurer nor the insured waives rights under the policy.

A **nonwaiver agreement** states that, while the insurer is investigating the claim, neither the insurer nor the insured waives any rights under the policy. This agreement, which must be signed by both parties, protects the insurer from estoppel by reserving the right to deny coverage based on information developed during the investigation. It also alerts the insured to a potential coverage problem. The nonwaiver agreement is usually used when the claim representative is concerned about investigating a claim before the insured has substantially complied with the policy conditions or when there appears to be a specific coverage problem or defense. Such concerns can be identified from the initial claim report, during initial contact with the insured, or at any point during the claim investigation. For example, a claim representative may offer a nonwaiver agreement when the insured reports the theft of an auto but refuses to make a police report about the theft. If the insured refuses to sign the nonwaiver agreement, the claim representative can use a reservation of rights letter to protect the insurer's rights.

Reservation of rights letter
An insurer's letter that specifies coverage issues and informs the insured that the insurer is handling a claim with the understanding that the insurer may later deny coverage should the facts warrant it.

Like a nonwaiver agreement, a **reservation of rights letter** is a letter signed and issued by an insurer and sent to the insured to indicate that the insurer is handling a claim with the understanding that the insurer may later deny coverage should the facts warrant it. It serves the same purpose as a nonwaiver agreement but is in letter form, and it is a unilateral document: it does not require the insured to sign or agree to the contents of the letter. It simply advises the insured of the potential coverage issue. Nevertheless, a reservation of rights letter can be as effective in protecting the insurer's rights to policy defenses as a nonwaiver agreement if the insurer has drafted the letter carefully and can show that the insured received it. Nonwaiver agreements and reservation of rights letters are usually sent by certified mail, return receipt requested, so the insurer has evidence that the insured received it.

Nonwaiver agreements and reservation of rights letters can be used only with the insured and can be used on any type of first-party claim. They are not sent to third-party claimants because third parties have no obligations under the policy.

The claim representative must take steps to ensure that the insured understands why an investigation is necessary to determine coverage and how the reservation of rights letter or nonwaiver agreement will facilitate the investigation. The strength of a reservation of rights letter or a nonwaiver agreement in protecting the insurer's policy defenses in court depends on the circumstances. For example, evidence that an insured received a reservation of rights letter and understood it may outweigh the insured's argument that the letter is invalid. On the other hand, an insured may sign a nonwaiver agreement but may not understand its meaning; in this case, the nonwaiver agreement would be less likely to be upheld in court.

> **APPLY YOUR LEARNING**
>
> **Adjusting Tip**
>
> The language in a nonwaiver agreement or a reservation of rights letter is often mandated by case law. The claim representative should consult with counsel to obtain the language for a specific state.

Investigating and Documenting the Claim

Another activity in the claim handling process is investigating and documenting the claim. Investigation and documentation are ongoing throughout the life of the claim. The investigation can take many different forms, and all aspects of it must be documented to create a complete claim file. This section provides an overview of investigations. The next chapter describes investigations in more detail, including how they are used to determine the cause of loss and the loss amount.

Claim representatives begin investigating a claim as soon as it is assigned. They can develop an outline or notes to logically organize the investigation and to ensure that information that may be available only for a short time is investigated first, such as any accident scene or damaged property that may be destroyed or discarded. Claim representatives should contact any third-party claimant early in the investigation. This contact can help establish rapport with claimants, and in turn facilitate the investigation and lead to a timely settlement.

Claim representatives must also know when they have sufficient information on which to base a decision. Investigations should be geared to obtain information that will help determine the cause of loss, the amount of loss, and liability. The insurer's claim handling guidelines help claim representatives determine the types and extent of investigation needed for a satisfactory claim settlement. Once sufficient information is obtained to make a reasoned determination, the claim representative does not need to continue the investigation, unless the determination is disputed.

This section provides a basic outline for the claim representative to follow to investigate any type of claim. Claim representatives must use good-faith claim handling practices and insurer guidelines to ensure a thorough investigation. Several types of investigations, including the following, are common to many types of claims:

- Claimant investigation
- Insured/witness investigation
- Accident scene investigation

- Property damage investigation
- Medical investigation
- Prior claim investigation
- Subrogation investigation and recovery

The following sections describe these common claim investigations and explains when and why they are important.

Claimant Investigation

In a first-party property claim, the claimant is the insured. In an automobile or liability claim, the claimant may be a third party who was injured in the accident or a third party whose property was damaged. In a workers' compensation claim, the claimant is the injured worker. Claim representatives conduct a claimant investigation, usually by taking the claimant's statement, to learn the claimant's version of the incident that led to the claim. This information can help the claim representative determine the value of the injury or damage, how it was caused, and who is responsible.

Insured/Witness Investigation

Claim representatives often take statements (either written or recorded) from the insured and witnesses because they can provide valuable information about the circumstances surrounding the loss. The insured is always the party named as the insured in the policy. Witnesses are any persons who have personal, first-hand knowledge of the incident that resulted in the claim. The witness investigation can support or refute an insured's version of an incident, affecting the liability determination. A statement can also serve as a means of attacking the witness's credibility if later testimony differs from the information given in the original statement.

Accident Scene Investigation

The accident scene offers crucial clues in automobile, third-party liability, and workers' compensation claims. By observing details such as tire tracks, curves in the roadway, and objects or conditions that may interfere with a driver's view or that may cause an accident (such as a pothole in the road), the claim representative can determine whether accounts of the accident are plausible or questionable. Claim representatives also consult weather or traffic reports in certain accident scene investigations to identify external factors that may have contributed to the loss.

Property Damage Investigation

An investigation of the scene at which property was damaged can be useful in automobile and property coverage claims to confirm the cause of loss and extent of damage. For business income claims, a property damage investigation is useful for determining lost profits or loss of business use resulting from covered property damage. The investigation can also help confirm the need to move operations to an alternate site or to temporarily replace damaged equipment with rented equipment so that business operations can continue while repairs are being made.

Medical Investigation

Claim representatives conduct medical investigations in all bodily injury claims, including worker's compensation claims. A medical investigation helps the claim representative determine the costs of the medical treatment, the expected duration of medical treatment and disability, the need for rehabilitation, and the suitability of medical care for the type of injuries the claimant suffered. This information is also used to evaluate the amount of pain and suffering that resulted from the accident or injury.

Prior Claim Investigation

Claim representatives conduct prior claim investigations on all claims to avoid paying for property damage or bodily injury that has been paid through prior claims by the same insurer or by other insurers. For example, a prior claim investigation may reveal that the claimant has a history of lower back injuries or that the insured's vehicle had sustained similar damage from a prior accident. By conducting a prior claim investigation, the claim representative ensures that the insurer pays only new claims for which the insurer has legal responsibility.

The prior claim investigation is usually performed by comparing the facts of the current claim to an industry database containing information from many different insurers. Insurers subscribe to these databases and also furnish them with claim information. The databases provide a quick way to check for similair prior claims. If the check returns a likely match, the claim representative should investigate the prior claim history in more detail to determine if the current claim is for the same injury or damage. If this is the case, the claim representative may have a basis for denying the claim or may adjust the investigation.

Subrogation Investigation and Recovery

During the course of an investigation, the claim representative may discover that the insured was not at fault and that a third party caused the accident. When an insurer pays a claim to an insured for a loss caused by a negligent third party, the insurer can recover that payment amount from the negligent third party through the right of **subrogation**. Subrogation rights are established by insurance policies and by law. When claim representatives investigate any loss, they must be alert to any subrogation possibilities; that is, they should be looking for ways to recover any money paid out on the claim. Claim representatives investigate subrogation possibilities concurrently with other investigations. The following examples describe losses for which a claim representative should investigate subrogation possibilities:

- Losses caused by the negligent operation of an automobile or a piece of construction equipment
- Fire, explosion, or water losses caused by the negligence of tenants

Subrogation
An insurer's right to recover payment from a negligent third party who caused a property or liability loss that the insurer has paid to or on behalf of an insured.

- Fire, explosion, or water losses caused by construction workers at a building site
- After work is completed, losses that result from poor workmanship of contractors
- Losses caused by defectively manufactured or poorly designed products

The subrogation clauses in most insurance policies require the insured to cooperate with the insurer by assigning the rights of subrogation to the insurer through a subrogation agreement. The subrogation agreement could be included in another form, such as a proof of loss form, that the insured completes for a property damage claim. Most subrogation agreements require the insured to give testimony and appear in court, when necessary, so that the insurer can establish the legal basis to recover from the negligent third party.

An insured may breach the subrogation agreement by impairing or interfering with the insurer's right of subrogation, by failing to cooperate in preserving evidence, by giving or failing to give testimony, or by releasing the responsible party from any liability after the loss. If an insured breaches the subrogation agreement, the insurer has the right to collect from the insured the amount that could have been recovered from the responsible third party.

When subrogating, the insurer has the right to recover only the amount that it has paid on the claim. The insurer has no right of recovery for losses that the insured has absorbed because of lack of coverage, exclusions, or coverage limitations under the policy. Therefore, both the insurer and the insured may have rights to recover from the responsible third party. When the insured has absorbed only the deductible amount, however, the insurer usually pursues recovery of that amount as well, as a courtesy to the insured.

Claim representatives must consider the costs required to pursue subrogation as well as the likelihood of success, and must be alert for any contract that may deny the right of subrogation (such as a lease agreement). Subrogation can be costly to pursue if litigation is required, and the insurer may in some cases decide that pursuing subrogation is not cost-effective. However, the insurer's decision does not affect the insured's right to pursue payment from the responsible party for the unpaid portions of the claim.

When the subrogation action is against a negligent third party who is responsible for a loss, the insurer can present a subrogation claim for payment to the third party's liability insurer. Usually, the liability insurer pays the entire loss or offers a compromise settlement on the claim, depending on the assessment of liability. When the two insurers cannot agree on the liability, they can agree to arbitrate the dispute, often through intercompany arbitration.

Intercompany arbitration is conducted by having one or more arbitrators review written submissions from both parties. The insurer submits the claim representative's claim file, usually with highlighted details or tabs on specific documents for the arbitrator's benefit. The file should be legible and in chronological order. An arbitration statement that outlines the insurer's position in the case should accompany the file. The decision of the arbitrator(s) is final and binding on both insurers.

File Review

Because they simultaneously handle many claims, claim representatives must have a system for working on and reviewing each claim. While the term for this system can vary (some call it a diary system, a suspense system, or a pending system), the purpose is the same. The system allows the claim representative to work on a claim one day and then diary it or calendar it for review. For example, the claim representative may send a letter to the insured requesting a repair estimate and diary that file for review on a date two weeks in the future. During that time the claim representative would expect to receive the requested estimate. If the estimate has not been received, the review prompts the claim representative to follow up.

Diary systems are usually maintained by the insurer's claim processing system, which may automatically set diary dates for the file based on the type of claim. Most systems allow claim representatives to override system-generated diary dates and set a review date manually. Claim representatives who set dates manually must ensure that their handling of the file meets the requirements of any applicable unfair claims practices acts. For example, a state law may require that the insured receive a status letter on the claim every thirty days. The automated system would set the diary dates to meet this requirement, but claim representatives should not reset dates that cause them to miss this or any other requirements.

File Documentation

In addition to reviewing claim files, claim representatives must document the files using both file status notes and reports.

File status notes (or an activity log) must accurately reflect and document investigations, evaluations of claims, decisions to decline coverage, or decisions to settle the claims. Because lawyers and state regulators can obtain copies of claim files, the file status notes and other file documentation must reflect the following:

- Clear, concise, and accurate information
- Timely claim handling
- A fair and balanced investigation considering the insured's and the insurer's interests
- Objective comments about the insurer, insured, or other parties associated with the claim
- A thorough good-faith investigation

Clear, concise, and accurate file status notes are essential because a claim file must speak for itself. The file status notes should be a chronological account of the claim representative's activities and can also include the claim supervisor's and the claim manager's activities relating to the claim. Ideally, an entry should exist for anyone who works on the file. Additionally, the file status notes should contain short summaries of reports and information received from outside sources. File status notes should be objective; they should not leave the reader with the impression that the claim representative is taking sides, such as in this statement: "The claimant obviously wasn't paying attention." File notes should not express prejudice of any sort, avoiding any remarks about race, religion, weight, or sex. Humor is also out of place in file notes. A note that seems innocuous when written can be devastating when read to a jury.

The box contains an example of some status note entries.

> **Example: Status Note Entries**
>
> 4/5/06 Received new assignment. Called insured at work and spoke to Mr. Smith. Took a recorded statement from Mr. Smith about the accident. He indicates that his car was struck from behind while stopped at a stop sign. No injuries reported. Assigned appraiser to inspect the vehicle, which is currently located at Sam's Auto Body, 123 Main Street, Anytown, Any State. Phone number is 555-1234. Requested police report.
>
> 4/6/06 Called adverse driver, Mr. Jones, and took his statement. He indicates he was traveling east on Main when he was blinded by the sun and struck Mr. Smith's car, which was stopped at the intersection.
>
> 4/10/06 Received and reviewed police report. Report states that vehicle 1 (Mr. Smith's) was stopped at a stop sign eastbound on Main at the intersection of Broad, when struck in the rear by vehicle 2 driven by Mr. Jones. Report confirms statement of the insured. Awaiting estimate from appraiser.
>
> 4/15/06 Received repair estimate from appraiser. The body shop agrees with the estimate. The amount of the damages is $5,250. Called Mr. Smith and advised him of the amount and that it was an agreed price with the body shop. Reached agreement with Mr. Smith and processed a payment for $5,000, which is the repair estimate, less the $250 deductible. Confirmed no lien-holder or other payee to be on the payment. Referred file to subrogation unit.

From these entries anyone reading this file can see that the claim representative received this claim on April 5, 2006, and began working on it that day. The file status notes indicate what activities the claim representative performed to investigate this claim and how long it took to settle the claim. These entries meet all the criteria for file status notes outlined earlier.

This example is simple and straightforward. Many claims are not. Some file status notes can be lengthy because they continue for as long as the claim remains open, which can be years in some cases. They can also be very detailed, outlining why reserves are set at a particular dollar amount or how settlement figures are determined. File status notes should not be cryptic or written in personal shorthand because the claim representative who writes them may not be available to interpret them later. Claim representatives should determine from their company guidelines if there are abbreviations for terms that are acceptable, such as "PR" for police report or "s/s" for stop sign.

File Reports

In addition to file status notes, claim representatives document claim activity using reports to various parties. One type of report is an internal report. Claim representatives prepare and distribute internal reports to parties within the insurance organization who have an interest in large losses or loss of a specific nature such as death, disfigurement, or dismemberment. Most insurers have guidelines outlining when and under what circumstances internal reports, such as file status reports and large loss reports, should be prepared. For example, large loss reports may be required for claims with reserves that exceed $500,000. These large loss reports summarize all the file status information for management and are updated as additional information is received or on a timetable set by the insurer.

In addition to the large loss report, claim representatives write three other internal reports while a claim is open: preliminary, status (or interim), and summarized (or captioned). These reports may have attachments, such as estimates, police reports, diagrams, photos, statements, and correspondence. If the claim is handled by in-house claim representatives, these attachments may already be included as images in the electronic claim file or included in the paper claim file. Often these reports are typed directly into a claim entry system (the electronic claim file) using an electronic form; distributed electronically to claim supervisors, managers, or underwriters; and then printed for any necessary outside distribution (such as lawyers).

An insurer may require preliminary reports within the first twenty-four hours, within seven days of the claim assignment, or only if the file remains open after thirty days. Preliminary reports acknowledge that the claim representative received the assignment, inform the insurer about initial activity on the claim, suggest reserves, note coverage issues, and request assistance, if needed. For small, uncomplicated claims that claim representatives settle quickly, the preliminary report may be the only report in the claim file.

Status reports tell the insurer how the claim is progressing on a periodic basis, generally every fifteen to thirty days. In these reports, claim representatives record the progress of the claim, recommend reserve changes, and request assistance and settlement authority when the amount payable exceeds their authority. Status reports are one way to confirm that the claim representative is working on a claim and progressing in a timely manner.

Summarized reports are often detailed narratives that follow an established format with captioned headings that give them structure. Claim representatives usually file a summarized report within thirty days of the assignment date. Insurers may require summarized reports for specific claims that require review by managers at regional or home offices. For example, suspected arson and insurance fraud claims are typically reported to the regional and home offices because of their potential for litigation. Managers may also review a file when the reserve exceeds a specified amount. Some insurers require summarized reports on certain types of claims because they want to track trends in certain types of business. Exhibit 2-5 is an example of a summarized report form.

EXHIBIT 2-5

Summarized Report Form

Claim #

Insured: Date of report:

Policy no: Adjustment firm:

Date of loss: Claim representative:

Producer:

1. <u>Assignment Date</u>

    Give date notice of loss received and how. Give date insured first contacted and how (phone or personal).

2. <u>Enclosures</u>

    List items attached (such as photos, estimates, fire/police reports).

3. <u>Activity Requested</u>

    List special requests (such as expense payments and coverage questions).

4. <u>Suggested Reserves</u>

    Suggested reserves should be shown net, by coverage, after any advances.

    List scheduled items separately, as in the following example:

    Collision $22,000

    Medical Payments $10,000

5. <u>Abstract of Coverage</u>

    Give forms applicable and amounts; identify deductible amount(s); identify other contributing insurance, if any; identify any limiting clauses.

6. <u>Ownership/Encumbrances</u>

    List title holder, mortgagee, loss payees, additional named insureds, and liens. Indicate source of information. Also include opinion as to current solvency, cash flow, receipts.

7. <u>Location and Cause of Loss</u>

    Give date, time, and place of loss. Relay cause as determined by authorities. If an outside expert has been employed, identify and give his or her findings. State claim representative's opinion.

8. <u>Insured/Employee Version of Loss</u>

    Give insured version—indicate if statement was secured. Indicate manager, guards, or service personnel on premises at time of loss.

9. <u>Witness Version of Loss</u>

    Give witness version—indicate if statement(s) secured. Indicate persons present at time of loss.

10. <u>Scope of Loss/Estimates of Damage</u>

    Describe property insured. Detail extent of damage. Cover any problems that may be encountered in reaching a settlement. List estimates received. Indicate whether an agreement regarding scope and procedures has been reached with the insured.

> 11. <u>Salvage/Subrogation</u>
>
>   Identify salvage and give an estimate of worth. Provide and explain theory of subrogation and what steps have been taken to protect the right of subrogation.
>
> 12. <u>Work Done to Date</u>
>
>   Itemize work done to date.
>
> 13. <u>Work to Be Done/Forecast of Closing</u>
>
>   Itemize work to be done. Give forecast of closing date. Estimate hours needed for completion of each activity.
>
> 14. <u>Risk</u>
>
>   Give your overall impression of the insured risk.
>
> 15. <u>Remarks</u>
>
>   Give comments on assistance of insured or employee in completing investigation. Identify attorney or public adjuster if involved.
>
> DATE OF NEXT REPORT

Insurers also document claim activity using external reports containing information collected by claim representatives. External claim reports inform interested parties about the claim and inform the public of the insurer's financial standing. These reports are prepared for producers, some states' advisory organizations, and others having an interest in the claim. Because insurers often write business through producers, losses are reported to the producer who sold the insurance. These reports provide details about the losses, such as the amount paid and the amount in outstanding reserve.

Determining the Cause of Loss and the Loss Amount

Claim representatives use the information gained during their investigation to determine the cause of loss, liability, and the loss amount. The facts of the loss determine the cause of the loss. For example, in a fire loss, the claim representative may find that a toaster caused the fire. The claim representative also determines the liability for the loss based on the facts of the case. For example, in an auto accident, the claim representative applies statutory and case law on negligence to determine liability of the parties invovled.

Concurrent to the determination of the cause of the loss and the liability for the loss, the claim representative may determine the amount of the loss. For a property claim, the claim representative investigates the amount of damage to the property and the cost to repair or replace it and may also investigate the amount of business income lost. To determine a loss amount in a bodily injury claim, the claim representative investigates the extent of the injury, the residual and lasting effects of the injury, and the amount of pain and suffering the individual has endured.

The activities required to investigate and determine the cause of loss, liability, and damages depend on the type of claim. The next chapter provides detailed descriptions of the investigations required to make these determinations in a property damage claim, a bodily injury claim, and a workers' compensation claim.

Having determined the cause of loss, liability, and loss amount, the claim representative can apply the policy coverages to the loss. Claim representatives can use the framework for coverage analysis, discussed earlier in this chapter, to assist them in this application.

Concluding the Claim

Generally, the last activity in the claim handling process is concluding the claim. Once the investigation is completed and all documentation is received, the claim representative must decide whether to pay the claim or deny it. If the claim is to be paid, the claim representative often must negotiate the amount with the insured or the claimant. Negotiation involves discussing disputed matters and mutually agreeing on a settlement. In some cases, alternative dispute resolution methods may be used to resolve a disagreement and, ultimately, the claim.

When an agreement on the settlement amount is reached, the claim representative secures the necessary final documents so that payment can be made. If the claim is denied, the insured or claimant may accept the denial or may choose to file a lawsuit to challenge the denial. Litigation may also be started if no agreement on the claim can be reached.

Payments

When a covered claim is concluded through negotiation or other means, the claim representative or claim personnel must issue a claim payment. Claim payments can be made by check, draft, or electronic transfer of funds.

A check creates a demand for payment on the insurer's bank account and can be presented for payment without further insurer authorization. A draft is similar to a check; however, when the claimant presents the draft to the insurer's bank (often through the claimant's bank transaction), the bank must verify that the insurer has authorized payment before disbursing any funds. Because of this required authorization, a claimant cannot present a draft at a bank for immediate payment. This delay in disbursing funds allows the insurer to confirm that the payment is proper. Funds can also be electronically transferred into an account of the insured's choosing.

When issuing claim payments, claim personnel must ensure that the proper parties are being paid. Many other parties, such as mortgagees on homes and loss payees on autos and personal property, can have a financial interest in the property. Parties named in the policy have rights, described in the policy, to be included as a payee under certain circumstances, such as for property that has been destroyed. For third-party liability claim payments, the claim representative must determine whether an attorney or a lienholder, such as a medical service provider, should be named as an additional payee on the payment. The claim representative is responsible for including all required payees when issuing a claim payment.

Claim representatives must also check various databases to ensure that the claim payment complies with federal and state laws. The Office of Foreign Asset Control, U.S. Department of the Treasury, requires all claim payors (insurers, self-insureds, and third-party administrators [TPAs]) to check the master list of potential terrorists and drug traffickers before making a claim payment. Claim payors may be prohibited from paying a claim to an individual or entity appearing on this list. Many insurers and TPAs have contracted with third parties to provide an automated means of performing this check. Failure to comply with this requirement can result in substantial penalties to the payor.

Insurers and other claim payors must also be aware of state child support enforcement initiatives that can affect claim payments. Many states have statutes that require a claim representative to check a database to determine if a claimant or beneficiary owes unpaid child support. If child support is owed, the claim representative must follow specific procedures when issuing the payment because the unpaid child support has priority. The claim payment goes toward reducing the amount of the child support in arrears rather than to the injured party. For example, Massachusetts law requires that an insurer licensed to do business in Massachusetts check the database before making payment on a claim of $500 or more. Failure to comply can result in financial consequences to the insurer. Many insurers and claim payors have created ways to automate the process.

Claim representatives handling workers' compensation claims and third-party bodily injury claims must be aware of the Medicare Secondary Payer Program and how this program can affect claim payments. The Center for Medicare and Medicaid Services (CMS) must approve a proposed settlement in specific situations. The settlement must be approved for claimants who are Medicare beneficiaries or who have reasonable expectations of Medicare enrollment within thirty months of settlement and when the settlement is $250,000 or more. Failure to gain CMS approval can expose the insurer to a bad-faith suit because Medicare goes directly to the claimant for reimbursement. Insurers are integrating this approval process into their claim practices to ensure compliance.

Claim representatives must ensure that all of these checks have been completed before issuing payment. If they are not, the insurer can be subject to fines, penalties, and possibly additional payments to satisfy these parties.

Claim Denial

A claim may conclude instead with denial. When claim investigations reveal that a policy does not provide coverage for a loss or when an insured fails to meet a policy condition, the claim representative must make a timely claim denial. Insurers often have strict guidelines that claim representatives must follow when denying claims, and some insurers require a claim manager's approval to issue a claim denial.

Before denying a claim, the claim representative must analyze the coverage carefully, investigate the loss thoroughly, and evaluate the claim fairly and objectively. Courts often favor insureds when a claim denial fails to meet these requirements, and the insurer can be assessed penalties in addition to the loss amount.

Once claim management gives authority to deny a claim, the claim representative must prepare a denial letter as soon as possible. Some denial letters are drafted by lawyers to ensure that they comply with the jurisdiction's legal requirements. For example, a denial letter must usually state all the known reasons for the claim denial. Specific policy language should be quoted, and the location of the language in the policy should be cited. The policy provisions should be described in relation to the facts of the loss. Also, an insured who disagrees with the denial should be invited to submit additional information that would give the insurer cause to reevaluate the claim. The denial letter should be signed and sent by the claim representative, even if it is drafted by a lawyer.

Insurers usually send denial letters by certified mail with a return receipt requested to be signed by the addressee. Some insurers also send a copy of the letter by regular mail, marked "personal and confidential," in case the certified mail is not claimed. These procedures help ensure that the denial letter reaches the correct party, and they provide documentation that it was received.

Alternative Dispute Resolution

If an insurer and an insured or a claimant cannot agree on the claim value or claim coverage, they may resolve the disagreement in court. However, court costs and delays in the court system have encouraged insurers, insureds, and claimants to seek alternative ways of resolving their disputes about claims that are less expensive and time consuming than litigation. Such processes also help relieve the courts of the burden of handling such disputes. **Alternative dispute resolution (ADR)** refers to methods for settling disputes outside the traditional court system. The most common ADR techniques are mediation, arbitration, appraisals, mini-trials, summary jury trials, and pretrial settlement conferences.

Mediation is an ADR method by which disputing parties use a neutral outside party to examine the issues and develop a mutually agreeable settlement. The mediator, often a retired judge or an expert in the field under dispute, manages the process. The mediator may be appointed by the court or selected by the parties. Each party presents its case to the mediator, who leads the parties through in-depth settlement discussions. The mediator points out the weaknesses in each argument or in the evidence presented,

Alternative dispute resolution (ADR)
Methods for settling disputes outside the traditional court system.

Mediation
An alternative dispute resolution method by which disputing parties use a neutral outside party to examine the issues and develop a mutually agreeable settlement.

proposes solutions, and helps the participants reach a mutually agreeable settlement. If mediation does not resolve the dispute, the parties may consider another ADR method or litigation.

Arbitration is an ADR method by which the disputing parties use a neutral outside party to examine the issues and develop a settlement, which can be final and binding. The arbitrator acts as a judge, weighing the facts of the case and making a decision based on the evidence presented. The advantage of arbitration is that someone other than the insurer and the claimant decides the case.

The type of arbitration determines whether the decision is binding on the parties. Under binding arbitration, which some states' laws require for arbitrated claim disputes, the parties must accept the arbitrator's decision. Under nonbinding arbitration, neither party is forced to accept the arbitrator's decision. However, the decision provides the "winner" with leverage for future negotiations. This method of alternative dispute resolution is cost-effective for all parties and relieves the courts of the burden of handling such disputes.

When two policies issued by different insurers cover the same loss, arbitration can be used to settle a dispute about which insurer should pay the claim and how much should be paid. Generally, one insurer settles with the insured. The case is then submitted to an arbitration service to determine what each insurer owes. Insurers may use an organization such as Insurance Arbitration Forums, Inc., or the American Arbitration Association. Insurer trade associations also offer arbitration services and other forms of ADR to member companies.

Property insurance policies include a provision that requires a form of ADR before litigation. This provision, called the **appraisal provision**, is used to settle disputes between insurers and their insureds over the amount owed on a covered loss. It is not used to settle coverage disputes, only the amount of damages. Almost all property insurance policies contain an appraisal provision. For example, the HO-3 provides that the insurer or the insured can demand an appraisal if they disagree on the loss amount. Each party chooses an appraiser, and the two appraisers choose a third appraiser to act as an umpire. Each party pays its own appraiser, and the two parties share the cost of the umpire. The appraisers can hear evidence that is typically excluded from trial. The two appraisers estimate the property damage separately. If their estimates match, the insurer pays the insured that amount. If the estimates are different, the umpire offers a binding decision on the loss amount.

Mini-trials are another form of ADR. At a **mini-trial**, an abbreviated version of a trial, representatives (usually lawyers) of the disputing parties present the evidence to a panel or an adviser who poses questions and offers opinions on the outcome of a trial, based on the evidence presented. A mini-trial enables parties to test the validity of their positions and continue negotiations. Parties can terminate the process at any time. The parties agree not to disclose in future litigation anything that occurs during the mini-trial, in order to preserve their rights in litigation if the negotiation fails.

Arbitration
An alternative dispute resolution method by which the disputing parties use a neutral outside party to examine the issues and develop a settlement, which can be final and binding.

Appraisal provision
A policy condition that provides appraisal as a mechanism for resolving disputes between insurers and insureds over the amount owed on a covered loss.

Mini-trial
An alternative dispute resolution method by which a case undergoes an abbreviated version of a trial before a panel or an adviser who poses questions and offers opinions on the outcome of a trial, based on the evidence presented.

The parties select an impartial adviser, often a retired judge, an executive, or an expert, and decide the role of the adviser, whether that of passive participant, arbitrator, or judge. The adviser has no authority to make a binding decision; however, he or she can pose questions that test the validity of each side's case and offer an opinion based on the evidence.

Before the mini-trial, parties can exchange information about their anticipated testimony and the documents that they plan to introduce as evidence. Such information may also be given to the adviser. Witnesses and experts may testify during the mini-trial. Lawyers are allotted a limited time to present their cases. The main advantage of mini-trials is that claimants and insurers can learn the likely outcome of their cases without having to contend with delays in the legal system.

Summary jury trial
An alternative dispute resolution method by which disputing parties participate in an abbreviated trial, presenting the evidence of a few witnesses to a panel of mock jurors who decide the case.

A **summary jury trial** is an ADR method by which disputing parties participate in an abbreviated trial, presenting the evidence of a few witnesses to a panel of mock jurors who decide the case. These trials offer a forum for deciding the merits of cases for court proceedings, and they may assist in negotiations. A summary jury trial is staged much like a regular jury trial, except that only a few witnesses are used to present the case. Mock jurors are pulled from a pool of persons selected to serve as possible jurors in an actual court case. Evidence and witnesses' testimony may be presented in both oral and written format for the mock jurors. Lawyers summarize information for the sake of brevity. The mock jurors decide the case based on the limited, though representative, presentation of evidence.

A summary jury trial can be concluded in a relatively short time, so legal costs are significantly reduced. Fewer witnesses mean less expense for witness fees. Although lawyers are required, the time required to develop the case and prepare for trial is considerably less. Summary jury trials can produce an effective settlement and control legal expenses.

Litigation

Even with the variety of ADR methods available, many cases are concluded through litigation. Litigation can occur at almost any point during the life of a claim. It occurs most often when the parties to the claim are unable to reach an agreement by negotiation or ADR, or when a claim is denied. ADR reduces, but does not eliminate, the chance that a claimant will sue and take a case to trial. Accordingly, insurers must be prepared to litigate some claims.

Many insurance policies require insurers to defend their insureds at trial. The HO-3, for example, states that the insurer must "provide a defense at our expense by counsel of our choice, even if the suit is groundless, false, or fraudulent." The duty to defend generally terminates when the amount the insurer has paid in settlements or judgments on the claim equals the insurer's limit of liability.

When litigation cannot be avoided, claim representatives participate in developing a litigation strategy for the insured's defense and for litigation expense control. Claim representatives must carefully select and direct defense lawyers. The lawyer's role is to be the insured's advocate; he or she must address every aspect of the claimant's case, from liability to damages, in order to mitigate the claim against the insured and to encourage the claimant to settle out of court. Litigation and the claim representative's role in litigation are described in detail in a later chapter.

Closing Reports

When a claim is resolved, the claim representative may complete a closing or final report, which can include the claim representative's recommendations on subrogation, advice to underwriters, and other suggestions. In some instances, these reports are used by subrogation claim representatives to evaluate the likelihood of a successful subrogation action. Claim supervisors and managers may use the reports to audit the claim representative's performance. These reports can also be submitted to reinsurers for reimbursement of loss payment. Claim representatives should be aware of claims that should be referred to reinsurers and must complete reports on those claims based on the insurer's internal guidelines and reinsurance agreements.

APPLYING THE FRAMEWORK FOR COVERAGE ANALYSIS AND THE CLAIM HANDLING PROCESS

Claim representatives can use the framework for coverage analysis and the claim handling process as guides for every claim they handle. The language of the policy and the facts of the claim will fill in the details. The following case study is provided as an example of how this can be done.

> ### Case Study
>
> Susan and Thomas Reed live at 104 Fremont Street, Malvern, Texas. They have two children: Ann, age 16, who resides at home, and John, age 19, who resides at home when not attending Columbus College in New Mexico. Susan's mother, Marie, also lives with them. Susan is a schoolteacher. Thomas is the owner of a small company, Universal Widgets.
>
> Susan and Thomas own their home and three cars. They have a mortgage on their home, held by ABC Loan Company. They also have a car loan, from Union Trust Company, on their 2006 Lexus. Their other two cars, a 2003 Toyota Camry and a 2003 Honda Civic, do not have lienholders.
>
> Susan and Thomas have an HO-3 (2002) policy covering their home. They have a Personal Auto Policy (PAP) covering all three cars.
>
> On April 12, 2006, Susan and Thomas receive a call from John's roommate informing them that John has been in an auto accident while driving the Honda Civic. John suffered minor injuries after running a stop sign and hitting another car. The driver of the other car, Karen Jones, has been hospitalized. After talking to John, Thomas calls his insurance agent and reports the claim. The agent reports the claim to the insurer, and claim representative Jim Smith is assigned to handle all aspects of the claim.

Continued on next page.

Upon receiving the claim assignment, Jim acknowledges receipt of the claim to the agent and sets up the claim in the claim-processing system. He identifies the Reeds' auto policy and performs an initial review, learning that the 2003 Honda Civic has liability coverage, collision coverage with a $1,000 deductible, and Personal Injury Protection coverage. Based on the limited information on the first notice of loss, Jim sets up the following parts of the claim with preliminary reserves:

- Liability claim from Karen Jones—reserve $5,000
- Property damage claim from Karen Jones—reserve $2,500
- Collision coverage for the 2003 Honda—reserve $2,500
- PIP coverage for John's injuries—reserve $1,000

Jim contacts Susan and Thomas Reed. They give him a brief description of the accident, but tell Jim to contact their son John for all of the details. While talking to Susan and Thomas, Jim confirms that they are the registered owners of the car, that the car was registered in Texas, and that John was using the car with their permission.

Jim calls John and takes a recorded statement from him that provides the following facts:

John is enrolled full time in college in New Mexico. He lives in a dormitory on campus. He has had the Honda at school since the beginning of the semester.

The accident occurred at 11:30 a.m. on a Saturday morning. John was on his way to the sandwich shop. He didn't see the stop sign because of the sun's glare. His car struck the car driven by Karen Jones on the driver's side door. John was wearing his seatbelt at the time of the accident. His air bag deployed on impact. He received a ticket for careless driving. He was taken to the emergency room, treated for minor cuts, and released. Karen Jones was also taken to the emergency room. John thinks she had a concussion and a bad cut on her forehead. The Honda is at Sam's Auto Body Shop in Columbus, New Mexico.

After concluding his conversation with John, Jim requests a police report and reviews the PAP to answer some questions he has regarding coverage for this claim.

Jim has already confirmed that the Honda is listed on the Reeds' policy and that it has collision coverage. (*Is the damaged property covered? Is the cause of loss covered?*) He has also confirmed that the accident date falls within the policy period. (*Did the loss occur during the policy period?*)

Jim determines who is covered by the PAP. According to the liability coverage part, "insured" is defined as:

1. You or any "family member" for the ownership, maintenance or use of any auto or "trailer".

According to the definition of insured, John is covered by the policy. (*Is the person involved covered?*) The insuring agreement says the insurer will pay damages for bodily injury or property damage for which any insured becomes legally responsible because of an auto accident. The insuring agreement also says that the policy will pay defense costs in addition to the limit of liability. (*Is the type of loss covered?*)

Part A exclusions are then checked. None of the exclusions appear to apply. (*Do any exclusions apply?*)

The PAP provides out-of-state coverage, which means that the policy will comply with New Mexico financial responsibility laws.

Next, Jim examines the policy period and territory provision of the PAP. The loss occurred during the policy period and within the policy territory of the U.S. (*Is the location where the loss occurred covered?*)

Based on the information obtained from Mr. Reed and John Reed, no other auto policies are applicable to this accident, as all of the Reeds' cars are insured on this policy. (*Does other insurance apply?*) Based on the limited medical information available at this time on Karen Jones, Jim believes that the liability limit on the Reeds' policy is sufficient to cover the bodily injury and property damage sustained by Karen Jones. (*Are the amounts of loss or damages covered?*) However, Jim will have to review this portion of the claim frequently as more information about Ms. Jones and her injuries becomes available. Jim will also have to continue his investigation in order to determine who is liable for the accident.

As part of his analysis of liability coverage, Jim has answered some of the questions to be asked when analyzing coverage for the damage to the Reeds' Honda, such as the date of loss occurring during the policy period, the loss location being covered by the policy, and no other auto policies applying to this loss.

Upon reviewing Part D—Coverage for Damage to Your Auto of the PAP, Jim confirms that the Reeds' Honda has collision coverage. Jim reviews the exclusions to Part D coverage and determines that none of the exclusions apply, based on the facts currently known. Jim assigns an appraiser to assess the amount of damage to the Reeds' Honda and to prepare an estimate to repair the damage. Based on the description of the accident that John gave in his statement, Jim decides that the $2,500 reserve is adequate. He will review the reserve when he receives the appraiser's estimate.

Jim reviews the Personal Injury Protection (PIP) endorsement attached to the Reeds' auto policy. This endorsement provides unlimited medical expenses coverage to covered persons. Jim confirms that the definition of insured applies to a family member. The insuring agreement states that PIP benefits will be paid to an insured who sustains bodily injury caused by an accident and resulting from the use of an auto. The medical expenses must be reasonable and necessary. John had indicated that he suffered a laceration above his eye, which was treated at the emergency room. He had also begun seeing a chiropractor to treat his sore neck and back. John will give his medical bills to Jim for review and reimbursement. Jim also reviews the exclusions in the endorsement and determines that none of them apply. Jim decides to raise the medical reserve to $2,500 to cover the emergency room bill and three months of chiropractic treatment.

SUMMARY

This chapter introduces the primary functions of a claim representative: analyzing insurance policies for coverage and handling claims using the claim handling process.

Claim representatives must be familiar with all the components of an insurance policy because they can each affect the coverage determination. These components include declarations, definitions, insuring agreements, exclusions, conditions, miscellaneous provisions, and endorsements. Claim representatives use a framework for coverage analysis that involves every policy component, ensuring that all parts of the policy will be considered when making a coverage determination. Using the framework, the claim representative answers the following questions:

- Is the person involved covered?
- Did the loss occur during the policy period?
- Is the cause of loss covered?
- Is the damaged property covered?
- Is the type of loss covered?
- Are the amounts of loss or damages covered?
- Is the location where the loss occurred covered?
- Do any exclusions apply?
- Does other insurance apply?

Claim representatives must also be able to apply the information contained in the policy to the activities in the claim handling process. These activities are performed on every claim, to some degree. Upon receiving a claim, the insurer acknowledges it and assigns it to a claim representative. The claim representative identifies coverage; contacts the insured or the insured's representative; investigates and documents the claim; determines the cause of loss, liability, and the loss amount; and concludes the claim.

The claim representative must perform all these activities with utmost good faith. By using good-faith claim handling practices, claim representatives can avoid situations in which they may waive defenses or be estopped from asserting defenses.

Claim representatives spend much of their time investigating and documenting claims. They often take statements from insureds, claimants, and witnesses. They can do scene investigations themselves or hire independent adjusters to complete them. They use the results of their investigation to determine the cause of loss, liability, and loss amount. With this information, the claim can be concluded.

Claim representatives use file review systems and submit status notes and reports to document the claim file. The timely review of the claim and the reserve noted in the file status notes is one means of showing good faith. Internal and external reports communicate the details of the loss and the loss adjustment process to those who need the information.

Many disputed claims are concluded by negotiation. Those that are not may be resolved by alternative dispute resolution (ADR) methods such as mediation, arbitration, appraisal, mini-trial or summary jury trial. In cases in which all else has failed, litigation is used to resolve the claim.

Because a claim representative's determination of cause of loss, liability, and loss amount can differ by the type of claim, these topics are discussed in greater detail in the next chapter.

CHAPTER NOTES

1. Includes copyrighted material of Insurance Services Offices, Inc., with its permission. Copyright, ISO Properties, Inc., 1999.
2. Includes copyrighted material of Insurance Services Offices, Inc., with its permission. Copyright, ISO Properties, Inc., 1999.
3. Includes copyrighted material of Insurance Services Offices, Inc., with its permission. Copyright, ISO Properties, Inc., 1999.
4. Includes copyrighted material of Insurance Services Offices, Inc., with its permission. Copyright, ISO Properties, Inc., 1999.
5. Includes copyrighted material of Insurance Services Offices, Inc., with its permission. Copyright, ISO Properties, Inc., 1999.
6. Includes copyrighted material of Insurance Services Offices, Inc., with its permission. Copyright, ISO Properties, Inc., 1997.
7. Includes copyrighted material of Insurance Services Offices, Inc., with its permission. Copyright, ISO Properties, Inc., 1999.
8. Includes copyrighted material of Insurance Services Offices, Inc., with its permission. Copyright, ISO Properties, Inc., 1997.
9. Includes copyrighted material of Insurance Services Offices, Inc., with its permission. Copyright, ISO Properties, Inc., 1999.
10. Includes copyrighted material of Insurance Services Offices, Inc., with its permission. Copyright, ISO Properties, Inc., 1999.
11. Includes copyrighted material of Insurance Services Offices, Inc., with its permission. Copyright, ISO Properties, Inc., 1997.
12. Includes copyrighted material of Insurance Services Offices, Inc., with its permission. Copyright, ISO Properties, Inc., 1999.
13. Includes copyrighted material of Insurance Services Offices, Inc., with its permission. Copyright, ISO Properties, Inc., 1997.
14. Includes copyrighted material of Insurance Services Offices, Inc., with its permission. Copyright, ISO Properties, Inc., 1997.

Chapter 3

Direct Your Learning

Investigation of Cause of Loss, Liability, and Damages

After learning the content of this chapter and completing the corresponding course guide assignment, you should be able to:

- Describe the three bases for legal liability.
- Explain why and how each of the following general investigative tools is used in claim handling:
  - Loss notice forms
  - Policy information
  - Statements
  - Diagrams, photos, and videos
  - Experts
  - Records and reports
  - Industry databases
  - Internet
  - Other investigative tools
- Explain how a claim representative investigates cause of loss, liability, and amount of damage in an auto physical damage claim.
- Explain how a claim representative investigates cause of loss, liability, and amount of damage in a property damage claim other than auto.
- Explain how a claim representative investigates cause of loss, liability, and amount of damages in a bodily injury liability claim.
- Explain how a claim representative investigates compensability, liability, and benefits in a workers' compensation claim.
- Define or describe each of the Key Words and Phrases for this chapter.

OUTLINE

Bases for Legal Liability

General Investigative Tools

Property Damage Claim Investigation

Bodily Injury Claim Investigation

Workers' Compensation Claim Investigation

Summary

Appendix

Develop Your Perspective

What are the main topics covered in the chapter?

To properly handle claims, claim representatives must understand the concept of legal liability and how legal liability may arise. This knowledge helps the claim representative plan and direct the claim investigation. Using general investigative tools that apply to every type of claim, the claim representative compiles the information needed to make a determination of cause of loss, liability, and amount of damage on a claim.

Identify the general investigative tools used in your office.

- Which tools help determine the cause of loss or liability?
- Which tools help determine the amount of damage on a claim?

Why is it important to learn about these topics?

Claim representatives spend a substantial portion of their time investigating to determine the cause of loss, the liability, and the amount of damage. That information, along with an understanding of the concept of legal liability, is essential to making a good-faith resolution of the claim.

How would you go about investigating a claim?

- Would you take statements and if so, from whom?
- What experts would you use to help you determine the cause of loss, liability, and amount of damage?

How can you use what you will learn?

Analyze a closed claim handled by someone else.

- Do you agree with the liability assessment? Why or why not?
- What, if anything, would you have done differently if you handled this claim?

Chapter 3
Investigation of Cause of Loss, Liability, and Damages

To handle a claim with good faith, a claim representative must investigate and determine the cause of the loss, the liability for the loss, and the amount of damages that result from the loss. The claim representative must have a thorough understanding of the concept of legal liability to decide what general investigative tools to use and what aspects of the claim to investigate.

Claim representatives use the same general investigative tools regardless of whether the claim is for property damage, bodily injury, or workers' compensation benefits. Each type of claim investigation can call for any or all of these tools, and each tool may provide different information about causes of loss, liability, and damages. In addition to explaining legal liability concepts and describing investigative tools, this chapter describes the investigation of a property claim, a liability claim, and a workers' compensation claim.

BASES FOR LEGAL LIABILITY

For first-party losses, claim representatives determine cause of loss, amount of damage, policy coverage for the loss, and amount payable under the policy. A third party may be responsible for some first-party losses. If this is the case, the claim representative must be able to apply legal liability concepts to subrogate against the responsible third party. For third-party liability claims, claim representatives focus on determining the liability, or establishing legal fault, among all parties involved, along with determining damages. The claim representative who handles workers' compensation must also apply legal liability principles for subrogation purposes.

Legal liability is different from criminal liability or criminal responsibility. Criminal liability or responsibility arises from laws that apply to wrongful acts that society deems so harmful to the public welfare that the government takes responsibility for prosecuting and punishing the wrongdoers. Criminal laws are always statutory. In contrast, civil law is based on the rights and responsibilities of citizens with respect to one another; it applies to legal matters not governed by criminal laws. Civil laws include common law, or case law, and administrative laws and regulations, as well as some statutory laws. Civil law governs liability for civil wrongs against people, entities, or property (torts), which include negligent acts, intentional acts, and strict

3.4 Claim Handling Principles and Practices

liability. It also governs liability for breach of contract. Contract law, a branch of civil law, deals with the creation and enforcement of contracts and settlement of contract disputes.

Legal liability
A person's or an organization's status as legally responsible for injury or damage suffered by another person or organization.

The term **legal liability** refers to a person's or an organization's status as legally responsible for injury or damage suffered by another person or organization. Although complex legal questions regarding liability require the professional expertise of an attorney, knowledge of some fundamental legal terms and concepts is essential for anyone dealing with liability loss exposures or liability insurance.

The legal system in the United States derives essentially from the following:

- The Constitution, which is the source of constitutional law
- Legislative bodies, which are the source of statutory law
- Court decisions, which are the source of common law

The supreme law in the U.S. is the Constitution, which specifies the structure of the federal government and outlines the respective powers of its legislative, executive, and judicial branches. The Constitution provides for a federal system of government in which powers not specifically granted to the federal government are reserved for the individual states. With its amendments, the Constitution also guarantees to all citizens certain fundamental rights, such as freedom of speech, freedom of religion, freedom from unreasonable searches and seizures, the right to a trial by jury, and the right to due process of law.

Constitutional law
The Constitution itself and all the decisions of the Supreme Court that involve the Constitution.

All other laws must conform to **constitutional law**, which is the Constitution itself and all the decisions of the Supreme Court that involve the Constitution. The courts interpret the Constitution when applying it to cases that raise constitutional issues. If the U.S. Supreme Court decides that a particular law conflicts with the Constitution, that law is invalidated. The Supreme Court is the highest court of appeal, and lower courts must follow the Supreme Court's decision in judging future cases involving the same issue.

Each state also has a constitution establishing the powers of the state government, as well as a supreme court to resolve legal conflicts and to hear appeals on matters of state law. However, states must ultimately follow the U.S. Constitution.

Statutory law
The formal laws, or statutes, enacted by federal, state, or local legislative bodies.

National, state, and local legislatures enact laws, or statutes, to deal with perceived problems. At the national level, Congress considers many newly proposed laws each year. Any member of the U.S. Senate or House of Representatives may introduce a bill, which may be referred to a committee for study or hearings before it is debated on the Senate or House floor. If the bill receives a majority vote in both the Senate and the House and the president signs it, the bill becomes law. State legislatures follow a similar procedure to make new laws. Laws made by local governments are often called ordinances. Collectively, these formal enactments of federal, state, or local legislative bodies are referred to as **statutory law**.

Numerous federal, state, and local government agencies derive their regulatory powers from authority granted by legislative bodies. Examples of such agencies include the Federal Trade Commission, the Environmental Protection Agency, state public utility commissions, and local zoning boards. These regulatory bodies issue detailed rules and regulations covering a particular public concern or relating to a particular industry. They also render decisions on the application of these rules and regulations in certain cases.

In contrast to statutory law, common law has evolved in the courts. **Common law**, or **case law**, is a body of principles and rules established over time by courts on a case-by-case basis. When the king's judges began hearing disputes in medieval England, they had little basis for their decisions except common sense and the prevailing notions of justice. Each decision, however, became a precedent for similar cases in the future. Gradually, certain principles evolved as the judges applied them consistently to all the cases they heard. These principles became known as the common law, or case law.

Common law, or case law
A body of principles and rules established over time by courts on a case-by-case basis.

These common-law principles guided judges not only in England but also in the English colonies in America. Thus, the English common law heavily influenced the U.S. legal system. When neither constitutional nor statutory law applies, judges still rely on precedents of previous cases in reaching their decisions. In many areas, laws have been passed that modify or replace common-law principles, but common law is still important in matters of legal liability.

The two major categories of U.S. law are not mutually exclusive. A particular act can often have both criminal and civil law consequences. Consider, for example, the following two incidents in the life of Susan Jones.

Because she is an entrepreneur who travels frequently, Susan usually has large amounts of cash in her purse. Once when she was walking down the street, a stranger grabbed her purse and ran off. When the police found the stranger, he still had some of the contents of Susan's purse, but the purse and the money were gone. The stranger was arrested, tried, and convicted of the crime of robbery. Susan might also have started civil law proceedings against the robber to recover her money, but that would have accomplished little because the robber had no money and was going to jail.

Another time Susan was returning from a business trip when her car was broadsided by another vehicle. Susan was injured and required medical care costing thousands of dollars; she missed two weeks of work, causing her to lose existing customers and to miss opportunities to secure new customers. Following the accident investigation, the other driver was charged and convicted of driving while intoxicated, a criminal offense. Susan's auto insurer paid most of her medical and auto physical damage bills. However, Susan did bring a civil suit against the other driver for her lost business opportunities, and the court ordered the other driver to pay an amount equal to the income Susan had lost.

In each incident, both criminal and civil law proceedings were possible results. The differing circumstances influenced the practical effectiveness of each type of legal action. Exhibit 3-1 illustrates the legal basis of a liability claim.

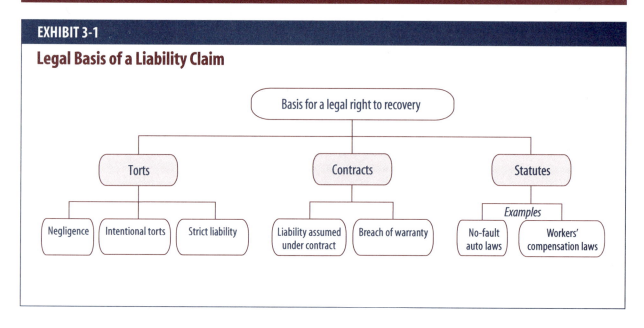

Liability Based on Tort

Tort
A wrongful act or omission, other than a crime or breach of contract, committed by one party against another, that causes harm and may lead to a civil lawsuit for damages.

A **tort** is a wrongful act or omission, other than a crime or a breach of contract, committed by one party against another, that causes harm and may lead to a civil lawsuit for damages. A person or an organization that commits a tort is called a **tortfeasor**. Tort law generally applies to civil actions for which damages may be awarded to the harmed person. The three types of torts are negligence, strict liability, and intentional acts.

Negligence

Tortfeasor
A person or an organization that commits a tort for which a civil remedy may be sought.

Negligence
The failure to exercise the degree of care that a reasonable person in a similar situation would exercise to avoid harming others.

Negligence is the most common type of tort that claim representatives encounter. **Negligence**, an unintentional tort, is the failure to exercise the degree of care that a reasonable person in a similar situation would exercise to avoid harming others. One individual may invade a legally protected right of another by committing an unintentional act through carelessness, neglect, or indifference. A person who fails to exercise reasonable care is held responsible by law for any injury, loss, or damage that results from that failure. For example, Josh is daydreaming while driving and runs a stop sign, hitting Emily's car. Josh does not intentionally hit Emily's car, but he is careless, and therefore negligent. Josh is responsible for the damage to Emily's car and for any bodily injury Emily suffers in the accident.

Liability based on negligence must establish each of the following four elements:

1. *One party's legal duty to use due care, owed to another party.* If there is no legal duty to use due care there is no negligence. For example, if a car thief is injured because the brakes fail on the car he stole, the car owner is not considered negligent and is not liable for the injury.

2. *A breach of the duty of care*, that is, a failure to conform to the standard of care required in the situation, creating an unreasonable risk of harm. To determine the degree of care that should be exercised, courts apply

a reasonable person standard: what a reasonable person, under similar circumstances, would do. For example, a motorist who runs a stop sign is not behaving reasonably. The motorist is negligent and can be held liable for any damages incurred if an accident results.

3. *Proximate cause*, that is, a causal connection between the negligent act and the harm or injury. The injury or damage must be a direct result of the failure to meet the duty owed. For example, Bill has a duty to keep his sidewalk clear of snow. He breaches that duty by not clearing the snow. While walking on Bill's sidewalk, Susan slips, falls, and breaks her arm. Bill's failure to clear the sidewalk is the proximate cause of Susan's injuries.

4. *Actual injury or damage*. If there is no injury or damage, then no liability for negligence exists. For example, while driving in stop and go traffic, Peter's car hits the back of Bob's car. When Bob looks at his bumper he does not see any damage; even though Peter caused the accident, no damage to Bob's car resulted from it.

APPLY YOUR LEARNING

Adjusting Tip

An easy way to remember the elements of negligence is:

- Duty owed
- Duty breached
- Proximate cause
- Damages

In some claims, not all the elements of negligence are present. All four elements of negligence must be present for a liability claim to be viable based on negligence.

Legal principles that affect liability based on negligence include vicarious liability, contributory negligence, and comparative negligence. **Vicarious liability** is the legal responsibility that arises when one party is held liable for another party's actions. The liability transfers to this party because of some relationship between that party and the party who is actually responsible. The most common vicarious relationship is that between an employer and an employee. Employers are held vicariously liable for the acts of their employees. For example, Sheila is a hairdresser at Sally's Salon. Sheila colors Jane's hair and it turns green. Sally's Salon would be liable for Sheila's negligence in turning Jane's hair green.

Vicarious liability
The legal responsibility that arises when one party is held liable for another party's actions.

The concepts of contributory negligence and comparative negligence may apply if a harmed party is partly responsible for the loss. These concepts are used as defenses in negligence cases; the person being sued can raise them to eliminate or reduce the damages that may be imposed or even to have the case dismissed. In a state that follows **contributory negligence** principles, a person who has been harmed cannot recover damages if his or her negligence contributed in

Contributory negligence
A common-law principle that prevents a person who has been harmed from recovering damages if that person's own negligence contributed in any way to the harm.

Comparative negligence
A common-law principle that requires both parties to a loss to share the financial burden of the bodily injury or property damage according to their respective degrees of fault.

any way to the harm. Even if the harmed party is only one percent at fault for an accident and the other party is ninety-nine percent at fault, the harmed party cannot collect anything from the other party. Most states have deemed this all-or-nothing approach unfair and have modified the concept of contributory negligence into one of comparative negligence.

In a state that follows **comparative negligence** principles, both parties to a loss share the financial burden of the bodily injury or property damage according to their respective degrees of fault. A harmed party who is partially at fault can recover from another negligent party but only to the degree to which the other party contributed to the loss. If the harmed party is one percent at fault for the accident and the other party is ninety-nine percent at fault, the harmed party can collect ninety-nine percent of his or her damages from the other party. Comparative negligence laws vary by state. Some states require the harmed party to be less than 50 percent at fault to recover. In other states, the harmed party can be 50 percent or more at fault and still recover the remaining percent of damages.

Strict Liability

Strict liability
Liability that arises from inherently dangerous activities resulting in harm to another regardless of the degree of care taken.

Claim representatives should also be familiar with strict liability torts. **Strict liability**, or liability without fault, arises from inherently dangerous activities resulting in harm to another, regardless of the degree of care taken. For example, because explosives are inherently dangerous, blasting operations create liability for bodily injury or property damage, even if the explosives are handled carefully. Another activity that may result in strict liability keeping dangerous animals. Allegations of strict liability also occur in many products liability claims. A harmed party can allege that a product was dangerous when the manufacturer, distributor, or retailer sold it. If the allegation is true, the court may impose strict liability against the manufacturer, distributor, or retailer for any resulting harm.

Workers' compensation laws create another type of liability without fault, similar to strict liability. An employer is liable for employee injuries sustained in the course of employment regardless of whether the employer's negligence caused the injuries.

Intentional Torts

Intentional tort
A tort committed with intent to cause harm or with intent to do the act that causes harm.

Another type of tort that claim representatives encounter is intentional torts. An **intentional tort** is a tort committed with intent to cause harm or with intent to do the act that causes harm. The tortfeasor may or may not have intended the consequences that resulted from the act. Examples of intentional torts include assault, battery, libel, slander, invasion of privacy, and trespass. Generally, insurance does not cover acts performed with the intent to cause harm because such a policy could encourage people to cause intentional harm with the expectation that insurance would cover it. However, claims alleging intentional injury may also include allegations of negligence, so the claim representative must conduct a good-faith investigation to determine if an act was intentional or negligent before making a coverage determination.

Liability Based on Contract

The other basis for legal liability under civil law is contractual liability. **Contractual liability** is liability imposed on a party by the terms of a contract. It arises when someone's rights under a contract's terms are violated. Contractual liability may be based on a written contract or an implied contract. Parties may be legally liable because of their failure to perform as agreed in the contract. For example, if a contractor is hired to construct a building and fails to build it or builds it improperly, the contractor is liable to the owner for damages associated with the failure to build the building. Even though the contractor is liable, insurance generally does not cover the damages from this breach of contract. However, insurance may apply to claims involving two types of contractual obligations: assumptions of liability stated in the contract and warranties stated in the contract.

Contractual liability
Liability imposed on a party by the terms of a contract.

Liability assumed by contract arises when, as a condition of a contract, a party agrees to assume financial responsibility for liabilities imposed by law on another party. The responsibilities assumed vary by contract and range from assuming all liability to assuming liability only for the negligence of one's own employees. For example, a landowner may hire a contractor to do specified work on a property. The owner may insist that the contractor assume all liability for the work. The contractor may agree to those terms and assume any liability imposed on the owner, whether the loss is caused by negligence of the contractor's employees, the owner's employees, or the owner.

Claim representatives often handle products liability claims that involve warranties. A warranty is a contractual promise that accompanies the sale of a product. Express warranties are promises made orally or in writing by the manufacturer or retailer. For example, a manufacturer of infant pajamas may guarantee that the fabric will not burn. An implied warranty is not specifically expressed, but a purchaser could reasonably infer that the warranty exists. For example, a parent who purchases baby food can reasonably expect that an infant will not become ill from eating the food.

Whether legal liability is based on tort or contract, understanding the concept allows the claim representative to conduct a thorough, good-faith investigation of a claim. Knowing the legal bases for a claim will help the claim representative determine the following:

- If the claim being presented is valid
- What investigation should be conducted
- Who is ultimately responsible for the claim

Liability Based on Statute

Statutory liability is legal liability imposed by a specific statute or law. Although common law may cover a particular situation, statutory law may extend, restrict, or clarify the rights of injured parties in that situation or similar ones. One reason for such legislation is to ensure adequate compensation

Statutory liability
Legal liability imposed by a specific statute or law.

for injuries without lengthy disputes over who is at fault. Examples of this kind of statutory liability involve no-fault auto laws and workers' compensation laws. In these legal areas, a specific statute (rather than the common-law principles of torts) gives one party the right of recovery from another or restricts that right of recovery.

In an effort to reduce the number of lawsuits resulting from auto accidents, some states have enacted "no-fault" laws. These laws recognize the inevitability of auto accidents and restrict or eliminate the right to sue the other party in an accident, except in the more serious cases defined by the law. Victims with less serious injuries collect their out-of-pocket expenses from their own insurers without the need for expensive legal proceedings.

A similar concept of liability without regard to fault applies to workplace injuries. Each of the fifty states has a workers' compensation statute that eliminates an employee's right to sue the employer for most work-related injuries and also imposes on the employer automatic (strict) liability to pay specified benefits. In place of the right to sue for negligence, workers' compensation laws create a system in which injured employees receive benefits specified in these laws. As long as the injury is work-related, the employer pays the specified benefits regardless of who is at fault.

GENERAL INVESTIGATIVE TOOLS

Claim representatives conduct investigations to determine who is insured by the policy, who suffered the loss, and who is responsible for causing the loss. They also investigate to determine what was damaged, when and where the loss occurred, how the loss occurred, and how much the loss is worth. The claim representative uses the same general investigative tools, regardless of the type of claim. Each of these tools helps the claim representative answer questions about the loss and determine the cause of loss, liability, and amount of damages. No matter what type of investigation claim representatives are conducting or what tools they are using, they should always be alert for indicators of fraud and investigate them.

Basic Investigative Tools

The general investigative tools available for the claim representative are as follows:

- Loss notice forms
- Policy information
- Statements
- Diagrams, photos, and videos
- Industry databases
- Experts
- Records and reports
- Internet
- Electronic tools

Loss Notice Forms

Generally, losses are reported to insurers on loss notice forms, which are the starting point of any claim investigation. ACORD Corporation produces standardized loss notice forms, in both print and electronic versions, that are used by many insurers. ACORD forms are available for each type of insurance: automobile, property, general liability, and workers' compensation. The claim representative uses information from the loss notice form to determine how to proceed with the investigation.

> **ACORD**
>
> ACORD (Association for Cooperative Operations Research and Development) is a global, not-for-profit insurance association that assists in the development and use of standards for insurance, reinsurance, and related financial services. ACORD serves as an independent advocate for sharing information. ACORD standards and services improve efficiency and expand market reach for insurers, reinsurers, producers, and other financial service providers.[1] Many insurance organizations use standardized forms proved by ACORD.

However, not every loss is reported on a loss notice form. An insurer may receive loss reports in letters, e-mail messages, or legal papers initiating a lawsuit. These methods of reporting a loss may not include all of the information that an ACORD loss notice contains. Consequently, the claim representative may have to make inquiries to obtain all the information necessary to begin the investigation.

Automobile Loss Notice Form

The ACORD Automobile Loss Notice (see Exhibit 3-2) is used to report both property damage and bodily injury claims involving motor vehicles. The form is divided into eight sections:

1. Agency
2. Insured
3. Loss
4. Policy Information
5. Insured Vehicle
6. Property Damaged
7. Persons Injured
8. Witnesses or Passengers

EXHIBIT 3-2

ACORD Automobile Loss Notice

ACORD®

AUTOMOBILE LOSS NOTICE

DATE (MM/DD/YYYY)

AGENCY | PHONE (A/C, No, Ext):
COMPANY | NAIC CODE:
MISCELLANEOUS INFO (Site & location code)
POLICY NUMBER | POLICY TYPE
REFERENCE NUMBER | CAT #
FAX (A/C, No):
E-MAIL ADDRESS:
CODE: | SUB CODE:
AGENCY CUSTOMER ID:
EFFECTIVE DATE | EXPIRATION DATE | DATE OF ACCIDENT AND TIME | AM | PM
PREVIOUSLY REPORTED | YES | NO

INSURED

NAME AND ADDRESS | SOC SEC # OR FEIN:
E-MAIL ADDRESS:
RESIDENCE PHONE (A/C, No): | BUSINESS PHONE (A/C, No, Ext):

CONTACT

CONTACT INSURED
NAME AND ADDRESS | WHEN TO CONTACT:
WHERE TO CONTACT
E-MAIL ADDRESS:
RESIDENCE PHONE (A/C, No): | BUSINESS PHONE (A/C, No, Ext):

LOSS

LOCATION OF ACCIDENT (Include city & state)
AUTHORITY CONTACTED:
REPORT #:
VIOLATIONS/CITATIONS
DESCRIPTION OF ACCIDENT (Use separate sheet, if necessary)

POLICY INFORMATION

BODILY INJURY (Per Person) | BODILY INJURY (Per Accident) | PROPERTY DAMAGE | SINGLE LIMIT | MEDICAL PAYMENT | OTC DEDUCTIBLE | OTHER COVERAGE & DEDUCTIBLES (UM, no-fault, towing, etc)
LOSS PAYEE
COLLISION DED
UMBRELLA/EXCESS | UMBRELLA | EXCESS | CARRIER: | LIMITS: | AGGR | PER CLAIM/OCC | SIR/DED

INSURED VEHICLE

VEH # | YEAR | MAKE: | BODY TYPE: | PLATE NUMBER | STATE
MODEL: | V.I.N.:
OWNER'S NAME & ADDRESS
RESIDENCE PHONE (A/C, No):
BUSINESS PHONE (A/C, No, Ext):
DRIVER'S NAME & ADDRESS (Check if same as owner)
RESIDENCE PHONE (A/C, No):
BUSINESS PHONE (A/C, No, Ext):
RELATION TO INSURED (Employee, family, etc.) | DATE OF BIRTH | DRIVER'S LICENSE NUMBER | STATE | PURPOSE OF USE | USED WITH PERMISSION? | YES | NO
DESCRIBE DAMAGE | ESTIMATE AMOUNT | WHERE CAN VEHICLE BE SEEN? | WHEN CAN VEH BE SEEN? | OTHER INSURANCE ON VEHICLE

PROPERTY DAMAGED VEHICLE? YES NO

DESCRIBE PROPERTY (If auto, year, make, model, plate #)
OTHER VEH/PROP INS? | YES | NO
COMPANY OR AGENCY NAME:
POLICY #:
OWNER'S NAME & ADDRESS
RESIDENCE PHONE (A/C, No):
BUSINESS PHONE (A/C, No, Ext):
OTHER DRIVER'S NAME & ADDRESS (Check if same as owner)
RESIDENCE PHONE (A/C, No):
BUSINESS PHONE (A/C, No, Ext):
DESCRIBE DAMAGE | ESTIMATE AMOUNT | WHERE CAN DAMAGE BE SEEN?

INJURED

NAME & ADDRESS	PHONE (A/C, No)	PED	INS VEH	OTH VEH	AGE	EXTENT OF INJURY

WITNESSES OR PASSENGERS

NAME & ADDRESS	PHONE (A/C, No)	INS VEH	OTH VEH	OTHER (Specify)

REMARKS (Include adjuster assigned)

REPORTED BY | REPORTED TO | SIGNATURE OF INSURED | SIGNATURE OF PRODUCER

ACORD 2 (2005/06) NOTE: IMPORTANT STATE INFORMATION ON REVERSE SIDE

The following is a detailed description of each section:

- Agency—name and address of the producer, the producer's phone number, and the agency code. This section also specifies the insurer's name, the policy number, the policy's effective dates, the date and time of the loss, and the date the notice was prepared. The claim representative should carefully review this information for every claim to detect errors before the investigation continues. The claim representative should also verify that the policy number is correct and confirm that the accident date falls within the policy dates. For example, a producer may send a loss notice to the wrong insurer or enter the current policy number on the ACORD form when in fact it is the insured's policy for the prior year that covers the loss.
- Insured—insured's name, address, and contact information.
- Loss—loss location, initial description of how the loss occurred, the name of the police department that responded to the accident, and the police report number. Claim representatives should use this description of the accident as a starting point of their investigation but should not consider it the definitive description. An insured's description of an accident given to the police may understate the extent of the insured's responsibility for the accident. For example, the accident description may read, "A pedestrian walked into my car," when it was really the car that hit the pedestrian.
- Policy Information—policy limits for the various coverages provided by the auto policy as well as the applicable deductibles. This section can also indicate whether another party, such as a lender, has a financial interest in the vehicle. The claim representative uses this information when making the claim payment. The section also lists other insurance that may apply to the loss. Such information can change the way a claim is handled.
- Insured Vehicle—the vehicle involved in the accident, the owner's name and contact information, the driver's name and contact information, the damage to the vehicle, and where the vehicle is located for inspection. The claim representative uses this information to verify that the vehicle described in the loss notice is insured under the policy. If the driver is not the vehicle's owner, the claim representative should investigate the relationship between the owner and the driver and whether the vehicle was used with permission. The claim representative also uses this information to arrange for an inspection of the damaged vehicle.
- Property Damaged—description of any property, other than the insured vehicle, that was damaged in the accident. This property can be another vehicle, an object, or a building. This section includes contact information for the property owner, a description of the damage, and where the damaged property is located. The claim representative uses this information to ascertain whether to assign someone to inspect the damaged property and to prepare an estimate.

- Persons Injured–name and contact information of anyone injured in the accident and whether each injured person was a pedestrian, was in the insured vehicle, or was in another involved vehicle. Space is provided for a brief description of the injury.
- Witnesses or Passengers—name and contact information of any witnesses to the accident or passengers involved in the accident who are not already accounted for on the form.

At the bottom of the form, the claim representative finds the name of the person who reported the loss to the producer and the name of the person who completed the report. Not all loss forms are thoroughly completed. Missing information must be obtained through investigation or additional contact with the preparer of the form.

Property Loss Notice Form

The ACORD Property Loss Notice form (Exhibit 3-3), used to report first-party damage to buildings and other types of property (other than autos), contains some of the same information as the Automobile Loss Notice form. However, because of the different types of losses associated with commercial and personal property, it contains more information on the damaged property than the Automobile Loss Notice form.

In the Agency section, the claim representative finds the producer's name and contact information, the insurer's name, the policy number, the policy's effective dates, and the date and time of loss. The section contains space for home, flood, and wind policy information. The claim representative should review this information to verify that the claim has been submitted to the correct insurer and that the policy effective dates cover the date of loss.

The Insured section provides the insured's name, address, and contact information. For a business loss, the name, address, and contact information of the insured's business is included.

The Loss section includes basic loss information, including the location of the loss and a brief description of how the loss occurred and of the resulting damage. Commercial policies often have many locations listed, and coverage can vary by location. The claim representative must verify that the loss location reported is covered by the policy and what coverage applies to that location. If the loss location does not appear on the policy, the claim representative should ask the producer and the underwriter whether the insured intended to include the location on the policy and omitted it inadvertently or whether the location was intentionally excluded from the policy. If it is a newly acquired property, the claim representative must review the policy to determine the length of time designated for the insured to report newly acquired property to the insurer. The insurer may be in the process of issuing an endorsement to add the location to the policy.

EXHIBIT 3-3
Property Loss Notice

ACORD® PROPERTY LOSS NOTICE

AGENCY	PHONE (A/C, No, Ext):		MISCELLANEOUS INFO (Site & location code)	DATE OF LOSS AND TIME	AM / PM	PREVIOUSLY REPORTED YES / NO

DATE (MM/DD/YYYY)

POLICY TYPE	COMPANY AND POLICY NUMBER	NAIC CODE	POLICY DATES
PROP/HOME	CO: / POL:		EFF: / EXP:
FLOOD	CO: / POL:		EFF: / EXP:
WIND	CO: / POL:		EFF: / EXP:

FAX (A/C, No):
E-MAIL ADDRESS:
CODE: SUB CODE:
AGENCY CUSTOMER ID:

INSURED
NAME AND ADDRESS OF INSURED
DATE OF BIRTH
SOC SEC # OR FEIN:
RESIDENCE PHONE (A/C, No)   BUSINESS PHONE (A/C, No, Ext)
E-MAIL ADDRESS:
NAME AND ADDRESS OF SPOUSE (IF APPLICABLE)
DATE OF BIRTH
SOC SEC # OR FEIN:

CONTACT   CONTACT INSURED
NAME AND ADDRESS
E-MAIL ADDRESS:
RESIDENCE PHONE (A/C, No)   BUSINESS PHONE (A/C, No, Ext)
WHERE TO CONTACT   WHEN TO CONTACT

LOSS
LOCATION OF LOSS
POLICE OR FIRE DEPT TO WHICH REPORTED

KIND OF LOSS: FIRE / LIGHTNING / FLOOD / OTHER (explain) / THEFT / HAIL / WIND
PROBABLE AMOUNT ENTIRE LOSS
DESCRIPTION OF LOSS & DAMAGE (Use separate sheet, if necessary)

POLICY INFORMATION
MORTGAGEE
NO MORTGAGEE

HOMEOWNER POLICIES SECTION 1 ONLY (Complete for coverages A, B, C, D & additional coverages. For Homeowners Section II Liability Losses, use ACORD 3.)

A. DWELLING	B. OTHER STRUCTURES	C. PERSONAL PROPERTY	D. LOSS OF USE	DEDUCTIBLES	DESCRIBE ADDITIONAL COVERAGES PROVIDED ON

COVERAGE A EXCLUDES WIND
SUBJECT TO FORMS (Insert form numbers and edition dates, special deductibles)

FIRE, ALLIED LINES & MULTI-PERIL POLICIES (Complete only those items involved in loss)

ITEM	SUBJECT OF INSURANCE	AMOUNT	% COINS	DEDUCTIBLE	COVERAGE AND/OR DESCRIPTION OF PROPERTY INSURED
	BLDG CNTS				
	BLDG CNTS				
	BLDG CNTS				

SUBJECT TO FORMS (Insert form numbers and edition dates, special deductibles)

FLOOD POLICY	BUILDING:	DEDUCTIBLE:	ZONE	PRE FIRM	DIFF IN ELEV	FORM TYPE	GENERAL	CONDO
	CONTENTS:	DEDUCTIBLE:		POST FIRM			DWELLING	

WIND POLICY	BUILDING	DEDUCTIBLE	CONTENTS	ZONE	FORM TYPE	GENERAL	CONDO
						DWELLING	

REMARKS/OTHER INSURANCE (List companies, policy numbers, coverages & policy amounts)/NY ONLY: PREVIOUS ADDRESS OF INSURED & WIFE'S MAIDEN NAME

CAT #   FICO #   ADJUSTER ASSIGNED   ADJUSTER #   DATE ASSIGNED
REPORTED BY   REPORTED TO   SIGNATURE OF INSURED   SIGNATURE OF PRODUCER

ACORD 1 (2005/06)   NOTE: IMPORTANT STATE INFORMATION ON REVERSE SIDE   © ACORD CORPORATION 1988-2005

Although the loss description can be a starting point for the investigation, the claim representative cannot rely on this description for a coverage determination. This description can be as generic as "water damage" or more specific, such as "sprinkler leakage." The description should direct the claim representative to review the portion of the policy dealing with water damage or sprinkler leakage before contacting the insured.

The loss description also gives the claim representative an idea about what type of expert may be needed to assist in investigating the claim. If the description says "extensive water damage to a retail clothing store," the claim representative may consider bringing in a restoration company to assist the insured in drying out the clothing. The loss section also indicates whether a police or fire department responded to the loss, and, if so, alerts the claim representative to request a report.

The claim representative must be aware of all parties who have a financial interest in the property in order to determine to whom to make claim payments. The Policy Information section specifies any mortgagees on the property. A mortgagee is a lender that loans money on a home building or other real property, thereby retaining an insurable interest in the property. Mortgagees are usually added to the policy as additional insureds. Other types of financial arrangements may also be reported in this section. If the reported loss is to a piece of equipment, such as a backhoe rented by the insured, then the name of the equipment's owner may appear in this section.

The Policy Information section also indicates policy limit and deductible information. Separate boxes for homeowners policy information and commercial property policy information include the applicable policy form numbers. The claim representative should obtain a copy of each policy form listed to determine coverage.

Coinsurance
An insurance-to-value provision in many property insurance policies providing that if the property is underinsured, the amount the insurer pays for a covered loss is reduced.

The commercial policy box may include information about multiple building locations or building contents, including whether the policy covers building and/or contents, the amount of the coverage, the coinsurance percentage, and the deductible. **Coinsurance** is a provision in a property policy that states that if the property is underinsured, the amount the insurer pays for a covered loss is reduced. The coinsurance percentage can vary by policy or by location within a commercial property policy. The claim representative must determine whether coinsurance will affect the final claim payment. The homeowners policy contains a similar provision, but the coinsurance percentage does not vary by insured, so it is not shown in the homeowners policy box. The policy information section also provides space for information specific to a flood policy and a wind policy.

At the bottom of the Policy Information section are several boxes. The first box is for the catastrophe number (CAT #). The box for the CAT # can also be found on the Automobile Loss Notice in the upper right hand corner. Catastrophes are single events that cause massive losses. Property Claim Services (PCS), a unit of Insurance Services Office, Inc., officially recognizes and assigns a **catastrophe serial number** to any single event that causes more than $25 million in insured damage for purposes of tracking and aggregating losses resulting from a catastrophe. Losses coded with a CAT # are aggregated, and the insurer may recoup these losses under a reinsurance agreement. Claim representatives record the CAT # in the claim processing system when it becomes available from ISO. Flood insurance uses a similar numbering system. When a flood occurs, the Federal Emergency Management Agency assigns it a Flood Insurance Coordinating Office number (FICO#) so that it can track the claims associated with the flood. This number is also recorded in the Policy Information Section of the loss notice.

Catastrophe serial number
A number assigned by ISO's Property Claim Services unit to a single event that causes more than $25 million in insured damage for the purpose of tracking and aggregating losses resulting from a catastrophe.

Some producers may have arrangements with the insurers they represent that allow them to assign independent adjusters to claims as soon as claims are received. In these situations, the name of the adjuster assigned and a code number (if applicable) are included at the bottom of the loss notice. The form also indicates who reported the loss and who received the loss notice. While a space for the insured's signature is provided, the insured usually does not sign the form because most claims are reported by phone rather than in person. The producer's signature is shown at the bottom of the loss notice.

General Liability Notice of Occurrence Claim Form

The ACORD General Liability Notice of Occurrence/Claim form (Exhibit 3-4) is used to report bodily injury and property damage for which the insured may be legally liable. For example, if the insured is a car dealership and a customer slips on oil on the showroom floor and is injured, the accident would be reported on a General Liability Notice of Occurrence/Claim. This form is used to report the following types of claims:

- Claims that occur on the insured's premises (premises liability)
- Claims that arise from the manufacture, distribution, or sale of products (products liability)
- Claims that arise from the insured's failure to properly practice a profession (professional liability)
- Claims for injuries to the insured's employees that fall outside the workers' compensation statutes
- Claims for damages that result from the insured's violations of workers' rights under various federal and state laws (employment practices liability)
- Claims for a loss of value to an organization resulting from the actions of a director or officer (directors and officers liability)
- Claims involving personal injury, such as reputation defamation or invasion of privacy, that may result from advertising or from other public statements (personal and advertising injury liability)
- Claims for the infringement of a copyright, trademark, or patent (intellectual property liability)
- Claims for damage as a result of pollution (environmental liability)

EXHIBIT 3-4

General Liability Notice of Occurence/Claim

ACORD®

GENERAL LIABILITY NOTICE OF OCCURRENCE/CLAIM

DATE (MM/DD/YYYY)

AGENCY	PHONE (A/C, No, Ext):	NOTICE OF OCCURRENCE / NOTICE OF CLAIM	DATE OF OCCURRENCE AND TIME — AM / PM
		DATE OF CLAIM	PREVIOUSLY REPORTED — YES / NO
		EFFECTIVE DATE	EXPIRATION DATE
		POLICY TYPE — OCCURRENCE / CLAIMS MADE	RETROACTIVE DATE
FAX (A/C, No):		COMPANY	NAIC CODE:
E-MAIL ADDRESS:		MISCELLANEOUS INFO (Site & location code)	
CODE:	SUB CODE:	POLICY NUMBER	REFERENCE NUMBER
AGENCY CUSTOMER ID:			

INSURED

NAME AND ADDRESS	SOC SEC # OR FEIN:
E-MAIL ADDRESS:	
RESIDENCE PHONE (A/C, No)	BUSINESS PHONE (A/C, No, Ext)

CONTACT — CONTACT INSURED

NAME AND ADDRESS	WHERE TO CONTACT
	WHEN TO CONTACT
E-MAIL ADDRESS:	
RESIDENCE PHONE (A/C, No)	BUSINESS PHONE (A/C, No, Ext)

OCCURRENCE

LOCATION OF OCCURRENCE (Include city & state)	AUTHORITY CONTACTED
DESCRIPTION OF OCCURRENCE (Use separate sheet, if necessary)	

POLICY INFORMATION

COVERAGE PART OR FORMS (Insert form #s and edition dates)

GENERAL AGGREGATE	PROD/COMP OP AGG	PERS & ADV INJ	EACH OCCURRENCE	FIRE DAMAGE	MEDICAL EXPENSE	DEDUCTIBLE	PD / BI

UMBRELLA/ EXCESS — UMBRELLA — EXCESS — CARRIER: — LIMITS: — AGGR — PER CLAIM/OCC — SIR/ DED

TYPE OF LIABILITY

PREMISES: INSURED IS — OWNER — TENANT — OTHER:	TYPE OF PREMISES
OWNER'S NAME & ADDRESS (If not insured)	OWNERS PHONE (A/C, No, Ext):
PRODUCTS: INSURED IS — MANUFACTURER — VENDOR — OTHER:	TYPE OF PRODUCT
MANUFACTURER'S NAME & ADDRESS (If not insured)	MANUFACT PHONE (A/C, No, Ext):
WHERE CAN PRODUCT BE SEEN?	
OTHER LIABILITY INCLUDING COMPLETED OPERATIONS (Explain)	

INJURED/PROPERTY DAMAGED

NAME & ADDRESS (Injured/Owner)				PHONE (A/C, No, Ext)
AGE	SEX	OCCUPATION	EMPLOYER'S NAME & ADDRESS	PHONE (A/C, No, Ext)
DESCRIBE INJURY — FATALITY		WHERE TAKEN	WHAT WAS INJURED DOING?	
DESCRIBE PROPERTY (Type, model, etc)	ESTIMATE AMOUNT	WHERE CAN PROPERTY BE SEEN?		WHEN CAN PROPERTY BE SEEN?

WITNESSES

NAME & ADDRESS	BUSINESS PHONE (A/C, No, Ext)	RESIDENCE PHONE (A/C, No)

REMARKS

REPORTED BY	REPORTED TO	SIGNATURE OF INSURED	SIGNATURE OF PRODUCER

ACORD 3 (2005/06) NOTE: IMPORTANT STATE INFORMATION ON REVERSE SIDE

One of the primary differences between this form and the others is that it serves as either a notice of occurrence or a notice of claim. General liability policies can be written either as occurrence policies or as claims-made policies, and this form is used to report losses for either type of policy. An occurrence policy covers only losses that occur during the policy period. A claims-made policy covers only losses that both occur and are reported within a time period specified in the policy.

In the first section of the form, the claim representative finds the producer information, the policy information, and information about whether the policy is claims-made or occurrence. Using this information, the claim representative determines whether the loss occurred during the policy period (for occurrence policies) or during the period specified in the policy (for claims-made policies).

As in the other forms, the Insured section provides the insured's identity and contact information. The Occurrence section, too, is similar the loss section in other forms, indicating where the loss occurred, describing the accident, and identifying any police or other authority from which a report can be obtained as part of the investigation.

The Policy Information section provides the form numbers and limits for the coverages provided. This section also contains information on the type of liability. It is divided into three sections: (1) premises liability, (2) products liability, and (3) other liability. Noting which section is completed gives the claim representative a preliminary idea about the type of claim submitted, but that information may not be complete. For example, if the premises liability section is completed, the claim representative may want an independent adjuster to visit the premises for more information. If a product is involved, the claim representative may want to arrange for the product to be sent to an engineer for testing.

The Injured/Property Damage section of the form provides information identifying persons or property damaged, the extent of injury or damage, and whom to contact.

The final section of this form lists any witnesses and identifies who reported the claim and who took the report. The claim representative uses this information to contact witnesses to the loss.

Workers Compensation Loss Notice Form

The ACORD Workers Compensation—First Report of Injury or Illness form (Exhibit 3-5) is used to report an accident or injury covered under a workers' compensation policy. This form looks very different from the other three forms. It contains more details about the injured party and the occurrence than the other forms because, in many states, this form is also submitted to a state regulatory body, such as the Department of Labor, which uses the information to

EXHIBIT 3-5

Workers Compensation—First Report of Injury or Illness

[ACORD Form 4 (2005/02): Workers Compensation - First Report of Injury or Illness. The form contains the following sections and fields:]

Header fields: Employer (Name & Address Incl Zip); Carrier/Administrator Claim Number*; Report Purpose Code*; Jurisdiction*; Jurisdiction Claim Number*; Insured Report Number; OSHA Case Number; Employer's Location Address (If Different); Location #; Industry Code; Employer FEIN; Phone #

CARRIER/CLAIMS ADMINISTRATOR: Carrier (Name, Address & Phone No); Policy Period (To); Claims Administrator (Name, Address & Phone No); Check If Appropriate — Self Insurance; Carrier FEIN*; Policy/Self-Insured Number; Administrator FEIN*; Agent Name & Code Number

EMPLOYEE/WAGE: Name (Last, First, Middle); Date of Birth; Social Security Number; Date Hired; State of Hire; Address (Incl Zip); Sex (Male/Female/Unknown); Marital Status (Unmarried Single/Divorced, Married, Separated, Unknown); Occupation/Job Title; Employment Status; Phone; # of Dependents; NCCI Class Code*; Rate; Per: Day/Week/Month/Other; Average Weekly Wages; # Days Worked/Week; Full Pay for Day of Injury? Yes/No; Did Salary Continue? Yes/No

OCCURRENCE/TREATMENT: Time Employee Began Work AM/PM; Date of Injury/Illness; Time of Occurrence AM/PM; Last Work Date; Date Employer Notified; Date Disability Began; Contact Name/Phone Number; Type of Injury/Illness; Part of Body Affected; Did Injury/Illness Exposure Occur on Employer's Premises? Yes/No; Type of Injury/Illness Code*; Part of Body Affected Code*; Department or Location Where Accident or Illness Exposure Occurred; All Equipment, Materials, or Chemicals Employee Was Using When Accident or Illness Exposure Occurred; Specific Activity the Employee Was Engaged In When the Accident or Illness Exposure Occurred; Work Process the Employee Was Engaged In When Accident or Illness Exposure Occurred; How Injury or Illness/Abnormal Health Condition Occurred. Describe the sequence of events and include any objects or substances that directly injured the employee or made the employee ill; Cause of Injury Code*; Date Return(ed) to Work; If Fatal, Give Date of Death; Were Safeguards or Safety Equipment Provided? Yes/No; Were They Used? Yes/No; Physician/Health Care Provider (Name & Address); Hospital or Offsite Treatment (Name & Address); Initial Treatment (No Medical Treatment / Minor: By Employer / Minor Clinic/Hosp / Emergency Care / Overnight Hospitalization / Future Major Medical/Lost Time Anticipated); Witnesses (Name & Phone #); Date Administrator Notified; Date Prepared; Preparer's Name & Title; Phone Number

ACORD 4 (2005/02)   SEE BACK FOR IMPORTANT STATE INFORMATION/SIGNATURE   © ACORD CORPORATION 1993-2005
REPRINTED WITH PERMISSION OF IAIABC

create statistics on industrial accidents. This form also differs from the others in that it has spaces, designated by an asterisk, that are not to be filled out by the employer who completes the form, but by the state regulatory body.

The first section of this form contains the employer's identifying and contact information. Other identifying information is the employer's Standard Industrial Classification (SIC) Code, taken from the SIC manual published by the Federal Office of Management and Budget, which represents the nature of the employer's business, and the employer's Federal Employer Identification Number (FEIN), also called the tax ID number.

The second section, entitled Carrier/Claims Administrator, identifies the entity providing insurance, whether an insurer, state fund, or self-insured; the carrier, third-party administrator, state fund, or self-insured responsible for administering the claim; and the name of the producer. This information is primarily used by the state regulatory body overseeing workers' compensation.

The Employee/Wage section contains details about the injured party, including identification; how much the person earns; and the basis for pay, such as day, week, or month. The claim representative uses this information in calculating the benefits owed to the injured worker.

More information to be used in calculating benefits appears in the Occurrence/Treatment section, including the date and time of the injury, the last day worked, and the date of initial disability. This section also indicates where the accident occurred, what the worker was doing at the time of the injury, what type of injury occurred, whether the injury resulted in a fatality, who the treating doctor is, and who, if anyone, witnessed the accident. The claim representative uses this information to plan the investigation. Finally, the form is signed and dated by the preparer.

Each type of ACORD loss notice form discussed gives the claim representative information essential to the claim investigation: information about the insured, the claimant, the type of injury or property damage, and the circumstances of the loss. Another useful source of investigative information is the policy itself.

Policy Information

Policy information may be contained in paper policies and underwriting files, or it may all be contained in an online database. Whatever the medium, the claim representative should review the policy to ascertain what is and is not covered. This is true of even those claims that seem simple and routine. Should the handling of a claim ever be challenged in court, a claim representative's admission that he or she relied on memory to determine policy coverage or exclusions could seriously harm an insurer's defense. Additionally, a review of the policy can reveal endorsements that can change the coverage, for example, by adding or deleting locations or changing limits.

The claim representative can use this preliminary review of the policy to help focus the investigation on the following:

- Who is covered
- What is covered
- When is coverage in effect
- What causes of loss are covered
- What is excluded

For example, if the first report of loss indicates that damage to a building occurred because of a faulty sprinkler, the claim representative should pay particular attention to the water damage portions of the policy. If the first report of loss indicates that the insured vehicle is a 2002 Toyota Camry, the claim representative should verify that this vehicle appears on the policy as a covered auto and determine what coverage applies.

For commercial policies, reviewing the policy and underwriting file can give the claim representative insight into the type of business the insured operates, whether conditions were noted that were to be corrected as part of the application for insurance, and what other types of losses the insured has had. Reviewing the policy and underwriting file can also provide information that may not initially seem pertinent but that may become pertinent as the investigation develops. For example, ABC Insurance Company issues a property policy to Acme Warehouse. Several months after the policy takes force, Acme Warehouse burns to the ground. The claim representative reviews the policy and learns that in its policy application, Acme stated that it stores only household goods. Several weeks later, the fire investigation indicates that the fire and extensive damage to the building resulted from the storage of a large amount of highly combustible and unstable chemicals used in a special manufacturing process. The claim representative realizes, based on the application, that more investigation into the loss and the policy is needed because of a potential increase in hazard from the storage of the chemical. While the nature of the insured's business initially did not seem to be an issue, it later became important in determining coverage.

Having gathered basic information about the loss from the first report and coverage information from the policy review, the claim representative usually contacts the insured to obtain a statement.

Statements

Depending on the type of loss, the claim representative may obtain statements from the insured, the claimant, witnesses, and other interested parties, such as an injured worker's supervisor. A statement is a record of the events surrounding an accident as told by the interviewee. Statements are best taken shortly after the loss occurs so that time does not diminish the person's memory of the event.

Statements are used for the following purposes:

- To gather information for claim decision making
- To memorialize the facts and loss circumstances as remembered by the interviewee
- To challenge the testimony of an individual who has furnished a statement previously, then changes the account of the loss

Insureds are often obligated by their policies to furnish statements. For example, the ISO Homeowners Special Form policy states that the insured must "submit to examination under oath, while not in the presence of any other 'insured.'" The policy also requires the insured to help the insurer "secure and give evidence…." Additionally, most policies have provisions that require the insured to cooperate with the insurer in the investigation or settlement of the claim or defense against a lawsuit. Claimants and witnesses have no such obligation to cooperate or to give the claim representative a statement. Claim representatives can attempt to gain their cooperation by explaining the importance of the statement to a thorough claim investigation.

A **sworn statement** is a signed record of events surrounding an event as told by the interviewee that contains language attesting that it is true. State laws vary regarding what constitutes sworn statements and whether they can be presented in court as testimony under oath.

Sworn statement
A signed record of events surrounding an event as told by the interviewee that contains language attesting that it is true.

Sworn statements can be either written or recorded. A written statement can be handwritten by the interviewee, or it can be dictated to the claim representative, who writes it down and gives it back to the interviewee to read and attest to. A written statement can also be a form, such as a proof of loss form used in property losses, that is completed by and attested to be true by the party completing the form. Claim representatives may also take recorded statements, either in person or over the phone, using a tape recorder or another recording device. The recording may be transcribed, or it may be maintained as a recording in the claim file.

An effective statement has four qualities. It is the following:[2]

1. Coherent—A statement follows a logical sequence.
2. Complete—A statement is thorough for the circumstances.
3. Objective—A statement reflects events as the interviewee remembers them.
4. Factual—A statement does not contain immaterial opinions.

To ensure that statements are coherent, complete, objective, and factual, claim representatives should prepare themselves, the interviewee, and the statement setting. The claim representative's personal preparation involves reviewing the claim file to compile appropriate questions and selecting a suitable setting for the statement.

> **Steps in Preparing for a Statement**
>
> The claim representative should take the following steps to prepare to take a claimant's, third party's, or witness's statement.
>
> Arrange the Logistics
>
> - Set a time and designate a place
> - Set an appointment with interviewee
> - Explain the procedures and consent process
> - Instruct the interviewee about documents to bring
> - Minimize distractions in the setting
>
> Review the Claim File
>
> - Note the loss information
> - Note the policy information
> - Outline the information to be learned from the statement
>
> Plan the Questions
>
> - Draft the questions that will lead to the desired information
> - Draw diagrams, if necessary

The questions a claim representative asks should reflect the specifics of the claim. For example, questions for an automobile claim would be different from those for a slip-and-fall claim. Questions for an insured may be different from those for a claimant or witness. In addition, the investigation may have uncovered facts that the claim representative should clarify in the statement. Thus, claim representatives should thoroughly review the claim file before taking a statement.

When taking a statement in person, the claim representative should select a location that is free from interruptions and excessive noise. During the interview, distractions should be kept to a minimum. The claim representative may have less control over distractions when taking a statement by telephone than during an interview in person. If, during a telephone interview, the claim representative notices background noise that may distract the interviewee, the claim representative should consider rescheduling the statement or asking the interviewee if the background noise can be reduced.

Before conducting the statement, the claim representative should attempt to develop rapport with the interviewee to reduce any anxiety the interviewee may be feeling. Engaging in a few minutes of casual conversation, rather than immediately starting the interview, can be calming. A review of the statement process also helps put interviewees at ease. The claim representative can explain the process for taking the statement and invite the interviewee to ask questions about the process. A further description of the question-and-answer format and of the information the claim representative is seeking also helps to prepare the interviewee. The claim representative should emphasize that only facts related to the claim will be discussed because the statement is meant only to memorialize the interviewee's recollection of the facts, and that unrelated issues, such as coverage under the policy and negotiations of the amount of damage, can be discussed after the statement has been concluded.

In some cases, the claim representative may want to have a drawing or sketch of the accident scene to refresh the interviewee's memory before the interview. For the statement itself, however, the claim representative should ensure that the interviewee carefully describes all aspects of the accident rather than simply referring to the sketch so that the statement itself, as written or recorded, is clear. The claim representative may also review some of the facts of the loss, such as the date, time, and location, so that the interviewee can quickly recall that information.

Interviewees may be more forthcoming with information if they know they can obtain a copy of the statements after they have been completed. Claim representatives should assure interviewees that copies will be provided.

Recorded Statements

Recorded statements can be taken in person or by telephone. The advantages of recorded statements for claim representatives include saving time and getting an account of the loss in the interviewee's own words. Recorded statements follow a format similar to written statements, except for the permission and closing portions. The permission acknowledges the fact that the statement is being recorded with the interviewee's permission. Generally, recorded statements are summarized, not transcribed (although transcriptions may be produced if requested by legal counsel). Recorded statements do not require written signatures. Instead, the recorded statement is closed with questions that elicit answers from the interviewee reiterating that permission was given to record and verifying that the facts are true to the best of the interviewee's knowledge.

The use of recorded statements offers claim representatives several advantages and disadvantages, shown in the box, compared to the use of written statements.

Recorded statements require more preparation on the part of the claim representative and the interviewee than written statements. The claim representative must make sure the recording equipment is working, and, because the interviewee may be nervous about being recorded, the claim representative may have to spend more time making the interviewee comfortable with the process. Following are some suggestions for introducing a recorded statement:

- "We ordinarily record these interviews so that we can obtain the facts quickly."
- "We use recorders so that we can get your version of the incident in your own words."

> **Advantages and Disadvantages of Recorded Statements as Compared to Written Statements**
>
> **Recorded Statements**
>
> *Advantages*
>
> - Recording is less time consuming.
> - The interviewee can be observed (if the interview is in person).
> - Exact wording is recorded.
> - Illegible handwriting is not an issue.
> - Telephone interviews are an option, saving additional time.
> - Recorded statements can be transcribed if written record is needed.
>
> *Disadvantages*
>
> - Equipment may fail.
> - Tapes must be stored.
> - Transcription adds to costs.
> - Transcript must be reviewed for accuracy.
>
> **Written Statements**
>
> *Advantages*
>
> - Interviewees may be less anxious.
> - Claim representative has more control.
> - Transcription is not required.
> - Interviewee's signature may be easier to obtain (because a written document exists).
> - Claim representative has an opportunity to evaluate the interviewee as a witness.
>
> *Disadvantages*
>
> - Handwriting may be illegible.
> - Producing a written statement takes more time.
> - Interviewees may claim they were misquoted.
> - Paraphrasing may lead to challenges of inaccuracy.

Adapted from "Effective Statements: A One-Day Course to Improve Investigative Interviewing" by Claims Training Services, 1999, pp. 58–59, 69–70.

- "We know your time is valuable, and recording is much faster than writing a report."
- "We can take a written interview in about an hour, or we can record one in about twenty minutes. I prefer and suggest the recording, but it's up to you."

The claim representative should instruct the interviewee to use verbal responses rather than nodding or shaking the head and to speak clearly and at a suitable volume to ensure that statements are audibly recorded. Others present during the interview should be asked not to interrupt.

The claim representative should inform the interviewee when recording begins, and asks the interviewee to acknowledge that he or she knows that all statements are being recorded and that he or she has given permission for the recording. Other than these verbal acknowledgements, the introductory information is the same as for a written statement. The claim representative states the date, day, time, and location of the interview; identifies the interviewee; and requests his or her name, age, address, telephone numbers, marital status, occupation, work address, and Social Security number. All proper names and any other words that may be unclear are spelled out in a recorded statement.

Despite careful preparations, interruptions can occur. Any interruptions must be explained in detail in the recording, for example, as follows:

"This recording will be interrupted while Bob [name of interviewee] leaves to answer the door [reason for absence]. It is 2:23 PM."

The claim representative then stops the recorder. When the interviewee returns, the claim representative starts the recorder and says,

"Bob [name of interviewee] has returned from answering the door [reason for interruption], and we will continue the interview. The time is now 2:45 PM. Bob, have we had any discussion while the recorder was off?"

After the interviewee answers, the claim representative states the time and continues the interview.

When the end of the tape is approaching, the claim representative may say,

"Bob [name of interviewee], we have reached the end of the tape and must interrupt the recording to change the tape. It is 3:05 PM."

The claim representative changes tapes the tape and begins recording,

"This is Jane Jones [name of claim representative] interviewing Bob Johnson [name of interviewee]. We will resume the interview. Bob, have we had any discussion while the recorder was turned off?"

After the reply, the claim representative states the time and proceeds with the interview.

At the end of the interview, the claim representative offers the interviewee a chance to make additions or corrections, asks the interviewee to confirm that the questions were answered truthfully to the best of his or her knowledge, and again verifies that the interviewee knew that the statement was being recorded. The claim representative plays back the last few words of the statement to ensure that the interview was recorded.

While recorded statements require more preparation time, recording a statement itself is less time consuming than completing a written statement. In addition, recorded statements are not routinely transcribed. Instead, the claim representative prepares a brief statement summary for the claim file. Such summaries should accurately reflect the statement's contents, not the claim representative's opinions. Written summaries refresh the claim representative's memory when the file is subsequently reviewed and enable others who review the file to quickly familiarize themselves with the statement contents. If the interviewee requests a copy of the recorded statement, it can be transcribed.

Written Statements

A written statement may be either a free-flowing description of events by an interviewee or, more commonly, an interviewee's answers to questions on a form provided by the insurer. The written form statement is more common than the free-flowing written statement because it need not be completed in person. However, the written form statement provides less information than the free-flowing statement because the person completing the form is only answering the questions that are asked. The free-flowing statement can be written by the interviewee, or it can be written by the claim representative, who takes notes during a personal interview and either writes out the interviewee's exact words or paraphrases them.

Written statements are often used when the interviewee has retained a lawyer. Lawyers may insist on written rather than recorded statements so that they can oversee the statement's preparation and content to ensure that it contains only the information necessary to the claim.

A written statement may also be preferred because signed, written statements are admissible in court proceedings. Recorded statements are generally not admissible unless accompanied by a signed affidavit (sworn statement under oath) from the interviewee. The written statement should begin with the identification of the interviewee, address, phone numbers (home and work), Social Security number, and driver's license number. It should also include place of employment, address, and name of immediate supervisor. The names and ages of all those residing at the same address as the interviewee should be included. All of this information is important in establishing the identity of the interviewee but is also useful in locating the interviewee at a later date should the need arise. The statement should also indicate that the information is being freely given. It should be written in the first person, regardless of who is doing the actual writing.

> **APPLY YOUR LEARNING**
> **Adjusting Tip**
> Leave the last line on each page of a written statement blank for the interviewee to sign and date.

Once the statement is complete, a closing, which includes signatures of the interviewee and the claim representative, must be added. The interviewee reads the entire statement and signs at the bottom of each page. On the last page, the interviewee writes that he or she has read the statement and understands it, and then signs below that. For example, "I have read the preceding two pages and eleven lines, and they are true and correct to the best of my knowledge." Any lawyer present during the statement, may also sign each page of the statement and, on the last page, add a signed statement indicating that he or she was present throughout the interview, has read the statement, and verifies that it is true. The lawyer's statement is not required and may be omitted if space is not available on the final page. The claim representative witnesses the signature(s) and signs at the end. If the interviewee is hesitant to sign each page, the claim representative may ease any anxiety by signing the statement pages first. An example of a written statement is shown in Appendix A.

The claim representative is responsible for writing the statement legibly and in such a way that alterations are not possible. This is crucial to a statement's admissibility in court. Each page should be numbered and dated, and no margins, indentations, or gaps should be left in the text. The statement should be written using a pen, typewriter, or computer and should contain no erasures. Errors are scored through with the corrections inserted above them. The interviewee initials any corrections. All words are fully spelled out in statements.

A written statement should also be chronological and complete, the interviewee's answers and statements should be recorded, in the interviewee's language, dialect, and figures of speech as much as possible.

Guidelines for a Written Statement

When preparing written statements, a claim representative should do the following:

- Write legibly
- Write in ink and on lined paper (if handwritten)
- Make one original and provide one copy to interviewee
- Date and number the top of every page
- Indicate the location at which the statement was taken
- Write from margin to margin, without any paragraphs
- Avoid legal jargon
- Use the interviewee's language/grammar
- Leave space for signatures
- Use first person
- Include opening and closing

Adapted from "Effective Statements: A One-Day Course to Improve Investigative Interviewing" by Claims Training Services, 1999, pp. 59–60.

Statement Content

With a few exceptions, statement content should be the same whether the statement is written or recorded. Statements generally follow a pattern to ensure that all relevant information is included. Claim representatives can use the Seven Part Method, breaking each statement into the seven parts described in Exhibit 3-6, as a guide to statement content.

> **EXHIBIT 3-6**
>
> **Seven Part Method**
>
> 1. Permission and introduction—date, time, and location of the interview, names of the parties involved in the interview, and an affirmation from the interviewee that the interview is given with permission
> 2. Identification—identifying information about the person being interviewed, such as name, address, phone number, Social Security number, and driver's license number
> 3. Setting—answers to questions such as who was involved in the loss, what was involved in the loss, when the loss occurred, where the loss occurred, and why the loss occurred
> 4. Incident—a step-by-step description of how the loss occurred
> 5. Post incident injuries/damages—description of the property damage and bodily injuries to individuals
> 6. Miscellaneous—any information the interviewee wants to add
> 7. Conclusion—reaffirmation that the statement was taken with permission

Adapted from "Effective Statements: A One-Day Course to Improve Investigative Interviewing" by Claims Training Services, 1999, p. 45.

The body of a statement is adapted for different types of losses and contains information specific to each type of loss. Exhibit 3-7 shows information that might be included in the body of an auto accident statement.

Whether the statement is written or recorded, the claim representative should have an outline of the questions that need to be asked. Many insurers provide their claim representatives with statement guides.

> **APPLY YOUR LEARNING**
>
> **Adjusting Tip**
>
> Instead of rigidly following the statement guide, a claim representative should let the interviewee's answer serve as a guide to the next appropriate question.

The closing varies for written and recorded statements. Appropriate closings are described in the later sections of this chapter.

Types of Questions Used in Statements

Claim representatives can develop statement-taking skills that encourage cooperation and elicit facts about the loss. One way claim representatives can produce sound statements is through a command of three different types of questions: direct, open-ended, and leading.

Direct questions elicit specific information and can often be answered with a short phrase or a yes or no response. These questions directly and objectively

Direct question
A question that seeks specific information and that can often be answered with a short phrase or a yes or no response.

EXHIBIT 3-7

Auto Accident Statement Information

1. Accident date, day, and time
2. Vehicle
   - Owner
   - Year, make, and model
   - Vehicle identification number (VIN)
   - License plate number
   - Defects or pre-existing damage
3. Accident location
   - Type of street or intersection (highway, residential, etc.)
   - Marking on street and lanes
   - Street surface
   - Traffic controls
   - Speed limit
   - Curbs and shoulders
   - Visibility (weather, obstructions such as buildings, trees, shrubs)
   - Street or traffic-control defects
4. Chronological accident description
   - Origin and destination of trip
   - Pre-accident activity involving driver or passengers (consumption of alcohol or drugs)
   - Vehicles' positions before, during, and after impact with respect to each other and to fixed objects
   - Speed of vehicles
   - Signals given
   - Skid marks or gouges left by vehicles
   - Points of impact on vehicles
   - Post-accident events (accusations; conversations; police, ambulance, and hospital involvement)
5. Passengers
   - Identification (name, address, phone number, relationship to driver)
   - Reason for being in car (personal or business)
   - Payment or other compensation to driver, if any
6. Damages
   - Description of property damage
   - Description of bodily injuries

address the issue, and do not reflect bias in the questioner, as leading questions may. Claim representatives use direct questions to clarify an interviewee's statements and help reduce the likelihood that the interviewee will change the statement later. An example of a direct question is, "Was the Chevy stopped at the light when you approached the intersection?" The answer is direct and objective, and it is difficult for an interviewee to change such an answer later.

> **Examples of Direct Questions**
>
> Automobile Claims
>
> - Were you involved in an automobile accident on (date)?
> - What was your car's speed immediately before the impact?
> - On the night of the accident, did you drink any alcohol?
>
> Premises Slip-and-Fall Claims
>
> - Were you looking at the floor just before you fell?
> - Where were you looking when you fell?
> - What—if anything—did you see on the floor?

Open-ended question
A question that seeks an answer that explains or elaborates on the circumstances under consideration.

Open-ended questions require explanation or elaboration. They seek descriptions using the interviewee's own words. Direct questions seek brief answers, while open-ended questions seek detailed answers. Open-ended questions tend to relax the interviewee and make the statement-taking process seem less threatening.

> **Examples of Open-Ended Questions**
>
> - How did the accident occur?
> - What happened next?
> - What was the condition of the premises?
> - How did the fall occur?

Open-ended questions allow the interviewee flexibility in responding. Also, open-ended questions sometimes lead to new follow-up questions. Consider the following example:

Claim Representative: "How did the fall occur?" (open-ended question)

Claimant: "I slipped on some water on the floor of the warehouse."

Claim Representative: "Did you see the water on the floor before you fell?" (direct question)

In this example, an open-ended question leads to a direct question asking for specific information.

However, open-ended questions can be time consuming and can allow the interviewee to wander to unrelated topics. If the answers do not provide specific information, it can be difficult to challenge the testimony. Using direct questions as follow-up to open-ended questions helps clarify the information and avoid these problems.

Direct questions and some open-ended questions can be phrased in such a way as to be leading questions. A **leading question** suggests to the interviewee that the questioner prefers a particular answer. Rather than allow the interviewee to answer based on memory, a leading question guides the interviewee to a particular answer. Leading questions often require a yes or no response and prevent the interviewee from explaining. Claim representatives should avoid leading questions and should give the interviewee an unbiased opportunity to relate information.

Leading question
A question that seeks or suggests a particular answer.

Exhibit 3-8 contrasts direct, open-ended, and leading questions. Leading questions can be blatant, as in the following examples, or subtle and seemingly neutral.

Consider the following exchange from a workers' compensation interview:

Claim rep:	"Where did you work on May 7?" (direct question)
Injured employee:	"Collins Construction Company."
Claim rep:	"Were you performing your regular job duties on May 7?" (direct question)
Injured employee:	"Yes."
Claim rep:	"Was there anything unusual in what you were doing?" (direct and leading question)
Injured employee:	"Yes."
Claim rep:	"What was unusual?" (open-ended question)

EXHIBIT 3-8

Direct, Open-Ended, and Leading Questions

Direct Question	Open-Ended Question	Leading Question
Did you see the red Pontiac stop at the stoplight?	What was the red Pontiac doing?	The red Pontiac stopped at the stoplight, didn't it?
At what speed would you estimate the Pontiac was traveling before impact?	Can you tell me what you observed regarding the Pontiac?	Did you see the Pontiac traveling at a high speed?
Did the Pontiac collide with Mr. Brown's car?	What did you see?	Did you see the Pontiac crash into the back of Mr. Brown's car?
Did the Pontiac skid before impact? How far?	What happened with the Pontiac before impact?	Did you see the Pontiac skid more than fifty feet before the crash?

The claim representative is trying to establish or rule out that the activity that resulted in the injury required an unusual exertion because this is a test for compensability in some jurisdictions. The claim representative uses direct questions requiring yes or no answers and then follows up with an open-ended question ("What was unusual?") based on the answer to a leading question. Rather than asking the second and third questions, the claim representative could have asked an open-ended question, such as "What job duties were you performing on May 7?"

Leading questions undermine the admissibility and credibility of statements at trial. Claim representatives should be careful to avoid sacrificing the admissibility of an entire statement by asking too many leading questions. In the previous example, the injured employee's case might be based on the answer to the open-ended question, "What was unusual?" But because this question was derived from the answer to a leading question, the entire portion of the statement may be tainted. If the claim representative had instead asked, "What job duties were you performing on May 7?", and the injured employee's response expressed that some duties were unusual, then the claim representative's questioning may be admissible in court.

Leading questions tend to reinforce the negative image that some people have about claim representatives. Claim representatives who use nonleading questions appropriately may encourage interviewees to confide in them and, as a result, may get more information in their statements.

Consideration for Special Interviewees

Whether statements are recorded or written, some circumstances require special considerations when taking statements, including the following:

- *Hospitalized interviewee.* Claim representatives must be familiar with state laws about taking statements from hospitalized people. Many jurisdictions prohibit or restrict taking statements from those hospitalized. Such people may be taking medicine or may be experiencing pain or stress from an accident. These circumstances may interfere with the patient's memory or concentration and make the statement less accurate. Furthermore, a hospital visit that is seen as an invasion of privacy can harm the claim representative's relationship with the injured person. Claim representatives should respect the wishes of the injured person and the person's family when it comes to scheduling and taking a statement.

- *Illiterate interviewee.* People who cannot read or write can give recorded statements. If a recorded statement is not feasible, the claim representative can write out a statement for the interviewee, taken in the presence of a disinterested party, that is, one who has no financial or personal stake in the claim outcome. The disinterested party can then read the statement back to the interviewee and attest that it accurately reflects the interviewee's words.

A special notation replaces the signature of an illiterate person who is interviewed for a written statement. The claim representative signs the interviewee's name, leaving a space between the first and the last names. Above the space, the claim representative writes "His" or "Her" and below the space, the representative writes "Mark." The disinterested party reads the statement to the interviewee. Then the claim representative explains that the interviewee should place an "X" in the blank space to verify that the statement is true. The disinterested party provides a separate statement verifying that the party has read the written statement to the interviewee and that the interviewee acknowledged that it was true by marking the "X."

- *Minor interviewee.* Laws about statements taken from minors (someone who has not reached the age of majority) vary by state. Most states require that the claim representative obtain permission from a minor's parent or guardian before interviewing the minor. Some states require that the parent or guardian be present during the interview of the minor or of children under a certain age. The parent or guardian and the minor should be identified on the recording, and the parent's or guardian's permission to interview the minor should be recorded. If a written statement is taken, the parent or guardian witnesses the minor's signature and provides a separate statement verifying his or her presence during the interview, that the minor's account of the event was accurately recorded, and that the statement was taken with the permission of the parent or guardian.

- *Foreign language interviewee.* When taking a statement from someone who speaks only a foreign language or who has limited understanding of the claim representative's language, the claim representative must arrange to have an interpreter assist with the statement. The interpreter can be a professional interpreter, but usually the claim representative can arrange for a family member or neighbor who is fluent in both the claim representative's and the interviewee's languages to assist. The claim representative should obtain the interpreter's contact information in case the interpreter is later needed to testify in court. During the interview, the claim representative should instruct the interpreter to repeat the interviewer's question in the interviewer's language and then translate it into the interviewee's language. This ensures that the interpreter completely understands the question before translating it. The interpreter should follow this same protocol for the interviewee's answer. When the statement is concluded, the interpreter should read the entire statement to the interviewee in the interviewee's language to confirm that he or she is satisfied with the statement. Both the interviewee and the interpreter should sign and date the statement, along with the claim representative.

Diagrams, Photos, and Videos

Claim representatives use diagrams, photos, and videos to illustrate what the loss scene looked like, how an accident happened, and the extent of the property damage and bodily injuries. Occasionally, photos and videos can be used as evidence of ownership, such as a wedding video showing the insured wearing the fur coat that was stolen or evidence that an item is missing, such as a photo of the dust ring around the base of the now missing television. They can also be used to show that the claim is fraudulent, for example, by videotaping a claimant who is claiming total incapacity in the act of painting a house. When taking a statement in person, the claim representative should ask the interviewee to make a diagram of the accident and then have the interviewee sign and date the diagram.

Some claim representatives visit the accident scene to make a diagram, take photos, or make a video. Others assign this task to a field adjuster or an independent adjuster.

Diagrams are useful to illustrate complex mechanical parts because they can provide more detail than photos. They can be prepared by an expert using a computer and scientific measurements. Diagrams can also be basic sketches drawn by the parties involved in the accident. It is up to the claim representative to determine what kind of diagram is necessary for the claim.

Photos and videos are widely used in lieu of or in addition to diagrams. Claim representatives may take photos and videos themselves or hire others to do so. Claim representatives should do the following to ensure the credibility of the photos or videos:

- When photographing property damage, such as a broken pipe, include a twelve-inch ruler in the photo to give the scale of the item.
- When photographing vehicles, include all aspects of the vehicle, not just the damaged portion, to provide an idea of what the vehicle's overall condition was at the time of the accident.
- When photographing an intersection, try to take the photos at approximately the same time of day and in the same weather conditions as the accident to provide evidence about lighting and visibility. Take photos from each direction so that visibility in each direction is shown. Photos should be marked with the date, time, and direction.
- When photographing structural damage, follow a sequence. Begin with the outside of the building, photographing all sides. Then move inside and photograph each wall.
- When photographing a scar, use lighting that will show the full effect of the scar.

A video can be a powerful means of explaining how an event occurred (by recreating the event), often used by experts, or of documenting damage or injury. For example, claim representatives can use a video to show the extent of damage in a large warehouse fire. Many lawyers use "day in the life" videos of injured people to show how their lives have changed. Like photos, videos must be substantiated with the date and time of the filming and the name of the videographer. Videos are usually not edited because that would detract from their credibility.

Experts

During the claim investigation, claim representatives may require the services of an expert to evaluate the cause or value of a loss, to investigate the possibility of fraud committed by an insured or a third-party claimant, or to provide legal advice.

The claim representative must determine when an expert is needed and which expert to use. Generally, guidelines are provided by claim supervisors, and most claim representatives discuss using an expert with their immediate supervisors before proceeding.

Many insurers have a panel of experts they use with some regularity. These experts have proven themselves to be impartial in their findings, respected in their field, and credible when testifying under oath. From this panel, the claim representative selects the expert that best fits the investigation's needs.

> **APPLY YOUR LEARNING**
>
> **Adjusting Tip**
>
> To select an expert, the claim representative must decide what the investigation needs to cover and what the budget is for the assignment. If the claim involves a fire, the claim representative may assign an origin and cause expert to determine what started the fire. If, for example, the origin and cause expert reports that the fire started in a toaster, the claim representative may then hire an engineer familiar with toaster fires to evaluate the toaster.

The claim representative should outline expectations for the expert—specifically, what the expert is expected to do and report on. Generally, expectations can vary with the type of expert but may include the following:

- *Documenting the investigation.* Experts document their investigations with photographs, videotape, and notes. Photographs must have captions and should match the description in the notes. Videotapes must indicate the video's time and date as well as the videographer's name. Notes of the investigation should be preserved until the claim is resolved.

- *Reconstructing the event or product that caused the loss.* An expert may be asked to reconstruct an accident scene or event. Reconstructions should be accompanied by a narrative describing the scene before the loss and the event that caused the loss. Computer assisted reconstruction has been used for automobile accidents to show the path of vehicle travel, for airline crashes to simulate weather conditions, and for fires to show where the fire spread. Photos and diagrams are useful in preserving reconstructions.

- *Eliminating other potential causes of the loss.* When experts determine a cause of loss, they eliminate certain other possible causes. The expert should document this process of elimination so that the conclusion cannot be challenged. Experts should also try to anticipate what an adversary may suggest as the cause of loss and document why it is not viable.

- *Demonstrating the link between the cause and the resulting damage or injury.* A demonstration of the event or cause of loss can be a physical demonstration or a computer-generated version of the event. A demonstration can be convincing to jury members or to the claim representative when reviewing the loss because they can see the sequence of events leading up to a loss and not have to rely on someone else's description of the events.

- *Preparing a report of the investigation.* The expert should prepare a report for the claim representative when the investigation is complete. In rare instances, the expert may be asked not to prepare a written report, but these occasions occur only when a claim is in litigation and the report would not assist in the preparation of the case. The expert's report may be either oral or written. In either form, it should be logical, easy to understand, and specific, and it should not use jargon or technical language unless necessary. The claim representative should ask the expert any questions about the claim or the damages that arise after reviewing the report, and, if necessary, ask the expert to submit a new report answering those questions.

- *Preserving evidence.* Finally, claim representatives expect experts to preserve the evidence they use or uncover in their investigation so that it will be available for use in litigation or subrogation. Without the evidence, the chances of successful litigation or subrogation are significantly diminished. Insurers can be penalized if the evidence is contaminated, tampered with, or destroyed. The responsibility for the preservation of the evidence is shared by the property owner, the insurer, and the expert.

Types of Experts

Claim representatives rely on various experts, depending on the nature of the claim. The following are some of the more frequently used experts:

- *Independent or outside adjuster.* One of the first experts a claim representative may use in the investigation of any type of claim is an independent or outside adjuster. While some insurers have staff field claim representatives, many hire independent adjusters or investigators to perform field investigations. The claim representative assigns certain investigative tasks to the outside adjuster that are best performed in person. For example, an outside adjuster can inspect a building or a vehicle to determine the extent of the damage and prepare a damage estimate. Claim representatives usually are given guidelines by their supervisors about what types of investigations should be handled by outside adjusters and investigators.

- *Special investigation unit.* A claim representative should refer claims that appear fraudulent to the insurer's special investigation unit (SIU), a department or division within an insurer created to investigate claims that raise suspicions of fraud. Insurers usually provide guidelines for when claims should be referred to the SIU. Claim representatives may also consult with SIU staff to discuss possible fraud indicators in a claim investigation.

- *Private investigator.* Private investigators have contacts and skills in obtaining information from witnesses, public records, and law enforcement agencies. They often conduct surveillance or find people who leave the area (called skip tracing). The claim representative can use the information gathered to reach coverage decisions, determine whether insurance fraud is being attempted, and document potential subrogation.
- *Lawyer.* Claim representatives may seek general legal advice from lawyers on all types of claims and specific legal advice about coverage issues and complex claims. Also, a lawyer's services may be required to gain access to an insured's books and records.

The independent adjuster, SIU investigator, private investigator, and the lawyer can all be used on any type of claim. Other experts have specific expertise related to specific types of claims, such as property damage claims or bodily injury claims.

Property Experts

Some experts are used primarily for property damage claims. They can assist the claim representative in determining how a loss was caused, such as, how a fire started or why a machine malfunctioned. They can also help determine the amount of the loss, such as the lost income resulting from a loss or the price a damaged item can be sold for as salvage. Property experts include the following:

- *Origin and cause expert.* Because determining the cause of loss is vital to property damage claim investigations, one of the most important experts who may assist the claim representative is an origin and cause expert. These experts use their background in fire science and arson investigation to determine whether a fire started accidentally or was deliberately set. Claim representatives may also consult origin and cause experts to investigate claims when subrogation is possible. This insurer may use these experts' reports to defend a claim, deny a claim, or bring a claim against another party.
- *Accountant.* Accountants help determine lost revenue for a business that has suffered a covered loss. The claim representative may consult an accountant who specializes in claims and legal matters to determine the financial stability of the business submitting a claim. These claim accountants are often used to verify the extent of business merchandise or stock losses and business income losses. They can discover a possible motive for fraud in the course of their investigations into the business's financial condition. Accountants can also help resolve cases in which insureds may have overstated or exaggerated the loss amounts, and they can determine whether the insured had the financial means to purchase the property that has been reported as stolen or destroyed.
- *Restoration specialist.* Claim representatives may consult with restoration specialists when windstorms, fire, water, or smoke damages property. Restoration specialists clean structures (including carpeting, walls, and floors), equipment, stock, merchandise, and personal or business property to preserve property value and to avoid further damage from mold or

other causes. Claim representatives may suggest that the insured use restoration specialists immediately to curtail subsequent damage.

- *Salvor.* Salvors separate damaged from undamaged inventory, business supplies and equipment; prepare inventories of damaged and destroyed property; and establish values of damaged or destroyed property. For example, in a water damage claim at a supermarket, a salvor would separate canned goods that are salvageable from paper goods that are not, determine what each can will sell for, and find a willing buyer, thereby reducing the overall cost of the claim to the insurer. Claim representatives may also employ salvors to sell salvage or, by special arrangement, to purchase salvage.

- *Construction expert.* Claim representatives may contract with construction experts, such as engineers, architects, and building contractors, to determine the cause of loss and the costs to repair or rebuild, or for related services. Engineers can help determine whether construction defects or malfunctions were the root cause of a loss. Architects sometimes draw plans or provide specifications for partial or complete reconstruction of structures or for specialized equipment and may also provide specifications needed to obtain remodeling or building permits. Building contractors can make emergency repairs to structures damaged by fire, water, windstorm, or other causes of loss.

- *Appraiser.* Claim representatives contact appraisers when investigating real and personal property losses. Appraisers help establish the value of personal property, merchandise, and equipment. For real property settlements, they resolve disputes over the loss amount. Some specialized appraisers assist claim representatives with general claim handling tasks. For example, auto appraisers inspect vehicle damage and prepare estimates for claim representatives as part of routine file handling.

Bodily Injury Experts

Experts are used in bodily injury claims to help determine how an injury occurred, how the injured parties are or will be affected by the injuries once they have recovered, and how much income they have lost as a result of their injuries. The need for any one of these experts is based on the claim's complexity. Bodily injury experts include the following:

- *Accident reconstruction specialist.* Claim representatives contact accident reconstruction specialists when injuries are serious and liability cannot be conclusively determined. These experts use details from an accident scene to draw scientifically and mathematically accurate conclusions on such details as the vehicle's speed and direction. Their findings can be used to assess negligence or comparative negligence.

- *Private investigator.* A claim representative who is suspicious of the injuries in a liability or workers' compensation claim may hire a professional private investigator. The private investigator can conduct surveillance and help determine whether a claimant is feigning or exaggerating injuries by documenting activity that is inconsistent with the reported injury.

- *Accountants or other financial or economic analysts.* Claim representatives may consult accountants or other financial or economic analysts in liability or workers' compensation injury claims to determine the value of a claimant's pre-accident ability to earn a living over the course of a working lifetime and to place a value on the loss of such earnings capacity.
- *Medical consultants.* Medical consultants, rehabilitation nurses, and other medical providers help insurers assess the medical requirements in injury claims. They arrange medical examinations, review medical reports, and audit bills from physicians and other medical providers to determine whether the treatment being provided follows the physician's treatment instructions. Rehabilitation nurses help claim representatives assess whether rehabilitation is possible for the claimant and, if so, the extent that is needed. Other medical professionals help by providing opinions on the medical necessity of treatments.

> **APPLY YOUR LEARNING**
>
> **Adjusting Tip**
>
> A thorough, expert investigation eliminates all possible explanations for a loss except for one. This information can reduce the credibility of an opposing opinion and can contribute to effective negotiations.

Records and Reports

The number and types of records and reports in a claim file depend on the claim's type and complexity. For example, a homeowner's burglary claim may contain only a police report, but an auto accident with injuries may contain a police report, emergency medical team report, hospital and emergency room records, treating physicians' reports, and a rehabilitation report. Claim representatives use records and reports to verify the facts of an accident or the nature and extent of damage or injury. A record or report may also reveal new information to the claim representative.

Police and fire reports can be found in both property and liability claims, but certain types of records and reports are found exclusively in property claims. For large property claims, property tax records from state and local government agencies can help a claim representative determine whether the taxes have been paid, whether the property has recently been sold, or what the property's appraised value may be. This information helps the claim representative determine whether fraud is involved in the claim. Local municipal inspection reports can provide information about a building's condition and maintenance. It is not uncommon in large property claims to request income tax records, inventory records, and bank records from the insured to verify the value of inventory involved in a claim. Motor vehicle title and registration records are used to verify the existence and ownership of vehicles. Shipping records can trace the path of cargo, as well as help determine ownership.

Workers' compensation claims and liability claims that deal with bodily injury can include any applicable police and fire reports. These claim files may also include medical reports and records, as well as reports that verify income. This information can be used to determine the extent of injury and disability or to determine potential payments.

Medical records can include those for emergency medical treatment, hospital treatment, emergency room treatment, and any diagnostic tests conducted on the injured party. Treating physicians issue reports, as do vocational and rehabilitation consultants. The injured party's employer can provide employment records, such as number of days worked, hours worked, wage rate, overtime rate, and bonuses paid. In some cases, the employer may also have pre-employment information such as a report of a physical exam or medical test that can shed light on the injured party's pre-accident condition.

To obtain much of this information, claim representatives use medical and wage authorization or release forms, which must be signed by the party before the information is released. Insurers, TPAs, self-insured businesses, and independent adjusters should all have authorization or release forms that conform to the various privacy laws.

In a claim for a fatality, the claim representative usually requests a copy of the death certificate and the autopsy report from the medical examiner's office. These documents are important to a bodily injury or workers' compensation claim because they can indicate cause of death and whether suffering preceded death. These facts can have a significant effect on the amount of compensation for pain and suffering.

Claim representatives who handle bodily injury claims also use records from state agencies, including birth, death, and marriage certificates. These records are particularly useful in verifying the existence of dependents. Because many of the agencies maintain these records online, claim representatives can access the records directly through the Internet or through a service such as ISO ClaimSearch.

Industry Databases

Industry databases, another investigative tool, contain claim information from insurers, TPAs, and industry organizations, which can be searched to detect fraud or find data on property, liability, auto, and workers' compensation claims. ISO ClaimSearch, the oldest and largest of these industry databases, receives claim information from participants such as insurers, TPAs, self-insureds, health and disability insurers and administrators, and workers' compensation funds. Fraud bureaus, fire marshals, and law enforcement agencies are generally provided access to the database to investigate fraud. Most ISO participants submit claim information directly from their own claim processing systems or by using the ISO ClaimSearch Web site.[3] ISO ClaimSearch automatically searches the database to find claims that match the submitted information.

For example, the following fields of data in a claim report can be searched automatically as part of the reporting process:

- Insured/claimant name
- Insured/claimant address
- Social Security number
- Telephone number
- Vehicle identification number
- Driver's license number
- Tax identification number
- Other parties to the loss, such as mortgagees, service providers, tenants, and witnesses
- Location of accident/loss
- Alleged property damage or bodily injury

ISO ClaimSearch automatically returns a report containing any matches to the submitting party. The report may indicate a pattern of claims, pre-existing conditions, unrepaired damage previously claimed, duplicate claims, or undisclosed duplicate insurance for the same loss.

Companies that participate in ISO ClaimSearch can also use the database to follow up on fraud suspicions by using the optional Claims Inquiry function. For example, a claim representative or fraud investigator who suspects a doctor of fraud in the treatment of auto accident victims could enter an inquiry in the system and obtain all claims reported that include that doctor's name. The claim representative could then evaluate the information and decide if further investigation is warranted. By using claim databases such as ISO ClaimSearch, the claim representative can perform a more thorough investigation and more effectively detect fraud.

Internet

The Internet is a powerful investigative tool for claim representatives. It allows them to obtain timely information from worldwide sources and to quickly share information with others outside their companies. The Internet allows online reporting and real-time loss notification. It can help claim representatives detect fraud or replace an unusual piece of equipment by locating possible suppliers. The Internet can also facilitate the inspection of a loss thousands of miles away by helping the claim representative contact a local representative who can inspect and report on the damage.

Hundreds of Web sites offer information useful to claim representatives. They provide links to information such as state vital statistics,[4] checklists for evaluating damages,[5] products that have been recalled,[6] and expert witnesses on various topics.[7] In addition, many business, healthcare institution, and medical college Web sites offer information on medical diagnosis and treatment options and outcomes.

Other Investigative Tools

Insurers and TPAs provide a variety of other investigative tools to their claim representatives to ensure consistent quality claim handling throughout the department. These tools can be fairly simple, such as an estimating program that uses room dimensions to calculate the amount of paint needed to repaint a room. Others can be complex, such as business rule engines that analyze claims for fraud indicators or coverage issues and then refer the claim to the appropriate party for response. Business rule engines use insurer-specific criteria to flag claims meeting those criteria. This process can assist claim supervisors in assigning the claim to the claim representative with the skills needed to handle the claim.

These investigative tools are meant to supplement the claim representative's basic investigation and offer options to facilitate the decision-making process. They gather data and present it for action, and they automate many tasks that are tangential to the primary claim handling functions of interviewing insureds and claimants, inspecting damages, and negotiating settlements. Expert injury evaluation tools can give the claim representative the benefit of many years' worth of historical data for use in evaluating an injury claim.

The claim representative must remember that the options these tools provide are not a substitute for a reasoned analysis of the claim. Overall, these tools save the claim representative time and effort in gathering data, but they do not replace the need for human reasoning in claim handling.

If claim representatives use all the investigative tools at their disposal wisely, the result should be a thoroughly investigated claim. But investigating the claim is only the starting point in the claim adjustment process. The investigation must give the claim representative sufficient information to make a well-reasoned decision about the cause of loss, liability for the loss, and the amount of damage. Because determining cause of loss, liability, and damages is different depending on the type of claim, the various types of claims—property, bodily injury, and workers' compensation—are discussed separately in the following sections.

PROPERTY DAMAGE CLAIM INVESTIGATION

For the purpose of this text, property damage claims are divided into two categories: auto physical damage claims and all other property damage claims. The main reason for this distinction is that many insurers have claim representatives who are dedicated to handling claims in only one of each of the two categories.

Determining Cause of Loss—Auto Physical Damage

Auto claims are usually divided among several different types of auto claim representatives. Some auto claim representatives handle only auto physical damage, while others handle bodily injuries that result from accidents. Because investigatory approaches are different for these two types of claims, this section discusses only the investigation needed for handling an *auto physical damage claim*, and the investigation of bodily injury claims is discussed in a subsequent section.

To determine the cause of loss in an auto physical damage claim, a claim representative requests either a written or recorded statement from the insured or the insured driver and obtains a copy of the police report, witness statements, and an estimate of damages. However, some claims may require more in-depth investigation. The claim representative may have to obtain photos of the accident scene or have an expert reconstruct the accident. If fraud is suspected, the claim representative involves the SIU to determine whether fraud has been committed.

Initial Contact and Statements

After receiving a loss report for damage to an insured vehicle, a claim representative usually contacts the insured, most often by phone, to obtain the loss details. Depending on insurer guidelines, the claim representative may take a recorded statement from the insured at this time to obtain the details of the loss or accident in the insured's own words. During the recorded statement, the claim representative asks the insured to verify ownership, describe the circumstances surrounding the accident, and describe any injuries sustained. The claim representative also learns what damage the vehicle sustained and where the vehicle is located. Additional information gathered at this time includes whether witnesses saw the accident and, if so, how to contact them, whether police responded to the accident scene, and whether the police completed an accident report. The claim representative may also take a recorded statement from the insured driver (if different from the owner) and any passengers or witnesses, which may corroborate the insured's version of how the accident occurred.

Some insurers use statement forms rather than have claim representatives take recorded statements. These statement forms ask for accident details and often ask for a diagram. Insurers send these forms to the insured, the insured driver, and any passengers or witnesses to collect as much information as possible.

Inspection

The claim representative usually arranges for an appraiser to inspect the damaged vehicles and prepare damage estimates. The appraiser may take photos of the vehicles to help corroborate the recorded statements.

The appraiser or the claim representative should verify the vehicle identification number (VIN), which uniquely identifies the specific vehicle and the registered owner as well as specific repair parts to be used. Verifying the VIN is particularly important if a vehicle has been stolen or destroyed because many fraudulent attempts to claim damages for stolen vehicles are made on vehicles that have intentionally been burned, dumped into a body of water, or entirely dismantled. Checking the VIN can uncover such fraud attempts by verifying that the burned, dumped, or dismantled vehicle is the one insured on the policy.

Decoding the Vehicle Identification Number (VIN)

The VIN is composed of seventeen numbers and letters. The following is an example:

WD24B76E32A435891

The first three characters are referred to as the World Manufacturer Identifier (WD2):

WD24B67E32A435891

- The first character identifies the country of manufacture, such as Germany (W).*
- The second character identifies the manufacturer, such as Mercedes Benz (D).
- The third character identified the vehicle type of manufacturing division.

The characters in the fourth through eighth positions identify the vehicle's attributes, such as body style, engine type, model, or series:

WD24B67E32A435891

The character in the ninth position is an accuracy check digit that is created by a mathematical formula:

WD24B76E32A435891

The tenth character identifies the model year, such as 2002 (2):

WD24B76E32A435891

The eleventh character identifies the assembly plant code, which is designated by the manufacturer:

WD24B76E32A435891

The last six characters identify the sequence of the vehicle in production. In this example, the last group of characters is referred to as the vehicle identifier:

WD24B76E32A435891

* The numbering system differs for manufacturers that produce fewer than 500 vehicles a year. In that case, the third character is always a 9 and the twelfth, thirteenth, and fourteenth characters identify and country and the manufacturer.

The appraiser prepares a damage estimate that includes the items to be repaired or replaced, the amount of labor involved, and the parts involved. This estimate is costed out (the price of materials and labor are added) and sent to the claim representative, the insured or claimant, and the repair facility. The claim representative uses this estimate to conclude the claim.

Documentation

The file documentation for an auto physical damage claim usually includes the following:

- Statements from the insured, drivers, and witnesses
- Photos of the damaged vehicle
- Police report

- Fire marshal report (if applicable)
- Damage estimates
- Any reports by experts (if applicable)

The file also contains any reports that the claim representative has prepared, the file activity notes, and copies of any correspondence sent or received. Much of this documentation is contained electronically in the claim file. If the vehicle is a total loss, whether from damage or from a theft, the file should contain an explanation of how the total loss was calculated. The file usually contains the vehicle title and a statement about how the vehicle was disposed of, whether taken to a salvage yard or returned to the insured.

Fire Claims

In the event of a fire, the claim representative may assign an origin and cause expert to inspect the vehicle and determine how the fire started. Fires are caused by either accident, intent (arson), or negligence. If the origin and cause expert determines that the fire started by accident, the claim representative may not need any further information to conclude the claim. If the origin and cause expert determines that the fire was intentionally set, the claim representative works with SIU staff to determine whether the insured was involved. If the origin and cause expert determines that the fire was caused by negligence, such as a faulty part, the claim representative investigates who put that part into the vehicle and whether that party is responsible for the loss. If the claim representative determines that the part was defective or installed incorrectly, the claim representative may subrogate against the manufacturer or installer.

Theft Claims

If a vehicle is allegedly stolen, the claim will have one of the following four outcomes:

1. The vehicle is not recovered.
2. The vehicle is recovered and repaired.
3. The vehicle is recovered but is a total loss.
4. The claim is denied because of fraud or another coverage defense.

When assigned a theft claim, the claim representative should immediately verify the existence of the vehicle and the loss circumstances by taking a recorded statement from the insured. When questioning the insured about the loss, the claim representative should consider all possible scenarios for the vehicle's disappearance. For example, the police may have impounded the vehicle if it was illegally parked, or the vehicle may have been repossessed by a bank. The statement should also include when and where the vehicle was acquired, the VIN, whether the vehicle was financed, and whether it had any recent repairs. The claim representative should ascertain the vehicle's overall condition, the vehicle options, and the mileage. This information helps calculate the vehicle's value.

When a vehicle is stolen, the insured has a duty to report the theft to the police. The claim representative should obtain a copy of the police report to help verify the loss. If a police report is not made, the claim representative should begin looking for other indicators of fraud, such as the following:

- Domestic problems—an unhappy spouse or child may have taken the vehicle.
- Significant debt—an insurance settlement may help alleviate debt.
- Invalid VIN—an invalid VIN could mean that the car insured was fictitious (the car does not exist) and was created for the purpose of submitting a claim.
- Leased vehicle with excessive mileage—the lessee would not have to pay the mileage penalty if the car is stolen.
- Major repair work needed—it is less expensive to get a new car paid for by insurance rather than pay for repairs.
- Unusual amount of personal property in the vehicle at the time of the loss—a claim for high value personal property is a way to collect more on the claim.

If the vehicle is recovered, some damage will probably require repairs. The claim representative should have the recovered vehicle inspected and the damage appraised. If the vehicle has not been recovered within a designated period, most insurers declare the vehicle a total loss, and the claim representative determines the vehicle's value at the time of the loss. The insured completes an affidavit of vehicle theft, an odometer statement, and other necessary documents so that the claim can be paid.

Determining Cause of Loss—Other Property Damage

The investigation of other property damage claims is similar to that of auto physical damage claims because such claims usually involve physical damage to a building or its contents or theft of property from a building.

Residential and commercial buildings and their contents can be damaged by numerous causes of loss, such as fire; lightning; explosion; windstorm; hail; smoke; vehicles; aircraft; riot or civil commotion; vandalism or malicious mischief; sprinkler leakage; sinkhole collapse; volcanic action; falling objects; water; and the weight of snow, ice, or sleet. The building's contents can be damaged by other causes as well, or they can be stolen. These causes of loss are described in the property policy as either covered causes of loss or excluded causes of loss. The policy also describes how the claim will be handled. The claim representative must investigate the cause of loss to determine if it is covered by the policy.

Initial Contact and Statements

On receipt of a claim, the claim representative contacts the insured to get initial information about the cause of the loss and the extent of the damage.

If the loss involves a theft, the claim representative usually takes a recorded statement to preserve the insured's description of the loss. If the loss involves only property damage, the claim representative interviews the insured to determine how the loss occurred and to discuss emergency repairs or temporary relocation with the insured. During these discussions, the claim representative must be careful not to waive any policy provisions.

Inspection

After contacting the insured, the claim representative often inspects the building or assigns an outside claim representative or an independent adjuster to do so. During the onsite inspection, the claim representative obtains detailed facts about the cause of the loss. The claim representative may photograph or visually record the damage and may draw diagrams to depict the damaged areas.

During or after the inspection, the claim representative creates a scope of the loss. The **scope** is a list of the areas damaged that includes the type of damage (such as fire, smoke, or water), a description of the proposed action to take regarding the damaged property (such as repair, replace, remove, or demolish), and the area's measurements. The claim representative may then use the scope to create the damage estimate or may send the scope to contractors who bid on the job. The estimate includes the quantity and price of materials and labor needed to complete the repairs.

Scope
A list of the areas damaged that includes the type of damage, a description of the proposed action to take regarding the damaged property (such as repair, replace, remove, or demolish), and the area's measurements.

Documentation

Documentation of a loss may include statements, inspection reports, estimates, and police and fire reports. In the event of a fire, the claim representative may interview witnesses, neighbors, and the police or fire personnel who were on the scene. If the loss involves a weather-related condition such as hail, lightning, windstorm, or heavy rain, then the claim representative often requests confirmation of the condition from a weather tracking source or a local television station.

Contents Claims

If a building has suffered physical damage, some or all of its contents may also be damaged. The insured and the claim representative create an inventory of the damaged items and determine their value. A similar inventory of missing contents is completed if a theft or burglary has occurred. For a business, inventory records show what was on hand and how much it was worth. Such records do not exist for homes. Receipts for items may no longer exist, but the insured may have photos or video tapes of the items. The claim representative evaluates the personal property claimed by the insured against the insured's circumstances and reasonable conditions. For example, if the insured claims that six sets of golf clubs were stolen from the car's trunk, the claim representative must consider why the insured would own six sets of golf clubs and whether the trunk would actually hold them all.

Loss of Income Claims

Commercial entities are subject to another type of property loss, to which homeowners are not. They can lose business income as a result of physical damage to the building or its contents. Some policies cover loss of business income, and adjusting such losses is a complicated process. Usually, only very experienced claim representatives handle business income losses, and they often request an accountant's assistance.

Determining Liability

Generally in a first-party policy, the claim representative does not have to make a liability determination to pay the insured's claim. However, during the investigation of a property claim, the claim representative may determine that a third party is responsible for the damage to the insured's property. Once the claim has been paid to the insured, the claim representative attempts to recover the amount of the claim payment (and usually the insured's deductible) from the responsible third party through subrogation. Usually, the claim representative notifies the third party that it is considered responsible for the damage, and the third party's insurer negotiates a settlement of the damages. In some cases, these subrogation claims are decided through arbitration.

Determining Amount of Damage

Claim representatives determine the amount of damage for property claims and apply the policy provisions to that amount to determine what is payable under the policy. Property damage is usually valued at **replacement cost**, which is the cost to repair or replace property using new materials of like kind and quality with no deduction for depreciation, or at **actual cash value (ACV)**, which is calculated by determining the replacement cost and subtracting depreciation.

Replacement cost
The cost to repair or replace property using new materials of like kind and quality with no deduction for depreciation.

Actual cash value (ACV)
A method of valuation of property calculated as the replacement cost minus depreciation.

Claim representatives can determine the amount of property damage by reviewing estimates provided by repair facilities such as auto body repair shops and building contractors. Some claim representatives are trained to prepare their own estimates of damage; others may rely on specialists within the claim department to prepare those estimates. Computers can also be used to estimate damage. A claim representative with access to a computer estimating system inspects the damage and enters the information into a computer. Using a database of prices and rates for materials and labor, the computer program performs calculations and prints an estimate.

In addition to the direct loss to property, an insured business may suffer other losses, such as the following:

- Expenses to expedite the replacement of damaged property that is no longer usable to keep a business going

- Expenses to expedite the repair of the damaged property to keep a business going
- Income lost because damaged property cannot be replaced or repaired quickly enough to avoid losing a sale

For example, a business may incur costs to ship repair parts overnight so that repairs can be completed quickly. A manufacturer may lose income while the factory is shut down because of damage.

Personal lines insureds suffer similar types of losses. For example, a personal lines insured may need to rent a car while the damaged car is being repaired. If a home is damaged and is unfit to live in, an insured may incur extra expenses to live in a hotel until repairs are completed.

Claim representatives can determine the amount of damages for some of these losses by reviewing bills, such as the rental car bill or overnight shipping bill. However, the amount of damages for lost income can be more difficult to determine and may require the services of an accountant or economist.

Auto Physical Damage

Auto physical damage claims generally involve one of the following three scenarios:

1. Vehicle is damaged and repairable.
2. Vehicle is damage beyond repair.
3. Vehicle is stolen and not recovered.

When a vehicle is repairable, the claim representative develops an estimate or obtains repair estimates from an appraiser or an auto repair shop. The claim representative concludes the claim by paying the insured the amount to repair the damage, minus the deductible.

Whether the vehicle is declared a total loss because it is not recovered or because of damage (either caused during a theft or in an accident) the claim representative must determine the vehicle's actual cash value at the time of the loss and any salvage value the damaged vehicle may have. Salvage value is the amount that a salvage yard pays for the damaged vehicle minus expenses such as towing and storage.

Claim representatives determine ACV at the time of loss by using reference material such as the *Kelley Blue Book* or the National Automobile Dealers Association (NADA) *Official Used Car Guide*. The claim representative must know the vehicle's make, model, and year, along with the various options on the vehicle and the vehicle's mileage to correctly determine the ACV.

Claim representatives determine salvage value by obtaining bids from various salvage dealers, either through a salvage pool or a bid process.

In some cases, repairing the vehicle may not be cost effective, and the vehicle is determined to be a total loss. To determine whether a vehicle is worth repairing, a claim representative must know the vehicle's ACV, the cost of the repairs, and the salvage value. Each insurer sets the threshold for a total loss, such as 75 or 85 percent threshold, and if the cost to repair the vehicle (including salvage value) exceeds that percent threshold, the vehicle is determined to be a total loss and the claim is paid accordingly. If the insured elects to retain ownership of a vehicle that is damaged beyond repair, the claim calculation includes a salvage value, as follows:

$$\text{Claim payment} = \text{ACV} - \text{Deductible} - \text{Salvage}.$$

If a vehicle is stolen and not recovered, it is declared a total loss, and the claim representative calculates the claim payment as follows:

$$\text{Claim payment} = \text{ACV} - \text{Deductible}.$$

All Other Property Damage

Claim representatives determine the value of damaged property using ACV or replacement cost. Some property, such as a work of art, may be paid on a stated value that is listed in the policy.

The definition of ACV for a building is similar to that for an auto, but the method of determining ACV is different. To determine the ACV for a repair estimate, the claim representative must know the useful life of building components and must be familiar with court decisions about ACV in the applicable jurisdiction.

The claim representative examines each item needing repair and quantifies the extent of betterment. Betterment is another way of expressing depreciation. The item's age, condition, and expected use affect the depreciation amount. An item's depreciation, or betterment, amount is how much better, or more valuable, a new item is compared to the older item.

If an entire building must be replaced, the ACV may be the fair market value. Some courts have interpreted fair market value to mean ACV. The **fair market value** is the amount at which a knowledgeable buyer, under no unusual pressure, would be willing to buy a building, and how much a knowledgeable seller, under no unusual pressure, would be willing to sell it. The claim representative must know the law in the applicable state to determine whether to use fair market value as a means of valuation.

Replacement cost of a building or personal property is somewhat easier to calculate. Replacement cost is the actual cost to repair or replace the building or personal property with a building or personal property of like kind and quality. The claim representative can determine this cost estimate by using a software package or, alternately, by consulting a general contractor who is bidding to perform the work.

Fair market value
The amount at which a knowledgeable buyer, under no unusual pressure, would be willing to buy property; and a knowledgeable seller, under no unusual pressure, would be willing to sell it.

After a first-party loss, an insured may need immediate money to pay for living expenses or medical expenses or to repair or replace damaged property. For example, if the insured's home has been destroyed, the insured may need to purchase clothing and personal care products. However, the claim representative needs time to investigate the loss, determine the total amount to which the insured is entitled, and pay the claim. To meet the insured's immediate needs, the claim representative may make an **advance payment** to the insured to cover the immediate expenses resulting from the loss.

Advance payment
Payment to the insured to cover the immediate expenses resulting from the loss.

Insurers that use advance payments require the insured to sign an advance payment receipt when each payment is issued. The receipt states that the advance payments will be credited to the total amount of the final settlement or judgment. The claim representative can then send checks or drafts directly to the insured, or the insured may authorize the payment to be sent directly to a contractor working on the property. Claim representatives should consult the insurer's procedure manual on how to use advance payments. In addition, claim supervisors can provide guidance on when and how advance payments should be made.

BODILY INJURY CLAIM INVESTIGATION

People can be injured in countless ways. They can be injured in car accidents. They may fall at a grocery store or in a neighbor's backyard. They can be injured by faulty products or get food poisoning from food served in restaurants. Those who are injured may pursue the responsible parties. While each of these losses may be covered under a different type of policy, the investigation of the cause of loss and amount of damage is generally the same because they are all liability claims against the responsible parties. The only bodily injury claims that are handled differently are workers' compensation claims, which are explained in a separate section.

Determining Cause of Loss

Bodily injury investigations to determine cause of loss focus on how the accident happened. The investigation is the same whether the injury is to an insured or to a third party. Most often, a claim representative receives a first report of loss that includes basic information on how the loss occurred and who was injured. However, the first notice that an injury has occurred maybe the insured's notice of a lawsuit alleging injury resulting from the insured's negligence.

When a lawsuit is the first report of loss, the claim representative assigns it to defense counsel while completing the investigation into the cause of loss. Claim representatives should follow the insurer's procedures on how these lawsuits should be handled.

Initial Contact and Statements

When an insurer receives a first report of injury, the claim representative's first action is to contact the insured and take a statement about the loss circumstances. The claim representative also takes statements from any witnesses and from the injured party, provided the injured party is not represented by a lawyer. If the injured party has retained a lawyer, the claim representative must contact the lawyer and get permission to take the statement. The statements establish what each party was doing at the time of the accident and assist the claim representative in determining who was at fault.

Documentation

To get a clear picture of the accident, the claim representative can obtain any documentation related to the loss, such as a police report or police photos and diagrams. The claim representative also obtains a copy of the reports of any emergency or rescue personnel who responded to the accident scene. With proper authorization from the injured party, the claim representative requests copies of medical treatment records in order to compare them to the various descriptions of the accident or injury. These records include the emergency room reports; physician bills and reports; hospital records that contain nurses' notes; results of lab tests, x-rays, and other diagnostic procedures; and reports from rehabilitation services. The claim representative may also request copies of any toxicology reports to determine whether the parties to the accident had any drugs, toxins, or alcohol in their bloodstreams at the time of the accident. Finally, a claim representative may obtain an autopsy report if death results from an accident or from a cause of loss that is not readily apparent.

Using Experts

If an accident is particularly complex or involves an allegation of a product defect or malfunction, the claim representative may want to hire an expert to assist in the investigation. As previously mentioned, an accident reconstruction expert can determine how an accident occurred using photos of the scene, witness accounts, measurements of the damage to the vehicles involved, and the nature of the injuries sustained. An engineer specializing in vehicles can inspect a vehicle and determine whether the brakes malfunctioned. An electrical engineer can inspect a product to determine whether wiring caused a malfunction. And a chemist may be asked to check for the presence of bacteria or other contaminants in food or beverages.

Determining Liability

Once satisfied about the cause of the loss, the claim representative can make a liability determination, that is, form an opinion about who is at fault or legally liable for the accident. If the facts show that the third party slipped and fell in a puddle of water in the insured's store and the insured had notice of the puddle and had not cleaned it up, then the insured may be 100 percent at fault for the accident. If the facts show that the insured and the third party both lost control of their vehicles because of an ice patch on the road, then they may each be assigned 50 percent of the fault. Assigning fault is an art rather than a science. The claim representative determines liability based on experience, case law, and the claim's facts. Ultimately, the final apportionment of liability is often negotiated between the claim representatives and/or lawyers representing the various parties. The negotiators use the principles of legal liability to determine the percentage of negligence apportioned to each party and how much each party must pay.

Determining Amount of Damages

While investigating the cause of the loss, the claim representative in a bodily injury claim also determines the amount of the damages. Note that there is a distinction made between the physical loss, injury, or deterioration of value (damage) and the monetary compensation for the loss or injury (damages). Bodily injury claims consist of two types of damages: special damages and general damages. Special damages or "specials" are out of pocket expenses that the injured person or the person's family incurs as a result of a loss, such as medical expenses, wage loss, funeral expenses, or repair bills. When determining special damages, the claim representative must do both of the following:

- Verify the amount of the damages claimed
- Verify that the special damages are related to the insured's accident

To verify the amount of damages claimed, the claim representative may call the party who provided the service to the injured party and confirm that the service was provided, and that the date and cost of the service shown on the bill are correct. For example, the claim representative may call a pharmacy to determine whether it rented a set of crutches to the claimant, for how long, and at what cost.

To verify that the special damages are related to the accident, the claim representative may have to consult a nurse or doctor who can give an opinion that a service, such as renting crutches, was necessary as a result of the accident.

General damages compensate a victim for losses, such as, pain and suffering that do not involve specific measurable expenses are more difficult to determine than special damages because they are subjective. General damages include items such as the monetary value associated with conditions, the injured party's pain and suffering, inconvenience, disfigurement, and other intangibles. Claim representatives use their experience and the experience of other claim representatives and lawyers to appropriately value general damages.

Insurers vary on the use of advance payments in liability claims. Generally, for liability claims, advance payments are used in cases of clear liability on the insured's part, when the claimant's injuries are serious, or when the claimant has demonstrated a financial need. When the claim representative offers to help relieve the claimant's concerns about financial obligations through advance payments, the claimant is more likely to view the insurer favorably. This can help foster cooperation and trust, and give the claimant a reason to believe that the claim has been handled fairly.

Future Damages

Future damages, which are damages that continue past the time of settlement, can be either special or general damages. For example, if a child has been scarred in an auto accident, a plastic surgeon may estimate the future expense of treating the scar. In a workers' compensation claim in which the employee is unable to work, the claim representative can estimate the future wage loss by estimating the length of the disability. If the claimant is permanently disabled, the claimant may recover damages for lost future earning capacity. Calculating lost future earning capacity can be difficult, and it often requires experts, such as accountants and economists. Pain and suffering also may continue into the future.

In some cases, the injured person may be willing to settle the claim but only with a specific allowance for future medical care. This settlement can be finalized with a special release called a "Release of All Claims—Open Future Medical" or an "Open End Release Agreement." The injured claimant releases the insured from future liability but the release specifies an amount of money for future incurred medical expenses. Typically, such a release specifies a deadline for discontinuing payments for medical expenses.

Punitive Damages

Punitive damages are payments awarded to punish a wrongdoer for a reckless, malicious, or deceitful act and to deter similar conduct. Such damages are awarded in addition to other damage awards. Liability insurance policies vary on whether they cover punitive damages. Also, state laws vary on whether insurers are required to pay punitive damages. Because standard liability policies do not define the term "damages," some courts have held that punitive damages are covered just as compensatory damages are covered, so they are insurable. Other courts have reasoned that insuring punitive damages defeats their purpose by allowing the wrongdoer to transfer financial responsibility for the wrongful act to the insurer. Courts in some states have not taken a position on the insurability of punitive damages.

In states in which statutes or court decisions prohibit insurance for punitive damages, the claim representative should inform the insured that the policy does not cover punitive damages. The claim representative should explain that, if a lawsuit is filed, the insurer defends the insured with respect to the general damages, but not punitive damages and that the insured can hire a lawyer, at his or her own expense, for representation relating to punitive damages.

Valuation of Special Damages

Claim representatives often use independent medical reviewers to determine whether medical expenses are reasonable and necessary. Incurred and future doctor and hospital bills are examples of medical expenses that are considered special damages in bodily injury claims. Travel expenses incurred going to and from healthcare providers and medical expenses that are reasonable and necessary are also special damages, as are Wage losses. Wage losses refer to the actual economic loss resulting from an inability to perform a specific job because of the injury. Wage loss is the loss of earnings from the date of the injury to the time recovery is complete. Loss of earning capacity is based on future estimated losses resulting from a permanent disability.

Valuation of General Damages

In bodily injury claims, the claimant may present a claim for general damages. Claim representatives consider future, as well as past, pain and suffering in this evaluation. To value general damages in a bodily injury claim, claim representatives should answer the following questions:

- What are the specific injuries, and what type of pain is associated with them?
- Are the injuries consistent with the accident?
- Did symptoms (and pain) preexist the accident?
- Do other causes contribute to the pain?
- Is pain severe, and is it acute or chronic?
- What is the resulting disability, and how does it affect the claimant's daily activities and ability to work and enjoy life?
- How significantly do the claimant's age and occupation affect the pain and suffering?

When valuing pain and suffering claims, claim representatives can break a claim down into three elements: (1) physical pain, (2) mental suffering, and (3) mental anguish. Physical pain can result from the injury itself, from effects of the healing process, from physical therapy, and from painful diagnostic procedures. Mental suffering can include the fear, anxiety, depression, and anger related to a physical injury as well as grief, despair, and humiliation. Mental anguish is the unpleasant mental consequence resulting from an injury. It is often used to describe the emotional or personal injuries not directly related to physical pain. The anguish over a scar and the embarrassment of being unable to perform normal activities are examples of mental anguish.

Damages for pain and suffering are proven by the testimony of medical providers; the individual's own testimony; and the testimony of others such as employers, clergy, family members, or friends. Such testimony can relate to the severity, intensity, and duration of the injured person's pain and suffering.

A claim representative should evaluate whether the injury will result in a permanent impairment or disability, which could increase the claim's value. The following are some issues to consider regarding permanent injuries:

- Have job/family and recreation been changed for the worse as a result of this permanent injury?
- Does chronic pain result from the injury?
- Does disability or disfigurement result from the injury?
- Has the person's personality been affected?

After determining the answers to these questions, claim representatives can contact experts to help value the potential losses resulting from the permanent impairment or disability.

Most legal jurisdictions treat loss of enjoyment as compensable general damages, distinguishable from pain and suffering. Loss of enjoyment claims are based on the claimant's reduced capacity to enjoy certain activities, including the loss of physical and intellectual gratification and other lifestyle losses. The term "hedonic damages" is sometimes used interchangeably with enjoyment damages. Loss of enjoyment damages has two components. The first is a medically determined permanent injury. The second is the comparison of what the person did before the accident and what the person can do after the accident.

Compensation for pain and suffering frequently constitutes the largest part of a bodily injury settlement. Insurers commonly find a two-to-one ratio of pain and suffering damages to medical expenses.

Methods for Determining the Value of a Bodily Injury Claim

Claim representatives may use one or more of the following methods for determining the value of a bodily injury claim:

- Individual case method
- Roundtable method
- Formula method
- Expert systems

The individual case method involves determining the claim's value based on all the claim's circumstances and the claim representative's experience in similar cases. Because of the numerous factors that go into this valuation, the individual case method may yield valuations that vary by claim representative. However, the following four factors are generally considered in determining a value:

1. The likelihood that the insured will obtain a favorable verdict
2. The insured's proportionate share of liability in the event of an unfavorable verdict
3. The numerous variables that affect a jury's likely award
4. A reasonable estimate of damages that the claimant will likely be able to prove in court

The roundtable method of valuing a bodily injury claim involves two or more claim representatives evaluating the claim file and each suggesting a settlement (or claim) value. After discussing the suggested values, the claim representatives may reach a consensus settlement range or calculated an average of all the figures to use as the basis for a settlement offer.

The formula method involves using a mathematical formula to set the claim value. This formula may be based on the assumption that a certain ratio exists between medical expenses and general damages. For example, the value of a claim with $1,000 in medical expenses and a "three times specials" formula would be $4,000 ($1,000 for medical expenses plus $3,000 for general damages).

Expert systems set a claim value by using computer software to, in theory, simulate the thought process of experienced, knowledgeable claim professionals. An expert system can be calibrated to match specific insurer guidelines and to the requirements of specific legal jurisdictions. The expert system contains the following components:

- A database of knowledge (facts) about particular types of claims.
- Relevant facts, information, assumptions, and procedures for solving claim valuation problems.
- A user interface that allows the user to present questions or answer prompts to help develop values. For example, a claim representative might input into the system that the claimant suffered a fractured right wrist. The system might respond with questions about whether the fracture required surgery or whether the person was right handed.
- An "inference engine" that controls how the expert system searches the knowledge base and produces conclusions.

WORKERS' COMPENSATION CLAIM INVESTIGATION

Workers' compensation claims involve the bodily injury, disease, or death of a worker. However, the investigation into the cause and the amount of the loss is distinguishable from that of other bodily injury claims because of the difference in the coverages. While most injuries are covered by the state workers' compensation statutes, some are not. The claim representative must know which injuries are and are not covered by the specific state statute and must conduct the investigation accordingly. For example, some states do not cover injuries arising out of the willful failure to use a safety device, such as the removal of a safety guard from a circular saw or a drill press.

In the investigation, the claim representative must determine whether the injury arose out of and in the course of employment. Workers can suffer injuries at work that are unrelated to employment, such as an office worker who faints from a viral infection while at work and breaks his arm in the fall. While the accident or injury takes place at work, the virus and fainting are unrelated to the job duties of the office worker. The injury also must occur in the course of the employee's employment. The claim representative must determine whether the injury occurred as a result of a work-related activity or was incidental to work. If an office worker is struck by a co-worker's car in the parking lot of their office building as they arrive for work, that injury is generally not considered to have occurred during the course of employment because generally, employment does not begin until workers are on the work premises.

Determining Compensability

Workers' compensation investigations focus on compensability and the payment of statutorily defined benefits. Compensability determination is similar to the cause of loss determination, but workers' compensation investigations examine additional issues. For a claim to be compensable (payable), the claim representative must determine whether the injured party is an employee under the workers' compensation statute, whether the injury is covered under the statute, and whether the injury arose out of and in the course of employment. Generally, the claim representative conducts the compensability investigation at the accident scene, which is most often the employer's location.

Initial Contact and Statements

As part of the process of determining compensability, the claim representative takes statements from the injured worker, any witnesses to the injury, and the injured worker's supervisor. These statements focus on what the injured worker was doing at the time of the injury and whether the activity that caused the injury was employment-related.

Documentation

The claim representative requests records from the employer, such as payroll records, to determine the employment status and wage loss. Copies of pre-employment physical reports, safety training records, and other pertinent documents can be obtained from the human resources department. The claim representative may also photograph the area in which the worker was injured or the piece of machinery that caused the injury.

Claim representatives may obtain medical reports from the emergency room, hospital, and treating doctor to document the injury. For some types of injury, rehabilitation and training reports may be available. The claim file also contains medical bills submitted for payment, wage loss calculations, and an explanation of how any final settlement was determined.

Using Experts

Claim representatives handling workers' compensation claims can use a variety of experts to assist them in determining compensability and the claim's value. These experts, usually from medical rehabilitation and vocational services, evaluate the extent of the injured worker's injury, length of disability, likelihood of recovery, and further employment possibilities. The claim representative may also use an outside investigator, if fraud is suspected. Also, if a piece of faulty equipment caused the injury, the claim representative may hire an engineer and an accident reconstruction service to document the loss for subrogation against the equipment manufacturer.

Determining Liability

The workers' compensation claim representative is usually not concerned with determining liability because workers' compensation statutes are not fault based, meaning that workers are compensated regardless of fault. However, claim representatives are interested in learning whether the injury was self-inflicted or the acts of a third party caused the injury. If the injury was intentional, the claim may be denied because most workers' compensation statutes do not cover intentional injuries. If a third party, such as the manufacturer of a machine, is found to have caused the injury, the claim representative can subrogate against the third party to recover any workers' compensation benefits paid to the injured worker.

Determining Benefits

Rather than determine general and special damages as in other bodily injury claims, a workers' compensation claim representative determines what statutory benefits the injured worker is entitled to receive and how much to pay for those benefits. The following benefits are payable under workers' compensation:

- Medical benefits
- Wage loss benefits
- Rehabilitation benefits
- Death benefits

A workers' compensation claim representative pays the injured worker's medical expenses after reviewing the medical records to determine that the treatments are related to the injury and are medically necessary. To make this determination, the workers' compensation claim representative must have a working knowledge of medical terminology and procedures. Based on the medical records, the claim representative also determines—often with the help of experts—whether the injured worker has suffered a permanent disability from the injury or whether the worker can return to work, either at the same job or another type of job. Vocational rehabilitation and physical rehabilitation expenses are payable under workers' compensation.

The claim representative uses the medical records and the treating doctor's records to determine how long the injured worker will be unable to work and to calculate the appropriate amount of wage loss benefit to pay. The claim representative may also pay death benefits, that is, funeral expenses or survivor's benefits if the injured worker has died.

SUMMARY

This chapter provides the claim representative with the tools to perform a good-faith investigation into the cause of a loss, liability for a loss, and the amount of damages resulting from a loss.

In preparation for performing a good-faith investigation, the claim representative must understand the concept of legal liability. Legal liability arises from civil law and is based on torts, contracts, and statutes. The three classes of torts with which the claim representative is concerned are: (1) negligence, (2) strict liability, and (3) intentional torts. The claim representative also handles claims based on contractual liability.

Regardless of the type of claim, the claim representative focuses on determining who was involved in the loss, what was damaged in the loss, when the loss occurred, where the loss occurred, how the loss occurred, and what the amount or cost of the resulting damage or injury is.

To make those determinations, the claim representative can use the following tools:

- Loss notice forms, which provide the initial investigative information about a claim, including identity of claimant, injured persons, other people involved, and witnesses; and property damaged
- Policy information, which describes who and what are covered by the policy, the duration of coverage, the causes of losses covered, and any exclusions to coverage
- Statements from the claimant, injured parties, and witnesses, which provide information about how the loss occurred
- Diagrams, photos, and videos of an accident scene, damaged property, or bodily injuries
- Experts who provide services, such as evaluating the cause or value of a loss
- Records and reports, such as police reports, workers' compensation accident reports, and medical reports
- Industry databases, which provide information that can be used to detect fraud or gather data on various types of claims
- The Internet, for access to Web sites that provide such information as vital statistics, checklists for evaluating damages, product recalls, and expert witnesses
- Other investigative tools, such as computer programs that calculate room dimensions or that analyze claims for fraud

These investigative tools and techniques are similar for all investigations, but each type of claim—property damage, bodily injury, or workers' compensation—is unique in how it is investigated and how damages are determined.

One type of property damage claim, damage to autos, may arise from auto accidents, fire, or theft. Other types of property damage claims may be for personal or commercial property and may involve contents of buildings in addition to buildings and land. Commercial property claims may also include loss of business income. For purposes of claim determination, damaged or lost property may be valued at replacement value or at actual cash value, depending on the type of property and on the insurance policy.

A bodily injury claim investigation focuses on determining how an injury occurred. Bodily injury damages include special damages and general damages. Punitive damages may also be imposed if the injuries result from malicious or outrageous conduct. Claim representatives may use one or more of the following methods for determining the value of a bodily injury claim: the individual case method, the roundtable method, the formula method, and expert systems.

For workers' compensation claims, the claim representative's investigation focuses on determining whether the injury falls under workers' compensation coverage as defined by state law and whether the injury arose out of and in the course of employment. The claim representative is usually not concerned with determining liability because the workers' compensation statutes are not fault based.

Insurance fraud costs insurers and policyholders millions of dollars each year. As the first line of defense against fraudulent claims, claim representatives must always be on the lookout for facts and circumstances that signal a fraudulent claim. Because fraud is a major concern for a claim representative, a thorough discussion of fraud and fraud investigation appears in the next chapter.

CHAPTER NOTES

1. Association for Cooperative Operations Research and Development (ACORD), "Mission," ACORD Global Insurance Standards, January 21, 2005, www.acord.com/about/mission.aspx (accessed November 10, 2005).
2. Adapted from "Effective Statements: A One-Day Course to Improve Investigative Interviewing" by Claims Training Services, 1999, p. 8.
3. ISO ClaimSearch, www.claimsearch.iso.com (accessed September 30, 2005).
4. For example, the National Center for Health Statistics, www.cdc.gove/nchs (accessed October 11, 2005).
5. For example, the Center for Forensic Economic Studies, www.cfes.com (accessed October 11, 2005).
6. For example, the Consumer Product Safety Commission, www.cpsc.gov (accessed October 11, 2005).
7. For example, ExpertPages, www.expertpages.com (accessed October 11, 2005).

Appendix

Written Statement

100 Lane Drive
Buckeye Lake, OH 43244
Friday, August 11, 200X
1:05 P.M.

I am Teddy Smith (no middle initial), age 32, married to Frances B. Smith, and we live at 100 Lane Drive, Buckeye Lake, Ohio. We have lived here for the past five and one-half years. My home phone number is 222-0000 and my business phone is 345-0000. For the past five years I have been employed as a plant supervisor for Good Food, Inc., located at 1508 Balsam Road in Columbus, Ohio. My manager's name is Edward Vance. I am paid a salary of $3,000 per month. My Social Security number is 125-00-9000. My Ohio driver's license number is NS 000 100, which was issued on March 16, 200X, and which is valid for X years. There are no restrictions to my driving, such as corrective lenses, etc., and I have been driving for 16 years. On August 8, 200X, at about 2:00 P.M., I was driving a 200X brown Chevrolet Corsica, which is titled in my name, on Connell Avenue in Buckeye Lake, Ohio. Mileage on my car at that time was about 22,000 miles, and my Ohio license plate number is ABC-162. I use the car to drive to work and as a family car. The car is in good shape with no previous damage, and I have had the car serviced regularly. I had my seat belt fastened at this time. No passengers were in my car. I was driving northbound on Connell Avenue to go back to work after having a late lunch at Angie's Restaurant, located at Connell Avenue and Revenue Road in Buckeye Lake. I did not drink any alcoholic beverages at lunch, nor was I taking drugs of any kind. The weather was fair and clear and the roads were dry as I approached the intersection of Connell Avenue and Main Street. I think the speed limit on Connell Avenue is 35 miles per hour. Connell Avenue is two lanes wide with parking lanes on each side of the street. Main Street is one lane in each direction with parking lanes on each side. The part of Main Street that is west of Connell Avenue curves somewhat and is not a straightaway as is the eastern side of the street. I would say that the curvature on Main Street begins near the doughnut shop on Connell Avenue. Connell Avenue traffic has a stop sign, and there are no stop signs for Main Street traffic. As I approached the intersection of Connell Avenue and Main Street I was driving approximately 30 miles per hour. I came to a full stop at the stop sign, looked to my left and right, and then pulled slowly into the intersection to cross Main Street. I believe I was in a stopped position for about one full second. To my left, a black van was parked, facing eastbound on Main Street. The van, combined with a line of parked cars and the curve in Main Street, hindered my view somewhat, so I had to pull slowly into the intersection. As I pulled into the intersection, I looked again to my left and then to my right and the way looked clear, so I proceeded through the intersection. All of a sudden I heard the screech of brakes to my left, and as I turned to my left, an Oldsmobile, which I later found out was driven by Ralph Morgan, struck my car in the left rear and spun the car around. I cannot estimate Morgan's speed. At the time of the impact, the front of my car was a few feet beyond the middle or center point of Main Street. At this point I couldn't have been traveling at more than 5 or 10 miles per hour since I had started from a stopped position at the stop sign. After the impact, my car came to a stop across the intersection at Star's Service Station. Ralph Morgan's car came to a stop over the curb on Main Street, facing in the opposite direction than he had been traveling. After my car came to a stop, I sat there momentarily as I was too emotionally shaken to move. Several bystanders came over to see if I was all right, and they finally helped me out of the car. An unknown bystander called the police and about five minutes later, two police cars from the Buckeye Police Department arrived at the scene along with an ambulance. During the crash, I bumped against the door and I must have hit my head on the steering wheel, as I had a large bruise on my forehead. Ralph Morgan was bleeding from the nose and holding his head when I first saw him, and he was very concerned for his passenger, who I later found out was Sandy Scott. Her face was bleeding and she was holding her nose. The Buckeye Lake Rescue Squad took Ralph Morgan and me to the Buckeye Lake Clinic. I don't know what happened to Sandy Scott. There were no accusations that I am aware of that were made after the accident by either me or Ralph Morgan. I did point out to the police officer that I thought the black van was illegally parked. I believe there were witnesses to the accident because immediately after it occurred, several people came to the scene trying to help, but I did not get the names of any eyewitnesses. As far as I know, neither Morgan nor I were cited for traffic violations as a result of the accident. The police questioned me briefly, and I told them I stopped at the stop sign, pulled slowly into the intersection, and the van had hindered my view. I do not know what Morgan told the police about the accident. At the clinic, I was X-rayed and released in about 45 minutes. The rear bumper of my car was hanging from the car, and the left rear quarter of the car was demolished. Ralph Morgan's car had extensive damage to the front end, and the windshield was cracked. There was debris from the accident lying in the intersection, and fluids were leaking from Morgan's car. Neither car was drivable after the accident. My car was towed to Tambourine Auto Body. I have read the preceding two pages and fourteen lines and they are true.

_____   _____
Claim Representative   Accident Victim

                                        _____
                                         Witness to Signing

Chapter 4

Direct Your Learning

Insurance Fraud

After learning the content of this chapter and completing the corresponding course guide assignment, you should be able to:

- Explain why insurance fraud is a threat to the financial stability of the insurance industry.
- Given a claim, identify the possible types of fraud involved.
- Describe the motives for insurance fraud.
- Given a claim, identify any fraud indicators present in the claim.
- Describe the anti-fraud efforts made by the following:
  - Insurers
  - Government
  - Industry organizations
- Define or describe each of the Key Words and Phrases for this chapter.

OUTLINE

Importance of Insurance Fraud Detection

Types of Insurance Fraud

Motives for Insurance Fraud

Factors That Influence Fraud

Fraud Indicators

Anti-Fraud Efforts

Summary

Develop Your Perspective

What are the main topics covered in the chapter?

The costs of insurance fraud to insurers and to the public continue to grow. This chapter explores issues surrounding insurance fraud, including the types of claim fraud, motives for committing fraud, factors that influence fraud, detection of fraudulent activity, and anti-fraud efforts.

Consider the effects of insurance claim fraud.

- How does insurance claim fraud affect insurance premiums?
- Who bears the costs of insurance claim fraud?

Why is it important to learn about these topics?

Because claim representatives may uncover potential fraud in their claim investigations, they play a key role in detecting and preventing insurance fraud. Claim representatives must be able to detect fraud and know when to make an appropriate referral to a special investigation unit (SIU) or law enforcement.

Compare some of the "red flag" fraud indicators to a claim you are handling.

- Does your claim contain any of these red flags?
- If so, what other information would you look at to either confirm or rule out the possibility of fraud?

How can you use what you will learn?

Evaluate a claim being handled by SIU.

- What type of activity constituted the potential fraud?
- What actions are SIU personnel taking to prepare the file for disposition?
- What actions would you take if this was your file?

Chapter 4
Insurance Fraud

Insurance fraud is any deliberate deception committed against an insurer or an insurance producer for the purpose of unwarranted financial gain. It can occur during the process of buying, selling, or underwriting insurance, or making or paying a claim. Insurance is intended to protect insureds against accidents or fortuitous events. When fraud is committed and is not detected, insurers pay for nonaccidental or nonfortuitous events. This drains vital resources and increases the cost of insurance for everyone.

Insurance fraud
Any deliberate deception committed against an insurer or an insurance producer for the purpose of unwarranted financial gain.

Insurance fraud is often described as a victimless, white-collar crime because it involves deception rather than violence and the "victim" is a company instead of an individual. In fact, the losses and adjusting expenses caused by fraudulent claims are eventually paid by the policyholders through increased premiums. Consequently, all policyholders are the victims of insurance fraud.

This chapter explains why fraud detection is important and describes types of claim fraud, motives for committing claim fraud, factors that influence claim fraud, claim fraud indicators, and anti-fraud efforts. It explores solutions to the problem of claim fraud and examines how the claim representative can help reduce fraudulent activity. This foundation of knowledge about fraud will help claim representatives reduce the effect of insurance fraud through detection and prevention.

IMPORTANCE OF INSURANCE FRAUD DETECTION

Fraud costs the insurance industry billions of dollars each year. The Coalition Against Insurance Fraud (CAIF) estimates that insurance fraud is the second most costly economic crime in America after income tax evasion.[1] The Insurance Information Institute estimates that the total cost of all insurance fraud is between $85 billion and $120 billion a year.[2] Some studies show that fraudulent claims account for 10 percent of all claim dollars; others suggest a much higher percentage. The Insurance Information Institute estimates that property-casualty fraud cost insurers $29 billion in 2003.[3] Some estimates suggest that property-casualty insurance fraud costs each household in the United States an extra $200–$300 per year in insurance premiums.[4] During the past decade, insurers, law enforcement officials, and state and local governments have invested considerable money and manpower in identifying and combating fraud and educating agents, brokers, employees, and policyholders about this problem. Despite these efforts, the problem of insurance fraud persists because of varying degrees of support from the public; insurers; and federal, state, and local governments.

Fraud must be detected and prevented by claim representatives because they are most familiar with individual claims. They must be able to identify fraud indicators ("red flags") and make the necessary referral to special investigation units (SIU) for review and action. Although a claim representative may suspect that a claim is fraudulent, he or she must behave ethically and in good faith at all times when dealing with insureds and claimants. Insurers, too, need to maintain a balance between preventing and detecting fraud and treating policyholders with dignity and trust.

TYPES OF INSURANCE FRAUD

In order to identify the types of insurance fraud, it is important to understand what constitutes fraud. Fraud occurs when all the following elements exist:

- An individual or an organization intentionally makes an untrue representation.
- The untrue representation concerns an important or material fact or event.
- The untrue representation is knowingly made.
- The untrue representation is intended to deceive.
- The victim relies on and acts on the untrue representation.
- The victim suffers some detriment, such as loss of money and/or property, as a result of relying upon and acting on the untrue representation.

Insurance fraud can be committed by anyone—insured, claimant, doctor, lawyer, mechanic, claim representative—involved in the insurance transaction or in a claim. For example, an applicant for workers' compensation insurance may deliberately under-report the amount of payroll to the insurance agent, broker, or underwriter. The underwriter relies on the payroll information provided by the applicant to set the premium amount. The applicant's misrepresentation causes the underwriter to charge a workers' compensation premium that is lower than the premium appropriate for the risk, and the insurer thereby suffers a loss of premium income. An agent, in collusion with an applicant, may over-report the square footage of a commercial building, permitting the applicant to purchase higher insurance limits with the intent of burning the building, collecting the insurance money, and splitting the proceeds with the agent. Or, an underwriter may provide an agent with a low premium quote in exchange for a payoff. Examples of fraudulent claims are staged accidents, inflated medical bills, and the intentional burning of an insured property. These are all examples of insurance fraud.

Insurance fraud can be classified as either hard or soft. **Hard fraud** involves actions that are undertaken deliberately to defraud. False claims or intentional losses are examples of hard fraud. **Soft fraud**, also known as **opportunity fraud**, occurs when a claim is exaggerated. The perpetrator uses the "opportunity" of a legitimate claim to obtain unwarranted personal gain.

Hard fraud
Actions that are undertaken deliberately to defraud.

Soft fraud, or **opportunity fraud**
Fraud that occurs when a legitimate claim is exaggerated.

Hard Fraud

Hard fraud involves schemes to defraud insurers by filing false claims for losses that have not occurred or by intentionally creating losses. Hard fraud can be a staged or invented accident, injury, or theft that results in a false claim. Hard fraud can also be an intentional loss, such as that resulting from arson.

False Claims

False claims arise when an insured pursues a claim for property damage or injury that has not actually occurred. Many types of false claims involving many types of insurance coverage can be made. For example, an insured may file a homeowners claim for stolen jewelry when no jewelry was stolen, or an employee may fake a back injury to get paid time off under a workers' compensation policy.

False claims can also include misrepresentation, concealment, or distortion of a material fact. In insurance, a **material fact** is a fact that would affect the insurer's decision to provide or maintain insurance or to settle a claim. **Misrepresentation** is a false statement of a material fact on which a party relies. **Concealment** is the intentional failure to disclose a material fact.

Material fact — Relevant
In insurance, a fact that would affect the insurer's decision to provide or maintain insurance or to settle a claim.

Misrepresentation
A false statement of a material fact on which a party relies.

Concealment
The intentional failure to disclose a material fact.

For example, store patrons who intentionally pull display items on top of themselves and then file bodily injury claims commit misrepresentation. Also, restaurants are frequently the victims of people who falsely claim injury or illness from improperly prepared food, another act of misrepresentation.

Some false claims can involve the insured's collusion with others. For example, an auto body shop may prepare a repair estimate for alleged damage to an auto when no damage exists. Workers at vehicle salvage yards may collude with others to purchase insurance on unrepairable vehicles; after the insurance is in effect, the "owner" files a false claim for damages when, in fact, the vehicle was already damaged at the time it was insured.

Intentional Losses

Another type of hard fraud is an intentional loss, one that is not accidental or fortuitous and that results from an intentional act. Intentional losses can be distinguished from exaggerated and false claims. An exaggerated claim is based on an actual loss, but the value of the loss is inflated. In a false claim, no loss has actually occurred. In contrast, intentional losses involve an actual incident with resulting damage. In this case, however, the incident is not accidental and the damage is intended.

Staged accident
An accident deliberately caused by a person who intends to feign injury and collect on the ensuing claim.

Arson committed by an insured or at an insured's direction is an example of an intentional loss. A business owner may burn his own warehouse and file a claim to recover the insurance proceeds. Another example of intentional loss, a **staged accident**, is deliberately caused by a person who intends to feign injury and collect on the ensuing claim. The intent of those who stage accidents is to defraud an insurer. Typical staged accidents include rear-end automobile collisions. When the collision occurs, the scammer claims to be severely injured and to require transportation to a hospital by ambulance, while feigning great pain. Alleged injuries from staged accidents vary, but the most common involve soft-tissue injuries to the neck and back because they are harder to medically disprove.

> **Staged Accidents**
>
> An insurer sued to recover more than $4.6 million in claim payments from participants in a staged car-accident ring in Texas. Most of the claims arose from collisions resulting when a car stopped suddenly in front of an innocent victim's auto, allegedly causing injuries. Lawyers, law-office employees, medical clinics, and others participated in the scheme.

Soft Fraud — OR OPPORTUNITY FRAUD

Soft fraud, or opportunity fraud, is the exaggeration or padding of a legitimate claim for the purpose of receiving greater reimbursement than would be received for the actual loss. Such claims may exaggerate the value of the property or the severity of an injury. For example, an insured may state that a stolen computer is six months old rather than its actual age of two years to increase the value of the claim.

Injury claims can be exaggerated or padded several ways. Some medical providers exaggerate claims by overtreating patients. Overtreatment involves performing more procedures, or more expensive procedures, than are medically necessary to treat an injury. These treatments may include additional or unnecessary diagnostic tests, such as X-rays, CT scans, or MRIs; extra office visits; or extended physical therapy. Overtreatment or unnecessary treatment by medical providers can occur with many insurance coverages, including automobile liability, workers' compensation, and homeowners liability.

Overtreatment is a form of medical provider fraud, that is, fraud that occurs when healthcare professionals help insureds file insurance claims for treatment that is unnecessary, is not related to the injury, or has not been rendered. For example, a doctor may recommend that a patient receive physical therapy three times per week for twelve weeks when three times per week for eight weeks would suffice. The patient may be aware of the deception and go along with it, or the patient may be unaware of the scheme and may simply be following the doctor's orders. The unnecessary treatment "pads" or exaggerates the true value of the claim, costing the insurer more money. The medical provider increases revenues by overtreatment.

Examples of Exaggerated/Padded Claims
- Overstated value of property
- Overstated severity of injury
- Overtreatment for injuries
- Unnecessary treatment for injuries

MOTIVES FOR INSURANCE FRAUD

People who perpetrate insurance claim fraud are as varied as the general population, and their motives vary as well. Motives for insurance fraud include the following:[5]

- Individual financial gain or profit
- Sense of entitlement
- Participation in organized crime

Individual financial gain or profit is the primary motive for insurance claim fraud. The person(s) committing the fraud may be motivated by financial difficulty or by greed. Concocting an insurance claim may appear to be an easy way to improve personal or business finances. An increasingly common type of fraudulent claim for financial gain involves leased motor vehicles. When a leased vehicle has excess mileage that will result in penalty fees when the lease expires, an unscrupulous lessee may have the vehicle shipped out of the country and claim it was stolen or burn it to avoid paying the excess mileage fee.

Arson is another insurance fraud scheme for financial gain. An arson-for-profit contractor is an individual hired to set fire to a business or residence so that the property owner may reap financial gain through insurance. The property owner establishes an alibi using witnesses who will testify that he or she was far from the fire scene. Any participation in such an arrangement is a criminal offense.

Arson-for-profit schemes occur in all areas of property ownership, but failing business enterprises account for many of the claims. According to the National Fire Protection Association, almost one-third of all restaurant fires raise suspicions of fraud. Because location affects a restaurant's success, problems with location can create a motive for fraud. For example, if a highway located near a restaurant is rerouted or closed for repairs, resulting in lost revenue for the restaurant, the owner may have a motive for insurance fraud. Similarly, a restaurant located next to a large factory may suffer financially if the factory closes or relocates. The owner may decide that burning the restaurant and collecting the insurance is an attractive, albeit criminal, way to recoup losses.

Obsolete, unsalable, or excess inventory, equipment, or supplies can also provide a financial motive for fraudulent claims. The owner may claim water, smoke, or fire damage to the unprofitable goods and attempt to recover the money invested in the useless inventory.

> **Example of Financial Motive**
>
> The chief executive officer of a software distributor allegedly used a severe earthquake as an excuse to destroy unmarketable merchandise. He received $840,000 of a $5 million claim before an employee reported the fraud.[6]

A sense of entitlement is another motive for insurance fraud. Some individuals believe that if something bad happens, someone should pay for it. They use that reasoning to justify exaggerating or padding a claim to cover their insurance deductible or to recover some of the premium. Some people consider their premium payments a sort of "fund" from which they can be repaid in the event of a claim. They further justify their sense of entitlement with the opinion that insurers are large, impersonal, wealthy institutions that will not miss a few extra dollars added to an auto claim or a workers' compensation claim. For those individuals, committing fraud is a means to collect what they believe is rightfully theirs.

> **Fraud Fact**
>
> In a survey conducted by Accenture in 2002, nearly one in four U.S. adults surveyed said they believe that overstating the value of claims to insurance companies is acceptable, and one in ten said they approve of submitting insurance claims for items that were not lost or damaged or for treatments that were not provided.[7]

Organized crime rings created for financial gain are responsible for many multi-million dollar insurance fraud schemes. Crime rings can involve many people and many business entities. A typical crime ring includes people who stage the accidents, medical providers who treat the victims, and lawyers who represent the victims and claimants who stage the accidents.

One example of an organized crime scheme is a network of "chop shops." A chop shop is an auto repair facility that dismantles stolen autos and either sells the parts or uses them to repair vehicles brought into the shop by unsuspecting patrons. An auto thief is paid a flat sum to steal a specific make and model of vehicle and deliver it to the chop shop. The auto is stripped, and the shell is sold as scrap or dumped back on the street for the city sanitation department or other city agency to haul away. The stolen parts may be used to repair an insured's vehicle at the repair facility, and a bill is prepared as if the parts had been ordered from a legitimate parts distributor. Thus the insurer is billed for the stolen parts and repairs.

In an effort to fight this type of organized insurance fraud, auto manufacturers stamp a vehicle identification number (VIN) on several component parts of new vehicles, including the trunk, hood, and doors. The VIN helps detectives who investigate suspected chop shops in tracking the distribution of stolen auto parts. Many law enforcement organizations have auto-theft task forces that specialize in identifying and investigating suspected organized-crime chop shop operations.

States address crime rings by setting strict penalties to reduce the profit that results from insurance fraud. For example, New York's Organized Fraud Unit concentrates on organized crime rings engaged in systematic, ongoing claim fraud.[8] The California Department of Insurance, Federal Bureau of Investigation, California Highway Patrol, and National Insurance Crime Bureau (NICB) spent four years investigating and tracking down members of a Chinese crime ring that allegedly shipped high-value luxury autos to Hong Kong and filed stolen auto claims totaling more than $6 million. Seventy-two individuals were arrested. The scheme involved recruiting people to purchase luxury autos, insuring the autos, and giving them to intermediaries who shipped them to Hong Kong. After the autos were out of the U.S., the owners would report a theft and file insurance claims, reporting that they parked their auto in a lot and that it was missing when they returned. In most cases, the autos were new and shipped within one month of purchase. However, in some cases, the intermediaries recruited lessees who were behind on lease payments and therefore had a motive to participate in the scheme.

Whether those committing insurance fraud are participating in crime rings or acting alone, financial need or the desire for financial gain are the most common motives. Coupled with these financial motivators, several factors can increase the likelihood that fraud will occur.

FACTORS THAT INFLUENCE FRAUD

Once someone has a motive to commit fraud, he or she may look for an opportunity to commit fraud. Several factors may create an opportunity for fraud. These include insurers' underwriting and claim practices, managed care practices, and public distrust of insurers. Recent efforts to cut costs associated with underwriting and claim adjustment, such as for on-site inspections, have made it easier for insureds to get coverage for property that does not exist as stated on the application and to receive claim payment quickly without inspection of the property or damages. Telephone adjusting activities further preclude the claim professional from initiating in-person contact and inspecting property. As a result, those predisposed to commit fraud see an opportunity to do so because their application or claim may not be thoroughly investigated. Additionally, some insurers hesitate to undertake the costs associated with denying suspected fraudulent claims and defending those denials. Other insurers consider fraud a cost of doing business that can be covered with increased premiums. These approaches may ultimately promote fraud.

Managed care pressures may lead medical providers to participate in fraudulent activity. Fee schedule guidelines exert ongoing pressure to reduce costs. Facing continuing threats to profits, unscrupulous providers may turn to fraudulent behavior, such as overtreatment or overbilling, to fund their businesses.

Consumers who believe they are being charged exorbitant insurance premiums may attempt to recover those premiums when a loss occurs (opportunity fraud). Distrust of the insurance business in general and insurance companies in particular has resulted in an "every man for himself" attitude, which has led to an increase in individual fraud and a tolerance of fraud by others.

To detect fraud, it is important to understand the factors that influence it. When this understanding is coupled with an awareness of fraud indicators, the claim representative is better able to detect fraud in insurance claims.

FRAUD INDICATORS

Insurers rely on claim representatives to notice certain elements in claims that are potential fraud indicators—called red flags—and to investigate any detected indicators thoroughly. Fraud-fighting organizations such as the National Insurance Crime Bureau publish lists of indicators of claim fraud.[9] Some insurers use software programs based on those lists to detect characteristics that are common to fraudulent claims. Such programs can analyze vast amounts of data across different lines of insurance to identify claim patterns and other similarities that may indicate fraud. Several organizations offer electronic anti-fraud databases that contain claim-related records or provide access to public records that may be used to gather evidence of fraud. Claim representatives who are aware of fraud indicators can more readily recognize cases that warrant review by an SIU investigator.

Claim representatives should watch for red flags in the insured's or claimant's behavior that indicate the possibility of fraud. Other red flags are specific to the type of claim, such as medical claims, lost earnings claims, fire claims, auto claims, or burglary and theft claims. The sections that follow provide examples of fraud indicators in each of these types of claims.

Behavioral Fraud Indicators

Claim representatives should be alert for potential fraud indicators in the insured's or claimant's behavior when the claim is first presented to the insurer. The NICB lists the following red flags related to insured or claimant behavior:

- *The insured is excessively eager to accept blame for an accident or is overly insistent in demanding a quick settlement.* This behavior may be an attempt to conceal a fraud by preventing the claim representative from conducting a thorough investigation. In the alternative, the insured may be seeking to resolve a claim quickly because the injury or loss has caused a financial hardship.

- *The insured or claimant is unusually familiar with insurance, medical, or vehicle-repair terminology and claim procedures.* The insured or claimant may have gained this familiarity from having submitted many prior claims or may be receiving "coaching" from a professional in order to perpetrate a fraud. In the alternative, the insured or claimant may have a legitimate reason for knowing this terminology; for example, his or her spouse may be a doctor, nurse, auto repair person, or claim representative.
- *The insured or claimant is willing to accept a small settlement rather than provide documentation.* This behavior may be an attempt to conceal a fraud. In the alternative, the insured or claimant may simply be attempting to resolve a claim for which documentation is legitimately unavailable.
- *The insured or claimant conducts transactions in person and avoids using the mail.* This behavior may indicate that the insured or claimant is trying to avoid a federal mail fraud charge if the insurance fraud is detected. In the alternative, the insured or claimant may simply want to ensure that documents are not lost.
- *The insured or claimant is recently separated or divorced.* Such a change in marital status can present a financial motive for fraud. However, it may have no bearing on the claim at all.

APPLY YOUR LEARNING

A Word of Caution

As shown, valid reasons may exist for any of the red flags listed in this chapter. Claim representatives should be aware of an increased risk of fraud when the indicators exist but also should avoid jumping to conclusions. Nothing surpasses the value of a good investigation in determining the validity of a claim.

Behavioral indicators of fraud can also come from other parties involved in the claim. If a claim representative suspects a fraudulent claim, contact with the producer can reveal additional fraud indicators. The NICB offers the following potential fraud indicators based on producer information:

- *The insured's business was unsolicited, new, or walk-in business not referred by a current policyholder.* In this case, the producer has no knowledge of or experience with the insured and can provide only a superficial assessment of the insured. The insured may be intentionally trying to hide information. In the alternative, the insured may have been seeking a new insurance producer and have selected a new one from a directory.
- *The insured arrived at the producer's office at noon or at the end of the day when staff are rushed.* This timing may be an attempt to hide information because the staff may not be as thorough at these times. In the alternative, it may be the only time the insured can get away from his or her job.
- *The insured neither works nor lives near the agency.* The insured may be attempting to hide information by making it inconvenient for the agent to drive to the insured's home or workplace to verify information. This

indicator may also suggest a hidden connection between the agent and the insured. In the alternative, it can mean that the insured was referred to this particular agent by a friend or relative.

- *The insured's stated address is inconsistent with employment or income.* This inconsistency may indicate that the address is false or that the insured is living beyond his or her means. In the alternative, it may mean the insured has another source of income.

- *The insured cannot provide a driver's license or other identification or has a temporary, recently issued, or out-of-state driver's license.* The insurer may be attempting to hide information, such as true name or address. In the alternative, the insured may not have such identification because he or she does not drive or has recently moved and has not acquired a new driver's license.

- *The insured paid the minimum required premium.* The insured may be trying to get an insurance policy, pay the minimum premium, and avoid making any other premium payments. This approach to insurance fraud occurs frequently in auto insurance because an insurance card is given out upon receipt of the minimum payment. The insured never pays the rest of the premium and the policy is canceled, but the insurance card remains in the insured's possession. If stopped by police, the insured will present the card as proof of insurance. In the alternative, the insured may be able to pay only the minimum premium because of financial issues and may fully intend to make all subsequent payments.

Medical Fraud Indicators

Claims for medical expenses can arise under several types of insurance coverage, including liability coverage; first-party coverages, such as automobile, medical payments, or personal injury protection; or workers' compensation coverage. Although policies differ, many medical fraud indicators are the same regardless of the type of coverage.

The wide variety of medical fraud indicators includes the following:

- *Exaggerated claims and claims for services that were never rendered.* The insured or claimant may be working with the medical provider to exaggerate the need for medical treatment. In the alternative, the medical provider may be overbilling the insurer without the knowledge of the insured or claimant.

- *The diagnosis is not consistent with the treatment.* For example, the claimant's diagnosis is diabetes, but the prescription is for an anti-convulsant drug. This discrepancy may indicate an attempt to pad the claim by choosing a diagnosis that would increase the medical bills. In the alternative, it may suggest the need for further investigation to determine whether the diagnosis and treatment really are inconsistent with one another, as the drug prescribed may have other less common or "off-label" uses.

- *The healthcare provider has a reputation for questionable claims.* This may indicate the provider's willingness to pad the claim. In the alternative, it may have no bearing on the claim.
- *Medical bills are summaries rather than itemized statements.* The provider may be attempting to hide information or create documentation for a fictitious injury. In the alternative, the medical provider may be able to supply itemized statements if asked to do so.
- *Medical bills are photocopies rather than originals.* Photocopies may have been made to camouflage alterations to the original bill. In the alternative, another insurer may have required an original.
- *Bills indicate that treatment was given on holidays or weekends.* Such bills may indicate an attempt to pad a claim by billing for treatment on dates when the medical provider is usually closed. In the alternative, the facility may have been open or the client may have been treated on an emergency basis.
- *All the claimants involved in one accident submit bills from the same healthcare provider.* The claimants may have been directed to a particular provider who is participating in a fraud scheme. In the alternative, all the claimants may be members of the same family and use the same provider.
- *The extent of medical treatment is not consistent with the damage to the automobile.* This discrepancy may indicate an attempt to inflate the value of the claim by overtreating the injury. In the alternative, the treatment may be legitimate if the person was physically susceptible to a more extensive injury.

Any of these red flags, when considered in the context of the entire claim, can be sufficient reason to refer the claim to an SIU investigator.

Lost Earnings Fraud Indicators

Workers' compensation insurance provides medical and wage-loss benefits to employees with injuries and illnesses that are work-related. Disability income insurance is designed to replace a portion of the income lost by a worker who becomes unable to work because of an accident or illness. Lost earnings fraud occurs when workers' compensation or disability insurance is used to pay for lost earnings that are not caused by covered illness or injury. Examples of lost earnings fraud include the following:

- An employee who is injured at home falsely claims that the injury is work-related in order to collect wage benefits from workers' compensation insurance.
- An employee stays home from work and continues to receive workers' compensation wage-loss benefits or disability income benefits after he or she has fully recovered from the injury and is capable of returning to work.
- An employee who has not been injured files a claim for workers' compensation benefits for a fictitious injury after a layoff is announced.

- An employee works a second job while claiming disability and receiving workers' compensation benefits or disability income benefits from his or her primary job.
- An employee seeks reimbursement under an employer-provided disability insurance policy for loss of wages that have already been reimbursed by the employer's workers' compensation insurer.

Like other fraud indicators, lost earnings fraud indicators can have legitimate explanations. Nevertheless, they can alert the claim representative to seek further verification. Lost earnings fraud indicators include the following:

- *The lost earnings statement is handwritten or typed on blank paper.* A lost earnings statement that is not on business letterhead may not have come from the insured business. In the alternative, all the business stationery may have been destroyed in the loss, and the documents were created from back-up records.
- *The business telephone number given to verify the claimant's lost wages reaches an answering machine or answering service during regular business hours.* This suggests that the number provided by the claimant may belong to someone other than the insured business. In the alternative, it can mean the business at which the claimant is employed is not a traditional business. It may be on run entirely out of the owner's home.
- *The business phone number is unlisted or the business has only a post office box for an address.* The business may be fictitious or the claimant may have provided false documentation. In the alternative, there may be a legitimate reason for the business number to be unlisted and the business's using a PO box. For example, it may be a temporary number and PO box because the insured location was destroyed by the loss.

Fire Fraud Indicators

Arson-related insurance fraud is committed when someone deliberately sets fire to property to collect on insurance. Although arson may also be committed for revenge or to conceal criminal activity, this section deals only with insurance-related arson.

Estimates of arson property losses range from $1.5 billion to more than $5 billion per year.[10] Arson has serious consequences because property is permanently lost. For example, a historic building can never be replaced. Even property that is not burned is often damaged by smoke.

Approximately 40 percent of all structure fires in the U.S. are intentionally set. Some sources indicate that nearly half the arsons committed involve damage to structures. The remainder is divided between damage to mobile units and damage to other property (for example, forest fires). Damage to structures resulting from arson is divided evenly between commercial and residential properties.[11]

Claim representatives should be alert to indicators of arson, such as the following:

- *The insured removes valuable inventory before a fire occurs, then claims damage to a large amount of old or out-of-season inventory.* The insured may be using the fire as a means of recovering some of the money spent to acquire inventory that did not sell. In the alternative, the insured may simply have had an unsuccessful year and was unfortunate enough to also have a fire that year.
- *The building or contents were offered for sale for a long period before the loss.* An unsalable building or contents can present a motive to commit arson. In the alternative, the cause of the fire may be unrelated to the failure of the property to sell.
- *The family pet was not on the property at the time of the fire.* The absence of the pet may indicate advance knowledge of the fire. In the alternative, there may be a reasonable explanation for the pet's absence, such as a visit to the groomer.
- *There are multiple mortgages on the property.* This situation may indicate that the insured was having financial difficulties. In the alternative, it may mean that the insured's business was expanding and lenders found the property to be valuable enough to sustain multiple mortgages.
- *Contents with sentimental value were not damaged.* The insured may have had advance knowledge of the fire and moved or secured the valued items. In the alternative, the insured may make it a practice of keeping items of sentimental value in a protected area.

Arson is often easy to prove because a telltale accelerant or ignition source is usually found at the fire scene. What is far more difficult to prove is that the insured started the fire or hired someone to start it. If a fire claim raises any suspicions of arson, the claim representative should involve SIU in the investigation.

Auto Fraud Indicators

Auto repair facilities that specialize in fraudulent insurance schemes have contributed to auto insurance fraud problems in many states. In some states, soaring auto insurance rates caused partially by fraudulent claims have influenced elections and have generated new legislation.

Red flags for auto fraud include the following:

- *For a serious accident, no police report is submitted or a police report is completed at the police station rather than at the accident location.* This situation may mean that the accident never occurred or was staged. In the alternative, there may be a valid reason that no police report was made, based on the circumstances.
- *No towing charge has been claimed, although repair estimates suggest that the vehicle could not have been driven from the scene of the accident.* This may indicate that the vehicle was previously damaged and was in the repair facility when the accident allegedly occurred. In the alternative, it may mean that the auto was still drivable.

- *The vehicle that is subject to the claim is reported to be an expensive, late-model automobile recently purchased with cash.* If the claim is for auto theft, the vehicle may be a "phantom" vehicle, existing only on paper. In the alternative, the insured may have had sufficient disposable income to purchase the auto with cash.
- *The accident occurred shortly after the vehicle was purchased or insured or after physical damage coverage was added to the policy.* The auto may have been purchased and insured solely for use in a staged accident. In the alternative, the insured may simply have been unlucky to be in an accident just after purchasing or insuring the auto.
- *All the vehicles in a multi-vehicle accident are taken to the same repair facility.* This may indicate collusion among those involved in the accident and the repair facility. In the alternative, it may be because this repair facility has the best service in the area.
- *An appraiser has difficulty locating the vehicle for an inspection.* This may indicate that the vehicle does not exist or that the damage is inflated or preexisting. In the alternative, it may mean the insured cannot afford to take the vehicle off the road for even a short period of time.

Burglary and Theft Fraud Indicators

Insurance fraud is common in burglary and theft fraud claims because the fact that the property involved is not available for inspection makes it difficult to detect claims that are exaggerated or false. The following red flags may indicate burglary and theft fraud:[12]

- *Losses are incompatible with the insured's residence, occupation, or income.* This incompatibility may indicate that the claim is exaggerated. For example, if the insured is a single mother working for a small lumber yard, it is unlikely that she will have high-end audio and video equipment. In the alternative, the insured may have another source of income, or the items may have been gifts.
- *Losses include appraised items or scheduled property, making proof of value readily available.* If only appraised or scheduled property was stolen, while other high value items were not, the claim may be false. In the alternative, items that are appraised or scheduled on a policy are usually high value, and those are most likely be the target of a thief.
- *Losses include many new items or gifts for which no receipts are available.* The absence of receipts to prove ownership or value makes it easy to exaggerate a claim. In the alternative, the insured may have received the gifts for a recent birthday or anniversary.
- *Loss inventory does not differ significantly from the original police report.* Initial police reports are usually made shortly after discovering the burglary or theft and before the victim has time to make a complete inventory. A complete inventory presented at the time the loss is reported may have been made in advance with the intention of filing a false claim. In the

alternative, the insured may simply be thorough and able to give the police an accurate initial inventory.

- *The insured does not remember when or where new items were purchased.* The insured may be attempting to conceal an exaggerated claim. In the alternative, the insured may just be forgetful, or the items may have been gifts.
- *Receipts have incorrect sales tax figures or no store logo, are numbered in sequence, or have the same handwriting.* The receipts may be false. Most stores use equipment that accurately calculates sales tax, and store receipts usually have an identifying mark, logo, or address. It is also unlikely that the insured would make consecutive purchases or that the same salesperson would handle all the transactions. In the alternative, there may be a logical reason for each of these circumstances.
- *The loss involves a stolen auto.* Improved auto anti-theft systems have reduced the frequency of automobile theft claims. However, those systems do not prevent vehicle theft fraud. Claim representatives should be aware of the types of vehicles that are most likely to be stolen, such as luxury autos and sport utility vehicles. Organized crime rings are especially interested in such vehicles. Claims for other types of vehicles can raise suspicions if any of the indicators listed in Exhibit 4-1 are present. As with all claims, the claim representative must conduct a balanced investigation to determine whether the existence of the indicator has a reasonable explanation.

EXHIBIT 4-1

Indicators of Vehicle Theft Fraud

Indicators of vehicle theft fraud related to coverage

- The loss occurs within one month of the issue or expiration of the policy.
- The loss occurs after the cancellation notice was sent to the insured.
- Coverage is for minimum liability with full comprehensive coverage on a late-model or an expensive vehicle.
- Coverage was recently increased.

Indicators of vehicle theft fraud related to reporting

- The insured has failed to submit or delayed submitting a police report.
- No report or claim has been made to the insurer within one week after the alleged theft.
- Neighbors, friends, and family are not aware of the loss.
- The license plate does not match the vehicle or is not registered to the insured.
- The title indicates that the vehicle is junk, salvage, or from out of state, or the title is photocopied or a duplicate.
- The title history shows nonexistent addresses.
- Repair bills are consecutively numbered or dates show work performed on weekends or holidays.
- An individual, rather than a bank or financial institution, is named as the lienholder.

Source: National Insurance Crime Bureau

Maintaining a Balanced Investigation

Claim representatives must maintain a balance between suspicion of fraud and the possibility that a claim is legitimate despite the presence of one or more fraud indicators. To achieve this balance, a claim representative can use the questions listed in Exhibit 4-2.

EXHIBIT 4-2

Questions to Help Maintain a Balanced Investigation

Having identified one or more fraud indicators in a claim, claim representatives should ask the following questions and conduct the investigation to obtain the answers:

- Given the circumstances of the loss, what would the reasonable or expected actions/responses be for any party involved in the loss?
- What part of the reasonable action or response is missing?
- What has been added to the reasonable action or response?
- Is there a rational explanation for the appearance of the fraud indicator?
- Is there physical evidence to support the reported version of the loss?
- Is the loss as reported physically possible?
- Would someone other than the insured, such as a retailer, supplier, or customer, have records that may confirm or refute the insured's version of the loss?
- Would a local or state governmental agency have records that may confirm or refute the insured's version of the loss?
- Is there a witness to the loss whose motives for coming forward may be suspect?
- Is there a rational or innocent explanation for all or some of the suspicions?
- Is any part of this analysis based on an assumption? If so, can it be proven?

An example illustrates how this analysis can work. Claim representative Marie Johnson is investigating a homeowners claim for the theft of personal items from the trunk of an auto the week before Christmas. The insured has submitted a lengthy list of toys and sports equipment that were stolen from the trunk. The insured stated that the items were all Christmas presents for his family and that the trunk was the only place no one in the family would look to discover the gifts. The insured also says that he paid cash for most of the items and left the receipts in their respective bags in the trunk. The insured claims that the total value of the items in the trunk exceeds $10,000. A partial list of the items reported stolen includes the following:

A set of Calloway golf clubs	$3,500
A Nike golf bag	$ 500
A motorized pull cart for the golf clubs	$ 200
A 27-inch TV/VCR/DVD	$1,000
A 21-inch computer monitor	$3,000

All items were in their original boxes, along with many smaller items.

Marie's conversations with the insured raises her suspicions about the veracity of the list. While she believes that hiding Christmas presents in an auto's trunk and keeping the receipts with the items could be considered reasonable behavior, she questions whether reasonable behavior would include paying cash for these items. She also questions whether physical evidence would support the claim that all the items, in their original boxes, would fit into the trunk of the insured's 1999 Toyota Camry with the trunk closed.

Marie contacts the insured to confirm that the listed items were in the trunk, that the trunk was closed at the time of the loss, and that the auto's back seats were not folded down. Marie also confirms that there is minimal damage to the trunk lock.

Marie asks the insured where he obtained the cash for the presents. He replies that he made the purchases over the course of several weeks after getting the cash out of his local automated teller machine (ATM). Marie then asks for a copy of his bank statement for that period or the ATM receipts to confirm the withdrawals. The insured is reluctant to supply them. Marie also asks for the dates and locations of each of the major purchases. The insured's answers are not specific enough for Marie to verify the purchases at the stores.

Finally, Marie decides to reconstruct the loss. She obtains boxes from various sources that match the size of the items claimed and asks the insured to place these boxes in the trunk of his auto in the same positions they were in at the time of the loss. The insured is unable to pack the trunk with all the items after several tries. Marie ultimately decides that the insured has exaggerated his claim and makes the appropriate denial.

This example demonstrates a balanced investigation. Marie seeks more information to determine whether there is a rational explanation for behavior that doesn't appear reasonable, and, testing her suspicions against the physical evidence, determines that the physical evidence does not support the claim.

A claim representative's detection of fraud on a claim-by-claim basis fits into a broader framework of efforts among the government, the insurance business, and the public to detect and prevent insurance fraud.

ANTI-FRAUD EFFORTS

Insurers; federal, state, and local governments; insurance industry organizations; and the public all play a part in countrywide anti-fraud efforts. Governments and insurers recognize that the enormous costs of insurance fraud reach far beyond an individual insurer or the insurance industry and can significantly affect an area's economic growth. Their anti-fraud efforts include not just detecting fraud and punishing those who commit it, but also raising public awareness of these costs and deterring fraudulent behavior.

Anti-fraud efforts must start with the public. A survey published in 2003 by the Insurance Research Council (IRC) found that many people find certain types of fraudulent activity acceptable. The study showed that when presenting a claim, some consumers believe they are entitled to collect the deductible and the amount of premiums they have paid by adding them to the claim amount (padding). One-third of respondents agreed that it is acceptable to pad insurance claims to compensate for the deductible that has been paid. One-fifth of respondents agreed that it is acceptable to pad claims to compensate for premiums paid.[13] While these figures represent a slight drop in acceptance from other years, tolerance of insurance fraud remains high. Exhibit 4-3 summarizes findings relating to the acceptability of different types of fraud.

EXHIBIT 4-3

Acceptance of Fraud and Buildup: Insurance and Other Areas

Percentage of Respondents Who Agree It Is All Right To...

	Total Agree	Strongly Agree	Agree	Probably Agree	Total Disagree	Probably Disagree	Disagree	Strongly Disagree
Insurance:*								
Increase claim amount to make up for deductible	33%	3%	17%	12%	60%	6%	32%	22%
Increase claim amount to make up for premium	22%	2%	10%	10%	71%	8%	34%	29%
Other areas:								
Exaggerate current income in a job interview to get a higher salary	15%	2%	8%	5%	84%	6%	51%	28%
Not report all income to IRS to lower taxes otherwise paid	11%	2%	7%	2%	88%	5%	48%	35%
Withhold information about debts when applying for bank loan	10%	1%	6%	4%	88%	5%	52%	31%
Exaggerate education or past experience on a job application	9%	1%	6%	2%	90%	4%	49%	37%

Note: Percentages may not equal totals because of rounding.

* 2002 data represent the average of findings from two separate telephone studies conducted in May and October 2002. The May 2002 sample of 1,000 respondents was conducted as part of the Insurance Research Council's *Public Attitude Monitor* series.

Source: Insurance Research Council, *Insurance Fraud: A Public View*, June 2003, p. 12.

However, in the same survey, respondents had much less tolerance for fraud in a few areas. Only 4 percent of the respondents found it acceptable to return to the doctor or chiropractor for treatment after an injury has healed, and only 4 percent found it acceptable to describe a stolen auto as having greater value than actual.[14]

Adding to the complexity of the insurance fraud issue is the fact that, according to a 2003 IRC survey, "respondents indicated that they recognize the economic effect that fraud has had on insurance costs and advocate strong measures against individuals who commit fraud. They appear less certain, however, about fraud's effect on accessibility of insurance coverage and are less committed to the idea of personally helping bear the costs associated with fighting fraud."[15] While most of those surveyed agreed that sterner measures need to be taken against those who commit insurance fraud, more than one-third of those surveyed are unwilling to contribute an extra dollar to their insurers for anti-fraud efforts.[16]

Public awareness of the costs and ramifications of insurance fraud, along with criminal penalties, appears to reduce the public's tolerance of fraud. Insurers, government, and insurance organizations work to raise public awareness in addition to detecting and deterring fraud and prosecuting and punishing those who commit it.

Insurers

Insurers are the first line of defense against insurance fraud because they are the most likely to detect it and report it. To assist claim representatives in detecting and reporting insurance fraud, insurers have created special investigation units (SIUs) to investigate claims that raise suspicions of fraud. Many states now mandate that insurers maintain an SIU as part of their anti-fraud efforts (see Exhibit 4-4).

SIUs use technology to help detect fraud. As mentioned previously, databases maintained by insurance-related organizations accumulate information on insurance fraud. These databases cross-index claims to pinpoint multiple filings and provide historical information about claimants. In addition to using such technology, many SIU personnel have law enforcement or investigative experience, and some have criminal justice degrees. Such qualifications help SIU personnel conduct the intensive investigations that are often necessary to substantiate claim denials based on fraud.

Claim representatives refer claims to SIUs based on criteria that vary by insurer. Some insurers refer every claim that raises suspicions to an SIU. Others refer claims based on the extent of the suspected fraud, the prospects of obtaining proof of the fraud, the size of the claim, or the type of coverage.

Insurers, as well as several states, require continuing education for claim representatives and appraisers. Such continuing education can include fraud awareness training. To the extent that continuing education focuses on preventing and detecting fraud, it contributes to the insurer's efforts to reduce fraudulent claims.

EXHIBIT 4-4

States That Require SIUs

These states require that insurers maintain a special investigation unit either in-house or vendor provided. At least two states have also set education requirements for investigators.

Florida and New Jersey have specifics regarding this mandate. In all other states, carriers are required to maintain an SIU regardless of premium or policy count.

* Florida: An SIU is required for insurers admitted to do business writing $10 million or more in direct premium.

Source: Adapted from GAB Robins, GAB Robins Risk Management Services, Inc., Insurance Investigation Unit's "Guide to SIU Regulatory Compliance," 2005 edition. Used with permission.

Resources are available to assist claim representatives in fraud detection, but the claim representative must know how to use the resources most effectively in combating fraud. In another recent IRC survey, 87 percent of responding insurers said that they offered fraud awareness training and 97 percent of responding SIU professionals said they spend time training company personnel. Claim representatives should take advantage of this training to become more informed and effective in fighting fraud.[17]

Insurers can also help combat fraud by educating the individual consumer about the costs associated with insurance fraud. Some insurers are making efforts to bring awareness of the problem to schools, organizations, and consumer groups.

Government

Responsibility for legal efforts to combat insurance fraud lies with a variety of city, state, and federal regulatory bodies, including state insurance departments, state fraud bureaus, and law enforcement agencies. Many states have enacted anti-fraud legislation that includes all or some of the following components:

- Expanding the definition of insurance fraud to include reckless conduct
- Increasing civil and criminal penalties for committing insurance fraud
- Requiring insurers to cooperate with law enforcement authorities in cases of suspected fraud
- Giving broad immunity from civil lawsuits to insurers that share information about suspected fraud
- Requiring insurers to form SIUs, develop anti-fraud plans, and place fraud warnings on all applications and claim forms

The Coalition Against Insurance Fraud (CAIF) advocates the following measures to detect, prosecute, and deter fraud:

- Make insurance fraud a specific crime with appropriate penalties, including restitution for victims.
- Require administrative action against licensed individuals or businesses—medical providers, lawyers, insurance agents, adjusters, contractors, and body shops—upon conviction of insurance fraud.
- Establish fully functioning fraud bureaus in states with moderate or severe problems of insurance fraud. The bureaus should have subpoena power and fining authority and should work with law enforcement and industry to investigate fraud.
- Require insurers to commit to specific plans to prevent and detect fraud.
- Require claim forms and insurance applications to display a warning that insurance fraud is illegal and treated as a serious crime.
- Provide immunity to insurers when sharing fraud information with other insurers, fraud investigators, and law enforcement.
- Require visual inspection of certain types of automobiles before insurance is granted to curtail the practice of insuring phantom vehicles and subsequently reporting them stolen. This requirement would also curtail the practice of insuring autos with existing damage.[18]

Pre-Inspection

To combat the dual problem of auto theft and fraudulent auto-repair facilities, some states and insurers require the insurer to physically inspect vehicles as a prerequisite to providing insurance. Pre-inspection programs prove to be effective in reducing theft claims for nonexistent or phantom vehicles. Pre-inspection can also deter inaccurate reporting of drivers and vehicle garaging locations that results in a lower than adequate premium. For example, a pre-inspection may reveal that the vehicle is routinely driven by someone other than the insured or that the car is rarely kept at the location designated as its principal garaged location. Some states also require photographic documentation as a part of pre-inspection. In Massachusetts, for example, an insurer must photograph a vehicle from the front and rear. The vehicle identification number is also photographed. This type of photographic documentation helps prevent attempts by the policyholder, insurance producer, or vehicle inspector to insure a phantom vehicle.

Mandatory Reporting

Cooperation and information sharing between insurers and law enforcement are essential in fighting insurance fraud. Most states have laws requiring insurers to report claims that raise suspicions to law enforcement or other authorities. New Jersey, for example, requires an insurer to report a fire loss from "other than accidental means" to the county prosecutor for investigation and prosecution. Mandatory reporting laws were enacted as a means to bring those who commit fraud to the attention of authorities for possible criminal or civil prosecution. These authorities may include the FBI or other law enforcement agency, district attorney's office, state fraud bureau, state insurance department, or NICB. Without these mandatory reporting laws, insurers may be hesitant to report suspected fraud because they may face a civil suit if they are unable to prove the allegation (see Exhibit 4-5).

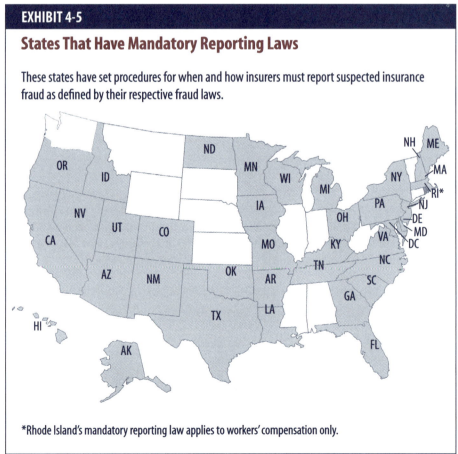

EXHIBIT 4-5

States That Have Mandatory Reporting Laws

These states have set procedures for when and how insurers must report suspected insurance fraud as defined by their respective fraud laws.

*Rhode Island's mandatory reporting law applies to workers' compensation only.

Source: Adapted from GAB Robins, GAB Robins Risk Management Services, Inc., Insurance Investigation Unit's "Guide to SIU Regulatory Compliance," 2005 edition. Used with permission.

Immunity Statutes

To further protect insurers who report potentially fraudulent claims, states have adopted immunity statutes. **Immunity statutes** allow insurers and law enforcement officials to share information about fraudulent activity without facing civil lawsuits for defamation, harassment, malicious prosecution, bad faith, or breach of privacy. Most statutes grant this immunity if the report is made in the absence of fraud, malice, or criminal intent. Statutes vary by jurisdiction and each should be reviewed before a report is made.

Sharing information about suspected fraudulent claims can help stifle fraud. For example, an individual purchases an auto and insures it with six different insurers. Allegedly, the auto is involved in an accident and destroyed. The claim representative investigating the claim is unaware that five other claim representatives are looking at the same vehicle for the same loss. The owner of the auto may have used six different names and addresses for the various policies on the same vehicle. Under the shield of the immunity statute, insurers can share information relating to the loss to determine whether the same claim has been submitted elsewhere, without the potential of a civil lawsuit. Database searches assist claim representatives and special investigators in detecting duplicate claims. For example, database queries may reveal that the same vehicle identification number was recorded six times in a one-month period or that one of the fictitious names was used previously in a fraudulent claim.

Immunity statute
A law that allows insurers and law enforcement officials to share information about fraudulent activity without facing potential civil lawsuits for defamation, harassment, malicious prosecution, bad faith, or breach of privacy.

Civil or Criminal Penalties

Civil or administrative action to punish people who make fraudulent insurance claims is increasingly used as an anti-fraud effort. For example, in 2002, twelve fraud bureaus reported taking civil action against people who committed fraud.[19] In New Jersey, medical practitioners convicted of insurance fraud must surrender their license for one year. If convicted again, the practitioners are permanently barred from their professions. A California statute (California Insurance Code §1871.7) has allowed several major property and casualty insurers to file multiple lawsuits for civil fines and damages against attorneys and doctors who knowingly pay runners (persons hired to steer accident victims to a particular attorney or doctor) or participate in submission of fraudulent claims.

The following are some advantages to pursuing civil action in fraud cases:

- Civil damages can be recovered from the wrongdoers.
- Organized fraud activity may be actionable, not only under common law, but under a number of different civil statutes relating to conspiracy or statutory fraud, including the federal Racketeer Influenced and Corrupt Organizations (RICO) statute.
- Civil prosecution may be easier than criminal prosecution because the burden of proof is less strict than in a criminal case.

- Civil litigation can focus attention on fraudulent activity of suspected individuals or organizations. Such action may alert law enforcement officials, who may pursue their own investigation into criminal activity.

- Civil litigation allows for greater discovery of information and broader subpoena power than criminal prosecutions do, making it easier to gather information.

A functional anti-fraud program uses all the tools available and includes processes for pursuing both civil and criminal remedies.

An Example of Civil Penalties for Fraud

Using all available anti-fraud tools, West Virginia authorities investigated and prosecuted an insurance fraud case that resulted in both incarceration and restitution. The fraud scheme took place over ten years and included sixty arsons across southern West Virginia that burned mobile homes, buildings, and automobiles. A husband and wife team was convicted. The wife was sentenced to fifteen years in prison, and the husband was sentenced to eight years and five months. The couple was ordered to pay $300,000 in restitution to fifteen insurers. The wife had three different Social Security numbers, and as many as seventeen aliases. She had been convicted on previous fraud-related felonies in the early 1990s.[20]

Fraud Prevention Bureaus

Another government anti-fraud effort involves the creation of fraud prevention bureaus. State fraud bureaus, which operate in thirty-three states representing approximately 75 percent of the U.S. population, evaluate potentially fraudulent cases submitted by insurers. After the referrals have been evaluated and enough evidence has been gathered, the information is presented to a prosecutor. Prosecutors can become involved during any phase of the investigation; when they become involved depends on the scope and size of the suspected fraud.

State fraud bureaus have a common goal of fighting insurance fraud, but their scope of operation may vary. Some were formed specifically to combat workers' compensation fraud. Some fraud bureaus are charged with enforcement activities beyond fraud, such as enforcing laws that require businesses to carry workers' compensation coverage. Virginia's insurance fraud bureau is part of the state police department, while Florida's is a division of the Department of Insurance.

Statistics show that fraud crimes increase in states located near other states that establish fraud bureaus or strengthen anti-fraud initiatives. For example, after California cracked down on fraud through legislation and the creation of a fraud bureau, fraud incidents in Arizona increased. Fraudsters tend to target states where tracking and monitoring systems are weak or nonexistent. This is known as migrating fraud.

Statistics show that anti-fraud efforts are working to some degree. The number of criminal convictions is growing, especially in states that have had fraud bureaus in place for many years. Those states have greater investigative experience, larger staffs, and more legal authority to prosecute criminals than states that do not have fraud bureaus. As shown in Exhibit 4-6, criminal convictions resulting from fraud bureau investigations rose nationally from 1,931 in 2001 to 2,535 in 2002.[21] Exhibit 4-7 indicates that civil prosecutions resulting from fraud bureau investigations have continued to increase nationally over the past several years. New Jersey accounted for 86 percent of all civil actions among the twelve states that reported such prosecutions in 2002.[22]

EXHIBIT 4-6

Criminal Convictions—total number, 2002

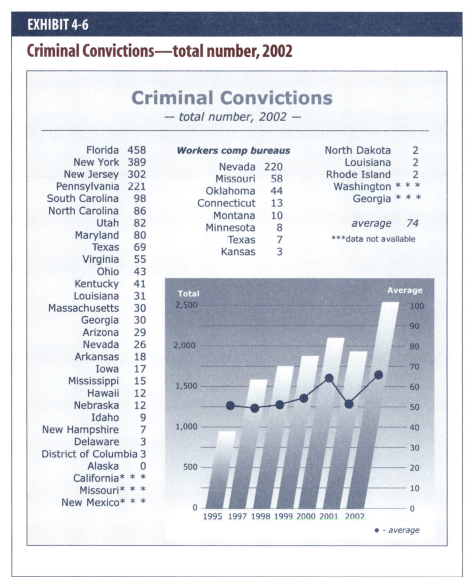

Reproduced from *A Statistical Study of State Insurance Fraud Bureaus: A Quantitative Analysis*, December 2003 edition, p. 16. © Copyright 2003 Coalition Against Insurance Fraud, Inc. Used with permission.

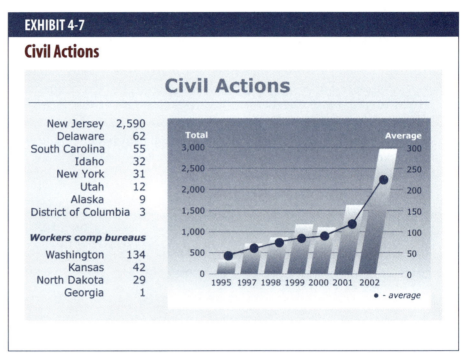

Reproduced from *A Statistical Study of State Insurance Fraud Bureaus: A Quantitative Analysis*, December 2003 edition, p. 18. © Copyright 2003 Coalition Against Insurance Fraud, Inc. Used with permission.

Fraud Plans

Certain states mandate that insurers draft and implement a written plan for combating insurance fraud. Some states exempt insurers that write small amounts of premium. Some states require insurers to submit their plans to the insurance department for review before implementing them. Exhibit 4-8 shows states that require a written fraud plan.

Industry Organizations

Many industry organizations are dedicated to the reduction of insurance fraud. Some, such as NICB and CAIF, are dedicated to the detection and prosecution of fraud. Others, such as the III and the IRC, compile statistical information on insurance fraud.

Even with the combined efforts of insurers, state and federal governments, and industry organizations, insurance fraud remains a pressing issue for insurers and claim representatives.

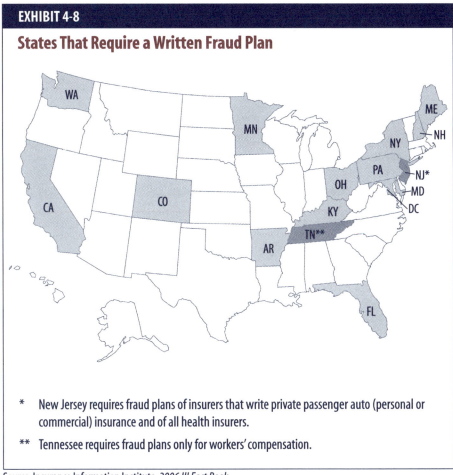

EXHIBIT 4-8

States That Require a Written Fraud Plan

* New Jersey requires fraud plans of insurers that write private passenger auto (personal or commercial) insurance and of all health insurers.
** Tennessee requires fraud plans only for workers' compensation.

Source: Insurance Information Institute, *2006 III Fact Book*.

SUMMARY

Insurance claim fraud is a threat to the financial stability of the insurance business. Many organizations, including insurers, law enforcement agencies, regulators, and legislators, are launching efforts to combat insurance fraud. Often viewed as a victimless crime, insurance claim fraud victimizes the average consumer, who pays for the crime through increased rates that may be charged to cover inflated claim payments.

Two categories of insurance claim fraud are hard fraud and soft fraud. False claims and intentional losses are examples of hard fraud. False claims are claims for events that never happened, such as the reported theft of a diamond ring that never existed. Many false claims involve several, or many, participants in a scam. For example, people other than the insured may participate in the fictitious diamond ring claim by creating a false appraisal and cash-register receipt. Intentional losses result from events that are purposely caused with the intent of defrauding an insurer. For example, several individuals may collude and intentionally cause an automobile accident, often with an unsuspecting motorist. Exaggeration, an example of soft fraud, occurs when a claim is filed with an insurer for reimbursement of a greater sum than was actually incurred in the loss. Describing property as more valuable than it really is or an injury as more severe than it really is are examples of exaggerated claims.

Common motives for insurance fraud are profit and a sense of entitlement. Organized crime is another motive. In addition to motive, other factors create an opportunity for fraud, including an insurer's underwriting practices and claim practices, managed care practices, and public distrust of insurers. Consumers who believe that insurers will not miss a few extra dollars added to a small auto claim or workers' compensation claim do not realize that those dollars collectively add up to millions that everyone pays for through increased rates.

Claim representatives should be trained to look for fraud indicators (red flags) that can help detect fraud before a claim is paid. These indicators can relate to behavior, medical losses, lost earnings, fire, auto losses, burglary, and theft. The claim representative must maintain a balanced investigation once fraud is suspected, because fraud indicators are not proof of fraud.

Anti-fraud efforts are conducted by insurers, the government, and insurance industry organizations. These efforts include pre-inspection, mandatory reporting, immunity statutes, civil or criminal penalties, fraud prevention bureaus, and fraud plans. Some anti-fraud laws mandate that insurers report claims that raise suspicions to law enforcement authorities. Immunity statutes permit insurers to discuss suspected criminal activity with other groups, including state fraud bureaus, law enforcement officials, and other insurers, without facing potential civil lawsuits. Anti-fraud legislation can expand the definition of insurance fraud to increase civil and criminal penalties for committing insurance fraud. Many states have formed state fraud bureaus to track and report the status of insurance fraud. Insurers have increased their internal efforts to combat insurance fraud by creating special investigation units (SIUs), which are responsible for investigating claims that raise suspicions of fraud. Some states require claim representatives to complete a certain number of hours of continuing education each year. Insurance fraud courses are offered as a way for claim representatives to stay informed of current trends in insurance fraud.

Many insurance industry organizations are dedicated to reducing insurance fraud. Some work to detect fraud and prosecute the people who commit it; others compile statistical information.

When dealing with suspected insurance fraud, claim representatives must balance their awareness of the potential fraud with the necessity of conducting a good-faith claim investigation. The insurance contract is a contract of trust between policyholder and insurer, and it guarantees that the insurer will always act in good faith and with the highest ethical conduct. Most policyholders are honest, but claim representatives have a duty to be alert for those who try to defraud insurers and their policyholders by submitting fraudulent claims, while using good-faith claim handling practices. These practices are the subject of the next chapter.

CHAPTER NOTES

1. The Coalition Against Insurance Fraud (CAIF) is an anti-fraud organization that includes as members many national and international organizations that represent insurers, consumers, regulators, legislators, and investigators. Its Web site is at www.insurancefraud.org (accessed October 25, 2005).
2. Insurance Information Institute, *2005 III Fact Book*, p. 126.
3. Insurance Information Institute, *2005 III Fact Book*, p. 126.
4. National Insurance Crime Bureau, "Insurance Fraud," www.nicb.org/public/publications/brochures.cfm (accessed October 25, 2005).
5. Robert A. DuBois, *Insurance Fraud and Motor Vehicle Collisions* (Rochester, N.H.: The Haven House, 1992), p. 2.
6. Margo D. Beller, "Group lists top 10 fraud cases of 1997," *The Journal of Commerce*, January 29, 1998, p. 5A.
7. "By the Numbers: Fraud Stats," Coalition Against Insurance Fraud.
8. "Fraud arrests up 140% since '95 in New York," *The Journal of Commerce*, February 6, 1998, p. 5A.
9. The National Insurance Crime Bureau (NICB), based in Palos Hills, Ill., is a not-for-profit organization dedicated to fighting insurance fraud and vehicle theft. The NICB is supported by approximately 1,000 property-casualty insurers and self-insured companies.
10. National Fire & Arson Report, March 1997.
11. From the Uniform Crime Report, Department of Justice, Federal Bureau of Investigation, 1996.
12. Adapted from *Indicators of Property Fraud*, National Insurance Crime Bureau, 2003.
13. Insurance Research Council (IRC), *Insurance Fraud: A Public View*, June 2003, pp. 3–4.
14. IRC, June 2003, pp. 16–17.
15. IRC, June 2003, p. 5.
16. IRC, June 2003, p. 27.
17. Insurance Research Council and Insurance Services Office, Inc., *Fighting Insurance Fraud: Survey of Insurer Anti-Fraud Efforts*, December 2001, pp. 19, 27.
18. Coalition Against Insurance Fraud Fact Sheet, and "Insurance Fraud: The Hidden Tax," April 18, 2000, p. 24.
19. Coalition Against Insurance Fraud, www.insurancefraud.org/downloads/fraud_bureau_study.pdf (accessed January 26, 2006).
20. The National Underwriter Company, *Claims Magazine*, Claims eNews, March 30, 2005, Florida 771 (accessed October 25, 2005).
21. Coalition Against Insurance Fraud, www.insurancefraud.org/downloads/fraud_bureau_study.pdf. p. 16 (accessed December 29, 2005).
22. Coalition Against Insurance Fraud, www.insurancefraud.org/downloads/fraud_bureau_study.pdf. pp. 16, 18 (accessed December 29).

Segment B

Claim Handling Issues

Chapter 5: *Good-Faith Claim Handling*
Chapter 6: *Ethics and Professionalism*
Chapter 7: *Negotiation*
Chapter 8: *Managing Litigation*

Chapter 5

Direct Your Learning

Good-Faith Claim Handling

After learning the content of this chapter and completing the corresponding course guide assignment, you should be able to:

- Explain how the law of bad faith relates to an insurer's duty of good faith and fair dealing and how the legal environment affects the law of bad faith.
- Describe the parties to a bad-faith claim.
- Describe the bases of bad-faith claims.
- Describe the damages that can be awarded for bad faith or extracontractual liability.
- Summarize the defenses available to an insurer in a bad-faith claim.
- Describe the elements of good-faith claim handling.
- Define or describe each of the Key Words and Phrases for this chapter.

OUTLINE

Law of Bad Faith

Parties to a Bad-Faith Claim

Bases of Bad-Faith Claims

Damages Resulting From Bad Faith or Extracontractual Liability

Defenses to Bad-Faith Claims

Elements of Good-Faith Claim Handling

Summary

Appendix

Develop Your Perspective

What are the main topics covered in the chapter?

To properly handle claims, claim representatives must understand the duty of good faith and fair dealing imposed on insurers through case law and statutes. The claim representative uses this knowledge to avoid bad-faith claim handling practices and to defend those bad-faith claims that arise.

Identify the good-faith claim handling practices in your state.

- Are these practices based on statutes or case law?
- Are these practices based on the NAIC Model Unfair Claims Settlement Practices Act?

Why is it important to learn about these topics?

Claim representatives who act in bad faith expose their employers to fines, penalties, and the possibility of significant monetary damage awards. Acting in bad faith also diminishes the reputation of the insurer, the claim representative, and the insurance industry.

Review the unfair claims settlement practices act of your state or the NAIC Model Act.

- Do you consistently handle your claims in compliance with the applicable act?
- What, if anything, do you need to improve on?

How can you use what you will learn?

Analyze a claim you are handling.

- What, if any, investigation activities have the potential to lead to an allegation of bad faith?
- How have you documented your file to avoid or mitigate this exposure?

Chapter 5
Good-Faith Claim Handling

A primary function of insurers is to pay valid insurance claims. Claim representatives should strive to handle claims with utmost good faith and in an ethical and professional manner. **Good faith** is broadly defined as giving consideration to the insured's interests that is at least equal to that given to the insurer's interests in handling a claim. Insurers have developed best practices or guidelines to help claim representatives act in good faith. Consequently, in the majority of insurance claims, no allegations of bad faith arise. Yet allegations of bad faith in insurance claims remain one of the most troublesome and controversial issues for insurers and claim representatives. This chapter contains examples of bad-faith allegations to make claim representatives aware of the complexity of such claims. These examples highlight the kinds of actions and activities that may lead to allegations of bad faith against an insurer.

Good faith
In insurance, consideration given to the insured's interests that is at least equal to that given to the insurer's interests in handling a claim.

Because interactions with claim representatives are often the only personal contacts that the general public has with an insurer, the claim representative's actions may be closely scrutinized and are often criticized. These criticisms, whether or not legitimate, can result in bad-faith allegations against an insurer. The claim representative's conduct is imputed to the insurer, which is legally liable for its employees' acts that are within the course and scope of employment. Consequently, bad-faith lawsuits usually name the insurer as the defendant, not the claim representative, even though it is the claim representative's actions that come into question. Therefore, claim representatives must understand what constitutes good-faith claim handling and what does not. In this chapter, the discussion of bad faith focuses on a claim representative's actions, which are, in reality, the insurer's actions.

No single widely-accepted definition of bad faith exists. However, Black's Law Dictionary (Eighth Edition 2004) defines "bad faith" in insurance as:

> An insurance company's unreasonable and unfounded (though not necessarily fraudulent) refusal to provide coverage in violation of the duties of good faith and fair dealing owed to an insured. Bad faith often involves an insurer's failure to pay the insured's claim or a claim brought by a third party.

Although some state laws define bad faith differently or more specifically, the Black's definition is useful for discussion of the issue because it is broad enough to encompass actions that courts nationwide have determined to constitute bad faith. Different courts also have reached seemingly contradictory decisions about actions that constitute bad faith. Therefore, claim representatives must be familiar with the bad-faith laws in all jurisdictions in which they handle claims.

State laws may also vary on who can sue an insurer for bad faith. In a claim context, bad-faith allegations can be brought by both first-party and third-party claimants. First-party bad-faith claims involve an insured's allegations of wrongdoing against an insurer in relation to the insured's own personal losses, such as property damage or uninsured/underinsurer motorist injuries. Third-party bad-faith claims arise in liability insurance and generally involve claims against the insured that the insured believes the insurer did not handle in good faith. The most typical third-party bad-faith claim alleges a failure to settle a third party's bodily injury claim within policy limits followed by a verdict that exceeds the policy limits. Only a few states allow third-party claimants to sue an insurer for bad faith.

To avoid bad-faith allegations, claim representatives must understand the law of bad-faith claims, who can make such claims, the bases of bad-faith claims, and the types of damages that courts can award. In addition, claim representatives should understand the defenses that insurers can use against bad-faith claims and how good-faith claim handling practices can make these defenses available to the insurer.

> **APPLY YOUR LEARNING**
>
> ### A Word of Caution
> The definition of bad faith and the actions that constitute bad faith vary by state. Claim representatives should be familiar with the bad-faith laws and any related regulations in all states in which they handle claims, so that they can follow good faith claim handling practices as defined in each state and avoid actions that could lead to a bad-faith allegation.

LAW OF BAD FAITH

The law of bad faith developed in response to the perception that insurers were placing their own interests ahead of their insureds' interests. In some cases, insureds became personally liable for losses or damages they believed were covered by their insurance, and they sued their insurers for breach of contract. **Breach of contract** is the failure, without legal excuse, to fulfill a contractual promise. The insureds alleged that, by wrongfully denying or mishandling their claims, the insurers had failed to fulfill their contractual promise.

However, in some of these cases, breach of contract remedies were perceived to be inadequate. The legal remedy for breach of contract is damages in amounts up to the contract's terms, or the policy limits. Consequently, if an insurer wrongfully denied or mishandled a claim, the policyholder would have to go through the expense, stress, and delay of a lawsuit to get the insurer to pay what it should have rightfully paid under the policy. Furthermore, if the insurer's actions caused the insured to be liable to a third party for damages above the policy limits, the insured would be responsible for those damages as well.

Breach of contract
The failure, without legal excuse, to fulfill a contractual promise.

Because contract remedies were considered inadequate in such cases, insureds brought lawsuits against insurers for alleged torts, such as fraud and intentional infliction of emotional distress. However, such cases often failed because of the difficulty of proving in court that the insurer's behavior was either fraudulent or outrageous enough to award damages for emotional distress.

Eventually, some courts decided that insurers have an implied duty of good faith and fair dealing when settling claims, requiring insurers to value their insureds' interests at least as much as their own. This duty applies by extension to claim representatives. Insurers' failure to comply with this duty can result in a bad-faith claim. Therefore, bad-faith law evolved from the special relationship between insurers and insureds based on the implied duty of good faith and fair dealing.

Insureds and claimants continue to seek new bases for bad faith claims, such as invasion of privacy, defamation, libel, or slander based on letters or documents in the claims files. In addition, the standard of conduct for proving bad faith continues to evolve. This section describes the duty of good faith and fair dealing, the legal environment of bad faith, and the standard of conduct required to sustain a bad-faith claim.

Duty of Good Faith and Fair Dealing

Most bad-faith claims for breach of the implied duty of good faith and fair dealing arise under insurance-related contracts rather than other types of contracts. Why have bad-faith claims developed to such an extent in insurance? Insurance contracts involve the public interest and require a higher standard of conduct because of the unequal bargaining power between the parties. The insured has less "bargaining power" than the insurer because the insurer not only dictates the terms of the contract (the policy), but also usually controls the claim investigation, evaluation, negotiation, and settlement.

Public Interest

As previously mentioned, states regulate insurers to protect consumers against illegal business practices and against insurer insolvency because it is in the public interest that insurers have the financial resources to pay claims. Courts also want to protect the public interest by ensuring that insurers pay claims they owe. In cases in which insurers have acted in bad faith and have harmed the public interest, courts require them to pay damages beyond their contractual obligations.

Higher Standard of Conduct

In comparison to other contracts, insurance contracts require a higher standard of conduct—utmost good faith. Because of the nature of insurance contracts, both the insured or applicant and the insurer must disclose all pertinent facts.

The insurer must disclose all the terms of the insurance policy, and the applicant must disclose all the information needed to accurately underwrite the policy.

As previously mentioned, the parties to insurance contracts have unequal bargaining power. Insurers are often perceived as powerful corporations with vast resources. Even if the insured is a large, financially strong corporation, insurers are considered to have greater bargaining power because they develop the insurance contract and settle the claims. When individual consumers purchase an insurance policy, they generally must accept the policy terms written by the insurer.

In addition, many insurance policies specifically state that the insurer controls the investigation and settlement of a claim. For example, Section II—Liability Coverages of ISO's homeowners policy states the following: "We may investigate and settle any claim or lawsuit that we decide is appropriate."[1] Because insurers control how claims are resolved, courts reason that insurers should be responsible for the outcome of their claim handling if they have acted in bad faith. Thus, courts hold insurers to a higher standard of conduct to discourage insurers from abusing their position of power. Consequently, filing and defending bad-faith lawsuits has become a specialty in the legal community.

To conclude that an insurer has acted in bad faith, courts must determine the standard of conduct to which the insurer should be held. Can an insurer be guilty of bad faith for unintentional mistakes or errors in judgment? Or, must an insurer's behavior be intentional, wanton, or reckless to constitute bad faith? Courts differ about whether bad faith should be based on negligence or on gross or intentional misconduct. In many cases, the results are the same regardless of the standard because insurers' actions can be considered both negligent and reckless or intentional.

Some courts use a negligence (sometimes called due care) standard in determining whether a claim representative's (and, by extension, the insurer's) actions constitute bad faith. Some courts may use negligence as a basis to award compensatory damages but award punitive damages only when the insurer has exhibited gross misconduct.

Many courts have rejected a negligence standard for bad faith. They hold insurers liable only if their behavior is found to be intentional or to constitute gross misconduct. To prove intentional misconduct, a complainant must show that the claim representative intended both the misconduct and the consequences, for example, denying coverage with the knowledge that coverage applies under the policy.

When applying a gross misconduct standard, courts have historically looked for signs of "dishonest purpose, moral obliquity, conscious wrongdoing… some ulterior motive or ill will partaking of the nature of fraud."[2] Bad faith may fall somewhere between simple error and outright fraud. Other courts have used terms such as "arbitrary, reckless, indifferent, or intentional disregard"[3] of a party's interests to describe bad-faith behaviors. Because these behaviors are judged on a subjective basis, courts attempt to determine the claim representative's state of mind at the time that bad-faith acts are alleged to have occurred.

Claim representatives should understand the subjective interpretation of negligence and gross misconduct. The difference between negligence and gross misconduct is determined by the court's or jury's interpretation of the facts. For example, a claim representative issues a coverage denial after performing an incomplete investigation. One court might consider the incomplete investigation to be the result of an oversight or of mere negligence. Another court might conclude that deciding coverage without being fully informed is clearly reckless and arbitrary and, therefore, constitutes gross misconduct on the part of the claim representative. Although the standard of care required varies by jurisdiction, some areas of bad faith, such as the parties to a bad-faith claim, remain stable.

Legal Environment of Bad Faith

Bad faith litigation is becoming more common, and the bases on which bad-faith claims can be brought are expanding. In this constantly changing climate, claim representatives must make an effort to stay informed about the bases of bad-faith claims so that they can provide good-faith claim handling in every instance. Although charges of bad faith are often unfounded, they drain insurer resources. Allegations of bad faith, legitimate or not, continue to proliferate.

> **APPLY YOUR LEARNING**
>
> ### A Word of Caution
>
> Even if a lawyer's initial letter to an insurer regarding a claim makes an allegation of bad faith, that does not mean that the insurer is guilty of bad faith. However, responses to such letters should be timely and carefully crafted. The claim representative may wish to consult with a supervisor or manager and possibly an attorney when drafting this response.

Although most bad-faith law is case law, state legislatures can pass laws that affect bad-faith claims. For example, in October 1999, the governor of California signed the California Fair Insurance Responsibility Act to take effect January 1, 2000. This Act would have allowed claimants to sue insurers for unfairly or fraudulently delaying or denying claim payments. The legislation was put to a popular vote as Propositions 30 and 31 in March 2000 and was defeated. Similar legislation was defeated by a Wyoming legislative committee in December 1999. These examples illustrate why claim representatives must be aware of the status of bad-faith laws in the states in which they handle claims and of additional circumstances that can put them and their employer at increased risk of bad-faith claims.

PARTIES TO A BAD-FAITH CLAIM

In bad-faith lawsuits, the insurer is usually the **defendant**, that is, the party against whom relief or recovery is sought in a lawsuit. Most states do not allow bad-faith claims against claim representatives because they are not parties to the contract. However, claim representatives can be held personally liable for fraud, conspiracy, or other torts in some states.

Defendant
The party (person or entity) against whom relief or recovery is sought in a lawsuit.

Plaintiff
The person or entity who files a lawsuit and is named as a party.

Several kinds of parties can be plaintiffs in bad-faith claims. The **plaintiff** is the person or entity who files the lawsuit and is named as a party. In addition to policyholders and claimants, excess insurers can pursue claims for bad faith against primary insurers. Excess insurers are insurers that offer policy limits to insureds above the limits provided by underlying policies. This section describes how these parties make bad-faith claims against insurers.

Policyholders

Policyholders are those persons or entities who own an insurance policy, whether or not they are the insured. In property-casualty insurance, the policyholder is usually the insured, but that is not always the case. Generally, insurers face two types of bad-faith lawsuits from policyholders: first-party lawsuits and third-party lawsuits. In a first-party bad-faith lawsuit, the policyholder sues its own insurer for bad faith in handling a first-party claim, that is, a claim for payment to the insured under the policy.

> ### Example of First-Party Bad-Faith Lawsuit
>
> The insured, a long-haul trucker, was involved in an accident that damaged his tractor-trailer. His insurance policy provided $30,000 coverage for collision damage, payable within sixty days after the insurer received a proof of loss or a damage appraisal. The trucker submitted the proof of loss but did not receive payment until almost nine months after the accident. The delay occurred because of a series of mistakes and inattention on the insurer's part and through no fault of the insured. The insured trucker was unable to work during those nine months and lost seniority status with his employer. He sued his insurer for negligent claim handling, breach of contract, and unfair and deceptive practices. He was awarded $70,000 in damages. The court stated that insurers have a duty to act "in good faith to effectuate prompt, fair, and equitable settlements of claims in which liability has become reasonably clear."[4]

In a third-party bad-faith lawsuit, the policyholder sues its own insurer for bad faith in handling a third-party claim. For example, the insurer may have provided an inadequate defense of the insured in a lawsuit by a third party (the claimant), or the insurer may have conducted an inadequate investigation. If, because of these actions, the insured is found liable for a judgment in excess of the insured's policy, a bad-faith lawsuit brought by the insured may result in the insurer's liability for the excess judgment. Or, rather than filing the lawsuit, the insured may assign the right to pursue a bad-faith claim directly to the claimant. Some states allow claimants who are not policyholders to sue the insurer directly.

> ### Example of Third-Party Bad-Faith Lawsuit
>
> Smith is involved in a car accident with Jones. Smith is insured by JKL Insurance Company. The facts of the accident clearly show Smith is at fault. Jones has suffered serious injuries as a result of the accident. Smith, who has a $300,000 auto policy limit, demands that JKL settle Jones' claim within the policy limit. Jones also makes a demand to JKL for the policy limit to settle the claim. JKL fails to respond to both Smith's and Jones' demands. Jones sues Smith for negligently causing the accident and wins a $1 million judgment. Smith, in turn, sues JKL for a bad-faith failure to settle Jones' claim within policy limits. At trial, the court holds that JKL's failure to respond to both Smith's and Jones' demands was bad faith because JKL had not given the insured's interests as much consideration as its own.

Claimants

When a claim representative's conduct results in a liability judgment against the insured that exceeds policy limits (referred to as an excess judgment), the insured is required to pay for the amount of judgment that exceeds policy limits, an obvious harm to the insured. However, the claimant (the party originally harmed by the insured) may also be harmed by having to collect the excess from the insured. Furthermore, if the insured has no financial resources to pay the excess, the claimant cannot collect the judgment's full amount.

Can a claimant sue an insurer for bad faith? Because the contract between the insured and the insurer is the basis for the implied duty of good faith and fair dealing, a claimant who is not a party to the insurance contract generally cannot sue an insurer for bad faith. There are exceptions, however.

For example, an insured can assign rights against the insurer to the claimant. The insured may do this to avoid paying the claimant. In exchange for this assignment, the claimant generally signs a covenant with the insured not to pursue recovery of the excess judgment from the insured. Thus, the claimant assumes the insured's rights to sue the insurer for bad faith for the excess judgment, and in return the insured protects its personal assets from the claimant.

Statutes or developing case law can also permit claimants to sue insurers for bad faith. For example, the California Insurance Code provides that a claimant who has obtained a judgment against an insured has a right of direct action against any insurer that issued a policy covering the loss.[5] In addition, a few states have unfair claims settlement practices acts that allow claimants to sue insurers. These acts are described later in this chapter.

> **Example of Bad-Faith Claim by a Claimant**
>
> Ann Johnson is severely injured in a car accident. The party responsible for the accident has a $100,000 auto policy limit. Ann demands the policy limit as settlement, but the insurer offers only $65,000. Ann sues the responsible party and obtains a $750,000 judgment. The responsible party assigns his rights against the insurer to Ann. Ann sues the insurer for bad faith and wins. The court rules that the insurer has acted in bad faith by failing to pay the policy limit demand, which exposed the insured to the $750,000 judgment. The court enforces the $750,000 judgment against the insurer.

Excess Insurers

Excess insurers write policies that provide coverage over the limits of the insured's primary policy. Excess insurance does not pay a loss until the loss amount exceeds the underlying policy limits (or a certain sum, if the underlying policy does not provide coverage). For example, a homeowners policy (in this context, the underlying policy) may have a liability limit of $300,000. An excess policy may provide coverage up to a $1,000,000 limit above the $300,000 limit of the underlying homeowners policy so that the insured has $1,300,000 in total coverage.

If a claimant wins a judgment in excess of the underlying policy limits, the excess insurer must pay the excess up to its policy limits. Thus, excess insurers have an interest in how insurers (called primary insurers) handle claims presented against the underlying policy. Bad-faith claims in this context arise when the excess insurer is different from the primary insurer.

An excess insurer can pursue a bad-faith claim against a primary insurer through equitable subrogation or through a direct action.

With equitable subrogation, an excess insurer has the same rights as an insured to bring a claim against an insurer because it is harmed in the same way an insured is harmed by a judgment in excess of the primary policy limits. Because the rights are the same, the primary insurer can use the same defenses against an excess insurer's claim as it can use against an insured's claim. Bad-faith claim defenses are described later in this chapter.

Some courts have ruled that excess insurers may bring direct actions against insurers for bad faith. These courts reason that an insurer should not be allowed to take chances with the excess insurer's money by risking an excess verdict. If courts impose on primary insurers a duty of care toward the excess insurer, then that duty encourages settlements, keeps the premiums for excess insurance low, and creates no extra burden for the primary insurer who is already under an obligation to settle the claim in the insured's interests.

> **Example of Bad-Faith Claim by an Excess Insurer**
>
> A federal court applied Illinois law to impose on the primary insurer a direct duty of care toward an excess insurer because "it is reasonably foreseeable that a primary carrier's [insurer's] unreasonable refusal to settle a claim against the insured may injure excess carriers of whose existence the primary carrier is aware during the settlement negotiations."[6] Claim representatives who learn that insureds have excess insurance should document that information in the claim file and discuss with their claim managers how to proceed regarding whether to provide a complete copy of the claim file to the excess insurer.

Just as there are limitations on who may bring suit for bad faith, there are limited bases on which a bad-faith lawsuit can be brought.

BASES OF BAD-FAITH CLAIMS

Generally, bad-faith claims arise from claim or coverage denials, verdicts in excess of policy limits, state statutes that create a bad-faith cause of action, or unfair claims settlement practices acts.

> **Bases of Bad-Faith Claims**
>
> - Claim denial
> - Excess liability claim
> - Statutory bad faith
> - Violations of unfair claims settlement practices acts

In each of these situations, an insurer's claim practices can be used as grounds for the bad-faith claim. Insurers' use of good-faith claim handling practices can help reduce the frequency and severity of an insurer's exposure to bad-faith claims.

Claim Denial

When insureds file claims, they expect their policies to provide coverage for the loss. A claim representative must thoroughly investigate a claim and determine whether the claim is covered. Sometimes after such an investigation, the claim representative finds that no coverage applies and denies the claim entirely. In other claims, a claim representative may find that part of a claim is covered and denies only the portion of the claim that is not covered.

When a claim is either fully or partially denied, the insured or the claimant may retain a lawyer to pursue coverage for the claim. Lawyers' involvement increases the possibility of a bad-faith claim because the lawyer has a better understanding of the actions (such as inappropriate claim denials) that can be the basis for a bad-faith claim. However, claim representatives who follow good-faith claim handling practices should not be overly concerned by the involvement of a lawyer.

In some jurisdictions, if an insurer denies coverage and a court finds that coverage does in fact apply, the insurer is liable for the full judgment regardless of having complied with good-faith claim handling practices. Therefore, an insurer can be liable for a judgment even if the claim representative believes in good faith that no coverage exists. Claim representatives should fully document the reason for their decision when fully or partially denying a claim because either action can present the possibility of a bad-faith lawsuit.

Excess Liability Claims

As previously discussed, bad-faith claims can also be based on excess liability. For an excess liability claim to be filed, a final judgment or settlement must have been entered against the insured and the amount of the judgment must be in excess of the insured's policy limit. The insured is not required to have paid the judgment before bringing suit; the judgment alone is enough for a bad-faith claim to be pursued.

In lieu of a final judgment, some courts allow a settlement in excess of the policy limit to be the basis of the claim. For example, if an insurer refuses to settle a claim, the insured can settle with the claimant, and the settlement may be in excess of the policy limits. The insured can then sue its insurer for the settlement amount including the amount above the policy limits. If the insured can produce evidence that the claimant would have settled the claim within the policy limits if the insurer had properly handled the claim, a court can find the insurer liable for the entire amount including the amount in excess of the policy limits even though the settlement was not fixed by a judgment.

Generally, excess liability claims arise from either of the following two situations:

1. The insurer refuses the opportunity to settle within policy limits.
2. The insurer refuses to settle.

Failure to Settle Within Policy Limits

An excess liability claim can arise when the insurer has an opportunity to settle the claim within the policy limits but fails to do so. This opportunity occurs when a claimant demands the policy limits or an amount within the policy limits to settle the claim. Some courts require that the claimant actually make this demand before the insurer can be faulted for failure to settle within the policy limits. However, other courts (and some state statutes) hold that an insurer has an affirmative duty to explore settlement whether or not a demand has been presented. Some courts weigh the chances that the insurer could have settled the claim within policy limits even though the claimant made no demand; they may impose excess liability if the insurer should have known that the chances of an excess verdict were high if the claim were not settled out of court. This duty to settle is not imposed upon the claim representative until he or she has had a reasonable opportunity to investigate the claim to determine liability.

Refusal to Settle

An excess liability claim can also be pursued when the insurer wrongfully refuses to settle the claim. The insurer may deny the claim (as discussed previously), or the failure to settle may result from the insurer's own negligence. For example, a court found an insurer liable for an excess judgment because the insurer did not use a standard of care at least equivalent to the care that a reasonable person would use in the management of his or her own affairs. A court may also find an insurer liable for an excess judgment if it finds no reasonable justification for the insurer's refusal to settle.

An important factor in evaluating an insurer's potential bad faith for failure to settle is the likelihood or foreseeability of an excess verdict. The greater the foreseeability that the verdict will exceed the insured's liability limits, the greater the likelihood of a finding of bad faith for refusal to settle. On the other hand, an insurer is not likely to be found at fault for failing to foresee an unexpectedly large verdict.

Strict Liability

Some insureds have attempted to pursue bad-faith claims based on strict liability, under which the insurer is liable for any excess settlement or judgment even though the insurer is not at fault. Almost all courts have stopped short of imposing strict liability, but some have placed burdens on the insurer or have used language which seems to support strict liability. If strict liability is imposed by courts for excess liability, an insurer is liable for the policy limit plus any excess liability if it has an opportunity to settle within policy limits and fails to do so, and if an excess judgment results. For example, a court may hold that an insurer has the burden of proving that its refusal to settle was based on reasonable and substantial grounds. To date, only one state has imposed strict liability on insurers for rejecting a reasonable written offer within policy limits. Claim representatives should determine whether the laws in states in which they handle claims impose strict liability on insurers under these circumstances.

Statutory Bad Faith

Some states have statutes that specifically define what constitutes insurers' bad faith and that allow a bad-faith cause of action. Under those statutes, plaintiffs have the right to pursue claims against insurers if they fall within the statutory definition of bad faith. For example, Pennsylvania enacted a statute in 1990 providing for recovery of punitive damages, interest, attorneys' fees and costs if an insured could prove bad faith.[7] Before that date, Pennsylvania did not recognize first-party bad faith as a cause of action against an insurer. In jurisdictions with bad-faith statutes, claim representatives should pay particular attention to the criteria outlined in the statute and the case law interpreting the statute.

Unfair Claims Settlement Practices Acts

Many states have unfair claims settlement practices acts, which specify what a claim representative can and cannot do when handling a claim. Such statutes may also require claim representatives to be licensed if they handle claims in that state. Claim representatives should be familiar with the provisions of the acts in any states in which they handle claims.

While the acts vary by state, many states base their unfair claims settlement practices laws on the Model Unfair Claims Settlement Practices Act developed by the National Association of Insurance Commissioners (NAIC). This act outlines the activities that are considered unfair claim settlement practices. A review of the Model Act provides a general understanding of the conduct that constitutes an unfair claim settlement practice.

Provisions of the NAIC Model Act

The NAIC Model Act specifies wrongful claim settlement practices. Some provisions apply to first-party claims only, and others apply to third-party claims. Violations of the Model Act are those "committed flagrantly and in conscious disregard of the Act" or "committed with such frequency to indicate a general business practice." Therefore, a single instance of carelessness or indifference typically does not violate the Act. To comply with the Model Act, claim representatives should treat both insureds and claimants with respect and professionalism. The provisions of this act are found in the appendix to this chapter.

Enforcement

The NAIC Model Act specifies that its provisions are to be enforced by state insurance departments. The stated purpose of the act is not to punish insurers and claim representatives but to elevate the standard of conduct for claim handling by all insurers for the benefit of all involved and to avoid bad-faith claims. However, state insurance commissioners can issue statements of charges or violations against insurers, require hearings on those charges, and impose appropriate penalties against the insurer if the charges are proven.

The NAIC Model Act allows regulators to impose one or more of the following penalties and sanctions on insurers found guilty of violating the act:

- Fines
- Interest on an overdue claim payment

- Payment of other fees and costs
- Injunctions or cease-and-desist orders
- Suspension of a claim representative's or insurer's license
- Revocation of a claim representative's or insurer's license

The act sets fines of up to $1,000 per violation and up to $100,000 in the aggregate. For example, if a claim representative violates several different provisions of the act in the same claim, each violation may be subject to a fine (assessed against the insurer, not the claim representative), and the total fines may not exceed the aggregate limit. If a violation is considered flagrant or in conscious disregard of the act, fines may reach $25,000 per violation and $250,000 in the aggregate. Insurers pay fines to the state department of insurance, not to the insured. Suspension and revocation of licenses are extreme penalties and are usually imposed only after other penalties have proved ineffective. An insurer can appeal an insurance commissioner's decision either through an administrative board or through the court system. Generally, insurers who have been penalized or sanctioned take corrective action to prevent further violations.

State Provisions

Most states have incorporated some or all of the Model Act's fourteen provisions into their state insurance codes. Some states have fewer provisions, but they are phrased in general terms to fit most situations. Other states have additional provisions that address the following:

- Misleading a claimant about the statute of limitations
- Requiring a polygraph test
- Causing a disproportionate number of complaints
- Requiring the use of a drive-in estimating service owned by the insurer
- Requiring more than two competitive estimates for property damage
- Failing to carry and exhibit an adjuster's license card
- Discriminating against claimants who are represented by a public adjuster

Whether a state unfair claims settlement practices act has a few provisions or many, the goals of those provisions usually fall into one (or more) of the following five categories:

1. Promptness
2. Honesty
3. Responsiveness
4. Fair-mindedness
5. Even-handedness

Keeping these categories in mind while handling claims may help claim representatives avoid exposing themselves or their employer to bad-faith claims.

Bad-Faith Lawsuits Under the Model Act

In addition to the case law and statutory bases for filing a bad-faith lawsuit, some states allow insureds and claimants to bring lawsuits against insurers for violation of the state version of the Model Act. Other states allow only insureds and not claimants to bring such a lawsuit. Courts in a few states allow a bad-faith lawsuit if the Model Act violation is part of a general business practice.

Many state laws either specifically prohibit bad-faith lawsuits based on violations of unfair claims settlement practices acts or are silent on the issue. If the law is silent, lawyers pursue bad-faith claims and ask courts to decide. Court decisions vary by jurisdiction, so claim representatives must know the laws on bad faith in every state and jurisdiction in which they handle claims.

> **APPLY YOUR LEARNING**
>
> **A Word of Caution**
>
> Violations of the Unfair Claims Practices Act are damaging even in states that do not allow them to be used as the basis for a bad-faith lawsuit. Evidence of behavior that violates an act is likely also evidence of the "malice," "reckless disregard," or "bad faith" necessary for bad-faith lawsuits.

Other Bases for Bad Faith

Insureds may use violations of other statutes or regulations as evidence of alleged bad faith and/or alleged extracontractual liability against an insurer. Bad-faith claims are sometimes based on fraud, deceit, conspiracy, defamation, libel, and slander. For example, an insured may bring a bad-faith lawsuit against an insurer because the claim representative told the insured's creditors that the insured had committed fraud, without having sufficient information to support this allegation. In addition, bad-faith allegations are sometimes made for violations of privacy rights.

Bad-faith claims are not the only risk insurers face from improper claim handling. They may also face extracontractual liability claims, that is, claims for damages outside the insurance policy, such as punitive damages, or in excess of the insurance policy. Such claims can be made as part of a bad-faith claim or they can arise under other state and federal statutes and regulations.

DAMAGES RESULTING FROM BAD FAITH OR EXTRACONTRACTUAL LIABILITY

Insurers found liable for bad faith or responsible for extracontractual liability are required to pay damages to the harmed party. Damages in bad-faith or extracontractual lawsuits may be based on common-law or statutory provisions, and they vary by jurisdiction. If a plaintiff wins a bad-faith or extracontractual lawsuit, the insurer may be required to pay the plaintiff compensatory damages, punitive damages, lawyers' fees and court costs, and prejudgment interest.

Compensatory Damages

Compensatory damages are a monetary compensation to a victim for harm actually suffered. Compensatory damages can include contractual damages, consequential damages, and/or emotional distress damages, which are damages for mental suffering without physical injury.

Contractual damages are the amounts payable under the contract according to the contract's terms. For example, in a coverage lawsuit, contractual damages are the full amount of coverage up to the policy limits.

Consequential damages are damages awarded by a court to indemnify an injured party for losses that result indirectly from a wrong such as a breach of contract or a tort. They can be out-of-pocket expenses that can be quantified and itemized, such as the following:

- Amount of an excess verdict over policy limits
- Verifiable business losses
- Expenses associated with filing the lawsuit and participating in the litigation process
- Interest or other statutorily prescribed damages for delay
- Lawyers' fees

In some jurisdictions, these expenses may not be considered consequential damages but instead may be prescribed by statute or common law.

In states that regard bad faith as a tort, courts may award emotional distress damages as part of compensatory damages. But courts have used different standards to determine when emotional distress is sufficient to incur damages. For example, some courts award damages if the insured suffers a property loss or an economic loss that causes emotional distress, even if the emotional distress is not severe. Some courts award damages when the insured suffers emotional distress, even when the insurer does not intend to cause the distress. Other courts award emotional distress damages only if a physical injury results or if the insurer's misconduct was intentional, malicious, or willful.

Contractual damages
The amounts payable under the contract according to the terms of the contract.

Consequential damages
A payment awarded by a court to indemnify an injured party for losses that result indirectly from a wrong such as a breach of contract or a tort.

Punitive Damages

Punitive damages, which are damages imposed in order to punish the wrongdoer, can result in very large monetary awards. Many bad-faith claims include a demand for punitive damages because the potential awards can be lucrative for both the claimant and the claimant's attorney. However, punitive damages are not always awarded in bad-faith claims. The standard for awarding punitive damages varies by jurisdiction but generally requires proof of insurer behavior that is worse than ordinary wrongdoing, such as malicious, fraudulent, or oppressive behavior. Some states require proof that the insurer's conduct was intentional, reckless, gross, wanton, or recklessly indifferent for punitive damages to be awarded.

When evaluating a claim for punitive damages, courts ask questions such as the following:

- Did the insurer intend to harm the insured?
- Did the insurer substantially harm the insured?
- Was the insurer's conduct so blatant that a reasonable person would foresee the harm to the insured?
- Does the insurer have substantial net worth?
- Do state laws influence when and what amount of punitive damages are allowed?

The amount of a punitive damage award can be influenced by a variety of factors. One factor may be the insurer's compensation or bonus plan. For example, if claim representatives receive incentive-based compensation to close claims quickly or to reduce claim payments, the insurer may run a greater risk of a punitive damage award, because this conduct may be contrary to public interest. Another factor that can influence a punitive damage award is an insurer's reaction to a bad-faith claim. A court may not look favorably on an insurer that shows no remorse for serious claim handling deficiencies. Candor in admitting mistakes and an open and honest approach to dealing with complaints can help insurers reduce their exposure to punitive damages.

Insurers generally support the following limits on punitive damages:

- Punitive damages should not exceed the amount of compensatory damages awarded except in unusual cases.
- Higher punitive awards are appropriate only in cases in which the plaintiff has not received a substantial award of compensatory damages and the defendant's conduct is outrageously reprehensible.
- Evidence supporting punitive damages must be specific to the harm suffered by the plaintiff and should not be based on misconduct occurring in other jurisdictions or at other times.

Lawyers' Fees and Court Costs

Among the types of consequential damages commonly imposed in bad-faith or extracontractual liability cases are lawyers' fees and court costs. Insureds or claimants incur lawyers' fees in bringing bad-faith lawsuits. In addition, if the insurer has refused to defend the underlying claim, insureds and claimants may incur lawyers' fees to defend the underlying lawsuit. In some states, statute or common law allows recovery of such lawyers' fees as part of damages in bad-faith cases. Even in states without such laws, individual courts may allow recovery of lawyers' fees as part of consequential damages resulting from the insurer's conduct. Those courts reason that when the insured must hire a lawyer to obtain the benefits the insurer wrongfully refused to provide, the lawyer's fees are an economic loss and are recoverable as consequential damages. Similarly, courts may allow the insured or claimant to recover court costs. However, some courts have refused to award attorneys' fees and costs if the claimant would have incurred the fees and costs regardless of the outcome of the suit.

Interest

If an insured pays an excess judgment and then wins a bad-faith lawsuit against the insurer to recover the payment of the excess judgment, the insurer may have to pay the insured the statutory interest rate on that excess judgment amount. Some courts award interest on the claimed damages because the insured was deprived of the money while the insurer had the money to earn interest. Some states' laws allow interest and penalties to be assessed against an insurer solely because of its failure to promptly pay a claim. In addition, some courts have allowed an excess insurer to claim prejudgment interest if the primary insurer was found to have negligently refused to settle.

The amount of damages resulting from a bad-faith or extracontractual liability claim can be sizeable because of all the different types of damages allowed. Claim representatives should be aware of these and other potential consequences of bad faith as they handle claims. Despite their best efforts to handle claims with good faith, bad-faith allegations will still be made, so the claim representative and the insurer must be prepared to defend against these claims.

DEFENSES TO BAD-FAITH CLAIMS

Insurers faced with bad-faith lawsuits have many defenses, some of which may be a total defense to the claim, others of which may be a partial defense to the claim. While any one of the defenses may be sufficient for the court to dismiss a lawsuit, an insurer that can assert more than one defense is more likely to succeed in defeating a bad-faith claim or reducing the amount of damages awarded. Each defense must be analyzed in relation to a specific lawsuit to determine whether it can be used.

Defenses to Bad-Faith Claims

Defenses That Result in Dismissal of Lawsuit

- Lack of right to sue
- Reliance on lawyers' advice
- Insured's collusion with the claimant
- Debatable reasonable basis
- Statutory defenses
- Fair dealing and good documentation
- Comparative bad faith

Defenses That Reduce Damages

- Comparative bad faith
- Contributory negligence
- Availability of higher limits

Statutes of Limitations

Statute of limitations
A statute that imposes time limits on when a cause of action can be brought, starting from the time the cause of action accrues.

One defense to a bad-faith lawsuit is the expiration of the statute of limitations. **Statutes of limitations** impose time limits on when a cause of action can be brought, starting from the time the cause of action accrues. These statutes apply to bad-faith claims. If the time limit specified in the statute of limitations has expired, the court will dismiss the bad-faith lawsuit.

The time allowed to file a lawsuit allowed by statutes of limitations varies depending on whether the lawsuit alleges a breach of contract or bad faith as a tort. The period also varies by state. Generally, the period ranges from two years to six years from the date the bad faith occurs. The claim representative and the insurer's defense lawyer should check state law to determine the statute of limitations that applies to a particular bad-faith lawsuit.

A common issue in cases involving a statute of limitations is the starting date of the statutory period. Some courts have held that the starting date for a bad-faith lawsuit begins when the insurer denies the claim or otherwise wrongfully withholds benefits. Other courts have held that the time does not begin to run (or toll) until the damages are ascertainable. For example, in excess liability cases, the statute begins to run when a final judgment in excess of the policy limit is awarded. If a bad-faith claim is based on an insurer's refusal to defend an insured, the statute begins to run when the insurer refuses to defend. Because these conditions vary by state, an insurer's lawyer should determine whether the statute of limitations is a valid defense in a given case.

Lack of Right to Sue

Policyholders, claimants, and excess insurers may have the right to sue (also called standing) for bad faith, depending on state law. If claimants and excess insurers do not have the right to sue for bad faith under the state's law, then the insurer can defend against the claim by challenging their standing to sue.

Several states, called direct action states, do allow a claimant to directly sue a tortfeasor's insurer. Claim representatives should check with their defense lawyers to determine whether the states in which they handle claims are direct action states.

One way for a claimant or an excess insurer to gain the right to sue is to obtain the policyholder's right to sue through an assignment. If a policyholder has assigned policy rights to the claimant, defense lawyers should ascertain whether the assignment is legal; an illegal or improper assignment can be a valid defense.

Reliance on Lawyers' Advice

Another possible defense against a bad-faith claim is reliance on lawyers' advice (often called the advice of counsel defense). If an insurer relies on the opinions and advice of competent, independent lawyers in reaching the decision that leads to a bad-faith lawsuit, the insurer can use that fact to build a defense. Evidence that an insurer obtained a lawyer's advice may be used to indicate that the insurer acted reasonably and with proper consideration in handling the insured's claim. Using lawyers' advice as part of a defense may require proof of the following:[8]

- The insurer acted on the lawyer's advice.
- The insurer disclosed all the facts to the lawyer.
- The insurer relied on the lawyer's advice in good faith.

Proof that the insurer followed a lawyer's advice may be effective in reducing or eliminating punitive damage awards. A court may reason that an insurer's good-faith reliance on a lawyer's advice eliminates the elements of oppression, fraud, or malice required for a punitive damage award. However, one drawback of relying on this defense is that doing so may waive any attorney-client privilege and thus allow the insured to review the file of the insurer's attorney.

Insured's Collusion With the Claimant

Another defense that can lead to dismissal of a bad-faith claim is collusion between the insured and the claimant. For example, an insured and a claimant may conspire to help the claimant recover an excess judgment in a lawsuit resulting from a claim and agree to split the proceeds if the lawsuit is successful. Such collusion is more likely to occur in the following situations:

- The insured and the claimant have an ongoing business relationship.
- The insured and the claimant are related or close friends.
- The insured will benefit indirectly from the claimant's recovery, such as in the case of a minor child suing a parent/insured.

Collusion can also occur when an insured enters into an agreement with the claimant, after a court awards damages above the policy limits, that the claimant will not collect the judgment from the insured's personal assets. Courts carefully scrutinize any such agreements before honoring them.

Another potential opportunity for collusion arises when there is a coverage issue in a claim. The insured may share the insurer's reservation of rights letter with the claimant for the purpose of coaching the claimant on how to assert an allegation so that it is covered and therefore payable by the insurer and not the insured.

The following are two indicators of possible collusion:

- The insured's attitude suddenly becomes more favorable toward the claimant during the claim process.
- The insured is uncooperative and does not appear to be concerned about possible personal excess exposure.

Courts are usually unsympathetic and intolerant of collusion and are likely to rule against the insured and claimant if collusive behavior is discovered.

Debatable Reasonable Basis

Another possible bad-faith defense stems from the existence of a debatable question. If an insurer has a reasonable basis on which to debate whether a claim is covered, the insurer should not be liable for a bad-faith refusal to pay a claim. For example, a claim representative makes a good-faith investigation and determines that a claim is not covered. The insured disagrees and sues for coverage, alleging bad faith in the original coverage determination. A court can find that the claim is covered and still find that no bad faith was involved if the court believes there was a reasonable basis for the original coverage denial. Some courts have held that a claim is "fairly debatable" if a reasonable insurer would deny or delay payment of a claim with the same facts and circumstances. If the questions are fairly debatable, the insurer is not acting in bad faith by seeking to resolve the questions before making payment. To use the debatable question defense, insurers must show that there is a reasonable justification in law or fact for denying or delaying payment of the claim.

Another measure of whether a claim involves a debatable question is whether the insured is entitled to a summary judgment on coverage. A court grants a **summary judgment** when it determines that no factual issue exists in a case. The insurer would a file for a summary judgment on the grounds that the policy does not cover the claim and that, therefore, there are no factual issues to be decided by the court. The court's refusal to grant a summary judgment would indicate that the factual issue of coverage is in dispute, that is, that it is a debatable question. In having attempted to resolve this question before making payment, the insurer would not, then, have been acting in bad faith.

Statutory Defenses

Federal and state statutes designate other defenses insurers can use to seek a dismissal of a bad-faith lawsuit. Any applicable statutes must be examined for any defenses that may apply to a particular bad-faith claim. For example, some states require insurers to report suspected insurance fraud to the state attorney general's office. To insulate insurers from angry insureds who are suspected of fraud and have been reported, these states offer the insurer immunity from related lawsuits. Obviously, there should be no bad-faith claim against the insurer for reporting suspected fraud in good faith if the suspicion is reasonable.

Fair Dealing and Good Documentation

Insurers can use fair dealing and good documentation as a defense to a bad-faith claim. Good-faith claim handling practices and supporting evidence can help defend bad-faith lawsuits by establishing that insurers have dealt fairly with insureds and claimants. Documentation in each claim file demonstrates how insurers conduct the claim investigation, evaluate claims, and negotiate claims. Activity logs; correspondence; and documentary evidence such as police reports, damage estimates, and medical bills can indicate that claim

---

Summary judgment
A judgment granted by the court when it determines that no factual issue exists.

representatives, supervisors, and managers are doing their jobs properly. Such evidence is part of a successful defense strategy for a bad-faith claim.

Fair dealing and good documentation are especially important in defending bad-faith claims resulting from claim denial and those resulting from claim representation errors. Claim representatives should have a thoroughly documented claim file before denying a claim. Investigative attempts should be documented irrespective of whether the results are good or bad for the insurer. Fair dealing practices and good documentation can also help claim representatives explain and correct errors. When an error is discovered, a sincere apology and quick action to correct it can help in avoiding and defending bad-faith claims.

Claim representatives should follow their company's procedures or best practices in documenting their files. They must operate as if every note, form, or letter in their claim files will be read to a jury. In addition, claim representatives should adopt the following practices from the first day of the claim handling process through the time the claim is closed:

- Request and obtain all necessary information or documentation before deciding to accept or deny a claim
- Include in their files detailed analyses of the coverage(s), the liability issues, defenses, percentages of liability for all parties, and damages issues
- Support their analyses with facts and documents in their files, not rumors or innuendos
- Avoid making derogatory or malicious comments about the insured, counsel, or witnesses
- Avoid exploiting or making comments about exploiting the claimant's or insured's financial hardship
- Avoid delays in handling a claim
- Avoid substantial variances between reserves and payments or offers made
- Avoid attempts to persuade public authorities to bring criminal charges against any person, but supply requested information about possible criminal activity as permitted by the applicable state
- Avoid attempting to coerce experts to change their testimony

The best defense to a bad-faith claim is sufficient evidence that the claim has been handled following good-faith practices. Good-faith claim handling must be thoroughly documented so that it can be made apparent to a jury or judge if a bad-faith claim is filed.

Comparative Bad Faith

The duty to act in good faith applies to both the insurer and the insured. Therefore, in some jurisdictions, evidence that an insured has acted in bad faith may allow the insurer to use the defense of comparative bad faith in a bad-faith lawsuit. The comparative bad-faith defense permits dismissal or reduction of a bad-faith claim if an insured failed to deal fairly with the insurer by breaching one or more implied duties. For example, an insured delays reporting an accident in which he or she is at fault and also fails to cooperate in the accident investigation. If the insured later sues the insurer for bad faith in handling that claim, evidence demonstrating that these actions prevented the insurer from properly handling or settling the claim against the insured may establish comparative bad faith as a defense. Comparative bad faith as a defense is recognized in only a few jurisdictions.

> **Example: Comparative Bad-Faith Defense**
>
> An insured's home was damaged by fire. The insurer paid the insured for the damage, although the insured claimed he was not fully compensated. Five months after the first fire, a second fire destroyed what remained of the home. The insurer denied the claim because the second fire was caused by arson. The insured sued the insurer for breach of contract, bad faith, and violations of the unfair insurance practices act. The court found in the insurer's favor because the insured had set the second fire, had made misrepresentations to the insurer, and had failed to protect the property after the first fire.[9]

Contributory Negligence

Another defense that may be used in a bad-faith lawsuit is contributory negligence. In some states, proof of any contributory negligence by the insured prevents recovery. However, most states use a comparative negligence approach, reducing the amount of damages that may be awarded. If the insured contributed to the damages, the insurer's bad-faith damages are reduced by the percentage that the insured contributed. Generally, a contributory negligence defense is available only in states that permit negligence as a basis for a bad-faith claim.

Availability of Higher Limits

Insurers can sometimes use the defense that higher limits of insurance were available to the insured to reduce the size of a bad-faith claim award. Because insurance coverage is readily available and insureds can purchase adequate policy limits through primary or excess insurers, an insured who has a policy with minimal limits may have difficulty putting all the blame for an excess judgment on the insurer. Evidence that the insurance producer encouraged the insured to purchase higher limits can help the insurer establish this defense. Although it is not a complete defense to a bad-faith claim, the fact that higher limits were available but were rejected by the insured may reduce the size of the award against the insurer.

ELEMENTS OF GOOD-FAITH CLAIM HANDLING

As previously mentioned, good faith is broadly defined as consideration given to the insured's interests that is at least equal to that given to the insurer's interests in handling the claim. This broad definition allows courts great leeway in deciding what constitutes good faith in a given situation. As a result, common sense and good judgment must underlie all claim handling.

Good-faith claim handling involves thorough and timely investigation, documentation, evaluation, negotiation, and communication. In addition, claim representatives should seek legal advice when appropriate. Finally, the insurer's management of all claims is important to good-faith claim handling.

Thorough, Timely, and Unbiased Investigation

Investigations that are thorough, timely, and unbiased are the foundation of good-faith claim handling. If claim representatives investigate claims adequately, they will have sufficient evidence of their good-faith efforts to conclude claims. That evidence is helpful in defending bad-faith lawsuits.

Claim representatives should thoroughly investigate claims and collect all relevant and necessary evidence. Investigation should continue as long as new facts develop or become available. Claim representatives should develop the information and documentation necessary to determine liability and damages and should make decisions once they believe they have sufficient information to do so. They should not delay decisions while trying to uncover or investigate what could be construed by a jury as unnecessary information.

A claim file must be organized so that the information is readable and easy to follow. For example, medical bills, doctors' reports, and other information on each claimant should be in a logical order. Photographs, police reports, and other documentary evidence should be sorted for easy reference.

In a thorough investigation, the claim representative is alert for new information that may change the course of the claim. For example, a homeowner files a claim for an injury to a visitor who fell on his front step. This may appear to be a simple claim. However, a claim representative may discover from the homeowner's statement that the visitor was actually a resident of the household or was on the premises as a business customer. Either situation may exclude coverage under the homeowner's policy. Without the additional investigation, the claim representative may have paid a claim that was not covered by the policy.

Claim representatives often determine when an investigation is sufficiently thorough, using their own judgment. For example, the insurer's claim handling guidelines offer guidance about which claims require statements and from which parties. However, a claim representative may decide a statement is necessary for a specific claim, even if the guidelines do not require it. In any case, an investigation should be thorough enough to satisfy a judge and jury that the claim representative followed good-faith claim handling procedures. Evidence of compliance with company procedures or best practices used in investigation helps convince the court or jury.

Investigation must also be timely. An insured who makes a claim expects prompt contact from the claim representative. Most insurers have guidelines requiring the claim representative to contact the insured and the claimant within a specific period, such as twenty-four hours after the claim has been submitted. Timely contact with the parties to the claim benefits the insurer in several ways. First, parties are more likely to remember the details of the loss accurately. Memory fades quickly over time; therefore claim representatives are most likely to get complete, accurate information from insureds and claimants if they contact them promptly. Second, the parties are more likely to share information if contacted promptly; prompt contact reassures insureds and claimants that their claims are important and makes them less likely to accept the advice of others who may encourage them to retain a lawyer or pursue unnecessary litigation. Documentation of timely contact in the claim file can help prove an insurer's use of good-faith claim handling procedures and/or the insurer's compliance with the provisions of the Model Act.

Finally, the investigation should not be biased. Bias in claim handling is a predisposition to a particular outcome. When investigating claims, claim representatives should pursue all relevant evidence, especially evidence that establishes the claim's legitimacy, without bias. They should avoid asking misleading questions that slant the answers toward a particular outcome, such as "The light was red when you saw it, wasn't it?" In addition, claim representatives should work with service providers that are unbiased and have no conflict of interest. As mentioned previously, courts and juries may not look sympathetically on medical providers or repair facilities that always favor insurers. Investigations should seek to discover the facts and consider all aspects of the claims so that decisions are impartial and fair.

When conducting a good-faith claim investigation, claim representatives must comply not only with state unfair claim practices acts, but also with federal statutes. These statutes, designed to ensure the privacy of confidential information, include the Health Insurance Portability and Accountability Act of 1996, the Gramm-Leach-Bliley Act, the Sarbanes-Oxley Act, and the Fair Credit Reporting Act.

Health Insurance Portability and Accountability Act of 1996

Claim representatives must be careful in handling confidential information learned about an insured or a claimant during the course of a claim investigation. Several statutes and regulations govern the handling of information. Congress established the Health Insurance Portability and Accountability Act of 1996 (HIPAA)[10] to address the use and disclosure of individual health information. HIPAA applies to health plans, healthcare clearing houses (that process health information), and healthcare providers, termed "covered entities" in the act. Its major goal is to protect individuals' health information while allowing the flow of information to provide and promote high quality healthcare. A major aspect of the primary rule in this act concerns the disclosure of medical information in connection with claims or potential claims.

HIPAA describes permitted uses and disclosures of protected information. A covered entity is permitted, but not required, to use and disclose protected health information, without an individual's authorization, as follows:

- When the information is disclosed to the individual
- When the information is used in treatment, payment, and healthcare operations, such as sending a patient's medical records to another doctor
- When the individual is given the opportunity to agree or object to certain disclosures
- When the information is incident to an otherwise permitted use and disclosure
- In the interests of public health
- As limited data for the purpose of research, public health, or healthcare operations

A covered entity may rely on professional ethics and best judgment in deciding which of these uses are permitted. Claim representatives must be aware of HIPAA restrictions and obtain the necessary authorizations to obtain HIPAA-protected information.

Gramm-Leach-Bliley Act

Congress enacted the Gramm-Leach-Bliley Act of 1999 (GLB)[11] to protect the security and confidentiality of customers of financial institutions. GLB sets forth requirements for protecting and using customer information. GLB applies to financial institutions such as banks, securities firms, insurers, and others who provide financial services and products to consumers and protects both current and prior customers of these institutions. The act includes requirements for handling confidential information and a disclosure provision, which requires companies to advise consumers of the company's information-sharing practices.

The protected information ranges from general biographical background information to information revealed in connection with a transaction. The act also provides several exceptions, including information required to be shared in administering a financial transaction authorized by a customer or made in connection with fraud prevention. Claim representatives must be aware of GLB because it may restrict their access to financial information obtained by their company for a purpose other than a claim, but which would be useful to the claim investigation.

Sarbanes-Oxley Act

Congress enacted the Sarbanes-Oxley Act[12] in 2002 in response to the financial and accounting scandals of the 1990s. This act requires publicly traded companies to meet and certify certain financial disclosure requirements. It requires commercial insureds and many insurers to conduct more intense investigations of their claims from an accounting standpoint to make sure they comply with the law. This requires more extensive reporting of claim information, greater accuracy in setting claim reserves, and more extensive audits of claims and claim files.

Fair Credit Reporting Act

Congress enacted the Fair Credit Reporting Act[13] in 1970 to promote the accuracy and privacy of personal information assembled by credit reporting agencies. The personal information includes credit reports, consumer investigation reports, and employment background checks.

The act requires reporting agencies to follow "reasonable procedures" to protect the confidentiality and privacy of personal information. To this end, procedures are established to handle personal information that includes the right to access and correct credit information.

Claim representatives should be aware of the restrictions imposed by the Fair Credit Reporting Act should they find it necessary to obtain or disclose an insured's or a claimant's financial information during a claim investigation. Claim representatives should check with their supervisors or managers to determine what "reasonable procedures" are in place to protect the confidentiality of this information.

While a violation of these statutes may not lead to a bad-faith claim, it may lead to a claim for extracontractual liability because the violations fall outside the scope of the policy but have occurred during the course of claim handling.

Complete and Accurate Documentation

A common saying among claim representatives is that if an activity, action, or event is not written in the claim file, it did not happen. A claim file must provide to anyone who reads the claim file a complete and accurate account of all the activities and actions taken by the claim representative. Claim representatives must remember that a claim file may be read by many different people, each with a different purpose. The claim representative's supervisor or manager may read the file to provide assistance to the claim representative. A home-office examiner or an auditor may review the file for compliance with claim handling guidelines. Claim department peers may review the file as part of a roundtable discussion of reserving. The underwriter, the agent, or the broker may review the file to determine whether the coverage determination or valuation is appropriate. A state insurance department may review the file in response to a complaint or during a market conduct study. Defense counsel, and maybe even the claimant's counsel, will review the claim file during the course of litigation. Mediators and arbitrators may review the file as part of a dispute resolution process. Regardless of who reads the file, no reader should be left wondering why something did or did not happen or how a conclusion was reached.

Fair Evaluation

Another aspect of good-faith claim handling is the fair evaluation of the claim. This is particularly important in liability claims. A fair approach to evaluating liability claims is to evaluate them as if no coverage limit existed. This approach helps claim representatives avoid the mistake of unfairly attempting to settle a claim for less than the policy limit when it may be worth more.

A crucial element of fair claim evaluation is a prompt evaluation. The evaluation of a claim usually takes place at the conclusion of the investigation, when the claim representative has received all supporting documentation. Unfair claims settlement practices acts often specify time limits within which evaluations of coverage and damages must be completed. Claim representatives' compliance with these requirements helps reduce the insurer's exposure to bad-faith claims.

Promptness is also important in responding to the claimant, the insured, or their respective lawyers' demands. If a letter specifies a time limit for reply, the claim representative should make every effort to respond within that limit or should respond by telephone and explain why more time is needed. The call should be confirmed promptly in a follow-up letter or e-mail. Any time extension agreed on should be documented by a letter and a copy should be placed in the claim file.

Courts have dismissed bad-faith claims based on unreasonable time limits. In some cases, the opposing side may set intentionally unreasonable limits to raise the inference of bad faith or to pressure a claim representative into settling before thoroughly investigating the claim. Prompt handling and constant attention help avoid these situations.

If a letter or another communication contains a demand that is at or near the policy limits, a prompt reply is particularly important. The lawyer may contend that the case is worth much more than the policy limits but that the client will accept the policy limits if the claim is settled quickly. If the claim representative has properly evaluated and documented the claim file, this time demand should pose no problem.

Claim representatives can perform a fair evaluation if they have conducted a thorough, timely, unbiased investigation and understand the jurisdiction of the claim. In addition, to assist in making a knowledgeable evaluation, they can consult with sources inside and outside the insurance company, including the following:

- Co-workers
- Supervisors and managers

- Defense lawyers who are already involved in the case
- Other defense lawyers who are not involved in the case
- People who represent a typical jury
- Computer-generated damage or injury evaluations
- Jury verdict research companies

Information about settlements or trial results from similar cases gained from any of these sources can help claim representatives knowledgeably evaluate the claim. However, each claim is unique and should be evaluated on its own merits.

Fair evaluations are based on facts, not opinions. A claim representative's statement in the file that "I think the case is worth $50,000" is of little value unless the investigation and file documentation substantiate that amount. Claim representatives determine a range of claim amounts based on the facts of the claim, the credibility of the evidence, and applicable laws. This is not an exact science. File documentation showing that the claim representative used best practices to evaluate a claim is evidence of good-faith claim handling. Of course, the amount of the eventual verdict or damages will be used to argue for or against a bad-faith claim.

Good-Faith Negotiation

Good-faith negotiations flow naturally from thorough, timely, unbiased investigations and prompt, fair evaluations. Courts in some jurisdictions have held that an insurer cannot be liable for bad faith for not settling a claim unless the claimant has made a settlement demand. However, claim representatives should take the initiative in making realistic offers when doing so is likely to promote a settlement. Such offers may include an offer to settle before a demand is ever made.

Although claim representatives must make realistic offers and carefully consider all demands, lawyers are not held to the same standard. They can make exaggerated demands in a vigorous representation of their clients, and their clients often expect them to do so, in the hope of obtaining the best settlement possible. Claim representatives should evaluate each claim fairly and respond to such demands by offering a settlement that is consistent with the evidence and documentation in the claim file. They should not trade unrealistic offers and demands with lawyers, as such behavior may result in an unrealistic settlement. All responses to demands should be reasonable and made in a courteous and professional manner.

Claim representatives should not allow their emotions or egos to affect negotiations. Unchecked emotions or egos can stop negotiations and prompt arguments. Judgment becomes clouded and the spirit of fair dealing can be replaced with bad feelings. When this happens, everyone loses, and it is more difficult for an insurer to prove that it has followed good-faith claim handling procedures.

Claim representatives should use policy provisions, such as arbitration clauses, when applicable, to resolve disputes over the settlement amount. Adherence to the policy provisions and payment of the amount determined through arbitration places the insurer in a better position to defend a bad-faith lawsuit.[14] Claim representatives should consider all possible forms of voluntary alternative dispute resolution, including mediation or a series of face-to-face negotiations to resolve claims.

Regular and Prompt Communication

Communicating with all parties to a claim (for example, the insured, the defense attorney, and the excess insurer) is a crucial aspect of good-faith claim handling and resolving claims. Keeping insureds informed is especially important because they expect it, they are most likely to make a bad-faith claim, and they may have the most important information about an accident. Regular and prompt communication with the insured achieves several important results, including the following:

- The insured feels like a part of the defense and can offer assistance.
- The insured can participate in discussions about the possibility of settlement and the handling of the claim.
- The correspondence with the insured documents the insurer's good-faith claim handling and the basis for its judgment about settlement.
- The correspondence establishes that the insured gave the insurer informed consent to take on the defense of the case and to decide how to defend it.

The defense attorney should also regularly and promptly inform the insured of all major events in the defense. Any request by an insured not to be informed of these events should be confirmed in writing. Claim representatives and lawyers should document telephone and personal communication in writing and confirm what they learn in such communications if it is crucial to the claim.

If defense lawyers fail to communicate promptly and regularly, claim representatives should contact them to solicit information and correct any misunderstandings. Claim representatives cannot abandon claims to defense lawyers and still meet good-faith claim handling standards.

Written communication from the defense lawyer to the insured may include the following:

- A letter advising that the insurer has received a demand for policy limits with an explanation of the insurer's planned course of action
- A letter indicating that negotiations have stalled, that the claimant has retained a lawyer, and what the insured should do if he or she receives a summons

- If suit is filed, a letter stating the defense lawyer's name, address, and phone number; identifying coverage questions or reservations of rights that result from the lawsuit; advising the insured of a possible excess verdict or punitive damages; and advising the insured of the right to hire a lawyer at the insured's own expense
- A letter stating that the claim has been settled without trial
- A letter stating that the court's decision is being appealed

If the insured has excess insurance, the claim representative should notify the excess insurer of the claim and provide the insured with copies of all communications. The excess insurer may request a copy of the claim file and may or may not want to be actively involved in the claim thereafter to protect its interests. Additionally, if the insured hires a lawyer, that lawyer will want to be kept advised of significant claim activity.

Competent Legal Advice

As previously mentioned, following the advice of competent lawyers can be considered evidence that an insurer acted in good faith. Lawyers who defend the insured should be selected based on their experience, knowledge of the law, and success in the courtroom. Lawyers have an ethical obligation to be loyal to the insured first and the insurer second, because the insured is the lawyer's client, regardless of who is paying the lawyer's fees. Defense lawyers who are overly optimistic about their chances of successfully defending a case may not be good choices, because their optimism may be unproven and can expose the insured and insurer to an excess verdict. Claim representatives should provide lawyers with all information and documentation necessary to reach a complete and accurate opinion and should avoid any attempts to influence the lawyer's independent judgment.

When resolving a coverage question, insurers should avoid conflicts of interest by using lawyers other than the defense lawyers hired to defend an insured. Asking a lawyer who defends an insured a coverage question creates an ethical dilemma for that lawyer because the answer may not be in the insured's best interest. Insurers that use in-house or staff lawyers (lawyers who are the insurer's employees) to defend insureds should be especially sensitive to the possibility of a conflict of interest and, if any appearance of such a conflict exists, should use outside lawyers.

Effective Claim Management

An insurer's claim management directly affects a claim representative's ability to handle claims in good faith. Claim management in this context refers to how claim departments are managed by claim managers and claim supervisors.

Claim management involves many duties. Although every duty is important, the following three are crucial to good-faith claim handling:

1. Consistent supervision
2. Thorough training
3. Manageable caseloads

Consistent Supervision

Supervisors and managers should work with claim representatives frequently and consistently to ensure that claims are investigated, evaluated, and resolved promptly and accurately. Supervisors and managers are responsible for quality control and for ensuring that claim representatives follow proper claim handling practices. They should make notes in files to document their reviews and to provide instruction and guidance. If a supervisor recognizes delays or improper claim handling practices, he or she must act to correct the problems and document those actions.

Managers also have a responsibility to maintain proper claim handling standards and practices. They develop guidelines for claim handling and are ultimately responsible for ensuring that the guidelines are followed.

Supervisors and managers have more settlement authority (the authority to settle a claim up to a specified dollar amount) than claim representatives. Therefore, they should become involved in the settlement evaluation and strategy when the claim representative's settlement authority is exceeded.

Thorough Training

Insurers should provide continuous and consistent training for claim representatives relating to all necessary claim handling procedures and best practices as well as to good-faith claim handling. Training is essential when a claim representative handles a new type of claim or a more complex, serious claim for the first time. Claim representatives should make an effort to continually improve their competence in handling claims, and training is one way to improve.

Manageable Caseloads

Supervisors and managers must monitor the number of claims assigned to a claim representative (referred to as caseload or pending) to ensure that the work is manageable. Situations arise when caseloads increase, such as when one or more claim representatives leave the company or are out of the office for an extended period. At some point, a claim representative's caseload may become unmanageable and increase the possibility of a bad-faith claim. Supervisors and managers must monitor caseloads to identify potential problems and reassign claims or provide support to ensure good-faith claim handling.

Claim representatives who practice good-faith claim handling know their job is to properly and expeditiously resolve claims according to the facts, law, and policy language. They do not delay or minimize claim payments. Some insurers summarize good-faith claim handling as "doing what is right." Claim representatives who adopt this attitude are likely to avoid or reduce the occurrence of bad-faith claims.

SUMMARY

Insurers and the claim representatives who work for them have a duty of good faith and fair dealing in claim handling. This requirement is imposed on insurers and claim representatives because of (1) the public interest in ensuring that insurers have the financial resources to pay claims and that they pay claims fairly and promptly, (2) the unequal bargaining power of the parties to the insurance contract, and (3) the insurer's control over the investigation and resolution of the claim. If insurers or their claim representatives do not live up to the standard of good faith and fair dealing, they are said to be acting in bad faith.

The definition of bad faith varies by state but can be generalized as any unfounded refusal to pay a claim. Courts have interpreted this definition in many ways, so claim representatives must be aware of the bad-faith law in every state in which they handle claims. Generally, a bad-faith lawsuit can be based on the claim representative's negligence or gross or intentional misconduct.

Bad-faith claims or lawsuits are usually brought by the insured against the insurer for the handling of the insured's first-party claim or the handling of a third-party claim against the insured. If the insured assigns the right to sue his or her insurer for bad faith to a claimant, the claimant can sue the insurer for bad faith. Bad-faith claims can also be brought against an insurer by an excess insurer that has had to pay a claim because of the insurer's bad faith.

Bad-faith claims usually result from a claim or coverage denial, a verdict in excess of the policy limit, or a violation of a state statute or of an unfair claims settlement practices act. In an effort to bring uniformity to the standard of conduct to which insurers and claim representatives are held, the NAIC created the Model Unfair Claims Settlement Practices Act, which act lists practices that are generally accepted as unfair claims settlement practices. Most states have adopted some or all of the Model Act's provisions.

Damages resulting from bad faith or extracontractual liability can vary by jurisdiction. Generally, they can include compensatory damages, emotional distress damages, and punitive damages. Among compensatory damages are lawyers' fees, court costs, and interest.

Insurers and claim representatives have several defenses available to combat a bad-faith claim or reduce the amount of damages awarded. The defenses include statutes of limitations, lack of right to sue, reliance on lawyers' advice, insured's collusion with the claimant, debatable reasonable basis, statutory defenses, fair dealing and good documentation, comparative bad faith, contributory negligence, and availability of higher policy limits.

To use these defenses, the insurer and the claim representative must be able to show they acted in good faith. The claim file must contain documentation of a thorough investigation; a fair, prompt, and knowledgeable evaluation of the claim; and a documentation of good-faith negotiation. The file should reflect prompt and adequate communication among the parties to the claim, the insurer's consideration of legal advice, and adherence to the insurer's claim management practices. The file should also show compliance with federal statutes such as the Health Insurance Portability and Accountability Act of 1996, the Gramm-Leach-Bliley Act, the Sarbanes-Oxley Act, and the Fair Credit Reporting Act.

Handling claims in good faith also means handling claims ethically. Ethics in claim handling is the topic of the next chapter.

CHAPTER NOTES

1. Form ISO HO 00 03 05 01, Copyright ISO Properties, Inc., 1999.
2. *Slater v. Motorists Mut. Ins. Co.*, 174 Ohio St. 148, 187 N.E.2d 45 (1962).
3. *Commercial Union Ins. Co. v. Liberty Mutual Ins. Co.*, 393 N.W.2d 161, 164 (Mich. 1986).
4. *Pickett v. Lloyd's*, 621 A.2d 445, 451 (N.J. 1993).
5. California Insurance Code Section 11580(b)(2).
6. *American Centennial Ins. v. American Home Assur. Co.*, 729 F. Supp. 1228, 1232 (N.D. Ill. 1990).
7. 42 Pa. C.S.A. §8371.
8. "Bad Faith in the 90's: Successful Tactics & Strategies for Defending the Insurer," sponsored by The CPCU Society's Golden Gate Chapter, presented by Ropers, Majeski, Kohn & Bently, a Professional Corporation, San Francisco, p. 33.
9. *Chapman v. Norfolk & Dedham Mut. Fire Ins. Co.*, 39 Conn. App. 306, 665 A.2d 112, cert. denied, 235 Conn. 925, 666 A.2d 1185 (1995).
10. Quoted and/or adapted from Department of Health and Human Services, *OCR Privacy Brief*, available at the department's Web site: www.hhs.gov/ocr/hipaa/ (accessed October 17, 2005).
11. 15 U.S.C. § 6801 et seq. (2005).
12. 15 U.S.C. § 7201 et seq. (2005).
13. 15 U.S.C. § 1681 et seq. (2005).
14. "Bad Faith in the 90's: Successful Tactics & Strategies for Defending the Insurer," p. 45.

Appendix
Provisions of 1990 NAIC Model Unfair Claims Settlement Practices Act

This appendix presents Sections 3 and 4 of the act, with illustrative examples.

Section 3—Unfair Claims Settlement Practices Prohibited

It is an improper claims practice for a domestic, foreign or alien insurer transacting business in this state to commit an act defined in Section 4 of this Act if:

A. It is committed flagrantly and in conscious disregard of this Act or any rules promulgated hereunder; or
B. It has been committed with such frequency to indicate a general business practice to engage in that type of conduct.

Section 4—Unfair Claims Practices Defined

Any of the following acts by an insurer, if committed in violation of Section 3, constitutes an unfair claims practice:

A. Knowingly misrepresenting to claimants and insureds relevant facts or policy provisions relating to coverages at issue;

> **Example**
> A claim representative tries to reduce claim payments by withholding information or misleading an insured on lesser-known coverages, such as additional living expenses, rental-car coverage, or business interruption.

B. Failing to acknowledge with reasonable promptness pertinent communications with respect to claims arising under its policies;

> **Example**
> A claim representative is too busy to answer telephone messages or to respond to letters from insureds and claimants. A short delay with proper explanations may be tolerated, but some state codes require telephone contact within forty-eight hours and responses to letters within ten days.

C. Failing to adopt and implement reasonable standards for the prompt investigation and settlement of claims arising under its policies;

> **Example**
>
> Most insurers require claim representatives to contact the parties within twenty-four hours. An insurer without such a rule may violate this provision by failing to adopt reasonable contact standards. Or insurers may have such standards and fail to implement them. For example, even though an insurer has a twenty-four-hour contact rule, claim representatives may know that supervisors never hold them to that standard. In addition, investigations that are unnecessarily prolonged may violate this standard of timely contact or investigation.

D. Not attempting in good faith to effectuate prompt, fair and equitable settlement of claims submitted in which liability has become reasonably clear;

> **Example**
>
> An accident occurs for which coverage is available under two policies from two insurers. If the two insurers pass the claim back and forth to avoid making payment even though each is clearly liable for at least a portion of the loss, they have violated this provision.

E. Compelling insureds or beneficiaries to institute suits to recover amounts due under its policies by offering substantially less than the amounts ultimately recovered in suits brought by them;

> **Example**
>
> A claim representative approaches an insured with a settlement offer that is only a fraction of what the claim is worth. This behavior is a blatant violation of the letter and the spirit of the Model Act and can therefore be a basis for a bad-faith claim.

F. Refusing to pay claims without conducting a reasonable investigation;

> **Example**
>
> A claim representative obtains incomplete facts about a loss, decides the damage is not covered, and denies the claim all in one phone conversation with the insured. If a reasonably complete investigation would show that the denial is incorrect, such a denial violates the Model Act.

G. Failing to affirm or deny coverage of claims within a reasonable time after having completed its investigation related to such claim or claims;

> **Example**
>
> A claim representative sends a coverage question report to claim management, who sends it to a lawyer, then to the home office. If each step takes a week, the process results in a substantial delay, which may be considered unreasonable under the Model Act.

H. Attempting to settle or settling claims for less than the amount that a reasonable person would believe the insured or beneficiary was entitled by reference to written or printed advertising material accompanying or made part of an application;

> **Example**
>
> An insured sees the terms "guaranteed replacement cost" on an advertising brochure. However, the policy has conditions that restrict the instances in which insureds can receive that benefit. If the difference between what is advertised and what the policy provisions are is too great or misleading, this provision of the Model Act may require the insurer to handle the claim according to what was stated in the advertising instead of the policy provisions. To do otherwise would be considered unreasonable under the Model Act.

I. Attempting to settle or settling claims on the basis of an application that was materially altered without notice to, or knowledge or consent of, the insured;

> **Example**
>
> After a policy is bound (coverage promised to the insured), the agent realizes that an expensive piece of jewelry requires a limitation on coverage. If the limitation was not explained to the insured prior to the policy being bound, that change in the policy must be promptly communicated to the insured. If not, the insured would be correct in assuming that any loss would be handled without the limitation.

J. Making claims payments to an insured or beneficiary without indicating the coverage under which each payment is being made;

> **Example**
>
> A claim representative settles a claim by mailing a check to the insured without an explanation. The claim representative may have mistakenly failed to include an explanation or may have done so deliberately under the assumption that, given an explanation, the insured might have challenged the amount.

K. Unreasonably delaying the investigation or payment of claims by requiring both a formal proof of loss form and subsequent verification that would result in duplication of information and verification appearing in the formal proof of loss form;

> **Example**
>
> An insured files a claim and completes several forms itemizing the damaged property. Several weeks later, the insurer requires the insured to comply with the conditions of the policy by filing a sworn statement and proof of loss that requests the same information already obtained. Redundant requests for information that cause unreasonable delay must be avoided even though a policy may allow for them.

L. Failing in the case of claims denials or offers of compromise settlement to promptly provide a reasonable and accurate explanation of the basis for such actions;

> **Example**
>
> An insured makes a claim for $2,500 for a damaged roof based on an estimate from a contractor. If the claim representative mails a denial letter to the insured but the letter does not provide an explanation of the reasons for the denial of coverage, he or she has probably violated the Model Act. There may be valid reasons for denial, but those reasons must be explained to the insured.

M. Failing to provide forms necessary to present claims within fifteen (15) calendar days of a request with reasonable explanations regarding their use;

> **Example**
>
> An insured needs personal property inventory forms to list damaged contents. When the insured requests blank forms from the insurer, the claim representative has fifteen days in which to provide them. This is the only provision in the Model Act in which a specific number of days is stated. Failure to comply with this provision is a violation of the Model Act.

N. Failing to adopt and implement reasonable standards to assure that the repairs of a repairer owned by or required to be used by the insurer are performed in a workmanlike manner;

> **Example**
>
> An insurer uses specific glass-replacement shops that provide discounts for the work done for insureds. If these shops do careless work, the insurer must act to improve their quality or discontinue doing business with them.

Adapted from the NAIC's Model Unfair Claims Settlement Practices Act, December 1990. Copyright National Association of Insurance Commissioners. Reprinted with permission. Further reprint or distribution strictly prohibited.

Chapter 6

Direct Your Learning

Ethics and Professionalism

After learning the content of this chapter and completing the corresponding course guide assignment, you should be able to:

- Explain why ethics and professionalism are important to a claim representative.
- Describe the ethical and professional dilemmas claim representatives can face.
- Explain how codes of ethics and quality claim practices can promote high ethical and professional standards.
- Given a claim, explain why a situation presents an ethical or a professional dilemma.
- Define or describe each of the Key Words and Phrases for this chapter.

OUTLINE

Importance of Ethics and Professionalism

Ethical and Professional Dilemmas

Ethical and Professional Standards

Summary

Appendix A

Appendix B

Develop Your Perspective

What are the main topics covered in the chapter?

Good-faith claim handling depends on the ethics and professionalism of the claim representative. This chapter describes the importance of ethics and professionalism, the ethical dilemmas claim representatives may face, and the standards claim representatives must abide by when addressing ethical dilemmas.

Consider the activities of everyday claim handling.

- Which activities could present a conflict of interest?
- How might competency present an ethical dilemma for claim representatives?

Why is it important to learn about these topics?

Claim representatives can frequently encounter ethical dilemmas. Claim representatives who make professional and ethical decisions better represent the insurer, provide better customer service, abide by consumer protection regulations, and may experience greater personal satisfaction.

Consider an ethical dilemma of claim handling. In resolving that dilemma:

- What stakeholder interests would you consider?
- Who else would you involve in the decision making?
- What activities would you avoid so that there is no appearance of conflict of interest?

How can you use what you will learn?

Evaluate the resolution of an ethical dilemma your employer handled in the past.

- How well did your employer consider the interests of all the stakeholders?
- What might you have done differently in resolving the dilemma?
- Have subsequent ethical dilemmas been handled differently based on lessons learned?

Chapter 6
Ethics and Professionalism

Ethics (a set of principles and values) and professionalism (the behavior or qualities that characterize a profession) are the foundation of good-faith claim handling. Good-faith claim handling means that claim representatives make an honest effort to determine whether and to what extent a claim is covered. Ethics is particularly important in good-faith claim handling because claim representatives face numerous ethical dilemmas trying to balance the interests of insureds and claimants, who are their customers, and the interests of insurers, who are their employers.

Ethics is the set of principles and values that determines what is the *better* course of action, given the choice of two or more legal courses of action. In today's business environment, being ethical is often equated with merely obeying the law; however, ethical behavior goes beyond merely obeying the law. Legality involves making a choice between what is lawful and what is unlawful. Ethics involves making a choice between an acceptable course of action and a better one. For example, it is not illegal for one person to remain silent when someone else, a competitor for example, is falsely accused of improper behavior. However, not speaking up could be considered unethical, particularly if the accusation causes the competitor harm and the party who remains silent thereby benefits.

Professionalism involves the behavior and qualities necessary to properly implement an ethical decision. In the example of the falsely accused competitor, professionalism requires the nonaccused party to speak up in a timely, objective manner. Professionals should also act knowledgeably, courteously, and empathetically.

In addition to emphasizing the importance of ethics and professionalism, this chapter examines dilemmas that claim representatives may face and possible responses, and suggests frameworks for the claim representative to use in making ethical decisions.

IMPORTANCE OF ETHICS AND PROFESSIONALISM

Ethics and professionalism are of utmost importance for insurers and claim representatives for three reasons. First, insurers and claim representatives are bound by the insurance contract to act in good faith, and, to do so, they must act ethically and professionally. They must keep the promises specified in insurance policies, as well as those created by law. In insurance transactions, the insured pays a premium for the insurer's promise to handle claims in good faith. The insurance policy states the terms of that promise. In fulfilling the promises insurers make in their policies, claim representatives encounter and attempt to satisfy a variety of parties, including insureds, claimants, producers, service providers, regulators, and the general public. When the needs of these parties conflict, claim representatives may be faced with dilemmas that require their understanding of and ability to apply ethical and professional principles.

In addition to the promises made in the insurance policy, claim representatives make many other promises to insureds, claimants, vendors, and their employers. For example, a claim representative may promise to contact an insured, claimant, or vendor within a specified time. Promises to employers may include a promise to follow an employer's code of business conduct, complete a course of continuing education, maintain appropriate licensing, or conform to dress codes. Claim representatives must keep these promises if they want to behave ethically and professionally.

Another reason ethics and professionalism are important is that claim representatives' behavior can affect public trust in and credibility of insurers. Unethical or unprofessional conduct can affect the insurer adversely. Although claim representatives handle thousands of claims ethically, professionally, and without complaint on a daily basis, one incident that violates the public's expectations of ethical or professional conduct may receive wide publicity and can damage the insurer's credibility and the public's trust. News about collusion between insurers and brokers to fix prices, inappropriate claim denials during catastrophes, and insurance executives' mishandling of corporate funds contributes to a negative public image of the insurance business. Consequently, most insurers recognize that abiding by ethical and professional standards of conduct is essential to improving their public image.

A third reason that ethics and professionalism are important is that consumer regulations create legal duties for insurers. Claim representatives have an ethical and professional responsibility to comply with these regulations to ensure that consumers are treated fairly through prompt, honest, and responsive claim handling. Some consumer regulations may also define the minimum expected ethical and professional standards for insurers and claim representatives. In addition, many insurers have good-faith claim handling guidelines in place that exceed these minimum standards, and such guidelines may also describe the insurer's philosophy regarding ethical and professional conduct. Both regulatory requirements and insurers' guidelines can provide guidance to claim representatives regarding ethical and professional claim handling conduct.

Ethical and professional conduct benefits claim representatives, insurers, consumers, and the general public. For the claim representative, ethical and professional conduct can be the foundation of a successful, satisfying career. For insurers, ethical and professional conduct can help retain customers and attract investors. Consumers who believe they have been treated fairly are more likely to renew their policies with the same insurer, thus reducing insurers' acquisition costs and improving financial performance. When insurers' financial performance improves, insurers can more easily attract investors.

Ethical and professional conduct can benefit consumers by encouraging fair treatment and prompt payment. Insureds and, by extension, society can reap the benefits of insurance—peace of mind, support for credit, efficient use of resources, and reduction of social burdens—only if the business of insurance is conducted ethically and professionally.

Behaving ethically and professionally is not without challenge; claim representatives often face difficult ethical issues. Recognizing these issues and responding appropriately is a lifelong learning process.

ETHICAL AND PROFESSIONAL DILEMMAS

In addition to the distinction made previously in this chapter between ethical dilemmas and legal dilemmas, a distinction can also be made between ethical dilemmas and moral dilemmas. Generally, moral dilemmas are characterized as right versus wrong and ethical dilemmas are characterized as right versus right. An example of a moral dilemma is keeping the money in a found wallet versus returning it to the owner. An example of an ethical dilemma is answering a question honestly versus keeping a promise to guard confidential information.

> **Values Conflicts in Ethical Dilemmas**
>
> Ethical dilemmas may raise conflicts in values, for example between being honest or keeping a promise, between an individual interest and a community interest, between immediate needs and long-term needs, and between fairness and compassion.

Ethical dilemmas usually provide more decision options than moral dilemmas do. In ethical dilemmas, the choices may be to do Act A, do Act B, do neither, or do both. In moral dilemmas the decision choices usually involve either doing or not doing a particular act. Several frameworks are available for resolving ethical dilemmas. One framework involves answering a series of questions about the ethical dilemma and possible solutions, assuming the options are legal. The questions could include the following:

- Who are the stakeholders, and what are their rights?
- Is the information about the dilemma reliable and accurate?
- Who should be involved in making the decision?
- Who might be harmed by each option and how?
- What are the long-term results of each option?
- What would be the consequences if the decision were made public?

In addition to these general questions, claim representatives can ask themselves personal questions, such as the following:

- How would I feel if my mother (or children) knew of my decision?
- What would a person whom I respect do in this situation?
- Am I using this decision for my own personal gain?
- Does anything about the decision not "feel right"?

Another framework claim representatives can use to help resolve ethical dilemmas is to evaluate three types of effects that decisions can have: maximizing effect, normalizing effect, and empathizing effect. With the maximizing effect, the claim representative focuses on the extent of the decision's effect. A decision that provides the greatest benefit to the greatest number of people would have a maximizing effect. With the normalizing effect, the claim representative focuses on determining the most common, acceptable standard of behavior. A decision to implement a legally acceptable business practice would have a normalizing effect. Finally, with the empathizing effect, the claim representative follows the golden rule: A decision that treats someone the way the claim representative would want to be treated in the same situation would have an empathizing effect. Of course, two different decisions can have more than one effect. For example, implementing a legally acceptable decision could have both a normalizing and a maximizing effect. Therefore, claim representatives can also consider the desirable combination of effects. This framework to evaluate ethical decisions can be an important tool for claim representatives because it allows them to evaluate the effects of different ethical decisions, each effect having merit.

Claim representatives can use these frameworks to resolve specific ethical dilemmas that arise in a variety of situations and those that arise in specific areas of claim handling. These types of dilemmas or situations include conflicts of interest, competency, continuing education, licensing, customer service, *ex parte* contacts, billing practices, privacy, and detecting fraud.

Many of these ethical dilemmas also raise issues of professionalism. For example, the conflict of interest that arises when a claim representative accepts an expensive gift from a service provider (an ethical dilemma) can adversely affect how others perceive the claim representative's level of professionalism. Other service providers may see the behavior as unfair and may conclude that the claim representative is capable of being unduly influenced. Ideally, insurers' claim handling guidelines provide guidance for claim representatives in how to appropriately respond to professional dilemmas. In the conflict of interest example, such guidelines might make it clear to the claim representative that accepting gifts from service providers is not professional behavior. Similarly, a claim representative who does not return phone calls in a timely manner will earn a reputation as someone who avoids work and is therefore not acting professionally.

Conflicts of Interest

Many ethical dilemmas arise from potential conflicts of interest. A conflict of interest is defined as a conflict between a private interest and official responsibilities. A conflict of interest can arise in many ways during claim handling, such as when employees have the opportunity to purchase salvage, when vendors offer claim representatives incentives for referring business to them, or when the insurer provides coverages for one or more insureds involved in the same claim (overlapping coverages or insureds). The conflict may be between the claim representative's personal interest and professional responsibility (in the first two examples) or between the insured's interests and the insurer's interests (in the last example). Generally, conflicts of interest situations involve individual versus community choices or short-term versus long-term choices.

Salvage

A conflict of interest can occur when a stolen item is recovered and is being sold as salvage. For example, a one-carat diamond recovered from a theft claim that sells for $5,000 in a retail store might have a salvage value of $600. A claim representative may be tempted to purchase salvage for a slightly higher amount than the highest bid from an outside salvage buyer. This presents a conflict of interest because the claim representative has an advantage over other potential buyers by virtue of knowing the salvage bids and being able to place a higher bid. Because of the potential conflict of interest in such situations, most insurers have specific guidelines that prohibit claim representatives from purchasing salvage. Violations of these guidelines can be grounds for dismissal.

Vendor Incentives

Claim representatives often refer insureds to vendors that can help them replace or repair lost or damaged property. A conflict of interest can arise when vendors offer gifts (such as vacations or hard-to-get tickets to special events), favors, gratuities, or other incentives in an effort to get more business referrals from claim representatives. Claim representatives should recommend and select vendors based strictly on the vendors' merits. Any other factor, such as friendship or gifts, that influences a claim representative's referral results in a conflict of interest.

Many insurers have guidelines that either prohibit the acceptance of incentives or that set dollar value limits on incentives that can be accepted. Compliance with such procedures helps the claim representative avoid situations in which their claim handling decisions are influenced by vendors' gifts.

Overlapping Coverages or Insureds

Another conflict of interest can arise from overlapping coverages or overlapping insureds. This situation occurs when the insurer provides multiple coverages for one insured that are triggered by the same occurrence or when the insurer covers several insureds involved in the same claim. A claim representative faced with decisions involving several coverages or claims for several insureds may encounter conflicting responsibilities, such as those related to apportioning liability among parties. To avoid this conflict of interest, insurers may have guidelines that require the claim to be bifurcated, or split into parts, with a different claim representative handling each part independently. Bifurcating the claim handling responsibilities between different claim representatives reduces the potential for a conflict of interest because each claim representative can focus on the assigned coverage or insured, thus protecting the insured's interests.

The following examples illustrate conflicts of interest involving multiple coverages or multiple insureds.

> **Overlapping Conflicts of Interest Arising From Overlapping Coverages or Insureds**
>
> An example of an *overlapping coverages* case involves an insured injured in a vehicle collision with an uninsured motorist who is responsible for the accident. The insured has personal injury protection (PIP) coverage and uninsured motorists coverage on his own policy. The claim representative's responsibilities in handling the PIP claim can conflict with those in handling the uninsured motorists claim because the latter relies on the medical expenses paid as a measure of damages. Some states may have case law that requires insurers to pay PIP benefits based on less stringent criteria than the policy language; for example, a payment for the insured's eyeglasses broken in the accident may be required as a PIP benefit.
>
> For the uninsured motorists claim, the claim representative would evaluate those same medical expenses and determine some of them, such as the glasses, to be an unrelated expense and, therefore, noncompensable. The claim representative's interest in properly paying the PIP claim can conflict with the interest to properly evaluate the uninsured motorists claim. To avoid this ethical dilemma, a different claim representative can be assigned to each part of the claim.
>
> An example of an *overlapping insureds* case involves two insureds, A and B, who have auto liability coverage from the same insurer. A and B are involved in an accident with Claimant C. Claimant C alleges that both A and B are responsible for the accident. The interests of Insured A conflict with those of Insured B. Each wants the other to be found responsible for the accident. The claims against Insured A and Insured B should be handled by different claim representatives, who can make liability determinations independently of one another.

Claim Handling Competency

Claim representatives who lack competency can commit ethical improprieties by paying claims that are not covered; overpaying claims because of poor investigation or negotiation; and denying claims that are covered, leading to increased customer dissatisfaction, turnover, litigation, and bad-faith lawsuits.

> **Factors That Can Affect Claim Handling Competency**
>
> 1. Changes in the claim environment
> 2. Changes in job responsibilities
> 3. Normal loss of knowledge over time
> 4. Lack of time or money
> 5. Inequitable rewards and promotions

Claim representatives must be aware of the following five factors that can affect their claim handling competency:

1. *Changes in the claim environment.* Consumer, social, and political forces influence insurance coverage, legal liability, damages, and technology. For example, insurers may broaden a coverage provided by a policy. New court interpretations of policy provisions and evolving liability standards can affect claim handling results. Changes in property damage evaluation can result from policy revisions, new laws, and changing technology, and changes in the auto repair field as a result of changes made by auto manufacturers. Relying strictly on one's memory of policy provisions and being unaware of changing liability and valuation approaches can lead to mistakes in evaluating damages and in settling claims. Consequently, claim representatives must continually update their knowledge.

2. *Changes in job responsibilities.* Claim representatives' responsibilities can change when they take a job with a new employer or in their current job through promotion, assignment to a different territory with different laws, or assignment of new types of claims. New duties usually require new knowledge and skills. Training can help claim representatives taking on new duties be more effective and avoid unethical or unprofessional behavior arising from lack of competency. Some employers offer little formal training beyond that given to new employees. Those promoted from within may be expected to rely on on-the-job training from managers or other colleagues who may lack experience or training skills. Outside educational sources, such as workshops and seminars, may also offer training. To ensure competency, claim personnel and their managers should identify the skills and knowledge required in new positions and implement plans for training and education. Human resources personnel can assist in the needs analysis and in suggesting training resources.

3. *Normal loss of knowledge over time.* Imperfections in human memory cause claim representatives to lose knowledge that they once possessed. The rate of knowledge can be graphed based on scientific research. Exhibit 6-1 shows the Dietz and Jones memory curve,[1] which illustrates the rapid loss of knowledge that occurs after original learning. The curve eventually flattens. Several years after learning, individuals retain only a fraction of the original information.

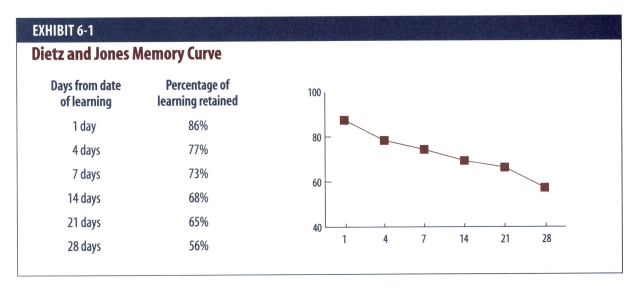

EXHIBIT 6-1

Dietz and Jones Memory Curve

Days from date of learning	Percentage of learning retained
1 day	86%
4 days	77%
7 days	73%
14 days	68%
21 days	65%
28 days	56%

Because of this normal loss of knowledge, even if the claim environment remained static, claim representatives would have to continue learning to maintain the same level of knowledge. Continuing education can reinforce the basics of claim work, refresh knowledge, and enhance skills already mastered.

4. *Lack of time or money.* Line supervisors stretched thin by downsizing have no time to train their staff, and claim representatives with ever-increasing caseloads may think they have no time for training. Such thinking overlooks the fact that training can improve a claim representative's efficiency and save time in the long run. Because investment in training and education is not shown as an asset on the financial statement, insurers may restrict such spending when facing the need to reduce expenses. However, saving money by eliminating or reducing training expenditures is false economy. Finding both the time and money to implement effective training programs can present ethical dilemmas for managers if other expenses must be cut to provide the training. To maintain their own ethical and professional standards, claim representatives may have to be responsible for their own training. Emphasis on reducing expenses may also prevent claim management from hiring before staff shortages occur or from retaining experienced staff. Research by consulting firms and universities indicates that the increased costs incurred for adequate, skilled claim staff are more than offset by the reduction in loss costs and increased customer satisfaction from superior claim service.[2]

5. *Inequitable rewards and promotions.* Claim representatives may be discouraged from improving their competency if they perceive that assignments, promotions, and raises are based on subjective rather than objective criteria. Rewards and promotions that match performance provide incentives for improving competency. Lack of competency and poor performance may become an ethical issue for managers and supervisors if they stem from inequitable rewards, inadequate recognition, or lack of incentives.

As discussed, continuing education is one method to maintain competency. Other ethical dilemmas can also arise from continuing education issues.

Continuing Education

In addition to conflicts of interest and claim handling competency, the need for continuing education can create ethical issues. Claim representatives faced with conflicting demands on their time may be reluctant to pursue continuing education, even where required by law. Continuing education may also be required by codes of professional ethics and insurers' internal codes of ethics. Two examples of codes of ethics relating to claim representatives, found in the appendixes to this chapter, refer to training or education. However, continuing education is valuable to claim representatives not just for complying with such requirements but for maintaining competency, enhancing professionalism and ethical conduct, improving their personal skills, and advancing their careers.

Continuing education can take many forms, including formal classroom education, informal on-the-job coaching from a colleague or manager, and current trade publications. States that require continuing education as a qualification for licensure may specify the form and types of continuing education that fulfill the requirement. Licensing requirements can also raise ethical dilemmas for claim representatives.

Licensing

State licensure laws vary in who is required to be licensed and in the procedures and requirements for licensure. Some states require licensure only for independent adjusters and public adjusters. Other states require staff claim representatives, vehicle damage appraisers, and property appraisers to have licenses. Licensing laws may require claim representatives to pass an examination, pay fees, and provide evidence of continuing education. States often grant temporary licenses to out-of-state claim representatives for catastrophe claim handling.

State laws relating to licensing inside claim representatives can be ambiguous. Some insurers assign groups of inside claim representatives to specific territories that cover more than one state; those claim representatives are licensed in the states in that territory that require licensing. Some insurers encourage or require their claim representatives to hold licenses from states beyond their territories in case their help is needed in a different territory. In the face of varying state licensing laws, such precautions help avoid any legal, ethical, and professional issues that can arise when claim representatives are assigned to new areas either temporarily or permanently.

Licensure-related ethical dilemmas can arise when a manager or supervisor asks a claim representative to assume claim handling responsibilities in a territory in which the claim representative is not licensed. For example, the claim representative who usually handles those claims is out of the office for an emergency. The supervisor believes that, under the state's somewhat ambiguous licensing law, the claim representative can legally handle the claim; the claim representative's interpretation of the law is that she cannot legally handle the claim. The claim representative faces the ethical dilemma of accepting the supervisor's interpretation of the law or following her own interpretation.

Customer Service

Customer service is another area in which claim representatives can encounter ethical dilemmas. Although thorough in describing insurers' promises about coverage, rights, and duties, insurance policies do not define the level of service that claim representatives should provide. Customer service includes prompt and courteous contact, good communication, and prompt payment. When customers receive a lesser quality of service than they expect, they may complain to their agent, the insurer, or the state insurance department. These complaints may call into question a claim representative's professionalism.

Common State Insurance Department Complaints About Customer Service

1. Claim representatives do not thoroughly explain claim procedures to the public.
2. Claim representatives take too long to settle claims after they have all the necessary information.
3. A lack of communication exists between insureds, producers, and claim representatives.
4. Claim representatives do not return phone calls.
5. Claim representatives do not explain how values are determined for vehicles when settling losses.
6. Claim representatives require insureds to furnish police reports, then later tell them they cannot rely on the police report information.
7. Claim representatives require insureds to obtain service from specific body shops and contractors.
8. Claim representatives refuse to help insureds by referring them to auto body shops or contractors.
9. Claim representatives do not explain how actual cash value is determined on homeowners claims.

As these complaints illustrate, customers have high expectations about the quality and timeliness of claim service. Customers who are accustomed to automated teller machines, online information about their utility bills, and instant access to information on the Internet expect the same level of fast, accurate service in their dealings with insurers. Such expectations can create ethical and professional dilemmas.

Because of caseloads and competing demands, claim representatives may be unable to provide the same level of service to all customers. For example, if asked to make a major insured's claim a priority, the claim representative may have to set aside the claim of a smaller insured. Claim representatives should try to treat all insureds equally, yet achieve a balance between the customer's demands and sound business practices, and to provide the level of service that people expect without compromising good-faith claim handling practices.

Ex Parte Contacts

Another area of ethical dilemmas relates to *ex parte* contacts. **Ex parte contacts** are contacts in which only one party is heard. In a claim context, an example of *ex parte* contacts is the claim representative's communication with a claimant without the knowledge of the claimant's attorney. While such contacts are not illegal, they are unethical and unprofessional. However, a claim representative may acquire information from a claimant, unaware that the claimant has retained legal counsel. On learning that legal counsel had been retained, the claim representative faces an ethical dilemma, particularly if the information would benefit the insured or the insurer. To avoid such dilemmas, claim representatives should routinely ask claimants if they have retained legal counsel and should review all claim file correspondence for any notification of legal representation.

Ex parte **contacts**
Contacts in which only one party is heard.

Another example of an *ex parte* contact is when a claim representative authorizes surveillance to determine the extent or validity of a claimant's injuries or disability. The claimant is unaware of the surveillance; therefore, it is a one-sided activity, but generally it is not unethical. Surveillance is often a legitimate and useful part of a thorough investigation. But surveillance used to harass, intimidate, invade privacy, or discredit someone's reputation may be considered unprofessional or unethical. In addition, if surveillance uncovers information that is unrelated to the merits of the claim, claim representatives must ensure that such information remains confidential.

Recording telephone calls also raises *ex parte* issues, for example, when a claim representative records a phone conversation without the other party's knowledge. Some states prohibit the recording of phone conversations without the knowledge of the parties. If state laws or claim department guidelines do not address such situations, the claim representative may encounter an ethical dilemma. The information gathered in a recorded phone conversation could benefit the insurer or the insured, but the party may not have provided the information with knowledge that the conversation was being recorded.

Billing Practices

Ethical dilemmas can arise from the billing practices of service providers and experts. Ethical dilemmas related to billing can also apply to independent adjustors who bill for their work and to claim representatives who allocate claim costs when more than one policy is involved.

When necessary, claim representatives hire service providers, such as lawyers, independent adjusters, or experts, to properly handle claims. Generally, service providers bill the insurer for services they provide on a time and expense basis. However, some bills may relate to more than one claim or to more than one insured involved in the same claim. In these cases, the ethical and professional billing practice may be to prorate the bill among all the involved claims or policies. Claim representatives have an ethical duty to make sure that such providers follow insurer billing guidelines and that they understand the scope of their assigned duties so that any unethical billing practices do not interfere with good-faith claim handling practices. Insurers can reduce the potential for service providers' unethical conduct by developing and following guidelines for billing practices that address such issues.

Time and Expense

Ethical dilemmas arise when time is billed in increments that do not reflect actual time spent. When billing is on a time and expense basis, the service provider must maintain accurate, detailed records of time spent and expenses incurred in providing the services. For example, an independent adjuster may bill in tenth-of-an-hour increments. If a phone call to leave a message with the claim representative takes two minutes, the adjuster will bill for six minutes (one-tenth of an hour) because that is the billing increment. The ethical issue arises when the independent adjuster makes a follow-up call that lasts two minutes: whether to bill another tenth of an hour increment for the follow-up call that lasts two minutes, having already billed for six minutes on the first call.

Allocation

Ethical questions related to billing can also arise when one insurer has written policies covering several parties in a claim. The claim representative must decide how to allocate defense costs and other claim costs among the policies. Should a claim representative be influenced by the fact that one policy provides defense cost coverage in addition to policy limits and another policy includes defense costs within the policy limits? If the insurer does not have guidelines in place that address these issues, claim representatives must decide using their own standards of ethics and professionalism.

Privacy

Matters of privacy can raise ethical dilemmas. Claim representatives have access to and acquire personal, medical, and financial information about others in the course of handling claims. Information may come directly from the insured or claimant or from other sources.

Information gathered by claim representatives may be protected by privacy laws or may be of such a sensitive nature that its disclosure would cause harm. In addition, some individuals may be concerned about information that may not seem personal or confidential to others. For example, an insured may not want a relative to know the value of her home, business, or other belongings. Even accidental or unintentional disclosure can be harmful. Claim representatives must therefore acquire only the information needed to investigate and settle a claim and should not misuse the information acquired or make it available to anyone who does not need it.

Ethical dilemmas arise when claim representatives acquire confidential information that, if disclosed, could benefit another. The obligation to protect privacy and an obligation to share information can conflict.

> **Example of Ethical Dilemma Involving Confidential Information**
>
> A claim representative discovers during an investigation that the insured has a serious communicable disease. The disease does not affect the claim's value, so the claim representative does not need the information to handle the claim. However, others in the insured's workplace and home could contract the disease. Should the claim representative tell those people who would obviously benefit if they were able to take precautions to avoid contracting the disease? Should the claim representative respect the insured's privacy and keep the information confidential at the risk that others might contract the disease? Use of one of the two frameworks may help resolve this dilemma.

Balancing the insurer's duty to investigate the claim and the claimant's right to privacy can be difficult in the best of circumstances. However, when fraud may be involved, that balance is even more difficult to maintain. Fraud causes huge losses that harm all policyholders; therefore, privacy rights may be given less weight when claim representatives suspect fraud. Nevertheless, claim representatives cannot ignore information security practices. They must still ensure that information is acquired only when necessary, that the information is accurate, that access to the information is strictly limited, and that the information is not communicated to others unnecessarily. The next section describes additional ethical dilemmas that arise when a claim includes suspected fraud.

Fraud Detection

Fraud is defined as an intentional deception or misrepresentation with the intent to cause another to give up a legal right or part with something of value. Fraud is illegal; therefore, it may seem that no ethical dilemmas are involved. However, the following examples illustrate how detecting fraud may lead to ethical dilemmas.

> ### Examples of Ethical Dilemmas Involving Fraud
>
> **Example 1**
>
> A claim representative suspects that an insured has committed fraud in submitting a claim for stolen property by including items that were not stolen. The claim representative believes that the insurer can deny the claim because of the fraud but does not have sufficient evidence to meet the legal standards to prove fraud. The claim representative considers offering less than a fair amount to settle the claim in hopes that the insured will accept the settlement. This course of action would reduce the insurer's loss from a fraudulent claim, close the claim, and avoid costs associated with trying to prove fraud. However, despite the claim representative's suspicions, the insured may not be guilty of fraud and may be entitled to the full amount of the claim.
>
> **Example 2**
>
> A claim representative is handling a claim for XYZ Company, written through a profitable and highly respected insurance agency. The agent, who is the claim representative's brother-in-law and who owns the agency, makes it clear to the claim representative that XYZ Company should be given special treatment because it is an important customer. The claim representative's estimate of damages shows that the policy does not cover about five percent of the damage, or about $2,000. The claim representative gives the agent this information, and the agent indicates that he will take care of it.
>
> Later, the insured submits a damage estimate from another source that is $2,000 higher than the previous claim. If the claim representative accepts the insured's damage estimate, the insured is compensated fully for the loss; the brother-in-law is happy and family harmony is maintained; and the claim representative can close the claim file with adequate documentation to support the payment. However, the ethical dilemma is that the later estimate may be inflated (fraudulent) in order to cover the entire amount of damages. The claim representative must determine the appropriate course of action based on ethical and professional standards.

When a claim representative suspects fraud, the claim may be assigned to a special investigation unit (SIU) for investigation. For some insurers, this means the claim representative no longer works on the claim. For other insurers, the claim representative may continue to investigate the claim to determine the cause of loss and the damage amount while the SIU conducts its investigations. In such instances, the claim representative may be tempted to set the claim aside or conduct a less thorough investigation because the SIU is involved. However, allowing the quality or thoroughness of the investigation to be influenced by unproved suspicions of fraud is unprofessional and may be unethical.

An example of a situation that may predispose a claim representative to suspect fraud is an auto accident in which the vehicle sustains only minor damage but the driver reports serious injuries. While staying alert for the possibility of fraud, the claim representative must investigate the case thoroughly, considering the claim on its own merits. Claim representatives should use good-faith claim handling practices in all instances, treating each insured and claimant fairly and professionally. Preconceptions based on race, gender, or national origin should also be avoided.

Clear guidelines from claim management can help avoid and resolve ethical dilemmas that arise during the claim handling process. Claim representatives also should not hesitate to consult with supervisors or managers about professional and ethical courses of action. Nevertheless, decisions about ethical and professional behavior in claim handling ultimately fall to the individual claim representative. In addition to the two decision-making frameworks previously discussed, ethical standards can serve as useful guidelines for developing appropriate responses to ethical dilemmas.

ETHICAL AND PROFESSIONAL STANDARDS

If everyone agreed on which behaviors were ethical and which were not, always acted in accordance with the values underlying those behaviors, and understood and agreed on how to resolve ethically ambiguous situations, there would be no need for ethical standards or codes of ethics. However, well-intentioned people can disagree about what constitutes ethical behavior in a given situation. One way to seek uniformity in ethical behavior, as well as to promote high ethical and professional standards, is to create codes of ethics. A second way is to define quality claim practices that exemplify professional and ethical behavior.

Codes of Ethics

Insurers can promote high ethical and professional standards in several ways, including the following:

- Define ethical practices in all business areas, communicate them to all employees, and require adherence to them
- Conduct independent reinspections of physical damage claims and perform file reviews of all types of claims at random intervals to detect and address any unethical behavior
- Encourage employees to consult with their supervisors and managers about ethical dilemmas and to report ethical dilemmas involving others, such as service providers
- Dismiss unethical employees
- Enforce a strict written policy or code of ethics, clearly stating the ethical and professional expectations for all personnel, and require every employee to sign it annually

Codes of ethics provide guidelines for addressing ethical dilemmas. They consist of broad principles rather than detailed specifics and set out minimum standards of compliance. Two examples of codes of ethics are the Society of Registered Professional Adjusters Ethics Guidelines, found in Appendix A to this chapter, and the Code of Professional Ethics of the American Institute for CPCU, found in Appendix B of this chapter.

RPA and CPCU Codes of Ethics

The Society of Registered Professional Adjusters has developed its Ethics Guidelines to emphasize integrity, competence, sensitivity, and legality. The Code of Professional Ethics of the American Institute for Chartered Property Casualty Underwriters (CPCU) contains canons of ethical performance for all professional activities of all CPCUs and CPCU candidates. Rules in the code set minimum standards of conduct to maintain the integrity of the CPCU designation. CPCUs and CPCU candidates who fail to meet the minimum standards may be subject to disciplinary measures. The Institute's Board of Trustees enforces the canons and rules and can revoke the CPCU designation or otherwise discipline CPCUs who violate the canons or rules.

In addition to ethical standards, professional standards play a major role in promoting ethical and professional behavior. Professional standards for claim representatives are the benchmarks by which they are evaluated, whether the evaluation is performed by a supervisor, manager, auditor, insured claimant, or a department of insurance. Yet no single set of professional standards exists for claim representatives, and unfair claim practices statutes and regulations vary by state. Although claim handling guidelines also vary among insurers, some practices are common to all. The next section examines some of the common practices, which, because of their widespread use, can be considered quality claim practices.

Quality Claim Practices

Insurers identify quality claim practices—those that reflect superiority and professional performance—by identifying customer needs and expectations. Quality-oriented insurers look to their customers, not their competition, to determine what services and products to provide. The following activities provide a foundation on which to build quality claim practices:

- Determining customer expectations
- Improving service based on customer expectations
- Developing claim practices to meet customer expectations

To measure and maintain quality claim practices, insurers use benchmarks—designated standards against which improvements can be measured—and compare practices to the benchmarks to monitor improvement.

Customer Expectations

Insurers begin the process of benchmarking for quality claim practices by reviewing customer expectations and determining how often those expectations are met. Successful insurers and claim representatives view good claim service as one of their best marketing tools. In addition to advertising their quality claim service, insurers hope that satisfied insureds and claimants will tell others about their good service. In contrast, dissatisfied customers who talk to others about their unfavorable experiences discourage people from becoming customers. A dissatisfied customer may personally complain to ten people. However, with access to the Internet, a dissatisfied customer can quickly and easily complain to thousands. A reputation for poor claim service is difficult for both an insurer and a claim representative to overcome.

Insurers attempt to measure customer satisfaction in the following ways:

- Analyzing complaints
- Obtaining customer feedback on individual claims through a closed claim follow-up
- Exploring customer attitudes about service through focus groups and surveys

Some complaints are unavoidable; not every insured or claimant will be satisfied with a claim settlement regardless of how well the claim is handled. Nevertheless, measuring customer satisfaction by analyzing complaints is a way both to measure claim department performance and to determine specific problems in individual cases. One measure of claim department performance is the percentage of claim files that produce complaints.

Individual complaints can also be a valuable learning tool for both the insurer and the claim representative because they force reviews of particular files. A supervisor's review may reveal that the claim representative overlooked insurance coverages or laws. Complaints also help the insurer identify training or supervisory needs.

A uniform and consistent complaint review process can optimize the potential benefits of complaints as learning tools and minimize potential damage that complaints can cause. When a complaint is received, it should be recorded and promptly answered. A tracking system helps ensure that complaints are addressed in a timely manner. Claim representatives, supervisors, or managers should respond to complaints based on facts, the insurance policy, and applicable law, not on personalities or emotion. The individual preparing the response should document a timely, well-reasoned, objective response. Such a response can reduce the likelihood that the complainant will file suit alleging bad faith and can also serve as evidence of good faith if such a lawsuit is filed.

Many insurers require an internal audit department to record all complaints and responses and to review and analyze complaints independently for trends and patterns. For example, the audit department may calculate the ratio of complaints to claims handled by claim representative or by type of claim. A chart showing complaints per month by region, division, unit, and claim representative can indicate problems, although managers should consider more than statistics to determine the nature and extent of the problem. For example, a specialized claim unit dealing with suspected arson and fraud may receive more complaints than a claim unit handling automobile windshield losses.

Complaints can also present an opportunity to mend a damaged relationship with a customer. Dissatisfied customers who complain give the insurer an opportunity to address the complaint and reestablish credibility. An insurer's prompt, competent, courteous response that exceeds the customer's expectations can convert dissatisfaction into satisfaction. The financial gain can be substantial if the insurer retains even a small number of such customers.

Another way to measure customer satisfaction is by obtaining customer feedback on individual claims through a closed-claim follow-up. When a claim is closed, the insurer mails a letter or postcard to the insured or claimant asking an open-ended question, such as "How was our service?" Polling both insureds and claimants provides a balanced view of claim performance.

The most valuable responses to a closed-claim follow-up suggest ways to improve service. The problem that prompted the suggestion may affect many insureds or claimants. Respondents may also comment on the performance of service providers (vendors) and others involved in the claim process. Comments about service providers should be evaluated and appropriate action taken. Managers often forward favorable responses to a closed-claim follow-up to the personnel involved with the claim. Good claim handling deserves praise.

An advantage of a closed-claim follow-up is that respondents may be more willing to share their comments after a claim is closed then they are while the claim is open. A disadvantage is that it may not yield adequate information about a claim department's performance. To gain a more complete picture of customer attitudes about service, insurers can use focus groups and surveys.

Focus groups are small groups selected from the broader population of the insurer's policyholders and interviewed through facilitator-led discussions, about their expectations and opinions of insurers and of the claim process, as well as their emotional responses to their experiences. Results are qualitative and are not statistically significant; nevertheless, they can help develop specific solutions. A disadvantage of focus-group feedback is that it represents the opinions of only a small number of customers. Nevertheless, it can reveal attitudes and expectations that were not previously recognized and that may apply to more customers than those involved in the group.

Process Improvement Plan

Using the results of customer satisfaction measurements, insurers develop process improvement plans. Complaint reviews, closed-claim follow-ups, focus groups, and surveys reveal customer expectations that have not been met. After gathering and assessing the information from customer satisfaction measurements, insurers can develop ideas and set professional standards for desired process improvements. A process improvement plan to overcome service deficiencies involves the following five steps:

1. Determining how things work and who makes them work
2. Developing and testing ideas for improvement

3. Implementing improvements (reengineering)
4. Setting and comparing performance standards (benchmarking)
5. Monitoring results

The first step in the process improvement plan is to determine how things work and who makes them work. Flowcharts and process diagrams can document the processes involved in handling claims and can reveal unexpected bottlenecks and redundancies that have evolved over time. The flowcharts and process diagrams are then used for the second step in developing a process improvement plan: developing and testing ideas for improvement.

In addition to ideas developed from the flowcharts and process diagrams, insurers can use investigative questioning and failure analysis to identify areas for improvement in the claim process. The following investigative questions may be useful in this process:

- What is the flow of work from one action to another?
- Are some activities unnecessary or of no value to the customer?
- Are activities duplicated that could be eliminated or combined?
- Can activities be completed more quickly?
- Can documentation be electronic rather than on paper?
- Can fewer people be involved in the claim process?
- Are the right people handling the claim work?

Example of Improvement Plan Developed From Investigative Questioning

Using the preceding questions, an insurer evaluated its claim department and developed ideas for process improvement. Implementation of the following changes could significantly improve the insurer's claim service:

- The department keeps paper copies of salvage logs, large loss information, and other records that are no longer valuable or that are stored in a new computer system. The department should eliminate redundant records.

- Claim representatives and supervisors enter redundant data into their processing system to generate reports. About 35 percent of the information entered by claim representatives was duplicated by supervisors. Clerical support personnel had already entered about 10 percent of the claim data. The department should eliminate duplicate entries.

- It takes four days to send file information to field claim representatives. Imaging technology could be used to send and store file material electronically to reduce the time involved.

- Senior claim representatives spend about 30 percent of their time handling small claims. Managers or supervisors should assign such small claims to claim representatives with less experience.

Failure analysis develops ideas for improvement by tracing the causes of failure. An example of a "failure cost" in the claim environment is an adverse verdict in a bad-faith lawsuit. Exhibit 6-2 shows one process improvement tool used to conduct a failure analysis, the Ishikawa (fishbone) diagram. This exhibit identifies the root causes of a jury award on a hypothetical bad-faith claim. In this case, a failure analysis reveals multiple causes for the adverse award: weak communication and human relations skills, inadequate supervision, lack of technical training, and ineffective negotiation skills.

Such an analysis of one claim may reveal flaws that are symptoms of a larger problem that must be corrected. The fishbone diagram is a good tool for identifying areas that need the most attention.

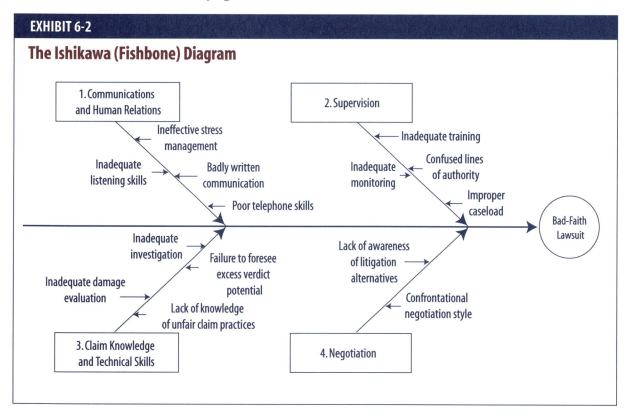

EXHIBIT 6-2

The Ishikawa (Fishbone) Diagram

Traditionally, insurers have relied on auditing as a failure analysis tool to detect problems. Audits may be conducted by claim staff or by staff from another department, such as a quality control department. If other failure analysis tools have identified a potential problem, files selected for the audit may target claims that are likely to be affected by the same problem. In other cases, a random audit may help identify failures that have not been detected through other tools.

Following the analysis, an insurer moves to the second step in the process improvement plan, developing and testing ideas for improvement. Tests may occur in one unit, branch, or department to ensure that it is feasible to implement an idea in the entire claim department.

The third step in the process improvement plan is implementing improvements. Strong management commitment is the key to successfully implementing improvements. Improvement plans often fail because management fails to devote the resources or encourage the necessary changes to support them. Management must make ethical and professional decisions about how to use resources to best accomplish its quality claim practices goals.

Reengineering, or analyzing and redesigning workflow, is one way to implement claim service improvements. The term "reengineering" is often interpreted to mean downsizing to reduce costs. However, businesses use reengineering to improve efficiency to improve customer service.

Another way to implement claim service improvements is to increase the competency of claim personnel through training. Insurers that make a commitment to high quality claim practices must also commit to ongoing training for their claim professionals.

After improvements are implemented, the next step in the process improvement plan is to establish performance measures, commonly called benchmarks. Effective benchmarks are internal or external performance standards based on specific customer needs and the insurer's philosophy on meeting them. Performance measurements such as closed claims per month and reopened claims per month allow insurers to compare performance from one period to the next and from one insurer to another. The following are other examples of common benchmarks:

- Contact with policyholder within a specified number of hours of receiving loss notice 95 percent of the time
- Response to correspondence within a specified number of days of receipt 100 percent of the time
- Claim expense ratio within a specified range for the calendar year

In setting benchmarks, insurers develop their own best practices or use industry best practices. Best practices define the most appropriate practice based on experience. The keys to identifying a best practice are to know what is most important for the organization and to know how to measure it. Answering the question "Does this practice lead to superior claim performance?" is crucial in identifying a best practice. Superior performance may be based on financial operating results, policyholder approval and loyalty, or employee retention and satisfaction. Managers must distinguish the tasks that really make a difference in the quality or effectiveness of fulfilling the insurance promise. With that information, any insurer can identify a best practice and determine how to implement it.

The final step in the process improvement plan is monitoring results. After establishing benchmarks, insurers must determine whether they meet them and, if not, why not. Insurers can monitor improvement by comparing results over time to the benchmarks and by taking steps to correct deficiencies.

SUMMARY

Ethics and professionalism are key elements in fulfilling in good faith the promises made within an insurance policy. To retain public trust and credibility, claim representatives should do their best to act ethically and professionally.

Ethical dilemmas involve choices between two courses of action, both of which may be right. Although choices between two right courses of action can be difficult, claim representatives can use frameworks for resolving ethical dilemmas. One framework is to answer a series of questions about the dilemma. Another framework is to evaluate the types of effects that decisions can have: maximizing effect, that provides the greatest benefit to the greatest number of people; normalizing effect, to determine the most common, acceptable standard of behavior; and empathizing effect, treating someone with in the same way one wants to be treated in the same situation.

In claim handling, ethical and professional dilemmas can arise in relation to conflicts of interest, competency, continuing education, licensing, customer service, *ex parte* contacts, billing practices, privacy, and fraud detection. How claim representatives respond to ethical dilemmas is a measure of the importance they place on professionalism and ethical behavior. Ethical and professional standards, such as codes of ethics and quality claim practices including customer satisfaction, continuous improvement, benchmarking, and best practices, can help claim representatives conduct themselves professionally and ethically to ensure that consumers receive the benefits of insurance that they expect.

CHAPTER NOTES

1. Sister Columba Mullaly, Ph.D., *The Retention and Recognition of Information* (Washington, D.C., The Catholic University of America Press, 1952), pp. 7–8.
2. Richard Cavalier and G. G. Hedges, "Improving Claims Operations—A Model Based Approach," The Service Productivity and Quality Challenge (The Netherlands, edited by P. T. Harker, 1995), pp. 281–310.

Appendix A
Society of Registered Professional Adjusters Ethics Guidelines

The work of adjusting insurance claims is a profession of public trust. Accordingly, RPAs must maintain a standard of integrity that will promote the goal of building public confidence and trust in the insurance industry.

RPAs will only discharge claims responsibilities for which they possess sufficient technical competence or can acquire adequate training.

RPAs will seek only information they believe to be relevant, timely and accurate, and use only legal and ethical means of obtaining that information. They will handle claims with no intent to mislead or misinform.

RPAs will be sensitive to individuals' rights of privacy, and will take reasonable measures to protect sensitive information from illegal or unauthorized examination.

RPAs will avoid illegal discrimination, and will strive to keep personal feelings and prejudices from influencing their judgment.

RPAs will maintain a courteous and sensitive attitude in their interactions with insureds and claimants, seeking to understand their concerns during times of distress. They will assist insureds in presenting and documenting their losses, and will not place the interests of their employer above those of the insured.

RPAs will maintain their business relationships with others in a manner that will promote the goal of bringing credit and honor to the profession. They will have no undisclosed financial interest in any direct or indirect aspect of an adjusting transaction.

RPAs will obey the laws and regulations related to handling claims.

They will resist fraudulent, unmeritorious or exaggerated claims, and support public and industry organizations involved in the detection and prevention of insurance fraud.

Recognizing that litigation is costly and time-consuming, when appropriate, RPAs will seek out all available alternatives to litigation to resolve issues in an expeditious and conciliatory manner.

Used with permission from "Society of Registered Professional Adjusters Ethics Guidelines" found on www.rpa-adjuster.com/ethics.html (accessed January 27, 2006). © 2004 Society of Registered Professional Adjusters.

Appendix B
The Canons and Rules of the Code of Professional Ethics of the American Institute for CPCU

Canon 1—CPCUs should endeavor at all times to place the public interest above their own.

> Rule R1.1—A CPCU has a duty to understand and abide by all Rules of conduct which are prescribed in the Code of Professional Ethics of the American Institute.
>
> Rule R1.2—A CPCU shall not advocate, sanction, participate in, cause to be accomplished, otherwise carry out through another, or condone any act which the CPCU is prohibited from performing by the Rules of this Code.

Canon 2—CPCUs should seek continually to maintain and improve their professional knowledge, skills, and competence.

> Rule R2.1—A CPCU shall keep informed on those technical matters that are essential to the maintenance of the CPCU's professional competence in insurance, risk management, or related fields.

Canon 3—CPCUs should obey all laws and regulations, and should avoid any conduct or activity which would cause unjust harm to others.

> Rule R3.1—In the conduct of business or professional activities, a CPCU shall not engage in any act or omission of a dishonest, deceitful, or fraudulent nature.
>
> Rule R3.2—A CPCU shall not allow the pursuit of financial gain or other personal benefit to interfere with the exercise of sound professional judgment and skills.
>
> Rule R3.3—A CPCU shall not violate any law or regulation relating to professional activities or commit any felony.

Canon 4—CPCUs should be diligent in the performance of their occupational duties and should continually strive to improve the functioning of the insurance mechanism.

> Rule R4.1—A CPCU shall competently and consistently discharge his or her occupational duties.

Rule R4.2—A CPCU shall support efforts to effect such improvements in claims settlement, contract design, investment, marketing, pricing, reinsurance, safety engineering, underwriting, and other insurance operations as will both inure to the benefit of the public and improve the overall efficiency with which the insurance mechanism functions.

Canon 5—CPCUs should assist in maintaining and raising professional standards in the insurance business.

Rule R5.1—A CPCU shall support personnel policies and practices which will attract qualified individuals to the insurance business, provide them with ample and equal opportunities for advancement, and encourage them to aspire to the highest levels of professional competence and achievement.

Rule R5.2—A CPCU shall encourage and assist qualified individuals who wish to pursue CPCU or other studies which will enhance their professional competence.

Rule R5.3—A CPCU shall support the development, improvement, and enforcement of such laws, regulations, and codes as will foster competence and ethical conduct on the part of all insurance practitioners and inure to the benefit of the public.

Rule R5.4—A CPCU shall not withhold information or assistance officially requested by appropriate regulatory authorities who are investigating or prosecuting any alleged violation of the laws or regulations governing the qualifications or conduct of insurance practitioners.

Canon 6—CPCUs should strive to establish and maintain dignified and honorable relationships with those whom they serve, with fellow insurance practitioners, and with members of other professions.

Rule R6.1—A CPCU shall keep informed on the legal limitations imposed upon the scope of his or her professional activities.

Rule R6.2—A CPCU shall not disclose to another person any confidential information entrusted to, or obtained by, the CPCU in the course of the CPCU's business or professional activities, unless a disclosure of such information is required by law or is made to a person who necessarily must have the information in order to discharge legitimate occupational or professional duties.

Rule R6.3—In rendering or proposing to render professional services for others, a CPCU shall not knowingly misrepresent or conceal any limitations on the CPCU's ability to provide the quantity or quality of professional services required by the circumstances.

Canon 7—CPCUs should assist in improving the public understanding of insurance and risk management.

Rule R7.1—A CPCU shall support efforts to provide members of the public with objective information concerning their risk management and insurance needs and the products, services, and techniques which are available to meet their needs.

Rule R7.2—A CPCU shall not misrepresent the benefits, costs, or limitations of any risk management technique or any product or service of an insurer.

Canon 8—CPCUs should honor the integrity of the CPCU designation and respect the limitations placed on its use.

Rule R8.1—A CPCU shall use the CPCU designation and the CPCU key only in accordance with the relevant Guidelines promulgated by the American Institute.

Rule R8.2—A CPCU shall not attribute to the mere possession of the designation depth or scope of knowledge, skills, and professional capabilities greater than those demonstrated by successful completion of the CPCU program.

Rule R8.3—A CPCU shall not make unfair comparisons between a person who holds the CPCU designation and one who does not.

Rule R8.4—A CPCU shall not write, speak, or act in such a way as to lead another to reasonably believe the CPCU is officially representing the American Institute, unless the CPCU has been duly authorized to do so by the American Institute.

Canon 9—CPCUs should assist in maintaining the integrity of the Code of Professional Ethics.

Rule R9.1—A CPCU shall not initiate or support the CPCU candidacy of any individual known by the CPCU to engage in business practices which violate the ethical standards prescribed by this Code.

Rule R9.2—A CPCU possessing unprivileged information concerning an alleged violation of this Code shall, upon request, reveal such information to the tribunal or other authority empowered by the American Institute to investigate or act upon the alleged violation.

Rule R9.3—A CPCU shall report promptly to the American Institute any information concerning the use of the CPCU designation by an unauthorized person.

Chapter 7

Direct Your Learning

Negotiation

After learning the content of this chapter and completing the corresponding course guide assignment, you should be able to:

- Describe the four different styles of negotiation and which style is generally best suited for use by claim representatives.
- Describe the steps in the claim negotiation process.
- Explain how claimant negotiation variables and claim representative negotiation variables affect claim negotiations.
- Describe the claim negotiation techniques that are the following:
  - Common to all parties
  - For use with unrepresented parties
  - For use with represented parties
  - Used by represented parties
- Describe the negotiation techniques claim representatives should avoid and the reasons those techniques should be avoided.
- Given a claim, identify the common pitfalls in claim negotiation and how to avoid them.

OUTLINE

Negotiation Styles

Claim Negotiation Process

Claim Negotiation Variables

Claim Negotiation Techniques

Negotiation Techniques to Avoid

Common Pitfalls in Claim Negotiations

Summary

Develop Your Perspective

What are the main topics covered in the chapter?

Successfully concluding claims requires effective negotiation skills. Although claim representatives may use several general negotiation styles, they can follow a specific process for negotiating claims. Within that process, a variety of negotiation techniques is available, some of which are effective and useful, and some of which should be avoided. Claim representatives should also be aware of common pitfalls they can encounter during claim negotiations.

Identify critical factors in negotiating claims.

- Is there one best style of negotiation?
- What are the key differences between negotiations with unrepresented parties (claimants and insureds) and negotiations with represented parties (attorneys and public adjusters)?
- How can good selling skills contribute to effective claim negotiation?

Why is it important to learn about these topics?

Effective negotiation skills can help claim representatives resolve claims quickly and fairly to the satisfaction of the parties.

Consider the negotiation techniques commonly used in your organization.

- Which additional negotiation techniques could help you and other claim representatives reach more satisfactory claim settlements?

How can you use what you will learn?

Examine a sampling of closed claims and look for any evidence of negotiation techniques that should have been avoided or pitfalls that may have affected the claim settlement.

- What techniques could the claim representative have avoided, and what other techniques could the claim representative have used to avoid those pitfalls?

Chapter 7
Negotiation

To resolve claims successfully, claim representatives must be able to negotiate effectively. A negotiation is any discussion conducted for the purpose of producing an agreement among parties. Negotiation occurs when differences arise between the insurer, or its representative, and the insured/claimant, or the claimant's representative. (Throughout the remainder of the chapter, claimant will be used to indicate either an insured or a third-party claimant.) The negotiation may resolve a single issue and allow the claim to move forward, or it may bring about the ultimate claim resolution.

Negotiation is a part of everyday life. People negotiate when they purchase cars, homes, and major appliances. A couple may negotiate which movie to see or which restaurant to dine in. Family or household members may negotiate vacation options or who will perform various household tasks.

Whether negotiations are formal or informal, individuals usually develop negotiation styles that reflect their attitudes toward the negotiation and the other parties. Although formal negotiators may choose a predominant style, most successful negotiators can adapt to a different negotiation style as the need arises.

Although negotiation is often seen as a way of concluding a claim, it can occur during any part of the claim process. For the claimant, the negotiation process includes the following three phases:

1. The crisis phase begins when a loss occurs. At that point, most people do not immediately consider the potential outcomes but are instead dealing with the immediacy of the loss and the desire to recover from the loss as quickly as possible.
2. The motivation phase begins when the insured recognizes the financial implications of the loss and starts to think about who will pay for the loss. As this motivational transition occurs, the claimant may begin to view the insurer as an adversary. Some claimants may consider exaggerating the claim or engaging in other forms of soft fraud. Ideally, during this phase, parties should work to establish rapport with each other.
3. The bargaining phase begins when the parties enter into serious settlement discussions. Parties arrive at this phase with preconceived notions and impressions developed in the earlier phases. During the bargaining phase,

the parties share their evaluations of the claim and determine any differences. Disagreements may erode any rapport previously established between parties. In successful negotiations, the parties resolve their differences and the claim is settled during this phase.

Negotiation skills are particularly important to claim representatives as a part of good-faith claim handling. Many claims do not have a set dollar value, and reasonable people can differ considerably in their opinions of claim values. Any part of a claim is negotiable, so no finite answer or value exists. The following are some examples of negotiated aspects of a claim:

- Damages in a bodily injury liability claim
- Percentage of comparative negligence attributable to the parties in any type of claim
- Amount of depreciation on a car or a piece of furniture
- Amount of lost sales in a business income claim
- Amount of recovery from the party responsible for an accident
- Payment arrangements with the uninsured responsible party in any type of claim

An examination of the four negotiation styles provides a framework for understanding negotiations and the parties who negotiate.

NEGOTIATION STYLES

Negotiators may use four distinct negotiation styles, commonly referred to as win-win, win-lose, lose-win, and lose-lose. These styles, shown in Exhibit 7-1, are derived from a negotiator's degree of concern for obtaining the best outcome relative to his or her ability to achieve rapport. Claim representatives should adopt a negotiation style appropriate to the claim and the parties involved.

Individuals who have no clear dominant style may typically compromise in negotiations. For example, a negotiator who prefers compromise settlements may suggest that the two parties split the difference or may offer to increase a proposed settlement if the other party decreases the demand. Compromise is not a style of negotiation; rather, it is the lack of a clear, dominant style.

Effective claim negotiators engage in activities and exhibit traits that demonstrate concern for obtaining the best outcome, and they are skilled in achieving rapport. The following qualities are important to claim representatives seeking to obtain the best outcome:

- Thorough knowledge of the claim file
- Persistence
- Firmness, coupled with fairness
- Thorough evaluation of the claim

The following qualities contribute to rapport in a claim negotiation:

- Good listening skills
- Humor
- Empathy
- Friendliness

EXHIBIT 7-1

Negotiation

Reprinted with permission from William Stewart Associates, Inc., Jackson, N.J.

Most good negotiators have an integrated style of negotiation that simultaneously seeks to obtain the best outcome and build rapport with the other party. A claim representative may focus on obtaining the best outcome in one phase of the negotiation process and, at another phase, may find that achieving rapport is more important in seeking a successful claim settlement. The integrated style gives the claim representative flexibility to shift focus depending on the circumstances and the claimant's needs and reduce the potential for conflict.

In claims, obtaining the best outcome does not mean taking advantage of the other party, settling for an unusually low amount, or providing an otherwise unfair settlement. Obtaining the best outcome means arriving at a settlement that is favorable to the insurer but that is considered equitable and fair by the other party. Negotiating parties seeking to obtain the best outcome may use a more direct negotiating style and may be less likely to make concessions than when they are working to build rapport.

Claim representatives may often negotiate with the same parties on different claims; they may be insureds, salvage buyers, or lawyers, for example. Impressions from prior negotiations can influence the outcome of current negotiations. In this situation, the claim representative may be more concerned with building rapport than with obtaining the best outcome and may, therefore, use a less aggressive, more cooperative negotiating style.

With an awareness of the various negotiating styles, claim representatives can select and adapt the style that will contribute most to a successful settlement in each case.

Win-Win

A claim representative using the win-win negotiation style seeks both to obtain the best outcome and to achieve rapport with the other party, resulting in a settlement that is satisfying to all parties. Win-win negotiators are simultaneously assertive and cooperative. They approach disagreements not as destructive or as conflicts but as tools to better understand the other party's wants and needs.

The following examples show how alternative repair proposals in property claims can be used in win-win negotiations:

- An insured scorched her Formica counter top when she placed a hot pan on the counter. The undamaged part of the two-year-old counter top is in good condition. Matching the Formica for a section repair is impossible because the particular pattern is no longer made. The insured expects that a repair will entail removing all the kitchen counter tops and replacing them with similar grade of Formica.

    Win-win solution—Because the kitchen counters are otherwise in good condition, the claim representative offers to replace the damaged section of the counter with a built-in cutting board that will also serve as a hot pad for hot items from the stove. The claim representative may even offer to waive the insured's deductible as an added incentive to proceed with this repair.

- Lightning strikes an insured's business office and damages the two-year-old telephone system, rendering it unusable. Because the telephone system is one of the insured's primary marketing tools, it must be replaced as soon as possible.

Win-win solution—Noting that it may be hard to locate the same make and model of equipment to replace the phone system, the claim representative offers to replace the system with a readily available newer model that has the same features, plus some enhancements. The insured will receive the phone system quickly and will benefit from an up-to-date system with additional features. The insurer will save not only the time it would have taken to replace the old system, but also costs because technological advances have resulted in lower prices for phone equipment.

Win-win negotiations can also occur in automobile physical damage claims, as the following example illustrates:

- The insured is driving her car when she strikes a large rock in the road, cracking the oil pan and causing an oil leak. As she continues to drive, the engine overheats and is damaged beyond repair. The car is four years old and has about 65,000 miles on it. A new engine will cost about $6,000. The insured's Personal Auto Policy, which has a $500 deductible, uses actual cash value (ACV, meaning the replacement cost less reasonable depreciation) as the valuation basis for a loss. Assuming that the car engine has a useful life-span of 130,000 miles, the ACV of the engine would be 50 percent of the cost of a new engine, or $3,000. Half the engine's useful life has been used, so the insurer reduces the loss amount by 50 percent to allow for depreciation. With the deductible of $500, the net settlement amount is $2,500, leaving the insured to pay the remaining $3,500 for the new engine.

    Win-win solution—The claim representative offers to replace the engine with a used engine of like kind and quality (LKQ) from a local salvage yard. Most repair shops provide a minor warranty on used auto parts. If the insurer has a direct repair program (DRP), and directs the claimant to a specific repair facility, most states' fair claims regulations require the insurer to guarantee the work. This solution eliminates the depreciation deduction and provides the insured with some warranty on the work performed.

Win-win negotiations may also be used in liability or workers' compensation claims. The following example is of a liability claim, but a similar approach can be used in workers' compensation claims:

- A six-year-old neighbor girl is playing with the insured's dog when the dog tries to grab a cap from the girl's head. One of the dog's teeth scrapes the girl's forehead causing a cut that requires twenty stitches. Although the dog is not known to be vicious, a law in this state creates strict liability (meaning liability regardless of negligence or intent) on the part of the dog owners in such cases. About a year after the injury, the scar has healed fairly well and no plastic surgery is anticipated. The claim representative is aware that injury claims involving unmarried females with facial scarring usually settle at high dollar amounts.

Win-win solution—During negotiation, the claim representative asks the parents whether they want their daughter to attend college. Both parents say they do but express concerns about their ability to pay for a college education. The claim representative suggests a structured settlement that will pay equal sums to the claimant during her four college years between ages eighteen and twenty-one. Such a settlement will have to be approved by a judge, he explains. An advantage of the settlement is that the daughter would be receiving the payments in the year she would spend them. If, instead, the family was to receive a lump sum payment, they might invest it for their daughter's education; consequently, they would have to pay taxes on the investment income, if any, and there would be no guarantee that the investment would not be lost. The claim representative may be able to negotiate a settlement that will cost less than a lump-sum settlement, so the insurer would benefit as well.

Another example of a win-win negotiation is the offer to settle a claim with a release that allows future payments for a claimant who may need additional treatment. The claimant receives immediate funds, and the insurer agrees that, if the claimant decides to have further treatment (such as plastic surgery), the insurer will pay up to a specified amount within a specified time after the claimant completes the treatment.

Although a claimant may decline a win-win offer, the claim representative who seeks a win-win settlement, at the very least, demonstrates an interest in resolving the claim to the claimant's satisfaction and may help build rapport as negotiations continue.

Win-Lose

Negotiators who use a win-lose style see negotiation as a contest between two opposing parties, each seeking to defeat the other. The parties' greatest concern is obtaining the best outcome for their side. They have little interest in achieving rapport with the other party. Negotiators may use this style of negotiation when other avenues of resolution have been exhausted, such as when a lawsuit has been filed and a trial is approaching. At that point, any rapport between parties has eroded because the settlement amount will ultimately be determined by the party that presents the best case to the judge and jury.

Claim representatives may use the win-lose style of negotiation in resolving claims that appear to involve fraud. While claim representatives must always act in good faith in all aspects of claim handling, they may be less concerned with achieving rapport with people they suspect of trying to defraud the insurer.

When fraud is suspected, insurers may require a formal proof of loss from the insured, followed by an examination of the insured under oath. Imposing these requirements does nothing to build rapport; however, this confrontational win-lose negotiation style can serve the insurer's need to prove or disprove suspected fraud.

Lose-Win

A negotiator using the lose-win style of negotiation is primarily concerned with achieving rapport with the other party; obtaining the best outcome is a low priority. This approach may sometimes result in a more expedient and more cost-effective settlement than other approaches. Generally, the lose-win style is best used when it is highly likely that the other party will hire an attorney or other representative to help resolve the issue.

The following examples illustrate the use of the lose-win negotiation style:

- The claimant is injured in an automobile accident with the insured, and the claimant's vehicle is not drivable. The claimant had no medical insurance. Assuming the insured is liable, the claim representative may offer to pay the claimant directly for a rental so that the claimant does not have to use his own money to rent the car and then submit the bills to the insurer for reimbursement.
- The insured's home is destroyed by fire, forcing the insured to stay in a hotel. The claim representative may offer the insured advance payment of part of the additional living expense claim while the claim investigation is pending rather than waiting until the entire claim can be resolved.

While the lose-win style initially meets the needs of the claimant, the insurer often achieves an equitable settlement in the long run because the claim representative began by engaging in rapport-building activities. Such activities may also shorten the amount of time that the claim is open.

Lose-Lose

A negotiator who has little concern either for obtaining the best outcome or for achieving rapport may be using a lose-lose negotiation style. The negotiator may focuses on a fast resolution without considering the other party's specific wants or needs. Used in claim negotiation, this approach can result in inequitable treatment of claimants and insureds. To avoid any inequity and potential bad faith actions, claim representatives should normally avoid this negotiation style.

Claim representatives who use a lose-lose style may be trying to avoid confrontational settlement negotiations. They may give in to demanding claimants and settle claims more quickly than they would with less demanding claimants.

Occasionally, the lose-lose negotiation style cannot be avoided in claim settlement. For example, some claimants offer unrealistic demands in negotiation and may not understand the logic of the claim representative's offer. Any explanation the claim representative offers only irritates the claimant. As a result, the claimant withdraws from the negotiation process and hires a public adjuster or a lawyer to continue the negotiations. Ultimately, the involvement of a third party will prolong resolution of the claim and result in less money for the claimant.

The following is an example of the use of the lose-lose negotiation style:

- A small kitchen fire has damaged some of the insured's personal property and left a smoky residue and a persistent foul odor in the room. The claim representative offers to settle with the insured for the cost to replace the personal property and the curtains and to pay a restoration firm to clean the residue from the ceiling. The insured is satisfied with the payment for the damaged property but demands complete replacement of the ceiling material. The claim representative explains that replacement of the material is more costly than cleaning and suggests that the cleaning be completed, and if it is not satisfactory, then the insurer will replace the ceiling. The insured persists with the demand that the ceiling be replaced.

    Lose-lose solution—The claim representative withdraws from settlement negotiations to give the insured time to consider the offer. The insured hires a public adjuster to handle the case on his behalf. The public adjuster charges a fee that, when subtracted from the final settlement amount, would reduce that amount to less than the cost to hire a restoration firm to clean the ceiling. The insured cancels the property policy. The result is that the insurer pays for the replacement of the ceiling material and the insured pays more of his own money for the repair than he would have had he accepted the initial offer. Both the insurer and the insured lose from this negotiation.

Claim representatives should choose the style that is appropriate based on the circumstances of a given negotiation, or they can integrate several styles as appropriate. The negotiation process generally involves several steps, and claim representatives can tailor the process to particular claims. The next section describes the steps of the negotiation process.

CLAIM NEGOTIATION PROCESS

Generally, all negotiators follow a process that breaks down into the following four steps:

1. Prepare
2. Develop and evaluate alternative outcomes
3. Identify and evaluate each party's interests
4. Make concessions and create appropriate resolutions

By being aware of and thoroughly completing each step, claim representatives can work towards more effective negotiations. The following descriptions apply these steps specifically to claim negotiations.

The first step of the negotiation process—preparation—begins long before the negotiation itself begins. For a claim representative, the process begins when the claim is assigned. The claim representative assembles information about the claimant's lifestyle, expectations, preferences, and likely behavior;

any previous claims handled by the current insurer or other insurers and their outcomes; and any information about the claimant's history that may be useful in the negotiation. For a commercial insured, the claim representative may assemble information about the claimant's business or employment policies, its supply contracts, and even its competitors. During this step, the claim representative also begins establishing rapport with the claimant.

In the second step of the negotiation process, both parties identify the settlement alternatives they consider appropriate and present the reasons why they are appropriate. The party with the greatest number of acceptable alternatives usually has the most leverage in the negotiation because the various alternatives can be used in making concessions that lead to satisfactory settlements.

To develop settlement alternatives, each party must identify the minimum and maximum dollar amounts acceptable for a claim resolution. Answering the questions in the box can help the negotiating parties establish these amounts.

Claim Representative	Other Party (Claimant)
What is the minimum amount I should accept for this claim in good faith?	What is the maximum amount I can demand without appearing outrageous?
What is the maximum amount for which I am willing to settle this claim?	What is the maximum amount the other party might pay for this claim?
What is the maximum amount the other party might demand for this claim without appearing outrageous?	What is the minimum amount the other party might pay for this claim without appearing outrageous?
What is the minimum amount the other party might be willing to accept for this claim?	What is the minimum amount I might be willing to accept for this claim?
What amount should I use for my starting offer?	

Source: Judith Gordon, *Organizational Behavior: A Diagnostic Approach,* Upper Saddle River, N.J.: Pearson Education, Inc., 2002), pp. 336–337.

The values determined through the answers to the minimum and maximum questions can be used to develop a best alternative to a negotiated agreement (BATNA). A BATNA is a standard against which a negotiator can measure any proposed agreement. It can help a negotiator avoid accepting unfavorable terms and rejecting favorable terms.[1] Stated simply, a BATNA is the choice a negotiator can make if the negotiation direction seems unlikely to result in a favorable outcome. If the BATNA is better than the likely outcome of the negotiation, the negotiator can walk away.

To determine the best alternative, the claim representative should consider the costs of the BATNA as well as the likely outcome. Any offers can then be compared against the cost of the BATNA. If an offer is less costly than the BATNA, the claim representative should seriously consider the offer. If the offer is greater than the BATNA, the claim representative should reject it.

The claim representative should also consider the claimant's likely BATNA and should compare the insurer's offers against it. For example, the claimant's BATNA may be the net outcome (after legal costs) likely from litigation. The claim representative should estimate the likelihood that the claimant will file a lawsuit based on information from the investigation. If the claimant suggests that a lawsuit would render a better settlement, then the claim representative, while acknowledging the claimant's right to file a lawsuit, should point out the legal costs that would reduce the settlement amount. If the claim representative's offer for a negotiated settlement is greater than the claimant's BATNA, then the claimant would be more likely to accept the offer.

In the third step of the negotiation process, each party's interests are identified. These interests can be based on essential needs, socialization needs, personal needs, or organizational needs. For example, an injured person's needs may include ongoing medical treatment, hospice care, income continuation, rehabilitation, social interaction, and financial provisions for dependents. A family's needs after a property loss can include temporary housing, food, clothing and personal necessities, toys or other entertainment, and allowance for public transportation of children to school. An organization's needs can relate to its reputation, relationships with its customers, organizational goals, and income.

Interests can be tangible, such as housing, or intangible, such as reputation, fairness, and socialization needs. Interests can be also subjective, that is, based on the claimant's perceptions. A claimant's interests can change intentionally or unintentionally during the claim settlement period.

In the final step of the negotiation process, successful negotiators recognize the need to make concessions to create appropriate resolutions. Concessions are trade-offs. For example, a claim representative may offer to increase the claim amount by $2,000 if the claimant agrees to concede on $4,000 worth of personal property reported stolen but for which the claimant has no proof of ownership. The settlement, then, would pay for fifty percent of the reported value of the allegedly stolen property.

Negotiators can assess prospective concessions by considering the best and worst possible claim resolutions for each party. They can examine the effect a concession would have on the claim resolution, and then they can determine whether the resulting claim resolution would better serve the interests of the claimant and the insurer. The parties' perceived value of the concessions may vary, as in the following example: An old vehicle is a total loss after an auto accident. The claimant, who repairs auto body damage as a hobby, values the car for sentimental reasons. As a concession, the claim representative offers to allow the insured to keep the damaged vehicle with a salvage title. If the insurer instead were to pay for a replacement vehicle, the claimant would have to pay sales tax on it. This concession can lead to a win-win resolution: the insured wins because he can keep a beloved car, and the insurer wins because it pays the value less the savage to the claimant. The insurer also saves by not having to dispose of the salvage.

In another example of concessions that can lead to win-win resolutions, a tornado tears the roof off a school, and most of the school's computers are damaged by the building's sprinkler system or rain. The claim representative offers to replace the mismatched older computers and printers with equipment of similar makes, models, and software configurations, including some refurbished computers and printers, along with refurbished network hardware and software. The insurer benefits from the convenience of getting all the equipment from one source and by receiving discounts for volume purchases and refurbished equipment. The school benefits from new, updated equipment and compatibility to enable better networking capability.

Successful claim resolution requires reviewing all the needs of both the claimant and the insurer to determine an optimum resolution for both parties. Options such as refurbished or used equipment, like-kind auto parts, and structured settlements can be negotiating tools for developing mutually satisfying claim resolutions.

Throughout the claim negotiation process, claim representatives must consider claim negotiation variables that affect their choice of negotiation style and the outcome of the negotiation.

CLAIM NEGOTIATION VARIABLES

Claim negotiation differs from many other types of negotiation. Claim negotiation often focuses primarily on the amount of money the insurer will pay for the claim. Other negotiations may involve a variety of negotiating variables. For example, negotiating variables for a homeowner seeking bids from contractors to replace an aging roof may include price, discount for cash payment, quality of materials, work start date, and work completion date.

If the roof requires replacement because of windstorm damage rather than age, the insured and claim representative usually negotiate only the loss amount; however, other variables may be negotiated. No two claim negotiations are exactly the same. The facts of two different losses may be similar, but the characteristics of the negotiation and the parties, as well as the outcome, can be dramatically affected by many negotiation variables. Claim negotiation variables may be distinguished between the claimant's variables and the claim representative's variables.

Claimant's Negotiation Variables

The variables the claimant brings into the negotiation influence the claim representative's choice of negotiation techniques and strategies. For the claimant, the most significant negotiation variables can include the following:

- Which phase of negotiation the claimant is in
- Claimant's financial needs
- Time pressures that the claimant may face

- Claimant's emotional reaction to the loss
- Claimant's experience with or knowledge of insurance claims
- Claimant's personality

The following sections explain these variables and how they affect the claim representative's negotiating behaviors and the outcome of the negotiation.

Claimant's Negotiation Phase

As described previously, claimants experience three phases during the negotiation process: the crisis phase, the motivation phase, and the bargaining phase. The claim representative does not become involved until the second phase. Understanding these phases can help the claim representative respond appropriately, resulting in smoother negotiations and contributing to successful claim settlements.

Crisis Phase—During the crisis phase, most claimants are primarily concerned with returning to normal. Although the claim representative does not become involved until later, understanding the claimant's experiences during this phase can help the claim representative work with the claimant in the remaining negotiation phases. The following examples suggest some thoughts a claimant may have immediately following a loss:

- The insured's thirty-five gallon fish tank ruptures in his living room at 2:00 AM on Sunday morning.
    - Can the fish be saved?
    - How will I clean up this mess?
    - How much will it cost to replace the ruined wall-to-wall carpeting?
- The claimant's new car is hit by an insured making a left turn at an intersection. The claimant has the right of way. Although nobody is injured, the claimant's car is not drivable and must be towed from the scene.
    - Who will pay for the damage to my car?
    - Who will repair my car?
    - How long will it take to get my car repaired?
    - How will I get to work while my car is being repaired?

In these examples, the claimants are motivated by a desire for life to be normal again rather than by the money they might make through the claim settlement process. As the claimant's desire for normalcy shifts to finding ways to return to normal, the motivation phase begins.

Motivation Phase—During the motivation phase of the negotiation process, the claimant recognizes that life will not be normal unless someone pays for damage. During this phase, the claimant files an insurance claim to seek payment for the damages. A quick response at this stage can establish the claim representative as an ally who will help the claimant return to normalcy as soon as possible. A quick response can also help establish the insurer's credibility.

Conversely, if the claim representative does not respond quickly enough after the claim is filed, the claimant may begin to view the insurer as an adversary that is delaying the return to normalcy.

When a claimant experiencing a crisis feels ignored by the insurer, he or she may begin to exhibit adversarial, and sometimes illegal, behavior, such as inflating the claim or engaging in other forms of soft fraud. This shift in claimant motivation is directly related to the time it takes the claim representative to contact the claimant, as illustrated in Exhibit 7-2.

EXHIBIT 7-2

Relationship Between Client Behavior and Claim Representative's First Contact

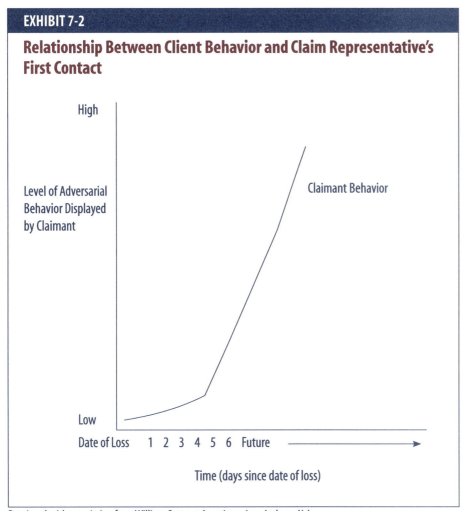

Reprinted with permission from William Stewart Associates, Inc., Jackson, N.J.

A claimant's adversarial behavior may lead a claim representative to pay more for the claim than the insurer would otherwise pay. Because prompt contact with the claimant can prevent such behavior, most insurers adopt contact standards that are more stringent than statutory legal requirements, which may allow up to ten days for an insurer to contact a claimant. Insurers recognize that prompt contact is a customer service issue that can directly influence the amount of a claim settlement.

A claim representative begins to establish rapport with a claimant from the first meeting. The first impression in the motivation phase of the negotiation affects the entire negotiation process.

Bargaining Phase—Negotiating parties carry all their preconceived notions, impressions, and perceptions into serious settlement discussions during the bargaining phase. A claimant brings his or her impressions of the claim representative and the insurer that have developed during the previous negotiation phases. During the bargaining phase, parties share their evaluations of the claim and determine any differences. Disagreements may arise, and any rapport previously built between the parties can disintegrate. In successful negotiations, the parties resolve their differences and settle the claim.

If the claim representative and the claimant do not communicate well or establish rapport during the earlier phases of the negotiation process, the bargaining phase may become adversarial. However, a smooth bargaining phase is not guaranteed even if the parties develop rapport during the earlier phases.

How Badly the Claimant Needs Money

A claimant's need for money in order to return to normal is a major variable that determines how the claim representative should approach negotiations with the claimant. The claim representative can use a claimant's financial need to encourage an early and reasonable claim settlement. A claimant may respond readily to a reasonable settlement offer that promises prompt settlement rather than delaying payment by seeking a greater settlement amount. Conversely, a claimant who has money or property available to meet temporary needs while the damaged property is being repaired or replaced may delay settlement. For example, a claimant who has a rental vehicle for use while his or her primary vehicle is being repaired may be slow to seek repair estimates and complete the necessary repairs, thus postponing the claim negotiation and settlement. To encourage a timely settlement, the claim representative may need to appeal to another of the claimant's needs.

Time Pressures That the Claimant May Face

Claim representatives should be aware of any time pressures the claimant faces, such as due dates on bills. Other examples of time pressures may include the claimant's desire to repair a damaged home before an approaching holiday or to repair an automobile for a daughter to use at college before the term begins.

Knowing of such time pressures, the claim representative can combine a reasonable offer with a promise of prompt payment to encourage the claimant to negotiate a claim settlement.

Claimant's Emotional Reaction to the Loss

The claim representative should allow the claimant to express the fears, concerns, frustrations, and needs evoked by the loss. Empathizing with the claimant can help establish rapport.

Sometimes claimants will direct their emotions at the claim representative with angry reactions or criticism. Such reactions should not be considered personal attacks. By maintaining flexibility and a professional demeanor, the claim representative can use any differences with the claimant to help find a satisfactory resolution for the insurer and the claimant. For example, if the claimant expresses a distrust of the insurer or the claim representative, the claim representative could regain some trust by making a prompt and reasonable offer for an advance payment that would be credited to the ultimate claim settlement.

Claimant's Experience With or Knowledge of Insurance Claims

The claimant's experience with or knowledge of insurance claims is a variable that can significantly affect the claim outcome. Claim representatives should ask claimants at the first contact whether they have ever filed a claim. The answer to this question helps the claim representative determine the claimant's experience in filing insurance claims and may provide clues to the claimant's motivation and how the claim will proceed. The claimant may respond with a variety of answers. For example, a claimant's asking why the claim representative wants to know about previous claims could indicate distrust of the insurer. The claim representative may respond that many people do not understand the claim process or have had a bad experience with it and proceed to describe how the claim handling process will help the claimant return to normalcy as soon as possible. In other cases, a claimant's previous bad claim experience may color his or her feelings about the present claim, and the claimant may worry that the payment in the current claim will not be sufficient to repair the damage. To counter this concern, the claim representative can differentiate the insurer's claim service from the service the claimant experienced previously and again emphasize the insurer's intention to meet the claimant's needs.

A claimant may know about insurance claims without having had personal experience with them. For example, the claimant may work for an insurer or a producer. If so, the claim representative may appeal to the claimant's knowledge in explaining the claim process and emphasizing the intention to reach a prompt and reasonable claim settlement.

Claimant's Personality

A claimant's personality can have a significant effect on negotiations. If the claimant is self-assured and easy-going, the claim representative may be able to establish rapport and resolve the claim quickly and satisfactorily. However, claimants may be insecure or distrustful of businesses or may be arrogant or aggressive. In responding to personality traits that can complicate negotiations, claim representatives can use empathy and patience and make continuing efforts to establish rapport.

The claim representative must be aware of the claimant's negotiation variables to develop creative claim resolutions but must also consider his or her own negotiation variables.

Claim Representative's Negotiation Variables

Negotiation variables for claim representatives can differ from the negotiation variables for claimants, but the two parties can be affected by common variables. The following are some of the most significant negotiation variables that can affect claim representatives:

- Claim representative's knowledge of the claim
- Claim representative's authority level
- Number of alternatives available for a satisfactory claim settlement
- Claim representative's time factors
- Negotiation settings
- Claim representative's personality

Because of the number of variables in a negotiation, no right way exists for claim representatives to conduct all negotiations. They cannot apply formulas that will produce successful claim resolutions the same way formulas can be applied to math problems. Negotiation strategies and tactics can vary based on the relative importance of the negotiation variables and the claim representative's ability to influence the variables. For example, claim representatives can ensure their own thorough knowledge of the claim and can influence the claim negotiation setting.

Claim Representative's Knowledge of the Claim

The claim representative's knowledge of the claim is one of the most significant negotiation variables. The more the claim representative knows about the loss details, the parties, and the results of the claim investigation, the better prepared he or she is to negotiate a satisfactory claim settlement based on the merits of the claim. Conversely, the claim representative's lack of knowledge of the claim can be a severe detriment to the claim negotiation.

Claim Representative's Authority Level

The claim representative's authority level is another crucial negotiating variable. Before beginning claim negotiations, the claim representative should be given sufficient authority to settle the claim up to its estimated maximum value. If the claim representative lacks sufficient authority, the claimant would be justified in seeking to negotiate with the claim representative's supervisor or someone with more negotiating authority. Delegating a claim representative adequate negotiating authority demonstrates an insurer's good faith.

Number of Alternatives Available for a Satisfactory Claim Settlement

Another variable that can significantly affect the negotiation is the number of alternatives available to the claim representative for a satisfactory claim settlement. Before reaching the bargaining phase, the claim representative should apply his or her knowledge of the claim and the claimant to devise as many settlement alternatives as possible. For example, if an insured's heirloom diamond necklace was stolen, but the matching bracelet and earrings were not, several alternatives may be available for settling this claim. Depending on the policy coverages, the claim representative could propose one of the following alternatives as a settlement offer:

- Replace the entire set with a set of like kind and value
- Replace only the necklace with one of like kind and value, matching the other pieces of the set as closely as possible
- Replace only the necklace with an exact match if one can be obtained through special replacement services available to insurers
- Pay the insured for the value of the necklace and allow the insured to keep the bracelet and earrings
- Pay the insured for the full value of the set and collect the bracelet and earrings to sell for salvage recovery

Any of these alternatives would achieve a satisfactory resolution for the insurer; the claimant's choice of alternatives is determined by the value of the set as a family heirloom.

In some cases, claim representatives can combine certain alternatives to best meet the claimant's needs. Some alternatives might cost the insurer very little but could be valuable to the claimant, and these alternatives could be added to other alternatives to create a more attractive settlement offer for the claimant.

Claim Representative's Time Factors

Claim representatives face time factors that are prompted by claim work in general. Time factors may be imposed by a claim manager or by department guidelines, by the insurer or a reinsurer, or by insurance regulators and state laws. These time factors become negotiation variables for the claim representative. The claim representative's caseload is also a variable because it determines the amount of time available to devote to any particular claim. A claim representative who faces deadlines in negotiating a settlement may be more flexible in accepting the claimant's demands and may take less time exploring alternative settlement options than one who has no deadlines.

As with claimant time factors, the claim representative's personal schedule can also influence the negotiation. For example, a claim representative preparing to take a two-week vacation may be eager to settle a claim before the trip. Or the claim representative's assignment to catastrophe duty for the next few months could become a variable in the negotiation process. Any factor that may prompt the claim representative to settle the claim more rapidly or to reduce the time devoted to the bargaining step in the negotiation process is a negotiation variable.

Claim Negotiation Settings

Many claims are settled entirely by telephone or by Internet tools and communication; the claim representative and the claimant may never meet in person. Although negotiating by telephone and the Internet is efficient and effective for most claim settlements, claim representatives may find that certain claims are better negotiated in person.

This section examines negotiation in the following settings:

- In-person negotiation
- Telephone negotiation
- Internet negotiation

In-person negotiation provides many advantages over other negotiation settings. Judges may require claim representatives to attend settlement conferences. Claims are often mediated in person, and claim representatives sometimes meet with unrepresented claimants to settle claims.

When people communicate in person, three channels of communication are available to them: words, tone, and body language. Of these three, the words used by one party may be the least significant aspect of communication. In face-to-face communication, words usually convey less of the total communication than any other aspect. The tone of voice is often far more significant than the words. However, the major component of face-to-face communication may be body language. When a person's words, tone, and body language appear in conflict, body language usually conveys the communicator's true meaning.

Personal appearance may offer the claim representative information about the claimant's economic status, education, and personal life. This information can be helpful in assessing the claimant's potential credibility at trial if the claim results in litigation. A potential disadvantage of in-person negotiation is that the claimant can observe the claim representative's body language and appearance and form an opinion of the claim representative's credibility as well.

In-person negotiation may also offer claim representatives the opportunity to take advantage of a group dynamic. When faced with the opinions of a claim representative, a defense attorney, and a judge or mediator, all advocating a particular settlement, the claimant may more readily agree. Conversely, if the claim representative suggests a lesser settlement than the other parties support, the group dynamic could be a disadvantage.

Another advantage of in-person negotiation relates to physical evidence. When the claim representative and the claimant see evidence such as photos or diagrams of the accident scene or visible scarring, they may change their opinions of the claim's value.

Claim representatives should follow some basic rules when conducting in-person negotiation, including the following:

- Arrive early or on time. Punctuality helps create a positive impression of the claim representative as someone who is organized and dedicated to settling the claim. It also presents a positive image of the insurer.
- When possible, become familiar with the negotiation site. When people are comfortable with their surroundings, their confidence generally increases. By spending a few minutes alone at the site, a claim representative can become familiar with any potential distractions so that when negotiation begins, he or she can concentrate on the negotiation itself.
- Do not bring the claim file to the negotiation. Claim files usually contain sensitive information, such as the claim reserve or extent of settlement authority. A claim representative should take only needed documents, such as physicians' reports and damage appraisals, to the negotiation.
- Be aware of the number of opposing negotiators. Generally, the party with the greater number of negotiators has an advantage. For example, before negotiations at a claimant's attorney's office, the claimant's attorney may ask if one or more associates may observe the negotiation. This move may be a ploy to add people to the party's negotiation team in order to outnumber the claim representative. The claim representative may object to the presence of additional people or may want to clarify the observer's role at the beginning of the negotiation. If an observer becomes involved in the negotiation, the other party has an opportunity to think and regroup or revise strategy. The lone claim representative has no such advantage. When faced with an unavoidable situation of being outnumbered, the claim representative should take as much time as needed to formulate answers to questions.
- When given the opportunity to choose a seating arrangement, the claim representative should choose a seat at the head of the table, which is considered a position of authority.

For reasons of convenience and efficiency, many claim negotiations are conducted by telephone. Telephone negotiators must rely on words and tone to communicate their messages. Without the body language component of communication, the parties are more likely to misunderstand each other. Active listening skills are useful to clarify the other party's meaning and avoid misunderstandings. With active listening, the claim representative periodically paraphrases the other party's communication. For example, the claim representative could say, "From our discussion, Mr. Brown, I understand that you are satisfied with the amount of the settlement we have offered for your totaled car, but we disagree on the value of contents of your car that were also damaged. Is that correct?"

Telephone negotiations are generally quicker and more convenient than in-person negotiations. Telephone conversations are usually shorter than the same conversation would be in person because the parties tend to get to the point more quickly and avoid casual conversation that often occurs in person. Nevertheless, even in telephone negotiations, claim representatives should take the time to develop rapport with the other party through some casual conversation.

Parties' behavior in telephone conversations differs from that in in-person conversations in several other ways. For example, the parties to a telephone conversation are more likely to compete with each other. Also, when people are unable to see one another, they may say things they would not say if they were communicating in person. These behaviors may create conflict during a negotiation.

While conducting telephone negotiations, claim representatives should be aware of their tone of voice. Absent body language, parties depend on vocal tone (the qualities of the sound of the voice). For example, if a person smiles while speaking, vocal tone tends to be pleasant and to convey a positive impression of the speaker.

In telephone negotiations, the party who places the call has the advantage of understanding what he or she wants to accomplish. A claim representative who is the receiver of a negotiation call has an immediate disadvantage because the other party has reviewed the facts and planned the call. Call initiators can also use the element of surprise to their advantage. If caught off guard, a claim representative may inappropriately yield to demands. Upon receiving an unexpected call from the other negotiating party, a claim representative should postpone the negotiation by offering to review the file and return the call at a mutually agreeable time. A return call gives the claim representative more control, and when a call is scheduled with the other party, both parties can prepare for a productive negotiation.

Internet negotiation, a third negotiation setting, adds another aspect to the negotiation. Internet systems of negotiation vary; however, they often offer some form of blind bidding process in which neither party knows the other party's offer or counteroffer. Some systems use a percentage of each offer and counteroffer to indicate an acceptable range; the counteroffer must be within the range established by the percentage. More complex systems allow parties to set priorities on some of the negotiating variables, such as the time to settle, the amount of the settlement, or the language of the settlement. These systems are designed to deliver an equitable settlement based on the positions of the parties in dispute.

Some vendors of these Internet systems incorporate the use of a live facilitator who can help the parties through the process. The facilitator summarizes the shared information but does not reveal the parties' offers or counteroffers.

Other systems offer a telephone facilitator. Some of these Internet companies also offer Internet mediation and arbitration services that may be initiated if the Internet negotiation fails to settle the claim.

The Internet systems' blind bidding removes the personalities from the negotiation process; body language, tone of voice, and rapport are no longer involved. These systems compare the negotiation figures submitted by both parties and use them to attempt to settle. For example, with one system, after completing an evaluation of the claim, the party making the offer (a claim representative) enters three acceptable offers. The party making a blind counteroffer (the claimant or the claimant's attorney) is notified of the offer via several methods (e-mail, fax, letter, and telephone) and then enters a counteroffer. If the claimant's demand is less than or equal to the claim representative's offer, the software calculates a median amount (the amount that is half the difference between the two amounts, added to the lesser amount) and declares the matter settled at that figure. If the claimant's demand is greater than the claim representative's offer, the claim representative can enter a new counteroffer that is compared against the claimant's original demand. The claimant can then make a new counterdemand against the claim representative's second offer. If the process does not result in a settlement, the offering party can start over with new offers or use some other form of settlement. Often the result is a much faster claim resolution (within days rather than months to years) with significantly lower legal costs. The fee for using the system is generally lower than the costs of litigation.

Only certain types of claims are good candidates for Internet negotiations. These systems are generally used in uncomplicated bodily injury claims when parties are primarily negotiating the value of the claim. They are not used in claims involving coverage issues or disputed liability because of the number of negotiation variables and alternatives in such claims.

Internet negotiation systems benefit insurers by making negotiations easier, less stressful, and less time-consuming for their staffs and by reducing legal costs. Such systems benefit claimants by reaching rapid settlement, providing funds to meet immediate financial needs and by eliminating the stress of the negotiation process.

Claim Representative's Personality

The claim representative's personality is another variable that can influence the negotiation. If a claim representative is self-assured, this trait is apparent in the negotiation, and the claimant may accept a settlement with little or no negotiation. If the claim representative is arrogant, the claimant may become defensive. Arrogance does not help establish rapport with the claimant and does not demonstrate good faith, which requires that the claim representative empathize with and respond patiently to the claimant throughout the negotiation process.

Conversely, if a claim representative's personality is insecure or submissive, the claimant may use those personality traits to influence the claim representative to accept a settlement that is unsatisfactory to the insurer. Thorough knowledge of the facts of the claim can help the claim representative be more confident and less submissive in the negotiation.

Armed with knowledge of the negotiating variables of both parties, claim representatives can apply a variety of claim negotiation techniques to effect successful claim resolutions.

CLAIM NEGOTIATION TECHNIQUES

Most negotiators repeatedly use the same techniques, particularly strategies and behaviors that have produced successful outcomes. However, by using a wider variety of negotiation techniques, negotiators can increase their chances of success. Claim representatives who are skilled in a wide variety of negotiation techniques can choose from them and adapt the ones they choose to the variables of the specific negotiation.

Some negotiation techniques tend to be more appropriate for unrepresented parties; others are more appropriate for represented parties. Some negotiation techniques work well with either type of party. Regardless of the techniques used, honesty is crucial in negotiation. Honesty does not require claim representatives to divulge the high and low figures of their settlement ranges, but they must be careful not to misrepresent facts. This section describes negotiating techniques that are appropriate for all parties, for unrepresented claimants, and for represented claimants.

Negotiation Techniques for Use by All Parties

Two negotiating techniques that can readily be used by all parties to a negotiation are the principle of yes and choicing. Because of their versatility, claim representatives may use either or both of these techniques to successfully negotiate claim settlements. They may also combine these techniques with techniques discussed subsequently to negotiate with specific parties.

Principle of Yes

The principle of yes is a negotiation technique that is often used in sales. This principle is based on the premise that if an individual answers "yes" to a question, he or she is likely to continue to answer "yes" to subsequent questions. To apply the principle of yes, claim representatives should begin negotiations with questions that will generate "yes" answers. Points on which the parties disagree should be avoided until all points of agreement are established. When parties begin a negotiation with items of disagreement, conflict is almost inevitable and may lead to failed negotiation.

In nearly all negotiations, the parties agree on certain facts—often basic facts such as the date of accident, the people involved, and the fact that injury or damage has occurred. When claim representatives focus on these areas of agreement, they apply the principle of yes, as described in the box.

Use of the Principle of Yes

Adjuster:	Good morning, Ms. Acton, this is Joe Schroder, a claim representative with XYZ Insurance Company. I was hoping that we could discuss settlement of your client's claim. Let's see; this accident happened approximately four months ago and it is my understanding that our insured struck the rear of your client's auto. Is that correct?
Claimant's attorney:	Yes.
Adjuster:	It is also my understanding that the damage to your client's auto was paid for by your client's collision insurance coverage. Is that correct?
Attorney:	Yes.
Adjuster:	I see that you have sent us three different medical bills, one from the emergency room where your client was taken following the accident, one from an orthopedist, and the third from a physical therapist. Are those all of the medical bills?
Attorney:	Yes.
Adjuster:	And finally, I see that you have sent us lost wage information and documentation that your client was disabled for one week. Is that correct?
Attorney:	Yes.
Adjuster:	So, the only thing left is for us to agree on a settlement value.

By using the principle of yes to focus on the areas of agreement, the claim representative can increase the motivation of all parties to the negotiation to work toward resolution as they begin to see how much they agree on.

Choicing

Choicing is a negotiation technique based on the principle that if someone is presented with a choice of possible solutions, one of those choices is presumably the correct choice. Choicing is based on the assumption that people feel empowered when given a choice. To use choicing, the claim representative first presents the choice the other party will find least desirable. This choice becomes a basis of comparison, making the next choice more appealing.

A claim representative who has developed rapport with the other party will usually be able to predict the other party's choice of solutions.

For example, the transmission on the insured's car has been severely damaged and needs to be replaced. The insured's Personal Auto Policy bases coverage for the loss on actual cash value. The insured vehicle has a life expectancy of approximately 120,000 miles; currently the odometer shows almost 60,000 miles. The claim representative's impression from previous conversations is that the insured can afford to pay little more than the $500 deductible toward the repair. The claim representative may use choicing with the claimant as described in the box.

> **Use of Choicing**
>
> Claim Representative: Mr. Nelson, I just received the appraisal on your car. The transmission is not repairable and needs to be replaced. We have a couple of options for repairing the car and the choice is yours.
>
> *Choice One* We could pay to put a new transmission in your car. This would cost approximately $4,000, but because your policy provides actual cash value coverage, we will have to depreciate the cost of the transmission. To explain, your car has an anticipated useful life of 120,000 miles and it already has 60,000 miles on it; so your transmission is approximately 50 percent worn. Therefore, we will pay only 50 percent of the replacement cost, or $2,000 minus the $500 deductible—$1,500 toward the transmission replacement.
>
> *Choice Two* As another option, I was able to locate a transmission at one of our salvage yards that has only 58,000 miles on it. This transmission is not an original manufacturer's part, but instead it is an LKQ (like kind and quality) transmission. If you agree to this option, you will have to pay only your deductible, $500. We will not subtract depreciation from your claim because this transmission is already depreciated. Which option do you prefer?
>
> The choices that can be presented are often limited only by the claim representative's imagination and resourcefulness.

Negotiation Techniques for Use With Unrepresented Claimants

Making a claim can be a stressful, anxiety-producing experience. Many people have little, if any, knowledge of insurance coverage. Unrepresented claimants may trust neither the claim representative nor the insurer. Many claimants have limited or no knowledge of settlement values, such as the value of a bodily injury claim. Media attention spotlighting excessively high verdicts and settlements tends to inflate the claimant's expectations for a loss settlement. A claimant's unrealistic expectations of the claim's value can make negotiating a settlement challenging for the claim representative.

Additionally, attorneys and public adjusters know and understand certain common practices observed in the negotiation process that unrepresented claimants would not observe. For example, they realize the insurer usually will not make a settlement offer until the attorney or public adjuster has provided the appropriate proofs and documentation. A claim representative and an attorney or a public adjuster may have a heated negotiation discussion and neither party will take it personally. Each sees this as part of the negotiation process. Conversely, unrepresented claimants with little or no knowledge of the claim process may assume that the claim representative, rather than themselves, is responsible for proving the claim. Claimants may be offended by heated discussions and may take them personally; emotions can flare and rapport can disintegrate.

Certain techniques, such as the following, can help smooth negotiations with unrepresented claimants:

- Collecting and using extraneous information
- Using sales techniques in negotiation
- Using needs analysis to effect a settlement
- Making the first offer

Collecting and Using Extraneous Information

Claim representatives collect and use extraneous information about the claim, the claimant, and the claimant's wants and needs that will help them develop creative settlements that meet those wants and needs. Claim representatives look for clues in information that claimants provide about themselves. For example, when telephoning the claimant, the claim representative may notice the sounds of children and pets in the background, providing information about the claimant's family situation. The claim representative may use this information to develop a settlement that meets family needs, such as prepayment for childcare and pet supplies. Conversations with the claimant can provide information about the claimant's level of education and understanding of the claim process. The claim representative may be able to propose a settlement for this claimant that pays for childcare or eldercare while the claimant pursues advanced education.

If a meeting can be arranged at the claimant's home, the claim representative can make observations about the claimant's lifestyle, hobbies, and other interests. Claimants and insureds may even disclose arbitrary or genuine deadlines for resolution of the claim. For example, if an insured says, "I need my car repaired soon because I leave for vacation in two weeks," the claim representative may propose replacing the damaged vehicle with a used vehicle, leading to a speedier resolution than requiring the insured to wait for repairs to be completed.

Claim representatives can sometimes use extraneous information to develop noncash settlements that meet the claimant's needs more adequately than cash settlements. For example, a claimant who has filed a products liability claim against a cereal maker because his daughter found a piece of plastic in her cereal may be satisfied with a year's supply of cereal instead of a cash settlement. Items used in such settlements must be tangible and must have some monetary value. For example, in a personal property claim for losses that include a broken article of fine china in a pattern that is no longer available, the claim representative may observe that the china has sentimental value for the insured. Rather than offering to replace the entire set of china with a new set of the same brand in a different pattern (and collecting the remaining pieces of the old set), the claim representative may use special replacement services available to insurers to obtain a replacement piece. The claimant, then, can keep the set of cherished china.

Using Sales Techniques in Negotiation

Real estate agents sell houses and automobile dealers sell cars; in a similar fashion, claim representatives "sell" settlements. The theories and philosophies used in sales apply in all sales situations, whether it is the sale of an automobile or the settlement of a claim. A knowledge of sales techniques can help claim representatives sell settlements.

All sales training courses begin with the same premise: to make a sale one must first understand the needs and wants of the customer. The claim representative uses the understanding of the claimant's wants and needs as the basis of the negotiation. Lacking that understanding, claim representatives may develop what they believe is an equitable settlement and then attempt to force it on the claimant.

Another sales technique is to mirror the behavior of the customer. For example, a clothing salesperson may suggest garments that are of similar style to the garments the customer has selected and make casual conversation on the topics that the customer introduces. People tend to like other people who are similar to themselves. A claim representative who mirrors the behavior of the claimant may develop greater rapport, leading to a better relationship and, ultimately, the sale of the claim settlement.

Using Needs Analysis to Effect a Settlement

A researcher of human behavior, Abraham Maslow established a hierarchy of human needs, often represented as a pyramid. The bottom of the pyramid represents basic needs and the top represents self-actualization needs.

Maslow theorized that people have different levels of needs, starting at the level of basic physiological needs (such as food, water, shelter, and clothing), and progressing to the need for safety and security, the need for belongingness and love (social acceptance), the need for esteem (mastery, competence, and status), and the need for self-actualization (autonomy, responsibility, and challenge). According to Maslow, individuals fulfill their needs in ascending order; they start with the most basic needs, and then move to the next need level when those needs are satisfied. Exhibit 7-3 depicts Maslow's Hierarchy of Needs.

EXHIBIT 7-3

Maslow's Hierarchy of Needs

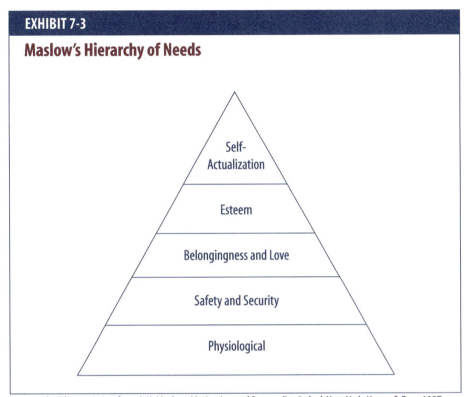

Reprinted with permission from A.H. Maslow, *Motivation and Personality*, 3rd ed. New York: Harper & Row, 1987.

All people operate at various levels of the hierarchy depending on the situation an individual is facing at the time. A person who has an annual income of $150,000 may be at the esteem level of the needs hierarchy, but if a fire destroys the person's home, he or she may revert to the physiological level or the safety and security level.

Claim representatives should be aware of the possibility that a claimant may be operating at a level at which money may not be the most important need. It may be easier to negotiate a claim involving a total loss house fire that has returned a family to the physiological level or safety and security level than to negotiate a minor burglary with an insured who is at the esteem level and is more concerned with not being taken advantage of by the claim representative than with replacing the stolen items. In the house fire claim, having lost most of its material possessions, the family is operating on a lower needs level and is motivated to conclude the claim. But in the minor burglary case, the claimant is motivated at a higher needs level and may hope to get as much money as possible to prove that he can do better than the insurer. In both cases the claimants' needs levels affect their motivation to negotiate the claims.

Making the First Offer

Generally, the party in a negotiation who makes the first offer holds a weaker initial bargaining position. The party who responds with a counteroffer holds a stronger bargaining position. If the original offer is significantly lower than expected, the party may increase the counteroffer. Consequently, negotiators try to avoid making the first offer. The circumstances of a specific case, however, may prompt one side or the other to make the first offer.

In negotiations with an unrepresented claimant, it may be best for the claim representative to make the initial offer. Most unrepresented claimants do not know the value of the claim and may suggest an inflated settlement amount on the assumption that it will be negotiated down. The claim representative is then put in the difficult position of responding to this posturing while seeking to retain the rapport established with the claimant.

To make the first offer, the claim representative can open with a statement such as the following: "I have taken the time to examine all the information you have shared and used it to develop an evaluation of your claim." Such a statement captures the claimant's interest. The claim representative can then explain the evaluation and how it was developed from the information provided. Allowing the claimant an opportunity to react, the claim representative should listen for information or he or she may not have considered in reaching the evaluation. Claim representatives should not concede merely because the claimant wants more money; any concessions made should be based on factual information related to the claim.

Because whether the claimant is represented or not represented affects how the claim is negotiated, claim representatives may use techniques that are different from those just discussed when negotiating with claimants' representatives, such as attorneys or public adjusters.

Negotiation Techniques for Use With Claimants' Representatives

Attorneys or public adjusters who represent claimants usually understand the claim process and claim settlement procedures. Public adjusters usually negotiate property claims; attorneys can negotiate any type of claim. The negotiation technique a claim representative uses in a particular case depends on the type of claim involved. For example, because liability claims for general damages (such as pain and suffering) have more subjective values than property claims (such as building damage), they require a different negotiation technique.

The following techniques are useful to claim representatives when negotiating with a claimant's representative:

- Using information obtained from the claim evaluation
- Establishing strengths and weaknesses

- Using timing in negotiation
- Making the first offer
- Making concessions

Using Information Obtained From the Evaluation

A claim representative's thorough knowledge of the claim is usually a strength in negotiation. Having investigated the loss, the claim representative usually has more detailed knowledge of the claim than the claimant's attorney, public adjuster, or other type of representative.

When the claimant's representative makes a demand in the negotiation, the claim representative should avoid an immediate reaction. Labeling a demand as too high or too low actually favors the other party. Instead, the claim representative should ask the claimant's representative to explain how the settlement value was determined and should listen carefully to the answer. The answer reflects the extent of the claimant's representative's knowledge of the claim and the level of thought that was put into the evaluation.

Claim representatives can use their thorough knowledge of a claim to develop initial offers or counteroffers and to explain the rationale based on the facts of the case. Just as with unrepresented claimants, the claim representative should insist that any changes in the settlement offer be justified based on the facts of the case.

Establishing Strengths and Weaknesses

The strengths and weaknesses of negotiation variables are often called negotiation "chips." Some chips may be more significant than others based on the claimant's wants and needs. The following example demonstrates the value of negotiation chips in a negotiation with a public adjuster and describes how the claim representative could play these chips.

An insured's three-bedroom ranch-style home is partially damaged by fire and sustains water damage caused by the fire department. One bedroom must be rebuilt, and a significant amount of damaged personal property must be replaced. The rest of the house has sustained severe smoke damage and requires extensive cleaning and replacement of wall coverings and carpets.

The day after the fire, the insured retains a public adjuster to handle the loss. The insured is currently staying in a hotel and wants to move back into his house as soon as possible. However, it appears that the house will be uninhabitable for at least three months. Coverage under the insured's homeowners policy is adequate to pay for the damage to the structure and the personal property and to pay the additional living expense. The claim representative has completed an estimate of the structural damage that totals $52,000. The public adjuster has submitted an estimate of $73,000 for structural damage and an inventory of damaged personal property totaling $24,000. Upon reviewing the public adjuster's estimates, the claim representative notes that construction prices and the prices of personal property in the inventory appear inflated.

The negotiation chips that favor the insurer include the following, in order of least to most significant and powerful for negotiating a satisfactory settlement for the insurer:

- The more difficult the public adjuster is to negotiate with, the longer the insured will be out of the house.
- The insured lacks proof of ownership (such as receipts, photos, or owner's manuals) of high value pieces of personal property (including cameras, a laptop computer, and stereo and recording equipment).
- The insurance policy contains a clause requiring appraisal if the loss value cannot be agreed on.

The claim representative should use the least significant chip first in seeking a concession because it is most likely the easiest concession to obtain. In this case, the claim representative would remind the public adjuster that the longer the insured is out of his house, the less satisfied the insured will be. This consideration may encourage the public adjuster to concede on some of the claimed loss.

Chips may also be replayed and combined. For example, in playing the second chip, the claim representative points out that the lack of proof of ownership for the damaged personal property could devalue the claim, and again reminds the adjuster that the insured will be without a house until the claim is settled.

Saving the most powerful chip for last preserves the value of the other negotiating chips. In this claim, if the public adjuster refuses to lower the counteroffer after the first two chips are played, the claim representative may suggest appraisal as an option to determine the value of the claim. Ideally, the possibility of appraisal will motivate the public adjuster to make some concession, such as decreasing the demand. The adjuster knows that appraisal may result in a lesser settlement, and a lesser settlement means a lower commission for the adjuster.

Using Timing in Negotiations

For many claims, the best time to settle with a claimant's attorney is just before the claim becomes a lawsuit. At that point, the attorney has usually spent only a couple of hours working on the claim. Although attorney fee agreements can differ, many claimant attorneys receive one-third of a settlement as their fee. Once the claim becomes a lawsuit, the plaintiff's attorney must invest much more time in the claim. Even though a higher settlement—and a greater fee—may result from a litigated case, the attorney's fee per hour of work decreases for each hour devoted to the case. The following example illustrates this result:

The claimant sustained a back injury as a result of an automobile accident that occurred when a vehicle driven by the insured struck the rear of the vehicle driven by the claimant. The claimant was taken to the hospital by ambulance and lost two weeks' salary because he missed work. In addition, the claimant saw an orthopedist several times over the course of a two-month period and required physical therapy three times per week. The bodily injury claim is valued at $4,500, and the claimant's attorney will receive a one-third contingency commission. If the attorney spent two hours interviewing the client, requesting and handling lost wage and treatment reports, and negotiating with the claim representative, the attorney's fee of $1,500 breaks down to $750 per hour. But if the claim becomes a lawsuit, the attorney must conduct pre-trial discovery, requiring significantly more time. The following table indicates some of the attorney's activities in preparing for trial with approximate times needed to complete them:

Attorney Activity	Time Required
File summons and complaint to institute litigation	1 hour
Send out and complete interrogatories	3 hours
Take depositions of defendant and plaintiff	6 hours
Attend mandatory settlement conference	3 hours

If the claim is settled for $6,000 during the pre-trial settlement conference, then the plaintiff attorney has invested 15 hours in the claim. The attorney will receive $2,000 (one-third of the settlement); however, the hourly breakdown for the work is $133.33 per hour. Compared to the original fee of $750 per hour, the prospect of an 82 percent drop in "hourly commission" may give the attorney an incentive to settle the claim before a lawsuit requires more time investment.

Making the First Offer

Which party should make the first offer depends on many variables, including personalities, comfort level with one another, insurer policies, and previous experience.

As discussed, the party making the initial offer of settlement takes a weaker negotiating position. The demand of a claimant's representative made before any offer may be higher than the mid-range initial offer the claim representative might propose. To entice a reasonable demand, the claim representative may begin the negotiation by asking the claimant's representative what fair settlement value would settle the case that day. For example, if the claim representative's pre-negotiation settlement range was from $4,000 to $6,500 and the claimant's representative demanded $6,500 to settle the claim that day, then the claim representative can make a more enticing initial settlement offer than if the claim representative had made an initial offer of $5,250 (mid-range).

Making Concessions

In a negotiation, the claim representative should make concessions only for one of the following three reasons:

- New information that affects the claim value has become available.
- The other party has made a concession.
- A concession by the claim representative would allow the claim to be settled that day.

Even after bargaining has begun, if the facts of the claim change because the claimant has introduced new information or because the claimant's condition has changed (usually for the worse), the claim representative should reevaluate the claim and, if appropriate, make a concession.

If the claimant lowers the counteroffer, the claim representative could choose to concede by increasing the insurer's offer in order to effect a settlement. That concession offer does not necessarily have to equal the other party's reduced counteroffer. For example, the claim representative may initially offer $6,000, and the other party counteroffers $10,000 to settle the claim and then drops to $8,000 (a $2,000 concession). The claim representative may concede with an offer of $7,000 (a $1,000 concession).

When there is a compelling reason to settle the claim immediately (such as before the claimant leaves for an extended vacation), the claim representative may make concessions to accomplish that settlement. If the other party demands a specific settlement amount that is within the pre-negotiation settlement range, then the claim representative may concede, accepting the demand to avoid prolonging the negotiation unnecessarily.

Negotiation Techniques Used by Claimants' Representatives

Claim representatives should be familiar with negotiation techniques commonly used by claimants' attorneys, public adjusters, and other claimants' representatives. Although some techniques are effective when used by attorneys and public adjusters, their use by claim representatives may be detrimental to negotiations.

Limited Authority Negotiations

In some negotiations, one or more parties may have authority to negotiate only up to a limited amount. To accept an amount above the limit, the party must consult some other authority. Car dealers are known for using the limited authority technique as a ploy. For example, a potential customer is in a showroom looking at a car that has a sticker price of $20,000. The salesperson opens the conversation with the customer and eventually asks what the customer would be willing to pay to take the car home that day. If the customer responds with an offer of $17,000, the car dealer says, "I need to talk to my manager. Please have a seat and I will be right back."

The salesperson's authority is limited, so the customer is really negotiating with the salesperson's manager, someone who is remote to the customer. The car dealership uses this technique to its advantage by making the customer wait for a response. While waiting, the customer is already considering how much more to offer if the $17,000 offer is not acceptable.

Attorneys, public adjusters, and other claimants' representatives may also use this technique. A claimant's representative can settle a claim legally and ethically only after speaking to the client, and in most cases the client is not present during the negotiation. The need to contact the claimant gives the claimant's representative the opportunity to leave the claim representative waiting. Upon returning, the claimant's representative may suggest that the claimant is willing to settle for $1,000 more than the current offer, for example. In most cases, the claimant's representative uses this technique in an effort to induce the claim representative into offering more money.

Generally, claim representatives should not use the limited authority technique. They should begin a negotiation with the authority needed to complete the negotiation. The perception that the claim representative does not have authority to settle the claim can undermine his or her negotiating position. For example, after learning about the limited authority, the claimant's representative could ask to speak with the claim representative's supervisor, implying that the claim representative has lost control of the negotiation. If the value of the claim increases as a result of newly discovered information, the claim representative with limited authority must consult a supervisor or manager to gain more authority to complete the negotiation.

Timing in Negotiations

As previously discussed, claim representatives can use timing to their advantage in negotiations because claimants' attorneys may prefer to settle claims before they go into litigation to avoid decreasing their hourly commission. Insurers also benefit from settling claims before litigation begins by avoiding additional court and legal costs. A claimant's attorney may use that fact to encourage a claim representative to accept a higher demand.

Having a thorough knowledge of the various negotiation techniques available, claim representatives should also be aware of which techniques to avoid. Some techniques provide no negotiation advantage to the claim representative; other techniques are inappropriate because claim representatives must demonstrate good faith when interacting with claimants and their representatives.

NEGOTIATION TECHNIQUES TO AVOID

Some techniques that work well in general negotiations do not work well in negotiations to settle claims and, in fact, may contribute to the failure of the negotiation. Claim representatives should be familiar with and avoid these techniques. In addition to limited authority negotiation, these techniques include using a first and final offer (Boulwarism) and using decreasing or limited offers.

Using a First and Final Offer—Boulwarism

Boulwarism, or making a first and final offer, is named after Lemuel Boulware, a former chief executive officer of General Electric Company. When negotiating union contracts with General Electric's labor unions, Boulware would make a single offer, telling the unions that it was the final offer and if they chose not to accept, then they should strike.

This technique is inappropriate for claim representatives. Presented with the first and final offer, the claimant may refuse it, ending the negotiation and possibly resulting in a more costly resolution for the insurer. Boulwarism invites conflict and prevents collaboration. In contrast, other negotiation techniques provide an opportunity for parties to collaborate to achieve a resolution.

Using Decreasing or Limited Offers

Another negotiation technique that claim representatives should avoid is making decreasing or limited offers. A decreasing or limited offer is an offer that changes simply because time passes. For example, a party to a negotiation may offer $4,000 one day, to decrease by $200 for each day acceptance is delayed. Similarly, a limited offer is withdrawn after the passage of a specified time. For example, the offering party may specify that if the offer is not accepted within forty-eight hours, it will be withdrawn.

Claim representatives should not use decreasing and limited offers. They invite conflict by placing unreasonable constraints on the other party. Once a claim representative makes an offer in a negotiation, it should stand unless a change is warranted by a change in the facts of the claim.

In addition to these detrimental negotiation techniques, a claim representative can encounter other pitfalls during the negotiation process.

COMMON PITFALLS IN CLAIM NEGOTIATIONS

Things can go wrong at any point in the negotiation process. Claim representatives, as well as other negotiating parties, can avoid some of these problems and can conduct more successful negotiations by being aware of some common negotiation pitfalls.

Allowing Personalities to Influence the Settlement

Claim representatives must sometimes negotiate with parties who are difficult to interact with. Personalities can interfere and the negotiation process can turn into a clash of egos. As emotions rise, rational thought diminishes, and negotiations come to a halt. For this reason, all parties to a claim negotiation should avoid allowing personalities to influence the settlement.

Claim representatives must maintain their focus on resolving the claim and avoid being swayed by the other party's personality. They should object to any form of abuse, but good-faith claim handling precludes retaliation to personal attacks. In response to a personal attack in the negotiation, the claim representative should inform the other party that, if the offensive behavior continues, the negotiation will cease until the party is prepared to negotiate in a civil manner. Offensive behavior should never affect the amount of the offer, the claim representative's willingness to negotiate, or any other factor that could prevent a fair claim settlement.

Trading Dollars

Trading dollars occurs when negotiators barter on the amount in dispute, not considering the facts of the claim. Claim negotiations should focus on the facts of the claim, and not on the offers and demands. If the facts of the claim change, the parties should increase or decrease their offers or demands according to the facts, but the settlement amount should be a byproduct of the negotiation.

Bidding Against Oneself

Parties to negotiation sometimes inadvertently bid against their own offer; that is, they increase their offer for no reason. For example, a claim representative could say, "We believe that this claim is worth $5,000, but if we settle the claim today, we would increase our offer to $5,500." In this statement, the claim representative has bid against the insurer's offer without any concession from the other party. Such an offer could signal that the claim representative lacks confidence in the claim evaluation or is overly eager to settle the claim. Generally, concessions in a negotiation should be offered only in response to a concession made by the other party and in a good-faith attempt to settle the claim for the appropriate amount.

Conceding as Deadlines Approach

As deadlines approach in negotiations, the number of concessions usually increases. For example, many union contracts are settled at 11:59 PM on the day of a deadline and, as described previously, many claims settle on the courthouse steps before a trial.

A party can gain significant power in a negotiation by determining any deadlines that may affect the other party. One such deadline for a claim representative to be aware of is the statute of limitations on a claim, which sets the time within which a claimant must file a lawsuit. Other deadlines can be determined through conversation and listening to the other party for such information. Some deadlines, such as impending holidays, may be "soft" deadlines; others, such as a tax deadline for a claimant who needs money to pay the taxes, may be "hard" deadlines.

Claim representatives also have hard deadlines with which they or the insurer must comply and which may increase their motivation to offer concessions.

For example, if the insurer gives its claim staff a directive to reduce pending claims by the end of the month, the claim representative may need to settle the claim and report the file closure by that deadline. As the deadline approaches, the claim representative may offer the highest amount in the settlement range in an effort to close the claim by the end of the month. Claim representatives should not make such settlement offers. Instead, their knowledge that a deadline might be imposed should induce them to work more quickly to settle claims sooner and avoid accepting excessive settlements to meet the deadline.

SUMMARY

A negotiation is any discussion designed to produce an agreement among opposing parties. Claim representatives negotiate many claim settlements.

Negotiators can adopt one of four different negotiation styles: win-win, win-lose, lose-win, and lose-lose. The choice of style for a given negotiation is determined by the negotiators' concern for obtaining the best outcome and achieving rapport. Whereas the win-win style usually renders more satisfactory, creative claim settlements, claim representatives may sometimes choose to use the win-lose and the lose-win negotiation styles for claim negotiations as the situation warrants. Except in rare circumstances, claim representatives should avoid using the lose-lose style of negotiation.

The negotiation process involves four steps: prepare, develop and evaluate alternative outcomes, identify each party's interests, and make concessions and create appropriate resolutions. The evaluation step should include establishing minimum and maximum settlement amounts acceptable for a claim resolution and developing a BATNA for comparison with other settlement options. Identifying each party's interests is crucial to making concessions and developing appropriate resolutions.

The variables that affect claim negotiations can be distinguished between the claimant's negotiation variables and the claim representative's negotiation variables. The claimant's negotiation variables may include the claimant's negotiation phase, how badly the claimant needs money, time pressures, the claimant's emotional reaction to the loss, the claimant's experience with or knowledge of insurance claims, and the claimant's personality. Some of the most significant variables that affect claim representatives are their knowledge of the claim and their authority level, the number of alternatives available, time factors, claim negotiation settings, and the claim representative's personality.

Many negotiation techniques can be used in claim negotiations. Some techniques, such as the principle of yes and choicing, can work well for all parties to a negotiation. When negotiating with unrepresented claimants, claim representatives find other techniques useful, including collecting and using extraneous information, sales techniques, needs analysis, and making the first offer. In negotiations with claimants' representatives, such as attorneys, public adjusters, or other representatives, other techniques are appropriate, including using information obtained from the claim evaluation, establishing strengths and weaknesses, using timing, making the first offer, and making concessions.

Claim representatives should be aware of techniques that claimants' representatives may use, such as limited authority negotiations and the counter-effect of timing. Claim representatives should avoid some negotiation techniques entirely because they do not produce satisfactory claim settlements for an insurer. Examples of such techniques are using a first and final offer and decreasing or limited offers.

Finally, claim representatives should be aware of common pitfalls in claim negotiations in order to avoid them. These pitfalls include allowing personalities to influence the settlement, trading dollars, bidding against oneself, and conceding as deadlines approach.

Claim representatives should expand their range of negotiation behaviors to be more successful. Knowledge of the negotiation process, variables, techniques, and pitfalls can help them adopt new negotiation behaviors.

When negotiation fails to effect a claim settlement, parties use various alternative dispute resolution techniques. When these techniques fail, litigation ensues. The final chapter examines a claim department's management of litigation.

CHAPTER NOTE

1. Judith Gordon, *Organizational Behavior: A Diagnostic Approach*, Upper Saddle River, N.J.: Pearson Education, Inc., 2002), pp. 336–337.

Chapter 8

Direct Your Learning

Managing Litigation

After learning the content of this chapter and completing the corresponding course guide assignment, you should be able to:

- Given a third-party lawsuit against an insured, describe the activities a claim representative would perform to manage the lawsuit.
- Given a bad-faith lawsuit against an insurer, describe the activities a claim representative would perform to manage the lawsuit.
- Explain how a claim representative can manage litigation expenses.
- Define or describe each of the Key Words and Phrases for this chapter.

OUTLINE

Managing a Third-Party Lawsuit

Managing a Bad-Faith Lawsuit

Managing Litigation Expenses

Summary

Appendix

Develop Your Perspective

What are the main topics covered in the chapter?

Claim representatives are responsible for managing litigation brought by either a third-party against an insured or by an insured against the insurer. To do so, they must actively participate in all aspects of litigation. They are also responsible for managing the expenses associated with litigation.

Review your company's policy for managing litigation.

- What do you do when a lawsuit is received?
- What steps do you take to manage litigation expenses?

Why is it important to learn about these topics?

Claim representatives routinely handle lawsuits against their insureds and the insurer. Mishandling of these lawsuits can result in bad-faith claims. Because claim representatives may also handle bad-faith lawsuits, they must understand the specific issues inherent in such claims. In managing the costs of lawsuits, claim representatives must avoid compromising the defense that is provided.

Consider how your organization manages litigation.

- Are the procedures for a third-party lawsuit different from those for a bad-faith lawsuit?
- How does your company handle the review of legal bills?

How can you use what you will learn?

Analyze a claim that is currently in litigation.

- What efforts has the claim representative taken to manage litigation expenses?
- What efforts might the claim representative take going forward?

Chapter 8
Managing Litigation

Most claims are resolved without litigation. Claim representatives are responsible for managing those claims that do result in litigation, and to do so, they must have a solid understanding of the legal system. They must handle and coordinate two aspects of managing litigation—the lawsuit itself and the expense of the lawsuit—in order to provide the insured or the insurer with an effective defense. In the process of litigation management, claim representatives must make decisions that can affect a lawsuit's outcome, including what to investigate, what to document, and how to settle claims. An understanding of the legal process can also help claim representatives avoid the kinds of errors in handling claims that can lead to bad-faith lawsuits.

Every claim has the potential to become a lawsuit. Such lawsuits usually come to the claim representative in one of three circumstances:

- While a claim is being investigated
- Before a claim is filed
- After a claim is closed

Most lawsuits are initiated on claims that are being actively handled by the claim representative. These lawsuits may be filed because the statute of limitations is about to expire or because negotiations have been unproductive. In this situation, the claimant (either the insured or a third party) is the plaintiff, that is, the party that files the lawsuit. The defendant, the party being sued, is usually the insured or the insurer, although other parties may also be named as defendants. If the insured is the plaintiff, then the lawsuit is a first-party lawsuit. If someone other than the insured files the lawsuit, it is a third-party lawsuit. For both first-party and third-party lawsuits, the claim representative has the advantage of using the information in the entire claim file to address the allegations.

In contrast to litigation that arises regarding a claim currently being handled, a lawsuit brought by an insured before a claim has been filed is the insurer's first notice of the claim. The insurer has no prior information about the accident or event giving rise to the lawsuit. The claim representative lacks the advantage of a claim file and has only the information contained in the lawsuit. The insured might have failed to report the accident or event alleged in the lawsuit for many reasons. The claim representative is responsible not only for investigating the allegations contained in the lawsuit but for investigating the reason the claim was not reported.

Lawsuits filed after claims have been closed are often coverage suits brought by insureds whose claims have been denied. To handle these lawsuits, the claim representative usually must reopen the claim file.

A claim representative may also receive a lawsuit when the insured (and in some states a third party) sues the insurer for bad faith. These lawsuits are generally received on active or closed claim files, but can also be received as the first notice of a claim. For example, the insured may file a bad-faith lawsuit alleging that the insurer failed to handle a claim in a timely manner, and the insurer may have no record of ever having received the claim. Because bad-faith lawsuits involve different allegations than third-party lawsuits, they are discussed separately in this chapter.

The process of managing the litigation of claims against the insured or insurer in any of these situations is the same. The process involves the following four steps:

1. Receiving the summons and complaint
2. Checking the summons and complaint to identify the parties, the applicable statute of limitations, the jurisdiction and venue, and the allegations
3. Referring the lawsuit to counsel, which involves selecting an attorney to represent the insured, preparing a suit transmittal letter, and notifying the insured of the selection
4. Assisting counsel in creating a litigation plan, answering the complaint, preparing evidence, preparing for trial, and managing pre-trial and post-trial activities

An important aspect of the claim representative's role in litigation management is managing litigation expenses. Failure to manage litigation properly can lead to adverse financial consequences for both the insured and the insurer.

Some insurers assign files involving litigation only to experienced claim representatives. However, because any claim can result in a lawsuit, an understanding of the litigation process is important for all claim representatives.

MANAGING A THIRD-PARTY LAWSUIT

Complaint, or petition
The initial document or pleading that is filed with the appropriate court to initiate a lawsuit and that specifies the grounds or allegations on which relief can be granted.

Summons
A document that directs a sheriff or another court-designated officer to notify the defendant named in the lawsuit that a lawsuit has been started and that the defendant has a specified amount of time to answer the complaint.

When claimants or insureds are dissatisfied with the outcome of a claim or the way a claim is being resolved, they can file documents with the appropriate courts. A **complaint**, or **petition**, is the initial document (or pleading) that is filed with the appropriate court and that specifies the grounds or allegations on which relief in the form of a judgment can be granted. This document may have other names, such as writ, depending on the state. For the types of lawsuits claim representatives handle, relief means money damages or the enforcement of a right. The complaint is delivered to the defendant via a **summons**, a document that directs a sheriff or another court-designated officer to notify a defendant named in a lawsuit that the lawsuit has been started and that the defendant has a specified amount of time to answer the complaint.

The delivery of the summons and complaint to the defendant by an authorized person is called **service of process**. If the defendant has insurance that covers or may cover the complaint's allegations, the defendant delivers the summons and complaint to the insurer to provide the defense. The Appendix at the end of this chapter contains an example of a summons and complaint.

Service of process
The delivery of a summons and complaint to a defendant by an authorized person.

Receiving the Summons and Complaint

An insured who has been served with a summons and complaint should immediately deliver them to the insurer or the producer, either by mail, by fax, or in person. If the insured delivers the documents to the producer, the producer should immediately forward them to the insurer. Time is of the essence in getting the summons and complaint into the hands of the claim representative because the summons contains a deadline by which the defense attorney must file an answer. An **answer** is a pleading or document filed in court by a defendant responding to a plaintiff's complaint and explaining why the plaintiff should not win the case. While the deadline to file the answer can be, and often is, extended by the plaintiff, it cannot be ignored.

Answer
A pleading or document filed in court by a defendant responding to a plaintiff's complaint and explaining why the plaintiff should not win the case.

When the insurer receives the summons and complaint, they may be given directly to the claim representative handling the claim or to the claim representative's supervisor. Information about the lawsuit may be entered in a tracking system, used by most insurers to compile data on lawsuit trends. The lawsuit is then matched to the existing claim, or if the lawsuit is the first notice of claim, a new claim file is created and referred to the claim representative for further handling.

Checking the Summons and Complaint

After receiving the summons and complaint, the claim representative must identify the parties in the complaint, determine the applicable statute of limitations and whether it has expired, and verify that the jurisdiction and venue are correct. The claim representative must also determine whether the insurance policy provides a defense against the allegations and coverage for any possible damages that may result from the allegations. Claim representatives cannot assume that all claims contained in lawsuits they receive are covered by the policy and are therefore eligible to be defended.

Generally, the insurer's duty to defend is broader than its duty to pay damages. If the allegations against the insured are fraudulent or potentially outside the coverage provided, the insurer usually is still obligated to defend the insured. Under such circumstances, the insurer may issue a reservation of rights to preserve its right to provide a defense only until such time as it is proven that the allegations are outside the policy coverage. Courts generally hold that an insurer's duty to defend is triggered if the lawsuit's allegations fall within policy coverage, regardless of whether the allegations are true.

However, an insurer is permitted to deny a claim and refuse to defend a lawsuit if the defendant is not insured. The claim representative's thorough review of the summons and complaint should determine whether the defendant is covered by the policy.

> ### Checking the Summons and Complaint for Coverage—Related Information
> - Identify the parties—Who was served and are they insureds?
> - Check how the service is accomplished—Was it proper?
> - Determine the time to answer—What is the deadline to file an answer?
> - Check the statute—Was the case filed within the statute of limitations?
> - Verify the jurisdiction and venue—Is the lawsuit filed in the appropriate court and location?
> - Examine the allegations—Are the allegations covered by the policy?

Parties

A complaint usually begins by identifying the parties in the lawsuit by name and address. It also gives the name and address of both the plaintiff's and the defendant's attorneys. The case caption "John Smith, Plaintiff v. Thomas Jones, Defendant" is used by most attorneys as an identifier in their correspondence and bills.

The claim representative must verify that the defendant is an insured under the applicable policy. Whereas verification is usually straightforward when dealing with a personal insurance policy such as auto or homeowners, it can be more complicated if the insured is a commercial entity that has various businesses insured by the same policy. When a commercial insured is involved, the claim representative may have to investigate the entities listed in the complaint to determine whether the defendant is an insured. For example, a general contractor may have an insurance policy that covers by endorsement every subcontractor the contractor has ever worked with. The claim representative must sort through all the endorsements to find the subcontractor named in the complaint. If the claim representative fails to verify the defendant is an insured on the policy, the insurer may erroneously provide a defense to an uninsured party.

Service

State and local laws specify who can be served with legal papers and how service is to be accomplished. For example, in Pennsylvania, a process server can accomplish service by handing the summons directly to the defendant or to an adult family member at the defendant's residence; to the clerk or manager of the hotel, motel, apartment house, or other place of lodging at which the defendant resides; or to the defendant's agent at the defendant's office or place of business. The Federal Rules of Civil Procedure set out the rules for service of federal lawsuits. To determine whether the appropriate party was served and the manner of service was correct, claim representatives should be familiar with the rules that apply in the jurisdiction of the lawsuit. If it appears that service was improper, the claim representative should advise defense counsel, who may file motions with the court relating to those issues or use them as a defense in the lawsuit.

Generally, two types of service are as follows:

1. Actual service
2. Substituted or constructive service

Actual service is hand delivery of the summons and complaint to the defendant. In the case of a corporation, the articles of incorporation designate the person authorized to accept service on behalf of the corporation, and that designation is filed with the secretary of state in the state of incorporation. **Substituted service**, or **constructive service**, is any method of notifying the defendant other than personal delivery of the summons and complaint. Most state statutes permit service by registered mail. Service can also be made by regular mail or may be delivered to the defendant's residence and left with a person of suitable age and discretion. Service by publication, usually in a newspaper, is the primary means of service on out-of-state defendants in some types of cases. In addition, if the defendant's whereabouts are unknown and there is no location to which the summons and complaint can be delivered, service by publication is appropriate.

Actual service
Hand delivery of a summons and complaint to a defendant.

Substituted service, or constructive service
Any method of notifying a defendant of a lawsuit other than personal delivery of a summons and complaint.

Time to Answer

Determining the deadline for filing an answer to the summons and complaint is an important aspect of handling litigation. If a complaint is not answered within the time specified, the insured and the insurer may face adverse consequences, such as losing the opportunity to defend against the allegations. The deadline to file an answer varies by state and usually ranges from ten days to twenty or thirty days from the date of service. Because the deadline is based on the date of service, the claim representative must determine when and how service was accomplished.

One common problem with insurance lawsuits is the potential for delay in getting the lawsuit into the hands of the claim representative. An insured named as a defendant who is unaware of the deadline for filing an answer may not report summonses and complaints to insurers promptly. If a summons and complaint are received close to the deadline for filing an answer, most states allow the claim representative to ask the plaintiff's attorney for an extension to answer the complaint. Some states require that defense counsel rather than claim representatives make such requests. In either case, attorneys usually grant the extension, usually for thirty days. If the extension is denied, the deadline in the summons stands. If a lawsuit is the first notice of the loss, the claim representative and defense counsel will have little time to investigate the claim before filing the answer. Formulating an answer on such short notice is difficult but not impossible.

Statute of Limitations

As previously explained, the statute of limitations defines the time limit for filing a lawsuit. The claim representative must check the complaint to determine the date the alleged offense occurred and then consult with counsel or otherwise determine the applicable statute of limitations. For example, if a summons and complaint alleges injury as a result of an auto accident, the claim representative can look up the statute of limitations for the state in which the complaint was filed. For example, the statute of limitations may be two years for a bodily injury claim. If the complaint alleges the accident occurred on May 18, 2004, and the complaint was filed on July 26, 2006, the statute of limitations has expired. If investigation reveals that a statute of limitations has expired, the claim representative should consult with counsel before taking any action.

Jurisdiction and Venue

The claim representative must next verify that the lawsuit's jurisdiction and venue comply with state or federal rules of civil procedure. An understanding of United States court systems is helpful in this analysis.

The U.S. has state and federal courts. State courts are created by each state's constitution. The single federal court system is created by the U.S. Constitution and acts of Congress. Whether a lawsuit is filed in state court or federal court depends on **jurisdiction**, a particular court's power or authority to decide a lawsuit of a certain type or within a specific territory. A court must have jurisdiction over a lawsuit to hear and decide it. Specifically, the court must have jurisdiction over the parties, the subject matter at issue, and the dollar amount at issue. The claim representative can make a preliminary review of the jurisdiction of the case and ask defense counsel to perform a more in-depth review.

Jurisdiction
A particular court's power or authority to decide a lawsuit of a certain type or within a certain territory.

In state court systems, the courts generally have jurisdiction over parties who reside or do business in that state. Most states also extend jurisdiction over anyone who operates a motor vehicle in the state. For example, a Pennsylvania resident who causes an automobile accident in New York is subject to the jurisdiction of the New York courts.

State court systems are similar to the federal court system, but the names of the courts at various levels may vary among U.S. states and territories. Every state has a trial court level at which most litigation starts. These courts of general jurisdiction have names such as court of common pleas, superior court, and district court. States may also have courts of limited jurisdiction, which hear specific types of cases. Examples are probate courts, which hear estate cases, and municipal courts, which hear cases involving limited amounts of money.

In addition to jurisdiction over the parties to a lawsuit, courts must have jurisdiction over the subject matter of the lawsuit. For example, a federal bankruptcy court lacks the subject matter jurisdiction to hear a lawsuit involving an automobile accident. Generally, state courts have subject matter jurisdiction over any legal dispute except those reserved by the U.S. Constitution for the federal courts.

Finally, the dollar amount at issue must also fall within the court's jurisdiction. Some courts can handle only lawsuits that do not exceed a stated dollar amount.

The federal court system has trial courts, called U.S. District Courts, and courts of appeal in thirteen multi-state judicial circuits. These courts handle lawsuits that deal with federal issues, such as those involving the U.S. Constitution, federal laws, and the U.S. as either a plaintiff or a defendant. In addition, there are special federal courts, such as the U.S. Customs Court, Bankruptcy Court, and the Patent Appeals Court, that have specific subject matter jurisdiction. Exhibit 8-1 shows the organization of the federal court system.

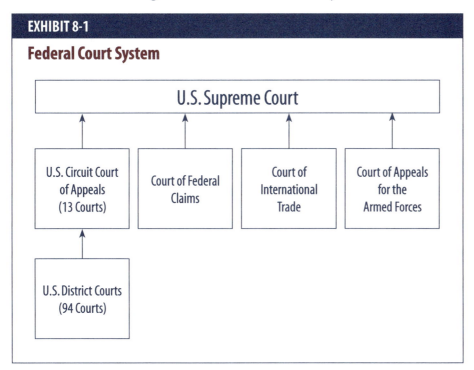

EXHIBIT 8-1

Federal Court System

U.S. District Courts also hear lawsuits involving diversity jurisdiction. Diversity jurisdiction is a federal court's authority to hear cases involving parties from different states that involve dollar amounts in controversy over a specified threshold. Claim representatives may find that some of their claims are heard in federal court because of diversity jurisdiction. This is often the case in a products liability claim when the insured is a corporation doing business in many states and when plaintiffs are from different states.

When reviewing the summons and complaint, the claim representative should note any possible jurisdictional question and bring it to the attention of counsel. Lawyers frequently seek to have a case dismissed on the grounds that a court does not have jurisdiction to hear a case.

A losing party in a lawsuit before a federal district court can appeal to the appropriate U.S. court of appeals. The losing party on a court of appeals case can appeal the case to the U.S. Supreme Court, the country's court of last resort, by filing a petition for a writ of *certiorari*, which asks the Supreme Court to consider the case. The Supreme Court grants review of a case solely within its discretion and chooses only about 100 cases to review annually.

Most states have an intermediate appellate-level court that hears appeals from trial courts. The decisions of a state's appellate-level court can be appealed the state's highest appellate court. Many states call this court the supreme court, but other states use different terms. Claim representatives should learn the names of the courts in the states in which they handle claims. Exhibit 8-2 shows the organization of state court systems.

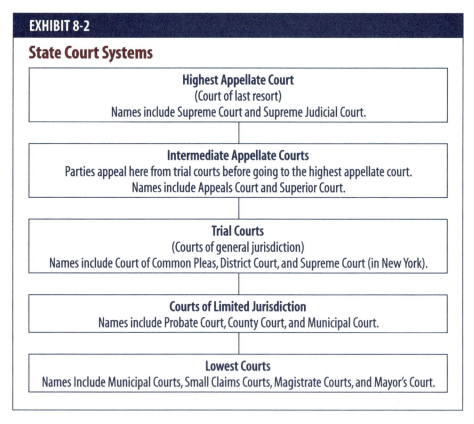

Venue
The locale in which the lawsuit may be brought.

Having reviewed the summons for jurisdictional issues, the claim representative should check the lawsuit's venue. **Venue** refers to the locale in which the lawsuit may be brought. Statutes usually require that a lawsuit be brought in the state in which the accident or occurrence took place, or in which either the plaintiff or defendant resides or does business. While jurisdiction designates which type of court will hear a case, venue designates the particular city, county, or state in which a court with jurisdiction will hear the case. Venue is important to the claim representative because when several different courts meet the requirements of jurisdiction and venue, the plaintiff chooses the court that is most likely to favor the plaintiff's lawsuit. This is an accepted practice; however, some plaintiffs may engage in a more questionable practice called forum shopping, manipulating the facts of a lawsuit to take advantage of a favorable venue, or forum. The claim representative should review the summons and complaint to determine whether the venue is questionable, and, if so, alert defense counsel. Defense counsel may seek to have the lawsuit removed to a more appropriate venue.

Example of Forum Shopping

Atley Corporation, incorporated and headquartered in New York City, is an international manufacturer and retailer of pesticide. The pesticide is shipped around the world in tanker ships. During a routine docking in San Francisco, the tanker runs aground and the pesticide leaks into the water, killing massive numbers of fish and game birds and contaminating miles of beaches. Atley spends billions of dollars cleaning up the spill, but Atley officials still expect to be sued by the commercial fishermen and local businesses affected by the spill. Atley Corporation is insured by Zelle Insurance Company, also headquartered in New York City. Atley submits a claim for the costs of the pesticide spill cleanup. Zelle Insurance Company denies the claim. Atley wants to sue the insurer for payment of the claim, but its attorneys do not believe it can win the case if it is heard in New York City. Research on jury verdicts in various states indicates that a Delaware jury may be more sympathetic to Atley's case. Consequently, Atley moves its corporate headquarters to Delaware and files suit against Zelle in Delaware.

Allegations

The body of the complaint contains the plaintiff's **allegations**, which are the claims the plaintiff expects to prove to obtain a judgment against the defendant. The body of the complaint serves the following four functions:

1. Gives notice
2. Reveals facts
3. Formulates legal causes of action
4. States the damages sought

The complaint gives the reader notice of who the parties are and where and why the lawsuit was filed. It lists each of the parties by name and states why the venue and jurisdiction are proper. It then presents the facts of the lawsuit and applies them to the issues of the plaintiff's cause of action (such as negligence or breach of contract). The facts must be sufficiently specific to give the reader fair notice about the basis for the lawsuit.

Allegations
Claims made in the complaint by the plaintiff, specifying what the plaintiff expects to prove to obtain a judgment against the defendant.

Claim representatives read complaints to determine whether some or all of the allegations are covered by the insurance policy. Allegations often include statements about the insured's actions or activities that may not be covered under the policy. If the policy clearly covers the allegations, then the claim representative refers the lawsuit to defense counsel to prepare an answer and defense. If the claim representative concludes that the policy does not cover the allegations, he or she should review that conclusion with a manager or supervisor. Some coverage questions may be so complex that an opinion from coverage counsel may also be sought. If the conclusion stands, the claim representative should issue a letter to the insured denying coverage and defense, stating specific reasons for the denial, and returning the lawsuit documents to the insured. If the complaint includes both covered and noncovered allegations, the insurer usually has to provide a defense for all the allegations but must indemnify only the covered allegations. In such cases, the claim representative sends the insured a reservation of rights letter reserving the insurer's right to withdraw the defense should facts clearly place the allegations of the lawsuit outside the policy coverage. Claim representatives should be aware that some states require insurers, when reserving their rights, to offer the insureds the option of choosing their own defense counsel.

When coverage of the allegations is an issue, the claim representative should select an attorney other than the attorney defending the insured to review the coverage issue. The defense attorney has an ethical obligation to act in the best interest of the insured. To be asked to render an opinion about coverage under the policy could present a conflict of interest for the defense attorney because the resulting opinion may be contrary to the insured's best interest.

Damages

The complaint concludes with a demand for damages. The claim representative should review this section carefully to determine whether the damages sought exceed policy limits. If so, the claim representative should advise the insured that the policy may not cover the total potential damages in the case. This information is usually contained in what is called an excess letter, and most insurers have a template for this letter that conforms to state law. The excess letter also gives the insured the option of hiring separate defense counsel to work with the insurer-appointed defense counsel in order to protect the insured's uninsured interests.

After deciding whether the insurer will defend the lawsuit, the claim representative is ready to select the defense counsel.

Referring the Lawsuit to Defense Counsel

Careful selection of defense counsel is an important factor in successful litigation and control of litigation expenses. Once the selection is made, the claim representative gives a copy of the claim file and the summons and complaint to the defense attorney, along with a lawsuit transmittal letter or set of instructions. The claim representative also notifies the insured that defense counsel has been assigned and provides the attorney's name and contact information.

Defense Counsel Selection

How defense counsel is selected varies by insurer. Defense counsel may be selected by one or more of the following: the claim manager, in-house legal counsel, a claim representative who is a litigation specialist, or the claim representative handling the claim. Generally, defense counsel is selected from a panel of attorneys, usually compiled by the home office claim staff in conjunction with the various claim offices. Selection of an attorney from the panel is usually based on a proven record of having represented insureds' interests well in previous cases and on an agreement to a fee schedule and billing guidelines set by the insurer. Some insurers may use staff attorneys, called in-house counsel, in the defense of insureds.

When selecting defense counsel, claim representatives should try to match the attorney's experience level to the subject matter and complexity of the lawsuit. For example, an attorney who specializes in workers' compensation cases may not be the best selection to defend an insured in a products liability case involving complex engineering issues.

Claim representatives should also select defense counsel who will meet the service needs of the insured and the insurer, for example, promptly returning phone calls and responding to the insured and the claim representative and submitting reports to the insurer throughout the litigation process. Defense counsel should be willing to work as a team with the claim representative in defending the insured. Often what distinguishes one attorney from another is this type of customer service.

Transmittal Form Completion

Once counsel is selected, the claim representative prepares a set of instructions and sends them to defense counsel in the form of a letter and report, along with the summons and complaint and a copy of the claim file. The transmittal form varies by insurer but generally provides a summary of the lawsuit and the claim investigation to date and includes the claim representative's opinions and expectations about the lawsuit's outcome. If the lawsuit is the first notice of the claim, the lawsuit transmittal letter informs defense counsel of how the claim representative intends to investigate the allegations.

The instructions set out a preliminary schedule of tasks to be accomplished, such as answering the complaint and completing outstanding investigation. They may also provide work and billing guidelines to which the attorney and the insurer have agreed. Details about these guidelines are described subsequently in this chapter.

> **Lawsuit Transmittal Letter Contents**
>
> A lawsuit transmittal letter should contain the following information:
>
> - Case caption
> - Title of the court in which the lawsuit is filed, along with the court's location
> - Claim number
> - Date of loss
> - Name and address of the plaintiff's attorney
> - Details of service of process
> - Name and address of the insured
> - Identity of all defendants to be defended by the appointed attorney
> - Policy number, insurer's name, and policy type
> - Policy limits
> - Deductible, if any
> - Presence of demand in excess of policy limits
> - Investigation conducted to date
> - Investigation remaining
> - Details of any settlement negotiations conducted
> - Reporting schedule
> - Billing guidelines
> - Request for a liability analysis
> - Request for a litigation plan

The claim representative should also prepare the claim file for transmittal. Some insurers photocopy the claim file and send it to the attorney with the summons and complaint. Others may give the attorney access to the electronic claim file via the Internet or company network/intranet. Whether the file is paper or electronic, the claim representative should ensure that it contains all documents pertinent to the claim, including copies of e-mail messages and activity notes. A copy of the insurance policy may be included. However, the transmittal should not include documents relating to any coverage issue, because such information can create a conflict of interest for the defense attorney.

Insured Notification

In addition to notifying defense counsel, the claim representative informs the insured that an attorney has been selected, providing name and contact information. The claim representative should instruct the insured to speak about the claim only to the claim representative and the designated attorney. This instruction is included to prevent the insured from making statements to others that could later be used against the insured in court.

Assisting Counsel

The claim representative's responsibilities in handling a claim do not end when the claim has been referred to defense counsel. The claim representative continues to be involved in all aspects of the defense. Even after litigation has begun, claim representatives continue to assess coverage, investigate liability and damages, evaluate the claim, and attempt to bring the claim to conclusion. Having defense counsel perform these tasks is not only too expensive but also, in many cases, inappropriate.

Claim representatives work with defense counsel to create litigation plans or plans for the insureds' defense. They may provide information that is useful to defense counsel in preparing answers to the complaints as well as certain types of evidence that can be used at trial. Claim representatives for some insurers take active roles in preparing evidence and witnesses for trial, and defense counsel may ask claim representatives to participate in the trials. In addition, claim representatives may handle negotiations, both during and after a trial, in an attempt to resolve the claim, and they may work with defense counsel on any post-trial motions or appeals. Because handling litigated claims can be complex and time-consuming, many insurers have a staff of experienced claim representatives dedicated to handling claims in litigation. Other insurers may assign only unusual or complex claims to such staff specialists so that other claim representatives can gain experience in assisting counsel with less complex claims.

Litigation Plan

After defense counsel has analyzed the information about the lawsuit provided by the claim representative, the two work together to develop a litigation plan or a plan for defense. They reach an agreement on what the ultimate outcome of the case should be and how to achieve it. This process can lay the foundation for effective communication between the claim representative and counsel throughout the trial, and the litigation plan itself can reduce the possibility of misunderstandings and disagreements with counsel. By agreeing on a goal at the outset, the claim representative and counsel can more easily work as a team to achieve the desired result. A litigation plan should also clarify the roles and expectations of the parties.

Both the claim representative and the defense counsel should view the litigation plan as a guideline rather than a rigid directive. They will probably adjust the plan several times as the litigation proceeds, and counsel should be aware that any deviations from the plan should occur only after consultation with the claim representative. Similarly, the claim representative should understand that the defense counsel owes the insured a duty of competent representation and that deviations from the plan should not jeopardize the attorney-client relationship by hindering the attorney's representation of the insured.

Generally, litigation plans outline a strategy to reach one of the following three possible objectives:

1. Defend the lawsuit
2. Settle the lawsuit
3. Obtain more information to decide whether to defend or settle the lawsuit

If the defense counsel and claim representative decide the lawsuit should be defended, they should agree on how to defend it. If they decide the lawsuit should be settled, for example, if the defendant is clearly liable, they should agree on a negotiation strategy. If, on the other hand, they decide they need more information before deciding whether to defend or settle, they must determine what additional information they need, how to obtain it, and who will obtain it.

When the litigation plan is complete, the defense counsel can draft an answer to the complaint.

Complaint Answer

The answer to the complaint contains the defendant's initial response to the complaint's allegations. A typical response is to deny the plaintiff's allegation of facts. For example, if the plaintiff alleges that the defendant negligently ran a stop sign at the corner of King Street and Main Street, on June 8, 2005, the defendant's answer may be a denial of the entire allegation or a denial only that the defendant negligently ran the stop sign.

The answer also presents affirmative defenses to the allegations, such as that the plaintiff failed to file the lawsuit within the appropriate statute of limitations, that the court in which the lawsuit was filed lacks jurisdiction, or that the venue is incorrect. Another affirmative defense is failure to state a claim for which relief can be granted (that is, the facts as alleged do not support the action). For example, in defense to a plaintiff's allegation of age-related employment discrimination, the defendant may assert that the plaintiff was not in a protected age class, was the youngest of all job applicants, and is ten years younger than the applicant who was hired for the job.

Counterclaim
A lawsuit brought by the defendant against the plaintiff that arises out of the same occurrence that is the subject matter of the plaintiff's lawsuit.

The answer also provides defense counsel with the opportunity to file a counterclaim, if the defendant has been wronged. A **counterclaim** is a lawsuit brought by the defendant against the plaintiff that arises out of the same occurrence that is the subject matter of the plaintiff's lawsuit. For judicial economy, courts usually hear both the original claim and the counterclaim simultaneously. For example, if the plaintiff claims the defendant negligently damaged the plaintiff's car, the defendant can counterclaim that the plaintiff negligently damaged the defendant's car and that the defendant's actions were in response to the plaintiff's negligent driving.

Defendants can also file lawsuits, called cross-claims, against other defendants in a case. A defendant's cross-claim alleges that another defendant should be at least partially responsible for any liability that may be imposed on the cross-claiming defendant. For example, in an indemnity contract with a general contractor, a subcontractor assumes responsibility for any damage that occurs while the subcontractor is working on the project. A plaintiff sues for damages and names both the general contractor and the subcontractor as defendants in the suit. The general contractor can cross-claim against the subcontractor for any award against the general contractor.

In a similar manner, a defendant can bring a third party into a lawsuit by filing a third-party complaint. The defendant alleges that the third party should bear some or all of the responsibility for the occurrence. For example, Driver B swerves into oncoming traffic and strikes Driver A. Driver A sues Driver B for negligence. Driver B files a third-party complaint against Driver C, alleging that Driver C stopped suddenly in front of Driver B, causing Driver B to strike Driver A.

Courts usually hear cross-claims and third-party complaints simultaneously with the original lawsuit.

Deciding when to use a counterclaim, cross-claim, or third-party complaint should be left to defense counsel. However, the claim representative should be alert for facts in the claim that may lead to any of these types of legal actions.

As previously discussed, promptness in answering the summons and complaint is important in order to avoid a default judgment. A **default judgment** is a judgment awarded to a plaintiff because the defendant has failed to respond to the summons and complaint by the deadline. Default judgments should be avoided because they automatically give the plaintiff all the damages asked for in the complaint.

Default judgment
Judgment awarded to a plaintiff because the defendant has failed to respond to the summons and complaint by the deadline.

A default judgment may occasionally be the insurer's first notice that a lawsuit had been filed. This is usually because an insured was served a summons and complaint and did not report it to the insurer. Although it is possible to have a default judgment vacated (withdrawn), such an outcome is not assured.

Discovery

Litigation plans outline the activities needed to accomplish the goals the claim representative and defense counsel have agreed on. For activities that are investigative in nature, the claim representative most likely can perform them more cost-effectively than the attorney can. If an activity can be performed only by the defense counsel, it is usually part of the discovery process.

Discovery is the process used to reveal facts and preserve testimony in a lawsuit. Discovery can also be used to narrow the issues of the lawsuit, which can lead to an early resolution. Both the plaintiff and the defendant use discovery to learn more about the case. Court rules generally permit attorneys to seek information in discovery that would not be admissible at trial; however, they must reasonably believe, and be able to show if asked by the court, that the information sought will lead to admissible evidence. A party may generally seek in discovery any evidence that is relevant to the subject matter

Discovery
The process used to reveal facts and preserve testimony in a lawsuit.

of the lawsuit as long as it is not privileged. Privileged evidence includes statements made by persons within a protected relationship, such as husband-wife, attorney-client, and doctor-patient. Examples of privileged evidence also include government records, grand jury proceedings, identity of informers, and attorney's work product. State statutes define the evidence and relationships that are privileged.

The following are the five most commonly used methods of discovery:

1. Request for production of documents
2. Interrogatories
3. Depositions
4. Physical or mental examinations
5. Admissions of facts not in dispute

Attorneys have the discretion to use discovery methods in any order. However, they generally use them in order listed because information gathered in one method is used in the next method. They may also use some discovery methods simultaneously, for example, sending a request for production of documents along with interrogatories.

A court's rules of civil procedure govern discovery methods, define each method of discovery, and set deadlines for exchange of discovery information and penalties for noncompliance with the rules. A court may also set a deadline for the completion of discovery in a specific lawsuit.

Request for production of documents
A request made by either the plaintiff or defendant in a lawsuit to the opposing side to provide all the documents and other tangible evidence it has in its possession relating to the facts of the case.

The discovery process usually begins with a **request for production of documents**, made by either the plaintiff or defendant to the opposing side to provide all the documents and other tangible evidence it has in its possession relating to the facts of the case. Other tangible evidence includes videotapes, diagrams, photographs, electronic records, and any other media used to transmit or preserve information. Any of the requested documents that the party possesses or can obtain without unreasonable effort must be produced, unless the party believes the document is privileged. To withhold a document as privileged, the party must identify the document, the parties communicating in it, and the basis for exercising the privilege. Lawyers may contest which types of documents are subject to privilege.

Interrogatories
Specific written questions or requests submitted by one party in a lawsuit requiring the opposing party to answer in writing.

After receiving and reviewing the requested documents, the attorney creates interrogatories. **Interrogatories** are specific written questions or requests submitted by one party in a lawsuit requiring the opposing party to answer in writing. Their primary purpose is to allow each side to discover the other side's position about the facts of the case and the applicable law. Because the answers are in writing, providing no opportunity for follow-up or clarifying questions, interrogatories are best used to identify specific facts and sources of information.

For example, an issue in a lawsuit is whether the lawsuit was filed within the appropriate statute of limitations. The defendant alleges in Paragraph #12 of its answer to the plaintiff's complaint that the driver was a permissive user of the plaintiff's vehicle. The plaintiff's interrogatory may state the following: "Please identify all the facts on which the defendant relies regarding Paragraph #12 of defendant's answer to plaintiff's complaint." This interrogatory seeks the information the plaintiff needs to determine the basis of the defendant's assertion of permissive use. The defendant must provide all the facts that support the allegation. Failure to respond completely to all questions in an interrogatory precludes the party from subsequently relying on information that was not disclosed. In this example, if the defendant withheld one of its reasons for believing the driver to be a permissive user of the vehicle, the defense would be unable to use that fact at trial.

Defense lawyers may call on claim representatives to assist in answering interrogatories, particularly when the plaintiff raises issues about the claim process. The claim representative should respond promptly because deadlines for answering interrogatories are usually short. Failure to meet filing requirements can result in sanctions, such as fines, or a finding in favor of the interrogating party. Exhibit 8-3 is an example of a simplified interrogatory.

Attorneys often use the answers to interrogatories as the basis for depositions. A **deposition** is an oral examination of a witness about his or her activities or knowledge of the subject matter of a lawsuit. This testimony is typed by a court reporter or videotaped. Depositions can be used at trials as evidence of what a person saw, heard, or did in relation to the dispute between the parties. Depositions are generally conducted at the office of the lawyer who requested the deposition.

Deposition
An oral examination of a witness about his or her activities or knowledge of the subject matter of a lawsuit.

Depositions have two purposes. First, they allow each party to the lawsuit to discover what the other party's witnesses know about the facts of the matter. Second, because the testimony is transcribed, it can be used to challenge any conflicting testimony given by the same witness at trial. Such a challenge can discredit the witness, and in some cases, expose the witness to a perjury charge.

Two types of witnesses can be deposed: party witnesses and nonparty witnesses. Party witnesses are parties to the suit, such as the plaintiff or the defendant or, in the case of a party that is a corporation, one of its representatives or employees. Nonparty witnesses include all other persons who have knowledge of the case. Nonparty witnesses may be eyewitnesses to an accident, claim representatives who investigated the loss, expert witnesses, or recordkeepers.

A party witness's lawyer usually reviews anticipated questions with that witness before the deposition. Such preparations may be time consuming if the witness has extensive knowledge that is important to the lawsuit. However, the review can help refresh the witness's memory and familiarize him or her with the types of questions that are likely to be asked. Claim representatives are frequently required to give depositions about claims they have investigated. In preparation for being deposed, a claim representative should refer to the claim's activity log to review the facts.

> **EXHIBIT 8-3**
>
> ### Sample Interrogatory
>
> SUPERIOR COURT OF
> DAWSON COUNTY
> COMMONWEALTH OF PENNSYLVANIA
>
> CIVIL ACTION NO. 1-77804
>
> James A. Dermont
> Plaintiff
>
> v.   INTERROGATORIES
>
> Hamilton W. Grind
> Defendant
>
> TO: HAMILTON W. GRIND
>
> Please take notice that the plaintiff, James A. Dermont, demands answers to the following interrogatories under oath within 30 days from the time service is made upon you.
>
> Question No. 1: Was the defendant legally intoxicated at the time of the accident?
>
> Question No. 2: Did the defendant fail to stop at a stop sign?
>
> Question No. 3: What physical evidence will the defendant present?
>
> Question No. 4: State the names and addresses of all the witnesses that the defendant will use to testify on behalf of the defendant in the trial of the case.
>
> s/s Jerry R. Fleetwood
> Jerry R. Fleetwood
> Attorney for Plaintiff
> 1200 Audubon Street
> New Haven, Pennsylvania
>
> Date: 10/15/200X

Attorneys preparing for depositions may not always have the name of the person who has the information they are seeking, particularly if the plaintiff or the defendant is a corporation, partnership, association, or government agency. In such cases, an attorney may request a deposition from the "person with most knowledge" about the allegations in the complaint and answer. For example, the lawyer of a plaintiff suing a large corporation may not know specifically which manager was responsible for developing and implementing a particular policy. Asking to depose the person with most knowledge eliminates the need to identify the specific individual.

During a deposition, the opposing lawyer is required to follow basic rules of professional courtesy. However, lawyers can ask questions out of order, repeat questions after rephrasing them, and engage in other tactics designed to catch the deposed party off guard to reveal contradictions in the testimony. Observing witnesses in the deposition setting also helps lawyers evaluate how they will testify in court.

Information obtained in a deposition or produced by another discovery method may lead defense counsel to request an examination of the opposing party's physical and/or mental condition. Requests for independent medical examinations (IMEs) are most common in bodily injury claims or claims for emotional or psychological injury and are usually initiated by the defendant in order to assess the physical or mental injuries claimed by the plaintiff. Generally, the rules of civil procedure require the injured party to submit to an examination. The claim representative and the defense attorney decide when an IME is needed, and the claim representative usually makes the necessary arrangements. After the need is determined, the claim representative should promptly contact the insured or claimant to request the IME and should follow the insurer's standards for selecting medical practitioners to conduct the IME.

With the information compiled from all other methods of discovery, one or both parties to the lawsuit may decide to request admissions. **Admissions** are factual statements that, unless denied, bind the party at trial. The purpose of this discovery device is to narrow the factual issues to those in contention and to reduce the number of facts the court or jury has to determine at trial. Facts that are usually admitted by the parties before trial include the names and addresses of the parties, dates of certain incidents, and other facts that are not in dispute but would otherwise need to be proven at trial.

Admissions
Factual statements that, unless denied, bind the party at trial.

The attorney representing each party must decide whether to admit certain facts. When the defense receives a request for admissions, the attorney may send it to the claim representative for review.

Attorneys are sometimes tempted to refuse to admit any facts, even those they know are true, on the premise that it is safer to deny everything. Such an approach can unnecessarily prolong litigation because it forces the opposing side to prove trivial details. For example, a complaint may allege that the insured owns a 2002 Toyota Camry. If there is no dispute over this fact, defense counsel could admit to it in the answer. Generally, facts that are indisputable should be admitted.

Once all methods of discovery have been completed, the claim representative and defense counsel should review the litigation plan to determine whether the information produced in discovery requires a change in the plan. If their initial assessment was that insufficient information was available to decide whether to defend or settle, discovery should have produced the needed information. If they initially considered the case to be defensible, they should review that decision in light of information obtained during discovery.

If the claim representative and defense counsel determine that the lawsuit is still defensible, then trial preparation begins.

Assisting at Trial

Throughout discovery, the defense attorney and claim representative have gathered information leading to the decision to try the case. This information must be incorporated into the trial strategy. The trial strategy is created by defense counsel and communicated to the claim representative, usually in the form of a pre-trial report that outlines the strengths and weaknesses of both the defendant's case and the plaintiff's case. The report may include a synopsis of applicable law and a range for possible settlement and/or jury awards.

In preparing the trial strategy, the defense attorney may research court decisions in similar cases to find a precedent for the defense position in the current case. The practice of using precedent is based on *stare decisis* (pronounced STAHR-ee di-SI-sis or STAIR-ee, meaning to stand by things decided), the principle that lower courts must follow precedents set by higher courts. Cases decided by a state's highest court become the common law of that state and set a precedent for later decisions in lower courts. Attorneys seek to distinguish their cases from unfavorable precedents in order to persuade judges that the precedents do not apply. Lawyers use favorable precedents to support their cases and may seek to have a precedent applied more broadly so that it applies to their case. For example, if a precedent-setting case involved an interpretation of a doctor's duties to a patient, an attorney might seek to use this precedent for a case involving a veterinarian's duty to an animal's owner even though, under the current common law, no such duty is required.

Stare decisis
The principle that lower courts must follow precedents set by higher courts.

A higher court can overturn a lower court's precedent. Such decisions are often made when a precedent becomes obsolete because of changes in statutory law, technology, or society.

Defense counsel often include case citations to precedent cases in their pre-trial reports or case analyses. Court opinions are chronicled in books called reporters or online in various legal databases. Case citations provide the following information:

- Name of the case
- Volume number, name of the reporter, and page number where the case can be found
- Court that decided the case
- Year the case was decided

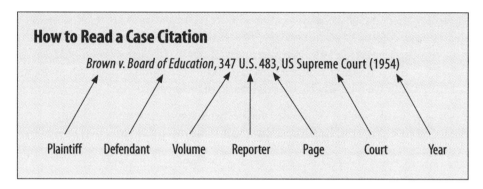

Courts publish their written opinions in official case reporters. Each state and each level of court may have its own reporter, the names of which are abbreviated in the case citation. The reporters have tables listing the abbreviations and the full names of the volumes. Commercial entities such as Westlaw or LexisNexis also publish compiled cases, and case law is available on the Internet at many different commercial, educational, and judicial Web sites.

Published court decisions usually start with a short case synopsis and a summary of the court's decision, or holding. They show the names of the attorneys involved and give a recitation of the facts. The court's decision is then set out in its entirety, followed by any concurring and dissenting opinions if it is a multi-judge court. Claim representatives may find it helpful to read court opinions not just in relation to a particular claim in litigation, but to stay abreast of changes in laws that may affect claims they will handle in the future.

After reviewing the trial strategy and case analysis with defense counsel, the claim representative and defense counsel should agree on any pretrial motions to be made. During litigation, the court must rule on disputes that arise relating to the case or the trial process. Some common issues are whether certain evidence can be admitted at trial, whether certain persons can be called as witnesses, and whether the lawsuit can be settled without further action by the parties. To bring these matters to a court's attention, lawyers file motions with the court. A motion is a written proposal for how a dispute should be resolved. Motions are governed by the rules of civil procedure, which designate when a motion can be brought, why a motion can be brought, what must be included in a motion, and when opposing attorneys must respond to a motion.

Attorneys can make many motions. Claim representatives should be familiar with the following three common pretrial motions:

1. Motion to dismiss
2. Motion *in limine*
3. Motion for summary judgment

Motion to dismiss
A request that a court terminate an action because of settlement, voluntary withdrawal, or procedural defect.

Motion *in limine*
A pretrial request that certain evidence be excluded from the trial.

Motion for summary judgment
A pretrial request asking the court to enter a judgment when no material facts are in dispute.

A **motion to dismiss** is a request that a court terminate an action because of settlement, voluntary withdrawal, or procedural defect. Among reasons for a motion to dismiss filed early in the proceedings are that the complaint is defective, the defendant has failed to respond to the summons, or the plaintiff has failed to state a legally recognized cause of action.

Either party can request that information gathered during discovery be excluded from the trial by filing a **motion *in limine*** (pronounced LIM-e-nee). Attorneys typically seek to exclude evidence that is harmful to their cases. For example, if the plaintiff offers photographs showing vehicle damage and bloodstains as evidence, defense attorneys may attempt to exclude the photos because they could unduly influence the jury's decision. Although the photographs may be admissible under the rules of evidence, attorneys may still seek to persuade the court to exclude them for the following reasons:

- They are highly prejudicial (bloodstains tend to influence jurors regardless of their importance in determining fault).
- They are cumulative (other photographs are available to show damage to the vehicle that do not show bloodstains).
- The fact is not in controversy (the defendant admits that the car was damaged).

At the close of discovery but before trial, the plaintiff or the defendant can file a **motion for summary judgment** asking the court to enter a judgment that no material facts are in dispute. The moving party submits a memorandum of applicable law that supports the motion. Supporting material can also include affidavits, answers to interrogatories, and replies to requests for admissions. In most cases, the nonmoving party responds to the motion for summary judgment and can file its own motion for summary judgment using the same facts but arguing for a different interpretation of the law.

After the motions and responses are filed, the court usually holds a hearing. The judge questions the attorneys about the bases for their respective motions or their opposition. In considering a motion, the judge assumes that all the pleadings of the party opposing the motion are true. For example, if defense attorneys bring a motion for summary judgment, the judge considers the motion in light of the allegations the plaintiff has presented in its complaint and other pleadings and from the standpoint that those allegations are correct. Courts apply strict standards when reviewing a motion for summary judgment because granting the motion deprives the nonmoving party (the party who has not made the motion) of a jury trial. To grant a summary judgment motion, the court must find that no genuine issues of material fact are in dispute and that the moving party (the party who made the motion) is entitled to judgment as a matter of law, and judgment is entered without a trial. If a motion for summary judgment is granted that covers the entire matter at issue, litigation is ended and a judgment for the moving party is entered. If the motion is denied or covers only some of the issues, the parties proceed to trial.

Defense counsel and the claim representative should agree in advance on pretrial motions. The claim representative should have a clear understanding of why defense counsel is proposing a motion and the likely outcome. This understanding is necessary because motion practice, as filing these motions is called, increases defense costs.

In addition to pretrial motions, there are pretrial conferences, called at the judge's discretion in an effort to settle the case. The judge and the parties' attorneys meet in the judge's chamber two or three weeks before the trial. In some cases, the judge simply inquires about the status of the case and whether any possibility of settlement exists. In other cases, the judge may use a pretrial conference to limit the issues to be heard at trial, much like a motion *in limine*. Exhibit 8-4 is an example of a pretrial order that might be issued at the conclusion of the pretrial conference to limit the issues in the case.

EXHIBIT 8-4

Sample Pretrial Order

SUPERIOR COURT OF
DAWSON COUNTY
COMMONWEALTH OF PENNSYLVANIA

CIVIL ACTION NO. 1-77804

James A. Dermont
Plaintiff

v.

Hamilton W. Grind
Defendant

PRETRIAL ORDER

A pretrial conference was held on January 15, 200Y, before me, with Jerry R. Fleetwood appearing as attorney for the plaintiff and William C. Havenship appearing as attorney for the defendant. The following proceedings were had:

1. Plaintiff and defendant were involved in an automobile accident on June 1, 200X.

2. Defendant was legally intoxicated at the time of the accident.

3. The issue remaining in the action is whether the defendant's brakes failed unexpectedly at the time of the accident.

s/s Anita S. Raimondi
Anita S. Raimondi
Judge, Superior Court
Dawson County

Date: 1/20/200Y

Claim representatives may be asked to attend the pretrial conference, either by the court or by the defense attorney. Before the conference, the claim representative and defense counsel should agree on the conference's expected outcome and the claim representative's role, if any, in the conference. The judge may attempt to settle the case by persuading the claim representative to make an offer or increase an offer, even though the claim representative and defense counsel have agreed that the case should be defended rather than settled.

As part of trial preparation, defense counsel may ask the claim representative to gather additional information, such as more photos of the accident scene or medical records. When they possess evidence, claim representatives may be involved in maintaining a chain of evidence (a record showing who has possession of or access to the evidence and when). In a claim against a potentially responsible third party, an insurer can be denied recovery if evidence has been intentionally or negligently lost or destroyed. Similarly, an insurer defending a first-party coverage lawsuit can be found liable if evidence is intentionally or negligently lost or destroyed. The claim representative shares responsibility for preserving evidence with the property owner, the defense attorney, and any expert given access to the evidence.

Trial Assistance

Depending on local practices, claim representatives may be asked to drive witnesses to court, participate in conferences between the parties, and observe the entire trial. They must be ready to assist as needed, and to hire others to assist, if necessary.

Most insurers use a litigation reporting process that requires the claim representative to file periodic status reports on the trial. These litigation reports inform the various interested parties (such as the underwriter and the home office claim department) and the insurer about the case's progress and outcome. In order to file accurate trial status reports, the claim representative should be familiar with the trial process.

A trial can be a jury trial or a nonjury trial. A jury is a group of people who hear and consider the evidence in a case and decide what facts are true. In a jury trial, the jury decides all questions of fact and the judge decides all questions of law. In a nonjury trial, the judge decides all questions of both fact and law. The right to trial by jury may depend on the amount in controversy or on the particular area of law that applies to the facts of a case. For example, in some states, questions about the actions of an insurer investigating a claim are heard not by a jury but by a judge. In a civil trial, the plaintiff and defendant may agree to have a case heard by a judge alone. A bench trial, also called a trial by court or judge, is a trial heard by a judge without a jury.

Depending on the amount in controversy and the jurisdiction, a jury may have six to twelve members. Alternate jurors hear the evidence but do not deliberate unless another juror is unable to serve throughout the trial. By using alternate jurors, the court ensures that after the trial starts, it continues to a verdict even if one or more jurors must leave the jury because of illness or undue hardship.

Jurors are selected from a jury pool. Potential jurors from the pool are questioned by the judge or lawyers about their knowledge or opinion of the parties to the litigation and the issues to be decided in the case. **Voir dire** (pronounced vwahr-deer) is the process of examining potential jurors about their possible interest in the matters presented at trial, their ability to decide the case fairly, and their competence to serve as jurors. During this process, attorneys attempt to determine the potential jurors that would most likely be favorable to their clients. Depending on the statute or a court rule, lawyers for each party are given a set number of peremptory challenges, which allow them to exclude a potential juror without stating a reason. After using the allotted peremptory challenges, lawyers may still exclude jurors but must state their reason for doing so.

Voir dire
The process of examining potential jurors about their possible interest in the matters presented at trial, their ability to decide the case fairly and without prejudice, and their overall competence to serve as jurors.

In some jurisdictions, people in certain occupations are automatically excluded from hearing a particular case. For example, attorneys and claim representatives may be excluded from hearing civil trials. Friends, relatives, and acquaintances of the parties to the lawsuit are also typically excluded.

In lawsuits against insureds, jurors and judges are not informed of insurer involvement in the case. That an insurer will pay the judgment or is providing the defense (unless, of course, an insured is suing an insurer directly) should not affect the judge's or jury's decision about liability. The trial should be conducted as though no insurers are involved, even when it is obvious that they are. For example, the parties involved in an automobile accident are likely to have insurance; therefore, it is likely that insurers are involved in civil trials related to such accidents. Nevertheless, any mention by a party that an insurer is involved is grounds for a mistrial.

The parties' respective burdens of proof have a bearing on why, how, and in what order evidence is presented at trial. **Burden of proof** is the duty of a party to prove that the facts it claims are true. To satisfy their burden of proof, plaintiffs must generally prove all the essential elements of their case by a **preponderance of evidence**; that is, the evidence supporting the jury's decision must be of greater weight than the evidence against it. For a judge or jury to determine preponderance of evidence, the basis and extent of witnesses' knowledge, the type and quality of information they possess, and their manner of testifying are more important than the number of witnesses. Determining preponderance of evidence is a subjective judgment.

Burden of proof
In a trial, the duty of a party to prove that the facts it claims are true.

Preponderance of evidence
Evidence supporting the jury's decision that is of greater weight than the evidence against it.

Once the jury is assembled, the trial begins with attorneys' opening statements. An opening statement is not evidence but a summary of the case and of the proof the attorney intends to present. Because the plaintiff has the burden of proof, the plaintiff's attorneys go first. They use this opportunity to summarize the facts of the case and the issues the jury will decide. The jury is usually told which witnesses will testify, how this testimony relates to the issues the jury is to decide, and why the jury should decide the case in the plaintiff's favor. After the plaintiff's opening statement, attorneys for the defendant can make an opening statement or reserve the opening statement until after the close of the plaintiff's case. Whether the defendant's attorneys reserve the opening statement is a matter of strategic planning and personal preference.

Following the opening statements, the plaintiff's attorneys introduce evidence by calling and questioning witnesses to establish the plaintiff's case. The defendant's attorney is entitled to cross-examine the plaintiff's witnesses. Cross-examination is an essential element of the trial. It allows opposing attorneys to test the truth of a witness's testimony, to further develop the testimony, or to question a witness for other purposes. Successful cross-examination may discredit testimony or reduce the weight a jury may give to the evidence.

After the plaintiff's attorneys have presented their case, the defense follows the same procedure, presenting an opening statement if it did not do so previously and then calling defense witnesses to testify. The plaintiff's attorney may cross-examine defense witnesses.

Witnesses may be lay witnesses or expert witnesses. Lay witnesses have no special expertise in the matters about which they testify but have first-hand knowledge of the matters, based on observation. For example, a witness to an automobile accident would be a lay witness. An expert witness has specialized knowledge in a particular field. The judge determines whether an expert witness is qualified. Often both parties produce expert witnesses in the same field who testify with different opinions about the same facts. Expert witnesses can include doctors, engineers, accountants, psychologists, and economists. Occasionally, an expert is required in an unusual field of expertise, such as an expert in identifying artistic forgeries.

During a trial, issues about the conduct of the trial arise that must be decided by the judge. These matters may include whether a particular piece of evidence should be presented to the jury, the scheduling of the proceedings, and the estimated duration of the trial. Because such issues do not concern the jury, and in some cases must be withheld from the jury, the judge and lawyers hold a bench conference, that is, a conference outside the hearing of the jury. For example, if an attorney wants to introduce specific evidence and opposing attorneys object, the judge hears arguments from both parties' attorneys about why the evidence should be admitted or excluded. The jury is barred from hearing these arguments to prevent prejudice if the judge decides to exclude the evidence. Bench conferences may be recorded by a court reporter so that a transcript is available if either party appeals the judge's decision. However, these conferences are not necessarily made part of the trial's written record.

Similar to pre-trial motions, the parties can make motions at other points during the trial. When the plaintiff's case has been presented, defense attorneys can move for a directed verdict, asking the court to dismiss the case because the plaintiff has failed to prove its allegations. The defense attorneys argue that the evidence is so clear and convincing that no reasonable trier of fact could find for the plaintiff. If the motion is granted, the verdict favors the defendant and the trial is concluded. Directed verdicts are rarely granted because a plaintiff's evidence is rarely so defective that it warrants such a ruling. Directed verdicts are often appealed.

After all evidence has been presented, attorneys for each side are given an opportunity to address the jury through closing arguments during which they typically summarize the facts presented in a light most favorable to their client. Like opening statements, closing arguments are not evidence. Because closing arguments promote a particular position, attorneys may attempt to influence the jury's decision by characterizing evidence adverse to their client's position as being "without weight."

Following the closing arguments, the judge instructs the jury about the law to apply in deciding the case. For example, in an automobile accident trial, the judge instructs the jury in the principles of negligence and fault and explains which party has the burden of proof. Attorneys usually submit written proposals for instructions, and the judge decides whether to incorporate them in the jury instructions. A losing party may appeal a case on the grounds that the judge instructed the jury incorrectly.

After receiving the judge's instructions, the jury retires to the jury room to decide the case. Jury members select a foreperson who acts as the leader. The jury's deliberations have no time limit; they continue until a unanimous verdict is reached. The jury returns to the courtroom, and the judge asks for their verdict. The verdict is read in open court, usually by a court officer or the jury spokesperson.

Post-Trial Activities

The court usually accepts the jury's verdict and enters a judgment to that effect. On rare occasions, the court can act on its own initiative or on a motion of the losing party and enter a judgment notwithstanding the verdict (judgment n.o.v.). This is a judgment in favor of one party even though the jury's verdict favored the other party. For example, if a jury finds a defendant liable for the plaintiff's injuries without evidence to support that verdict, the court can enter a judgment for the defendant, notwithstanding the verdict. Sometimes the losing party must file a motion for a directed verdict before a judge can grant a judgment n.o.v.

The court can grant a new trial on its own initiative or on the losing party's motion. Typical grounds for a new trial include insufficient evidence, erroneous rulings on instructions, newly discovered evidence, and a verdict contrary to the judge's instructions. However, trial judges seldom grant new trials.

The court can adjust the damages awarded by the jury. A judge who considers the jury award excessive or insufficient may decrease or raise it. This typically happens when a jury awards an extraordinarily high judgment that is disproportionate to the damages.

Either party can appeal a court verdict to a higher court, although it is commonly the losing party that appeals. Appeals courts hear no new evidence from witnesses and do not consider whether the finder of fact (the judge or the jury) in the lower court was correct in determining the facts. Rather, appeals courts usually limit their opinions to a review of the application of law to the facts decided by the jury or the judge. The distinction between the facts and the law can be subtle. For example, if the trial court found a motorist to have driven thirty-five miles per hour in a twenty-five-mile-per-hour zone, an appeals court could not dispute that finding if it was reasonable. However, the appeals court could determine whether the judge gave correct instructions to the jury on the law of negligence as it applied to the fact that the motorist was speeding.

Appeals are most commonly based on evidentiary matters. During a trial, a judge rules on many matters concerning the admissibility of evidence. A party may appeal on the grounds that the judge's decision to admit or exclude certain evidence altered the outcome of the trial. For example, defense attorneys may argue that excluded evidence about the plaintiff's reputation should have been allowed in order to show that the plaintiff is not a truthful person.

An appeal may be based on the judge's instructions to the jury. A judge's error in stating the law is grounds for an appeal because the jury uses these instructions to apply the law to the facts. For example, if a judge misstated the law of negligence, lawyers may have grounds for a successful appeal.

Another common ground for appeal is that the verdict is "against the weight of the evidence" and that, therefore, some influence from outside the trial must have caused the jurors to reach their verdict. Because jurors are entrusted to make all findings of fact, such an appeal requires a heavy burden of proof: that no reasonable trier of fact could have reached the verdict at issue.

The appeals process is lengthy. A complete trial transcript must be certified and transmitted to the appeals court along with all physical evidence introduced at trial. After the parties file appeals briefs, a hearing is held, and attorneys for each party argue for or against the appeal and answer questions raised by the appellate justices. The decision of a state's highest appeals court is final and concludes the matter. Exceptions involve cases appealed based on the U.S. Constitution, which can be appealed to the U.S. Supreme Court. Unlike most state supreme courts, the U.S. Supreme Court chooses the cases it will hear.

Once a judgment is final, the plaintiff moves to enforce the judgment. In most instances, the defendant makes arrangements to pay the plaintiff. If the defendant is indigent or unable to pay in full, the plaintiff may file a lien with the court to enforce the judgment should the defendant later be able to pay.

Exhibit 8-5 summarizes the process of a typical lawsuit.

EXHIBIT 8-5
Process of a Typical Lawsuit

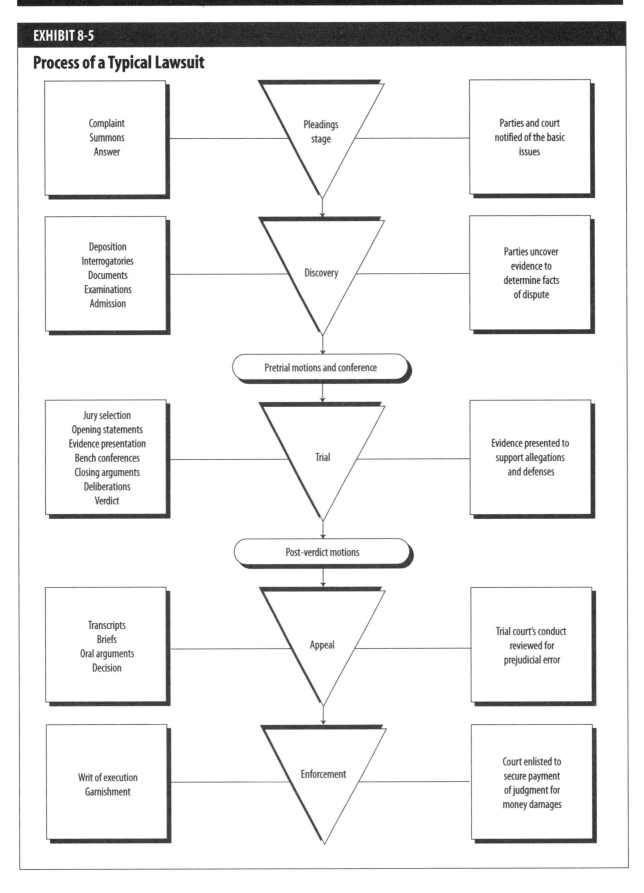

MANAGING A BAD-FAITH LAWSUIT

Although the trial process is the same for third-party lawsuits and bad-faith lawsuits, the claim representative's roles and responsibilities differ. Bad-faith lawsuits are often referred to specific claim representatives who are also attorneys. Most insurers believe that bad-faith lawsuits should be handled by someone other than the claim representative who handled the claim, whose actions are the basis for the lawsuit. Many insurers create a new claim file for the bad-faith lawsuit that is separate from the underlying claim file. In some circumstances, the bad-faith allegation has no reasonable basis, and the insurer prefers not to reassign the claim to another claim representative.

Receiving the Summons and Complaint

Because a bad-faith lawsuit is usually filed against the insurer, the summons and complaint may be served on the insurer's corporate office, the local office, or an insurer representative. Insurers have guidelines about who should receive the summons and complaint and how to respond. The guidelines may direct the lawsuit to the claim representative's supervisor or manager or to a corporate claim person who specializes in bad-faith lawsuits. The time limit for answering a bad-faith lawsuit is the same as for any other lawsuit; therefore, the summons and complaint must promptly reach the designated person.

Checking the Summons and Complaint

Similar to other lawsuits, on receipt of a bad-faith lawsuit, the claim representative must check the summons and complaint to identify the parties in the complaint, determine the applicable statute of limitations, verify the jurisdiction and venue, and check the allegations to determine what defenses may be available.

Parties

Generally, bad-faith lawsuits are brought against the insurer and not against the individual claim representative because the insurer has sizable assets available to satisfy a judgment. However, a claim representative may be named as a defendant. If so, the claim representative should verify that the insurer will handle his or her defense. If the insurer refuses to provide the defense, the claim representative must retain personal counsel to protect his or her interests.

The claim representative handling the bad-faith lawsuit should confirm that the defendant insurer is correctly identified in the summons and complaint. A policyholder could get the name of the insurer incorrect, or the name of the actual insurer could be different from the parent company that has been named in the lawsuit. This occurs when an insurance company writes policies under many different names to comply with insurance admission laws in various states. These errors should be pointed out to defense counsel, who will move to correct them.

Service

The claim representative handling the bad-faith lawsuit should determine how service of the summons and complaint on the insurer and other related defendants was accomplished. The rules of service for a bad-faith lawsuit are the same as those for any other lawsuit. A potential problem in a bad-faith claim is that the service may have been accomplished at a location far from where the claim is being handled. For example, service may have been made at the insurer's corporate headquarters rather than at the local claim office. Particularly when service has been made at a distant location, the claim representative must determine who received the service and whether it was proper.

Time to Answer

The statutory time in which to file an answer in a bad-faith lawsuit is specified in the summons and complaint. The claim representative handling the lawsuit should make every effort to comply or to secure an extension from the opposing party.

Statute of Limitations

The claim representative handling the bad-faith lawsuit should check the applicable statute of limitations in the state in which the bad-faith lawsuit is filed to determine whether the lawsuit has been filed within the time limit. The claim representative should also determine whether the policy applicable to the underlying claim specifies a time limit for filing a lawsuit if the bad-faith claim is included in a lawsuit for coverage.

Jurisdiction and Venue

As for other lawsuits, the claim representative checks jurisdiction and venue for a bad-faith lawsuit. Forum shopping may be an issue in a bad-faith lawsuit. The plaintiff may have filed the lawsuit in a jurisdiction that was more favorable to insureds than to insurers, even though another jurisdiction might have been more convenient for all parties.

Allegations

The allegations in a bad-faith lawsuit provide details of the activities on which they are based. These allegations may be specific to how the underlying claim was handled, or they may be general, alleging a pattern or practice occurring with many different claims. In contrast to the relative simplicity of investigating allegations that involve a single claim, investigation of a pattern of practice over many years can be complicated, possibly requiring review of computer printouts, archived claim files, and other claim department documents.

Damages

Because damages in bad-faith claims are punitive in nature, the dollar value of damages sought is often extremely high. The claim representative handling the bad-faith lawsuit should not be surprised or alarmed by these amounts, because they may be unrealistic. A familiarity with customary bad-faith damage awards in the lawsuit's jurisdiction can put the demand into perspective. If a claim representative has not yet acquired this information from experience, the attorney assigned to the case should be able to provide it.

Such information is also helpful for reporting. The claim representative must keep various members of corporate claims and finance apprised of the lawsuit and the potential for a judgment against the insurer. Generally, insurers do not set up claim reserves to cover potential judgments against them, because bad-faith lawsuits are not claims against policies. However, if the potential for a sizable bad-faith judgment is significant, corporate finance may want to show the lawsuit as a liability on its financial statements.

Referring the Lawsuit to Defense Counsel

Just as in other lawsuits, the claim representative handling the bad-faith lawsuit must assign it to defense counsel for handling. Most insurers have a list of attorneys they prefer to defend bad-faith lawsuits. These attorneys are usually experienced litigators with knowledge of the insurer's claim practices.

As in other cases, the claim representative provides defense counsel with a set of instructions and a copy of the claim file and associated material. The content of the instructions does not differ markedly from that used in other lawsuits. Because it is the subject matter of the lawsuit, the complete claim file must be given to counsel, including any e-mail and voice-mail messages and any other messages stored in an electronic format that may pertain to the underlying claim but that are not part of the file.

Assisting Counsel

In comparison with other lawsuits, the claim representative who handles a bad-faith lawsuit may be more actively involved in the discovery and trial preparation. In a bad-faith lawsuit, the attorney's client is the insurer, and the claim representative handling the lawsuit is the primary point of contact with the client. Because most of the material to be discovered in a bad-faith lawsuit exists within the insurer, the claim representative must comply with the discovery requests.

Litigation Plan

A litigation plan should be created for the defense of the bad-faith lawsuit just as for other lawsuits. The claim representative and defense counsel must review all information available about handling the underlying claim to determine if a bad-faith loss exposure exists. They must communicate openly with one another about the contents of the claim file, and they must be realistic about the potential for significant financial consequences and loss of public trust that may result from a bad-faith lawsuit.

The litigation plan for a bad-faith lawsuit has the same goal as the plan used for other lawsuits: defend, settle, or obtain more information to decide whether to defend or settle. To determine whether the insurer faces a bad-faith loss exposure in the case, the claim representative and defense counsel evaluate the actions of the claim representative who handled the underlying claim in light of the bad-faith law in the jurisdiction.

They may decide to settle the case whether or not an exposure exists. Bad-faith litigation can be expensive and time consuming, draining the insurer's resources that are better used elsewhere. Bad-faith litigation can also be invasive, requiring the insurer to produce records and documents that it would prefer not to become part of the trial record. Testimony of corporate officers may be called for, requiring them to fit depositions and trial testimony into their business schedules. Producing a corporate officer for deposition can also lead to the disclosure of information that is not really pertinent to the case. Bad-faith litigation can also harm the insurer's reputation with the general public.

If the claim representative and defense attorney decide that the lawsuit should be defended, they must agree on how this is to be accomplished. If they decide the lawsuit should be settled, they must agree on a negotiation strategy. If insufficient information is available to decide whether to defend or settle the case, they must agree on what additional information is needed and how to obtain it.

Complaint Answer

Procedurally, answering a bad-faith complaint is no different from answering any other lawsuit. The answer must respond to the allegations raised in the complaint and provide affirmative defenses. It must be filed within the statute's deadline or within the extension granted by the opposing party. Failure to file a timely answer can result in a default judgment.

Some insurers may have corporate guidelines to assist defense counsel in answering bad-faith complaints. Such guidelines usually seek to ensure company-wide uniformity of the insurer's answers to lawsuits. Inconsistency of answers to similar allegations in different lawsuits and in different states does not serve the insurer well.

The biggest challenge in a bad-faith lawsuit is providing the content of the answer to the complaint. It must be accurate and consistent with corporate policy. Formulating an answer to allegations in a bad-faith complaint can require substantial research by the claim representative. An allegation may be broad, for example: "All claims in the state of New Jersey involving red cars were wrongfully denied." This example is exaggerated to make a point. To answer this allegation, the claim representative would need to research all New Jersey claims to select those involving red cars and then determine the outcome of each claim. Depending on the type of data contained in the claim processing system, it may or may not be possible to electronically sort accident claims by the color of the cars involved. The claim representative or the insurer's data managers may also have to review thousands of claim files to find the data because no time period is specified in the allegation. Such a search can be time consuming and costly. If a complaint contains overly broad allegations, defense counsel can object or can include a statement in the answer asserting that the research required in ascertaining the information is too difficult, time-consuming, or costly to perform.

When drafting the answer, the claim representative and defense counsel also discuss whether the insurer should file a counterclaim against the plaintiff or whether a declaratory judgment action is appropriate. A counterclaim may be useful if the insurer suspects that the plaintiff acted in bad faith. A declaratory judgment action may be appropriate if the bad-faith lawsuit resulted from a coverage denial based on the insurer's good-faith opinion that the policy did not cover the loss. This reason for denial can also be used as a defense to the bad-faith allegation. Whether any of these actions can be taken depends on the facts of the case and the applicable state law.

Discovery

Discovery in bad-faith claims can be very demanding. Claim representatives who handle bad-faith claims must be able to locate information from many sources within the insurer. Depending on the allegations and the applicable state law, the discovery may concern only one claim, or it may be so broad that it encompasses the patterns and practices of the insurer in similar claims. Defense counsel usually objects to extremely broad discovery requests. In some cases a court may require justification for the objection; therefore, the claim representative should be prepared to explain to the court why a request is prejudicial, irrelevant, or burdensome.

Three areas of discovery can cause significant concern for insurers and defense counsel: (1) the discovery of corporate financial information, (2) the discovery of documents believed to be privileged, and (3) the discovery of the claim file itself. The discovery of corporate financial information and the discovery of privileged documents is best left to the claim representative handling bad-faith lawsuit and the insurer's defense attorney. Because the claim file is the record of their claim activities, claim representatives should be aware that any claim file may be subject to a discovery demand.

Bad-faith lawsuits are filed long before the plaintiff's attorney receives a copy of the claim file. They are based on the actions and communications of the claim representative. Once a lawsuit is filed, the plaintiff's attorney uses the claim file to prove the allegations. The claim file's content can be the insurer's best defense or its worst nightmare. Even the most innocent of entries in a claim file can be used by the plaintiff's attorney to sway a jury.

Traditionally, much of the claim file has been protected from discovery by state and federal rules of civil procedure that protect attorney work products (materials prepared in anticipation of litigation) and attorney-client communications from discovery. Work product information is generally not discoverable unless those demanding it can prove substantial need or an inability to obtain the information through other sources without undue hardship.

However, in jurisdictions that permit bad-faith causes of action, some courts have held that the bad-faith allegations themselves create a substantial need for information that cannot be obtained from another source. Other courts have held that claim file materials are part of an insurer's normal business operations and are not created in anticipation of litigation. Therefore, these courts have concluded, such materials are not entitled to protection. Consequently, plaintiffs in bad-faith lawsuits can see all or almost all the claim file's contents, including relevant e-mail and voice-mail messages, text messages, and data back-ups.

Tips for Keeping the Claim File Objective and Balanced

- Do assume that the entire claim file and related documents are discoverable and may be seen by a jury.
- Do not make gratuitous comments on any topic.
- Do not make entries in the file that show self-interest on the part of the claim representative or insurer.
- Do not use language that gives the impression that the claim representative has already taken a position about the validity of the claim.
- Do justify reserve amounts and ensure that reserve changes reflect new or additional information received.
- Do not use color highlighters, punctuation, or any other method to emphasize a point.
- Do not use descriptive terms when stating facts. Imagine having to clarify the distinction between the following two entries: "The claimant carried two bags of groceries from the car to the house very easily" and "The claimant carried two bags of groceries from the car to the house."
- Do not erase, white-out, or otherwise alter claim documents. If a correction is necessary, merely put a line through the wording to be corrected and write the correction in the margin. Do not attempt to conceal the original entry or writing in any way. If possible, attach an explanation in for the correction in the document.
- Do not discard material from the claim file.
- Do not put material belonging to another claim in the claim file. Only the documents relating to the specific claim belong in the file.
- Do not put personal notes in communications. This tends to happen in e-mails, such as "looking forward to lunch next week."
- Do not include facts that are not material to the claim. If the claim involves water damage, the file should not include facts about the insured's poor driving record.
- Do not include humor in the claim file. Light-hearted comments would not be well received by the insured or the jury.

It is likely the claim representative will be deposed on the claim file's contents at some point during a bad-faith lawsuit. This deposition may occur years after the claim representative made the entries in the claim file. Explaining opinions, gratuitous comments, corrections or deletions, unrelated material, and humor years after the fact is extremely difficult. It is far easier to explain the basic facts as reflected by the documents and entries in the claim file.

Trial Preparation

Once discovery is completed, the focus shifts to trial preparation. As with other lawsuits, all information gained during discovery must be reviewed to determine whether the original litigation plan should be revised. If the insurer decides to settle the bad-faith lawsuit, then the claim representative and the defense attorney initiate settlement discussions. If the insurer decides to defend against the bad-faith lawsuit, the claim representative and defense attorney begin their trial preparations. These preparations usually begin with a report from counsel outlining the case's strengths and weaknesses and the applicable case law. It may also include information about verdicts from similar cases.

After reviewing the trial strategy offered by defense counsel, the claim representative and counsel decide whether to make any pretrial motions. Such motions are particularly important in bad-faith lawsuits because they can narrow the issues to be tried and minimize the likelihood of the unnecessary disclosure of information.

During trial preparation, the claim representative may be asked to re-verify and update information that was used in discovery. The claim representative may also be asked to participate in witness preparation. This activity is important because many of the witnesses in a bad-faith lawsuit are insurer executives, not just the original file handler.

Trial Assistance

The trial assistance the claim representative provides in bad-faith lawsuits is similar to that provided in other lawsuits. In a bad-faith lawsuit, it is extremely important for the claim representative to report to the insurer regularly on the trial's progress. It is also important to keep the lines of communication open with the plaintiff in the event that a sudden turn in the case may make settlement more likely.

Post-Trial Activities

The post-trial activities for a bad-faith lawsuit mirror the post-trial activities for other lawsuits, as follows:
- Possible judgment notwithstanding the verdict
- Motion for a new trial
- Adjustment of damages awarded
- Appeal to a higher court
- Enforcement of the judgment

Bad-faith litigation is a relatively common occurrence. At some point in their careers, most claim representatives will receive complaints that contain bad-faith allegations. Properly handling the underlying claim and any bad-faith allegations that arise are key in mitigating any exposure.

Managing litigation, for bad-faith claims as well as for insured and third-party claims, is a significant part of a claim representative's job. Crucial to managing litigation is effectively managing the costs associated with litigation.

MANAGING LITIGATION EXPENSES

In recent years, substantial public discussion has centered on the volume and cost of litigation in the U.S. For the fiscal years 2002 and 2003, more than 512,000 civil cases were filed in federal district courts. Twenty percent of these cases were tort cases, and 2 percent of these tort cases were resolved at trial.[1] More than 16 million civil cases were filed in state courts in 2002. Jury trials accounted for less than 1 percent of all civil dispositions in state courts.[2] The cost of the U.S. civil tort system was $233.4 billion in 2002 (this amount includes the cost of legal defense and claim handling, payments to plaintiffs and claimants, and administrative costs of all claims, including those settled out of court).[3]

Managing the costs associated with litigation is only one aspect of a claim representative's duties, but it can have noticeable financial effect on the insurer. The use of a litigation plan, a litigation budget, legal bill audits, and evaluation of defense counsel's performance can contribute to an effective defense of the insured at a reasonable cost.

Creating a Litigation Plan

A litigation plan is essential to the insured's defense and to managing the cost of the litigation. The prior discussion of the litigation plan focuses on how it provides a defense to the insured (or the insurer in a bad-faith case). This discussion examines how the litigation plan can save costs while enhancing the insured's defense.

By working with defense counsel to establish a litigation plan, the claim representative fosters a sound relationship with counsel. The need for continual review and updating of the plan ensures that the claim representative and the defense counsel frequently communicate with one another and that they are always aware of major activity in the litigation.

Many of the activities in a litigation plan relate to discovery. The claim representative and the defense attorney agree on the discovery needed for the case and on who will perform the discovery. For example, medical records may be sufficient to provide needed information, rather than a deposition of a doctor. If the defense attorney agrees, the claim representative can obtain the medical records more cost-effectively than the defense attorney can simply because the attorney bills for the activity. Claim representatives should never hinder an attorney's representation of the client by refusing to allow a deposition, research, or any other activity the attorney deems necessary. However, defense counsel should be able to explain why an activity is necessary to provide the insured with a professional defense and how the activity fits into the overall litigation plan, and should be able to estimate the cost of the activity.

The litigation plan can help reduce costs because it ensures that the claim representative and defense attorney are working toward a common goal. If these two parties direct their activities toward different goals, they may end up working at cross purposes, resulting in duplicated effort, unmet expectations, and additional legal expense to rectify the situation.

Creating a Litigation Budget

In addition to the litigation plan, the attorney and the claim representative should create a litigation budget. Most attorneys are comfortable working within a litigation budget because they know they can make reasonable adjustments as the needs of the case change during the course of litigation. The budget depends on the type of fee arrangement the attorney has with the client/insurer. The most commonly used fee arrangement is the hourly fee; the attorney submits an itemized bill for the hours spent on the case. However, other fee arrangements can be used, such as **flat fee** (the attorney agrees to handle the case from start to finish for a specified, or flat, fee) or **phased fee** arrangements (the attorney agrees handle each phase of litigation for a specific fee.). Most insurers have agreements with the attorneys most frequently retained in litigation about how the fees are to be handled. Such agreements relieve the claim representative of having to negotiate the type of fee arrangement.

Flat fee
A fee arrangement in which the attorney agrees to handle the case from start to finish for a specified amount.

Phased fee
A fee arrangement in which the attorney agrees to handle each phase of litigation for a specific fee.

Having reached agreement about the goal of the litigation and the type of fee for the case, the claim representative and the attorney can establish the tasks required to reach the goal. In establishing a litigation budget, the claim representative and the attorney should consider the activities that must occur to provide the best defense. These activities can be broken down into several categories, as follows:

- Case review, including initially reviewing material from the claim representative and interviewing the insured and other involved parties
- Legal research
- Initial pleadings, including drafting an answer to the complaint, and cross-claims or counterclaims
- Discovery, including drafting interrogatories, answering the opponent's interrogatories, preparing for and attending depositions, and complying with document production requests
- Locating and retaining experts
- Motions
- Negotiations and conferences
- Trial

Within each of these categories are numerous tasks that must be completed. The tasks and costs should be recorded in a table, such as the following example showing the tasks that may be required in the case review category:

Task	Responsible Party	Time
Initial review of file	Primary attorney	2 hours
Interview insured	Primary attorney	3 hours
File appearance	Paralegal	0.5 hour
Obtain police report	Claim representative	0.5 hour

Each task should include the name of the party assigned to perform the task. The claim representative should determine which people on the attorney's staff will actually work on the case. In many cases, it is cost-effective to have an associate or paralegal perform some tasks rather than the defense attorney.

The table should show a time estimate for each task. An additional column may show the cost estimate. The cost estimate may be a simple calculation of the number of hours multiplied by the hourly rate, or it may be a "not to exceed" estimate, which places a limit on the amount the attorney can spend without first discussing it with the claim representative. Legal research often uses a "not to exceed" figure. Outside expenses, such as travel costs, court reporters' fees, and expert witness fees, should also be budgeted.

The litigation budget is a tool the attorney and claim representative can use to ensure the best representation of the client. The budget should be reviewed periodically and changed to reflect case developments.

Auditing Legal Bills

As previously mentioned, most insurers have billing guidelines for the attorneys who defend insureds or the insurer. These billing guidelines usually require a detailed, itemized record of work performed, which includes the task performed, how long the task took in tenth-of-an-hour increments, the name of the attorney or paralegal who performed the activity, and any expense associated with the task. The billing guidelines also specify the hourly rate to be charged by each attorney and paralegal; travel expenses allowed; and associated expenses, such as overnight mailing or photocopying charges, that can be charged to the case. Agreeing to these details at the outset of the relationship with the attorney allows the claim representative and the attorney to focus fully on the defense of the insured or insurer instead of negotiating fees during litigation.

Even with billing guidelines in place, the claim representative should carefully review legal bills for compliance with fees and agreed-to guidelines. Any bill that does not provide sufficient information for review or does not comply with the billing guidelines should be returned to the attorney for explanation. The following box lists some of the items a claim representative should look for when reviewing a legal bill.

> **Checklist for Reviewing Legal Bills**
>
> - Dates of the major activities on the bill should correspond with dates of the same activities in the claim file. For example, if the bill lists a thirty-minute phone call with the claim representative on a specific date, the claim representative should have a corresponding entry in the claim activity log.
> - Only the work of parties (partner, associate, paralegal) agreed to in advance by the handling attorney and the claim representative should be included on the bill.
> - Mathematical computations should be checked for accuracy. Despite law firms' use of computerized billing systems, errors do occur.
> - Only authorized investigative activity should be included on the bill.
> - Only authorized attorneys should have appeared at depositions, hearings, motions, or trials. Billing for any additional attorneys or legal staff should be questioned.
> - Itemized incremental billing should be based on a reasonable time for the specific activity billed. Attorneys bill in tenth-of-an-hour increments, so 6 minutes equals 0.1 hour, 12 minutes equals 0.2 hour, 18 minutes equals 0.3 hour, and so on. For example, unless a letter is extremely long, it usually does not take someone 18 minutes to review it.
> - Absent a compelling reason, most attorneys should not bill more than 10 hours per day.
> - Administrative costs, such as general postage, local travel, word processing, and other items of overhead, should not be billed unless specifically agreed to, either in the billing guidelines or by the claim representative.
> - Airfare, hotel, and meal charges should comply with the billing guidelines.

Because reviewing legal bills can be time-consuming, many insurers have designated specific staff, usually attorneys themselves, to perform the review. In some states, insurers may use outside bill auditing firms to perform these reviews. Usually, insurers' billing guidelines address who is to perform the bill review.

Claim representatives should not hesitate to request an explanation of any item or charge on a legal bill. Usually the explanation is sufficient to resolve any questions the claim representative may have. However, when some portion of a legal bill must be challenged, the claim representative should be prepared to explain the reason for the challenge to the attorney and suggest a realistic amount to be paid. To determine a reasonable amount, the claim representative should carefully weigh the merits of the particular item, the fee associated with it, and any circumstances that may affect the fee.

After reviewing a legal bill and determining the amount that should be paid, claim representatives should make every effort to ensure that the bill is paid promptly. Prompt payment helps maintain a good relationship with counsel. If there is a reason for delayed payment, the claim representative should advise the attorney.

Evaluating the Litigation Plan and Counsel Performance

Once a claim in litigation has been resolved, the claim representative may evaluate the litigation plan and the attorney's performance on the case. A review of the litigation plan should cover the original plan and any subsequent revisions. The following questions may be helpful to the claim representative in the evaluation:

- Was the final outcome of the case satisfactory?
- Was the case's final outcome the outcome that was specified in the plan at the beginning of the case? If not, why not?
- Was the original plan realistic, given the facts known at the time?
- Was the plan revised in a timely manner to reflect changes in facts as they became known?
- Were the plan and any subsequent revisions agreed on by both the claim representative and the attorney, or were changes made unilaterally?
- Did the attorney adhere to the plan?
- Were any expenses incurred that were unanticipated by the plan and the budget? If so, how could this be avoided in the future?

It is possible that a case may be resolved satisfactorily even if the litigation plan is not followed; however, adhering to a plan can usually reduce the overall cost, duration, and stress of the case.

The claim representative begins the attorney's performance evaluation by looking at the result of the case. Was it satisfactory? Was it the agreed upon resolution? Another item to consider is whether the attorney was cooperative and responsive to the claim representative throughout the case and whether the attorney's handling of the case was cost-effective. The claim representative should share the results of the performance evaluation with the attorney. Some insurers may have a formal means of providing this feedback, such as a mid-year and yearly review process. Others may have the claim representative provide the feedback directly, shortly after the case has been resolved. Most attorneys welcome the feedback because they want to have a good working relationship with their clients. They would also like to have a long-term relationship, so they have a vested interest in keeping the claim representative and the insurer satisfied with their performance.

SUMMARY

Many claims turn into lawsuits, so claim representatives must be prepared to handle these lawsuits. The activities involved in handling litigation are similar for third-party lawsuits and bad-faith lawsuits. When a summons and complaint (or similar documents) are received, the claim representative usually logs the lawsuit into a tracking system or database and reviews the complaint. The claim representative reviews the summons and complaint to determine the following: whether the parties are covered by the insurance policy, how service of process was accomplished, what the deadline is for filing an answer, whether the case has been filed within the appropriate statute of limitations and in the appropriate jurisdiction and venue, and whether the allegations contained in the complaint are covered by the policy.

The claim representative then selects the defense attorney best suited to handle the case and refers the lawsuit to defense counsel for handling, along with a transmittal form or letter outlining the facts of the case. The claim representative then notifies the insured that a defense attorney has been selected and provides identifying information. The claim representative assists the attorney by continuing to perform investigation as needed and works with the attorney to create a litigation plan to guide their activities throughout the case.

The claim representative can be involved in many aspects of the defense, including assisting in preparing the answer, gathering information to respond to requests for production of documents and interrogatories, attending depositions, and arranging for IMEs and other expert reports. The claim representative may also attend the trial to assist the attorney. At the trial's conclusion, the claim representative discusses possible post-trial actions with the attorney.

The process of handling the trial portion of a bad-faith lawsuit is the same as that used for third-party lawsuits. However, the handling of the lawsuit by the claim representative differs. Many insurers create a separate file for the bad-faith lawsuit and assign it to a claim representative other than the one who handled the underlying claim. The claim representative handling a bad-faith lawsuit must be diligent in providing accurate information for the answer to the complaint that is also consistent with corporate policy. Discovery can be difficult because it may involve requests for corporate financial information and privileged documents and because the entire claim file is subject to discovery.

Managing litigation includes managing the cost of litigation. For each case, the claim representative and the attorney prepare a budget that works in conjunction with the litigation plan. The budget, like the plan, is revised as circumstances dictate. During and after the case, the claim representative reviews the legal bills submitted to ensure that they adhere to billing guidelines. Any part of the legal bill that is in question should be addressed with the attorney. When the issues are resolved, the claim representative should pay the attorney's bill promptly.

Once the case has been resolved, the claim representative should evaluate the success of the litigation plan and budget and the performance of the attorney. Most attorneys welcome this feedback because they want to maintain good working relationships with insurers and claim representatives.

CHAPTER NOTES

1. "Federal Tort Trials and Verdicts, 2002-03," Bureau of Justice Statistics bulletin, August 2005, NCJ 208713, www.ojp.usdoj.gov/bjs, p.1 (accessed August 19, 2005).
2. Court Statistics Project, "Examining the Work of State Courts 2002," National Center for State Courts, www.ncsonline.org/D_Research/csp/2003_Files/2003_Main_Page.html, p. 10 and p. 18 (accessed August 19, 2005).
3. U.S. Tort Costs: 2004 Update, "Trends and Findings on the Cost of the U.S. Tort System," Towers Perrin, www.towersperrin.com/tillinghast/publications/reports (accessed August 19, 2005).

Appendix

Sample Summons

IN THE COURT OF COMMONS PLEAS FOR THE STATE OF _____
IN AND FOR _____ COUNTY

```
Name (s)                           )
                                   )
                                   )
              Plantiff (s),        )
      V.                           ) Civil Action No.
                                   )
                                   )
Names (s)                          )
              Defendant (s).       )
```

TO THE SHERIFF OF _____ COUNTY,
YOU ARE COMMANDED:

    To summon the above named defendant(s) and serve upon said defendant(s) a copy of this summons and complaint.

TO THE ABOVE NAMED DEFENDANT(S):

    Within twenty (20) days after you receive this summons, excluding the day you receive it, you must file an Answer to the attached Complaint if you want to deny the allegations. The original of your answer must be filed with the Clerk's Office of the Court of Common Pleas, _____ _____, Delaware and must include proof that a copy of the Answer was served on the plaintiff or his/her attorney who is named on this Summons.

    Failure to file an answer denying the allegations will result in a judgement against you, and action may be taken by the plaintiff or his/her attorney to satisfy the judgement.

DATED: _____ _____
                                                                                                  Clerk

Plaintiff's Attorney Name
Address
Telephone Number

Sample Complaint

In the Court of Common Pleas of _____ County, Delaware
Civil Division

Plaintiff's name,   )
        Plaintiff,)
)
   v.   )
)
Defendant's name,   )
        Defendant.)

<u>Complaint</u>

AND NOW comes Plaintiff _____, by its undersigned attorneys, and brings this civil action against (defendant's names), Defendants, of which the following is a statement:

1. Plaintiff, _____ is a resident of the state of _____.
2. Defendant, _____ is a resident of the state of _____.
3. On or about March 31, 200X Defendant _____ did negligently operate her vehicle in such a manner as to strike the vehicle of Plaintiff _____.
4. The accident occurred at the intersection of Main Street and Roosevelt Boulevard, in _____.
5. As a result of the negligence of the Defendant, _____ Plaintiff, _____ suffered serious bodily injury and damage to property.
6. At the present time the value of the property damage is $10,000.
7. The Plaintiff, _____ seeks damages in the amount of 1 million dollars for the bodily injury sustained.

WHEREFORE, Plaintiff, _____ seeks judgment for the property damage and bodily injury sustained and costs of this action, together with reasonable attorney's fees.

Name of Plaintiff's Law Firm
By _____
Signature of Lawyer

Index

Page numbers in boldface refer to definitions of Key Words and Phrases.

A

Accident, staged, 4.6
Accident scene investigation, 2.34
ACORD (Association for Cooperative Operations Research and Development), 3.11
Actual cash value (ACV), **3.50**
Actual service, **8.7**
Actuarial, 1.21–1.22
Admissions, **8.21**
Advance payment, **3.53**
Allegations, **8.11**–8.12, 8.33
Allocation, 6.14
Alternative dispute resolution (ADR), **2.44**–2.46
American Institute for CPCU, Canons and Rules of the Code of Professional Ethics of, 6.27–6.29
Answer, **8.5**
    complaint, 8.16–8.17, 8.35–8.36
    time to, 8.7–8.8, 8.33
Anti-fraud efforts, 4.19–4.29
Appraisal provision, **2.45**
Arbitration, **2.45**
Association for Cooperative Operations Research and Development (ACORD), 3.11
Audit factors, qualitative and quantitative, 1.18
Auditing legal bills, 8.41
Auto fraud indicators, 4.15
Auto physical damage, 3.51–3.52
Automobile Loss Notice form, 3.11–3.14
Average value method, **2.25**

B

Bad faith, **1.35**
    comparative, 5.23–5.24
    law of, 5.4–5.7
    legal environment of, 5.7
    statutory, 5.13–5.14
Bad-faith claims
    bases for, 5.11–5.16
    defenses to, 5.19–5.24
    parties to, 5.8–5.11
Bad-faith lawsuit
    first-party, 5.8
    managing, 8.32–8.39
    third-party, 5.9
    under the Model Act, 5.16
Behavioral fraud indicators, 4.10
Benefits, determining, 3.61
Bidding against oneself, 7.37
Billing practices, 6.13–6.14
Bodily injury claim
    investigation, 3.53–3.59
    methods for determining value, 3.58–3.59
Bodily injury experts, 3.40
Boulwarism, first and final offer, using, 7.36
Breach of contract, **5.4**
Building, damaged, inspection of, 3.49
Burden of proof, **8.27**
Burglary and theft fraud indicators, 4.16
Business risk, **1.5**

C

Canons and Rules of the Code of Professional Ethics of the American Institute for CPCU, 6.27–6.29
Caseloads, manageable, 5.33
Catastrophe serial number, **3.17**
Cause of loss
    auto physical damage, determining, 3.44–3.48
    bodily injury, determining, 3.53–3.55
    is it covered?, 2.15–2.16
    and loss amount, determining, 2.41–2.47
    other property damage, determining, 3.48–3.50
Choicing, 7.25–7.26
Civil or criminal penalties, 4.25
Claim
    acknowledging and assigning, 2.22
    concluding, 2.42–2.47
    denial of, 2.43–2.44, 5.11–5.12
    excess liability, 5.12
    function, 1.12–1.19
    investigating and documenting, 2.33–2.41
    management, effective, 5.32
    personnel, 1.14–1.15
    workers compensation investigation of, 3.59
Claim department structure, 1.12–1.13
Claim file, objective and balanced, tips for keeping, 8.37
Claim handling competency, 6.8–6.11
Claim handling process, 2.3–2.50
    activities in, 2.21
Claim negotiation
    process, 7.10–7.12
    settings, 7.20–7.23
    techniques, 7.24–7.35
    variables, 7.13–7.24
Claim practices, quality, 6.18–6.19
Claim representatives
    authority level of, 7.18
    knowledge of claim of, 7.18
    negotiation variables of, 7.18
    personality of, 7.23–7.24
    staff, 1.14
    time factors of, 7.19
Claim settlement, satisfactory, number of alternatives for, 7.18–7.19
Claimant
    emotional reaction of to loss, 7.16–7.17
    experience of with or knowledge of insurance claims, 7.17
    negotiation phase of, 7.14–7.16
    negotiation variables of, 7.13–7.16
    personality of, 7.17–7.18
Claimants, 5.9–5.10
Claimant investigation, 2.34
    bodily injury, 3.53–3.59
    property damage, 3.45–3.53
Claims
    contents, 3.49
    exaggerated/padded, examples of, 4.7
    theft, 3.47–3.48

Closing reports, 2.47
Code of Professional Ethics of the American Institute for CPCU, 6.27–6.29
Codes of ethics, 6.17–6.18
Coinsurance, **3.16**
Collusion with claimant, of insured, 5.21
Combined ratio, **1.16**
Common law, or case law, **3.5**
Communication, regular and prompt, 5.31–5.32
Comparative bad faith, 5.23–5.24
Comparative negligence, **3.8**
Compensability, determining, 3.60
Compensatory damages, **2.18**, 5.17
Competition, destructive, prevention of, 1.27
Complaint, or petition, **8.4**
Complaint, sample, 8.48
Complaint answer, 8.16–8.17, 8.35–8.36
Concealment, **4.5**
Conceding as deadlines approach, 7.37
Concessions, making, 7.34
Concluding the claim, 2.42
Conditions, 2.10–2.12
Conflicts of interest, 6.7–6.8
Constitutional law, **3.4**
Consumer protection, 1.32
Consumers, protection of, 1.26
Contents claims, 3.49
Continuing education, 6.11
Contract, breach of, 5.4
Contractual liability, **3.9**
Contributory negligence, **3.7**, 5.24
Costs of insurance, 1.10
Counsel, assisting, 8.15–8.31, 8.34
Counterclaim, **8.16**
Court system
 federal, 8.9
 state, 8.10
Coverage
 special form, 2.15
 specified cause of loss, 2.15
Coverage analysis, framework for, 2.12–2.10
Coverage analysis and the claim handling process, framework for, 2.47
Customer expectations, 6.18–6.20
Customer service, 6.12–6.13

D

Damage, determining amount of, 3.50–3.53
Damages, 8.12, 8.33–8.34
 compensatory, 2.18, 5.17
 future, 3.56
 general, 2.18, 3.55, 3.57–3.58
 punitive, 2.18, 3.56, 5.17–5.18
 resulting from bad faith or extra-contractual liability, 5.16–5.19
 special, 2.18, 3.55, 3.57
Debatable reasonable basis, 5.22
Declarations, 2.7
Decreasing or limited offers, using, 7.36
Default judgment, **8.17**
Defendant, **5.8**
Defense counsel
 referring lawsuit to, 8.12–8,13, 8.34
 selection, 8.13
Defenses, statutory. 5.22
Defenses to bad-faith claims, 5.19–5.24
Deposition, **8.19**
Diagrams of loss scene, 3.35–3.36
Direct loss, **2.17**
Direct question, **3.30**
Discovery, **8.17**–8.22, 8.36–8.38
Documentation,
 auto physical damage, 3.46
 bodily injury 3.54
 complete and accurate, 5.28–5.29
 other property damage, 3.49
 workers' compensation, 3.60
Duty of good faith and fair dealing, 5.5–5.7

E

Endorsements, 2.12
Estoppel, **2.31**
 waiver and, 2.30
Ethical Guidelines, Society of Registered Professional Adjusters, 6.18, 6.25
Ethical and professional dilemmas, 6.5–6.17
Ethical and professional standards, 6.17–6.23
Ethics and professionalism, importance of, 6.3–6.5
Evaluating litigation plan and counsel performance, 8.43
Evaluation, fair, 5.29–5.30
 information obtained from, using, 7.31
Ex parte contacts, 6.13
Excess insurers, 5.10–5.11
Excess liability claims, 5.12
Exclusions, 2.9–2.10
 do they apply?, 2.19–2.20
 seven purposes of, 2.10
Expert system method, **2.26**
Experts, 3.37–3.41
 bodily injury, 3.40–3.41
 property, 3.39–3.40
 types of, 3.38–3.39
 using, 3.54, 3.60–3.61
Extraneous information, collecting and using, 7.27–7.28

F

Factors that influence fraud, 4.9
Failure to settle within policy limits, 5.12–5.13
Fair Credit Reporting Act, 5.28
Fair dealing and good documentation, 5.22–5.23
Fair market value, **3.52**
False claims, 4.5
Federal court system, 8.9
File documentation, 2.37–2.38
File reports, 2.39–2.41
File review, 2.37
Finance and accounting, 1.22
Fire claims, 3.47
Fire fraud indicators, 4.14
First and final offer—Boulwarism, using, 7.36
First offer, making, 7.30, 7.33
First-party claim, **1.8**
Flat fee, **8.40**
Formula method, **2.25**
Forum shopping, example of, 8.11
Framework for coverage analysis, 2.12–2.20
Framework for coverage analysis and claim handling process, applying, 2.47–2.49
Fraud
 detection, 6.15–6.17
 hard, 4.5–4.6
 plans, 4.28
 soft, 4.6–4.7

Fraud indicators, 4.10–4.17
    auto, 4.15–4.16
    behavioral, 4.10–4.12
    burglary and theft, 4.16–4.17
    fire, 4.14–4.15
    lost earnings, 4.13
    medical, 4.12–4.14
    vehicle theft, 4.17
Fraud prevention bureaus, 4.26
Future damages, 3.56

G

General damages, **2.18**, 3.55
    valuation of, 3.57
General Liability Notice of Occurrence Claim form, 3.17–3.19
Good faith, 2.30, **5.3**
    claim handling, elements of, 5.25–5.34
    and fair dealing, duty of, 5.5–5.7
    negotiation, 5.30
Government, anti-fraud efforts of, 4.23–4.29
Gramm-Leach-Bliley Act of 1999, 1.24–1.25, 5.27

H

Hard fraud, **4.5**
Hazard risk, **1.5**
Health Insurance Portability and Accountability Act of 1996, 5.26–5.27
Higher limits, availability of, 5.24

I

Immunity statute, **4.25**
Incurred losses, **1.16**
Independent adjuster, **1.14**
Indirect loss, **2.17**
Individual case method, **2.23**–2.24
Industry databases, 3.42–3.43
Industry organizations, 4.28
Information technology (IT), 1.22
Initial contact and statements, 3.45, 3.48, 3.54, 3.60
Insurable interest, **1.8**

Insurance, **1.7**–1.12
    benefits of, 1.8–1.10
    costs, 1.10–1.12
Insurance agent, **1.15**
Insurance broker, **1.15**
Insurance company functions, other, 1.19–1.23
Insurance fraud, **4.3**–4.10
    detection, importance of, 4.3–4.4
    factors that influence, 4.9–4.10
    motives for, 4.7–4.9
    types of, 4.4–4.7
Insurance Fraud Protection Act, 1.24
Insurance guaranty funds, **1.31**
Insurance policy
    regulation, 1.31–1.32
    structure of, 2.3–2.12
Insurance regulation, 1.23–1.35
    activities of, 1.27–1.28
    evolution of, 1.23–1.25
    purposes of, 1.26–1.27
    types of, 1.28–1.35
Insurance regulators, activities of, 1.27
Insured, **1.7**
Insured or insured's representative, contacting, 2.28–2.33
Insured notification, 8.14
Insurer solvency, maintainence of, 1.27
Insurers, anti-fraud efforts of, 4.21–4.23
Insuring agreement, **2.8**–2.9
Intentional losses, 4.5
Intentional tort, **3.8**
Interest, 5.19
Internet, 3.43
Interrogatories, **8.18**–8.22
Interviewees, special, consideration for, 3.34–3.35
Investigating and documenting claim, 2.33–2.41
Investigation
    accident scene, 2.34
    balanced, maintaining, 4.18–4.19
    claimant, 2.34
    insured/witness, 2.34
    medical, 2.35
    prior claim, 2.25
    property damage, 2.34–2.35
    thorough, timely, and unbiased, 5.25–5.26
Investigative tools
    basic, 3.10
    general, 3.10–3.44
    other, 3.44
Ishikawa (fishbone) diagram, 6.22

J

Jurisdiction, **8.8**
    venue and, 8.8–8.11, 8.33

L

Law of bad faith, 5.4
Law of large numbers, **1.7**
Lawsuit, process of typical, 8.31
Lawyers
    reliance on advice of, 5.20–5.21
    fees and court costs, 5.18–5.19
Leading question, **3.33**
Legal advice, competent 5.32
Legal bills, auditing of, 8.41–8.42
Legal liability, **3.4**
    bases for, 3.3–3.10
Liability
    based on contract, 3.9
    based on statute, 3.9–3.10
    based on tort, 3.6–3.8
    for bodily injury claims, determining, 3.54
    for loss of income claims, determining, 3.50
    strict, **3.8**, 5.13
    vicarious, **3.7**
    for workers' compensation claims, determining, 3.61
Licensing, 6.11–6.12
Limited authority negotiations, 7.34
Litigation, 2.46–2.47
    budget, creating, 8.40–8.41
    and counsel performance, evaluating, 8.43
    creating, 8.39–8.40
    expenses, managing, 8.39–8.43
    plan, 8.15–8.16, 8.34–8.35
Location of loss, covered?, 2.19
Lose-lose, 7.9–10
Lose-win, 7.9
Loss
    are amounts covered?, 2.18–2.19
    indirect, 2.17
    types of, is it covered?, 2.19
Loss, cause of, *See* Cause of loss
Loss control, 1.21
Loss or damages, are the amounts covered?, 2.17
Loss of income claims, 3.50
Loss notice forms, 3.11–3.14

Loss ratio, **1.16**
Loss ratio method, **2.26**
Loss reserves, **1.16**
Losses
    incurred, 1.16
    intentional, 4.5–4.6
Lost earnings, fraud indicators for, 4.13

M

Mandatory reporting, 4.24
Manuscript policies, **2.6**
Marketing and sales, 1.20
Maslow's Hierarchy of Needs, 7.29
Material fact, **4.5**
McCarran-Ferguson Act, 1.24
Mediation, **2.44**
Medical fraud indicators, 4.12
Medical investigation, 2.35
Mini-trial, **2.45**
Misrepresentation, **4.5**
Moral hazard, **1.11**
Morale hazard, or attitudinal hazard, **1.11**
Motion to dismiss, **8.24**
Motion in *limine*, **8.24**
Motion for summary judgment, **8.24**
Motives for insurance fraud, 4.7

N

NAIC (National Association of Insurance Commissioners), role of, 1.25
NAIC Model Act, 5.14–5.15
    bad-faith lawsuits under, 5.16
    enforcement of, 5.14–5.15
    provisions of, 5.14. 5.37–5.40
        state, incorporated, 5.15
Needs analysis to effect a settlement, using, 7.28–7.30
Negligence, **3.6**
    comparative, 3.8
    contributory, 3.7, 5.24
Negotiation
    good-faith, 5.30–5.31
    process, claim, 7.10–7.12
    styles, 7.4–7.10
Negotiation techniques
    to avoid, 7.35–7.36
    for use by all parties, 7.24–7.26
    for use with claimants' representatives, 7.30–7.34
    for use with unrepresented claimants, 7.26–7.30
    used by claimants' representatives, 7.34–7.35
Negotiations
    in claims, common pitfalls, 7.36–7.38
    limited authority, 7.34
    timing in, 7.35–7.35
Noninsurance transfer, **1.7**
Nonwaiver agreement, **2.32**
Notification, insured, 8.14

O

Offers, decreasing or limited, using, 7.36
Open-ended question, **3.32**
Other insurance, does it apply?, 2.20
Overlapping coverages or insureds, 6.7–6.8

P

Payments, 2.42
Penalties, civil or criminal , 4.25
Performance measures, 1.15–1.19
Person involved, covered?, 2.13–2.14
Phased fee, **8.40**
Photos, 3.35–3.36
Physical construction, 2.4
Plaintiff, **5.8**
Policy
    components and their functions, 2.6–2.12
    form numbers, 2.5
    identifying, 2.22–2.28
    information, 3.21–3.22
Policy condition, **2.10**
Policy period, did loss occur in?, 2.15
Policyholders, 5.8–5.9
Possibility, 1.4
Post-trial activities, 8.29–8.31, 8.38–8.39
Pre-inspection, 4.23
Pre-trial order, sample, 8.25
Preponderance of evidence, **8.27**
Principle of indemnity, **1.8**
Principle of yes, 7.24–7.25
Prior claim investigation, 2.35
Privacy, 6.14–6.15

Probability, 1.4
Process improvement plan, 6.20–6.23
Producers, 1.15
Profitability measures, 1.16–1.17
Property damage
    claim investigation, 3.44
    investigation, 2.34
    other, 3.52–3.53
Property, damaged, is it covered?, 2.16–2.18
Property experts, 3.39
Property Loss Notice form, 3.14–3.17
Public adjuster, **1.15**
Public interest, 5.5
Punitive damages, **2.18**, 3.56, 5.17

Q

Quality claim practices, 6.18
Quality measures, 1.17–1.19
Questions used in statements, types of, 3.30

R

Rate regulation, 1.29
Reasonable basis, debatable, 5.22
Recorded statements, 3.25
Records and reports, 3.41–4.42
Refusal to settle, 5.13
Regulation,
    consumer, 1.32–1.35
    insurance, 1.23–1.35
    insurance policy, 1.31–1.32
    rate, 1.29
    solvency, 1.30–1.31
Reinsurance, 1.21
Reinsurer, **1.21**
Replacement cost, **3.50**
Request for production of documents, **8.18**
Reservation of rights letter, **2.32**
Reserve, **2.23–2.28**
    case, common methods of setting, 2.23
    errors, causes of, 2.27–2.28
Retention, **1.6**
Right to sue, lack of, 5.20
Risk, **1.3**–1.7
    business, 1.5
    hazard, 1.5

Risk control, 1.6
Risk financing, 1.6–1.7
Risk management techniques, 1.5–1.7
Roundtable method, **2.25**

S

Sales techniques in negotiation, using, 7.28
Salvage, 6.7
Sarbanes-Oxley Act, 5.27–5.28
Scope, **3.49**
Service of process, **8.5**–8.7, 8.33
    actual, 8.7
    substituted, or constructive, 8.7
Settlement
    personalities, allowing to influence, 7.36
SIUs (special investigation units), 4.21–4.22
Society of Registered Professional Adjusters Ethical Guidelines, 6.18, 6.25
Soft fraud, 4.5-4.6
Soft fraud, or opportunity fraud, **4.5**
Solvency regulation, 1.30–1.31
Special damages, **2.18**, 3.55
    valuation of, 3.57
Special form coverage, **2.15**
Special investigation units (SIUs), 4.21–4.22
Specified causes of loss coverage, **2.15**
Staff claim representatives, 1.14
Staged accident, **4.6**
Standard of conduct, higher, 5.5–5.7
Stare decisis, **8.22**
State court systems, 8.10
State provisions, NAIC Model Act, 5.15
Statements, 3.22–3.35
    content, 3.29–3.30
    information, auto accident, 3.31
    questions, types used in, 3.30–3.35
    recorded, 3.25–3.29
    steps in preparing for, 3.24
    sworn, 3.23
    written, 3.28–3.30
Statute of limitations, **5.20**, 8.8, 8.33
Statutory bad faith, 5.13
Statutory defenses, 5.22
Statutory law, **3.4**
Statutory liability, **3.9**
Strengths and weaknesses, establishing, 7.31–7.32

Strict liability, **3.8**, 5.13
Subrogation, **2.35**
    investigation and recovery, 2.35–2.37
Substituted service, or constructive service, **8.7**
Summarized report form, 2.40
Summary judgment, **5.22**
    motion for, 8.24
Summary jury trial, **2.46**
Summons, **8.4**
    sample, 8.47
Summons and complaint
    checking, 8.5–8.12, 8.32–8.34
    receiving, 8.5–8.12, 8.32
Supervision, consistent, 5.33
Sworn statement, **3.23**

T

Theft claims, 3.47–3.48
Third-party administrator, **1.12**, 1.14–1.15
Third-party claim, **1.8**
Third-party lawsuit, managing, 8.4–8.31
Time to answer, 8.7–8.8, 8.33
Time and expense, 6.14
Time pressures claimant may face, 7.16
Timing in negotiations, using, 7.32–7.33
Tort, **3.6**
Tortfeasor, **3.6**
Trading dollars, 7.37
Training, thorough, 5.33
Transmittal form completion, 8.13–8.14
Trial
    assisting at, 8.22–8.26, 8.29, 8.38
    preparation for, 8.38

U

Underwriting, 1.20–1.21
Unfair claim practices acts, **1.35**
Unfair claims settlement practices acts, 5.14–5.16
Unfair trade practices acts, **1.33**–1.35

V

Valuation of general damages, 3.57
Valuation of special damages, 3.57
Values conflicts in ethical dilemmas, 6.5
Vehicle, damaged, inspection of, 3.45–3.46
Vehicle Identification Number (VIN), decoding, 3.46
Vendor incentives, 6.7
Venue, **8.10**
Vicarious liability, **3.7**
Videos, 3.35–3.36
Voir dire, **8.27**

W

Waiver, **2.30**
Waiver and estoppel, 2.30–2.33
Win-lose, 7.8
Win-win, 7.6–7.8
Workers Compensation Loss Notice form, 3.19–3.21
Workers' compensation claim investigation, 3.59–3.61